T0072064

Peace of Mind

BIBLE
WORD SEARCH

PSALMS

LINDA PETERS

Good Books®

New York, New York

Copyright © 2020 by Hollan Publishing

All rights reserved. No part of this book may be reproduced in any manner without the express written consent of the publisher, except in the case of brief excerpts in critical reviews or articles. All inquiries should be addressed to Good Books, 307 West 36th Street, 11th Floor, New York, NY 10018.

Good Books books may be purchased in bulk at special discounts for sales promotion, corporate gifts, fund-raising, or educational purposes. Special editions can also be created to specifications. For details, contact the Special Sales Department, Good Books, 307 West 36th Street, 11th Floor, New York, NY 10018 or info@skyhorsepublishing.com.

Good Books is an imprint of Skyhorse Publishing, Inc.®, a Delaware corporation.

Visit our website at www.goodbooks.com.

10 9 8 7 6 5 4 3

Library of Congress Cataloging-in-Publication Data is available on file.

Cover design by Joanna Williams
Cover image used under license from Shutterstock.com

Print ISBN: 978-1-68099-627-2

Printed in the United States of America

All scripture quotations are taken from the following sources:

The Holy Bible, New International Version®, NIV®. Copyright © 1973, 1978, 1984, 2011 by Biblica, Inc.™ Used by permission of Zondervan. All rights reserved worldwide. www.zondervan.com The "NIV" and "New International Version" are trademarks registered in the United States Patent and Trademark Office by Biblica, Inc.™

The ESV® Bible (The Holy Bible, English Standard Version®), copyright © 2001 by Crossway, a publishing ministry of Good News Publishers. Used by permission. All rights reserved.

The New American Standard Bible® (NASB), Copyright © 1960, 1962, 1963, 1968, 1971, 1972, 1973, 1975, 1977, 1995 by The Lockman Foundation. Used by permission. www.Lockman.org

New Revised Standard Version Bible, copyright 1989, Division of Christian Education of the National Council of the Churches of Christ in the United States of America. Used by permission. All rights reserved.

Holy Bible, New Living Translation, copyright © 1996, 2004, 2015 by Tyndale House Foundation. Used by permission of Tyndale House Publishers, Inc., Carol Stream, Illinois 60188. All rights reserved.

The Holy Bible, King James Version. New York: American Bible Society: 1999; Bartleby.com, 2000.

Psalm 1:1-2

```
B W N N M S S S L O R D D Q
D B B B X T E B K Y R T Z Y
M W L Q A C G T N L H D B D
K W I N V G O J A G A N V R
B N D C T S R U I T S W B B
T S I D K T I L N R I W D Y
N Q B G Q E E N E S P D J D
S W N Y H D D F N B E B E Y
D E M Y L T F G J E L L M M
A K A B L O D J G E R W D M
Y G Y T C Z D V S R A S W L
W Y Y S W V Y S T L M W Z D
Y V N T J T E J R N T R M N
P B N G X D R Q G Z M T Y N
```

Blessed is the man
who walks not in the counsel
   of the wicked,
nor stands in the way of sinners,
nor sits in the seat of scoffers;
but his delight is in the law of the Lord,
and on his law he meditates day
   and night.

BLESSED	SCOFFERS
WALKS	DELIGHT
COUNSEL	LAW
WICKED	LORD
STANDS	MEDITATES
SINNERS	DAY
SEAT	NIGHT

Psalm 2:10-11

```
N T K E C I O J E R
T H E R E F O R E B
T R E M B L I N G N
W D S M E S O H M M
E A N G R V T R R Z
S D R E N R R A D X
I R L N A I E E J J
W U V E E F K W S Q
R Q K Q D D J D L T
```

Now *therefore*, O *kings*, be *wise*;
be *warned*, O *rulers* of the *earth*.
Serve the *Lord* with *fear*,
and *rejoice* with *trembling*.

THEREFORE	SERVE
KINGS	LORD
WISE	FEAR
WARNED	REJOICE
RULERS	TREMBLING
EARTH	

Psalm 3:3-4

```
S Y S N P L M A Z T
H R M T L B N B R N
I O N A F S G D G Y
E L C I W I R R L P
L G A E A O L O M W
D D R R L T H G I H
Z S Q Y O E N D M P
M B R D A U Y U D W
K L Q D L N N R O N
V Z B N L T T D N M
```

But you, <u>Lord,</u> are a <u>shield</u> <u>around</u> me,
my <u>glory</u>, the One who <u>lifts</u> my
 <u>head</u> <u>high</u>.
I <u>call</u> out to the Lord,
and he <u>answers</u> me from his
 <u>holy</u> <u>mountain</u>.

LORD   HIGH

SHIELD   CALL

AROUND   ANSWERS

GLORY   HOLY

LIFTS   MOUNTAIN

HEAD

Psalm 4:6-8

```
Y D R E T T E B B
E S R E P S W W T
Q C T O T E A N L
X S A S L A A F N
T M N F E D E C E
Y I R I N V W R E
O L M U A O R N G
J E B E H R I A R
N A J S S W G J H
```

Many people say, "Who will <u>show</u> us
   <u>better</u> <u>times</u>?"
Let your <u>face</u> <u>smile</u> on us, <u>Lord.</u>
You have given me <u>greater</u> <u>joy</u>
than those who have <u>abundant</u> <u>harvests</u>
   of <u>grain</u> and new <u>wine.</u>
In <u>peace</u> I will lie down and sleep,
for you alone, O Lord, will keep me <u>safe.</u>

SHOW	JOY
BETTER	ABUNDANT
TIMES	HARVESTS
FACE	GRAIN
SMILE	WINE
LORD	PEACE
GREATER	SAFE

Psalm 5:11-12

```
R E J O I C E S X Y T T
D A E R P S U K W M B L
R X Q W N R M G G D N J
L R Z R R B F R O O W N
P R K O L G E I I D P P
J D U E Q F F T L R L L
Y N S T U O C E A L B Y
D S D G R E I I S N E L
B B E E T H S Z P I O D
P D V O S E Y Y Z V N J
D E R M S T W N E N O G
R P M Z M M R L X Y G K
```

But let all who take <u>refuge</u> in you <u>rejoice</u>;
let them <u>sing</u> joyful <u>praises</u> <u>forever</u>.
<u>Spread</u> your <u>protection</u> over them,
that all who love your name may be
  <u>filled</u> with <u>joy</u>.
For you <u>bless</u> the <u>godly</u>, O Lord;
you <u>surround</u> them with your <u>shield</u>
  of <u>love</u>.

REFUGE	FILLED
REJOICE	JOY
SING	BLESS
PRAISES	GODLY
FOREVER	SURROUND
SPREAD	SHIELD
PROTECTION	LOVE

Psalm 6:2-4

```
G B R L W K T N M M
N O S E O F A I N T
I N O G V R N R U T
L E U P L I D B H D
I S L O L M L S L X
A E N Y E X I E Y Y
F G V R H U G N D E
N B C A G E O N V Y
U Y T N S G A O X P
N W A W A L L L L D
```

Have _mercy_ on me, _Lord_, for I am _faint_;
heal me, Lord, for my _bones_ are in _agony_.
My _soul_ is in deep _anguish_.
How _long_, Lord, how long?
Turn, Lord, and _deliver_ me;
save me because of your _unfailing_ love.

MERCY	ANGUISH
LORD	LONG
FAINT	TURN
HEAL	DELIVER
BONES	SAVE
AGONY	UNFAILING
SOUL	LOVE

Psalm 7:9

```
X R B S M I N D S M J T
T Y D U N R T Z O Y X E
T V I O L E N C E G R Z
P W S E W E K A M U K G
R N X T Y I V J C D N M
O V Q H R R C E D I L M
B W G G D A S K R N W N
E D R I P R E B E L E P
S P Y R M R D H J D Q M
```

*Bring to an end the violence of
    the wicked
and make the righteous secure—
you, the righteous God,
who probes minds and hearts.*

BRING	SECURE
END	GOD
VIOLENCE	PROBES
WICKED	MINDS
MAKE	HEARTS
RIGHTEOUS	

Psalm 8:3-5

```
Q Y L A J L K Y F Z T J
R H D W N R L I E R A C
D E L D O G N H U M A N
E A D W N G E V R Y K R
N V X I E I T L R V B M
W E S R S R K O S R N Y
O N S T E N L N O P T B
R S M W A G O N A M R D
C N O O M R O C D M B X
D L M J X H S D X D T R
```

When I _consider_ your _heavens_,
the _work_ of your _fingers_,
the _moon_ and the _stars_,
which you have set in place,
what is _mankind_ that you are mindful
   of them,
human beings that you _care_ for them?
You have made them a little _lower_ than
   the _angels_
and _crowned_ them with _glory_ and _honor_.

CONSIDER	HUMAN
HEAVENS	CARE
WORK	LOWER
FINGERS	ANGELS
MOON	CROWNED
STARS	GLORY
MANKIND	HONOR

Psalm 9:9-10

```
B Z D T I M E S T G R B
X N E N W N R R G E B N
K W S P M T U R V D E Y
T N S D B S R E L K D R
N D E Z T M N O A K B Q
K D R O L G H S U M J X
D Z P N W G R N K B M Q
K R P T N O B E A E L P
T M O O F V N V F M E E
R R R D W N Z K N U E S
P T B M Z K G N Y D G N
S X Y B Z R L T N N K E
```

The _Lord_ is a _refuge_ for the _oppressed_,
a _stronghold_ in _times_ of _trouble_.
Those who _know_ your _name_ _trust_ in you,
for you, Lord, have _never_ _forsaken_ those
who _seek_ you.

LORD	KNOW
REFUGE	NAME
OPPRESSED	TRUST
STRONGHOLD	NEVER
TIMES	FORSAKEN
TROUBLE	SEEK

Psalm 10:14

```
M W V G B C Z N K A J B
B S Y I O Y T M F R C J
E W S M C Y M F R O R T
K T M E G T L T N D H J
A I R R L I I S Z E B V
T K I O C R I M L G D L
W E S T U D E P S N T Q
F E E L E B E H A N Y G
E D L R P R L H T D O G
Y D P V T B R E R A P K
L R D J T B D Z X L F D
```

*But you, <u>God</u>, <u>see</u> the <u>trouble</u> of
  the <u>afflicted</u>;
you <u>consider</u> their <u>grief</u> and <u>take</u> it
  in <u>hand</u>.
The <u>victims</u> <u>commit</u> themselves to you;
you are the <u>helper</u> of the <u>fatherless</u>.*

GOD	TAKE
SEE	HAND
TROUBLE	VICTIMS
AFFLICTED	COMMIT
CONSIDER	HELPER
GRIEF	FATHERLESS

Psalm 12:5-6

```
D B S R B Q T V G T K Z K
K Q O E T R I E U C S E R
X O Z S S O E C A N R U F
P B R S L I G F D Z B T L
B K Y E D D M R I R T M V
Z W N L T E R O O N O Q D
L C Y P L T G A R A E L Q
E S I L V E R N E P N D K
R B D E P R N K O H K S R
B R L H I U P Y Q L J V K
L M N S D Y R J D Z V D D
G P E T J M G E W G W T R
```

The Lord replies, "I have seen violence
  done to the helpless,
and I have heard the groans of the poor.
Now I will rise up to rescue them,
as they have longed for me to do."
The Lord's promises are pure,
like silver refined in a furnace,
purified seven times over.

LORD	RESCUE
VIOLENCE	LONGED
HELPLESS	PROMISES
HEARD	PURE
GROANS	SILVER
POOR	REFINED
RISE	FURNACE

Psalm 13:5-6

```
U S E C I O J E R L
P N O I T A V L A S
R R F M D S R R Y R
A U M A L L U J T G
I O D O I H B R G T
S Y V D E L G N T K
E E R A T O I G D Q
P O R M O S B N V G
L T L D R M X Y G D
```

But I <u>trust</u> in <u>your</u> <u>unfailing</u> love;
my <u>heart</u> <u>rejoices</u> in your <u>salvation</u>.
I will <u>sing</u> the <u>Lord's</u> <u>praise</u>,
for he has been <u>good</u> to me.

TRUST	SALVATION
YOUR	SING
UNFAILING	LORD
LOVE	PRAISE
HEART	GOOD
REJOICES	

Psalm 16:9-11

```
S P G L Y L U O S R
E R Y N I T D Y E J
R E E O I F E V P T
U S W C J T E F R P
S E G L I R N A A R
A N W R O O E A E S
E C D F A H J S R M
L E N A O V T E K G
P T J L L S E L R B
L N Y R T G T L T B
```

No wonder my _heart_ is _glad_,
   and I _rejoice_.
My body _rests_ in _safety_.
For you will not leave my _soul_ among
   the dead
or allow your _holy_ one to rot in the _grave_.
You will show me the way of _life_,
granting me the _joy_ of your _presence_
and the _pleasures_ of living with
   you _forever_.

HEART	GRAVE
GLAD	LIFE
REJOICE	GRANTING
RESTS	JOY
SAFETY	PRESENCE
SOUL	PLEASURES
HOLY	FOREVER

Psalm 17:6-7

```
J P V X U N N M P N J T R D
Y A Y M W N Y L D N L G R K
L R N E Z Y F N B N D Y D T
G U V S N V E A V V Q R Y B
M O F Y W B G N I Y A R P S
L R D R T E D E B L M J H N
E L R V E H R B G Y I O T V
W N D E Z D G Q L U W N N Z
Y V E W S W N I T P F T G Y
M T M M V C S O M D O E N B
K W D X I T U M W J Y W R V
B O Q T E E R E R Q T R E R
G V N N N Q S Q D B T Z Q R
```

I am <u>praying</u> to you because I know you
   will <u>answer</u>, O <u>God</u>.
<u>Bend</u> down and <u>listen</u> as I pray.
<u>Show</u> me your <u>unfailing</u> <u>love</u> in
   <u>wonderful</u> ways.
By your <u>mighty</u> <u>power</u> you <u>rescue</u>
those who seek <u>refuge</u> from their
   <u>enemies</u>.

PRAYING	LOVE
ANSWER	WONDERFUL
GOD	MIGHTY
BEND	POWER
LISTEN	RESCUE
SHOW	REFUGE
UNFAILING	ENEMIES

Psalm 18:1-3

```
S A L V A T I O N D L M P J
E T L D D Y S S E R T R O F
I L R L L R D L Z S D L L K
M W Z O Q E I D T R O C K T
E R O B N V I R E G U F E R
N S M R E G E H P R A I S E
E L A R T N H T S L O V E L
Q O E V G H D O Z D L N M X
T R B T E X Y X L N R B R M
D D H B G D R W X D R R R V
```

I *love* you, <u>Lord</u>, my <u>strength</u>.
The Lord is my <u>rock</u>, my <u>fortress</u>
   and my <u>deliverer</u>;
my God is my rock, in whom I
   take <u>refuge</u>,
my <u>shield</u> and the horn of my <u>salvation</u>,
   my <u>stronghold</u>.
I called to the Lord, who is <u>worthy</u>
   of <u>praise</u>,
and I have been <u>saved</u> from my <u>enemies</u>.

LOVE	SHIELD
LORD	SALVATION
STRENGTH	STRONGHOLD
ROCK	WORTHY
FORTRESS	PRAISE
DELIVERER	SAVED
REFUGE	ENEMIES

Psalm 18:35-36

```
T E E F M N B X J
S U P P O R T S G
V I C T O R Y N T
D G G M R H I R H
L R I R R P E A M
E E K V P I N L P
I A D I E D G A P
H T L I D N T H V
S S Y V W H Q L T
```

You have *given* me your *shield* of *victory.*
Your *right* *hand* *supports* me;
your *help* has made me *great.*
You have made a *wide* *path* for my *feet*
to keep them from *slipping.*

GIVEN	HELP
SHIELD	GREAT
VICTORY	WIDE
RIGHT	PATH
HAND	FEET
SUPPORTS	SLIPPING

Psalm 19:9a-11

```
E S L T F D E N R A W
N D E I N L G I K S B
D P R E O A G O W Z J
U M R R H V E L W D
R D D E T C E R V D X
I M R E C T E Y E F V
N P O A E I E D E S Z
G U U R W N O A W T Z
S T G R O E R U B R L
P M D H E L R D S Y Z
```

The _fear_ of the _Lord_ is _pure_,
enduring forever.
The _decrees_ of the Lord are _firm_,
and all of them are _righteous_.
They are more _precious_ than _gold_,
than much pure gold;
they are _sweeter_ than _honey_,
than honey from the honeycomb.
By them your _servant_ is _warned_;
in keeping them there is great _reward_.

FEAR	PRECIOUS
LORD	GOLD
PURE	SWEETER
ENDURING	HONEY
DECREES	SERVANT
FIRM	WARNED
RIGHTEOUS	REWARD

Psalm 20:7-8

```
C H K R X D R K D B P
H O M T S I N G T P P
A R V O S E G H L Q W
R S M E E U G O N Y D
I E S S D U R A D L L
O S J T O D M T L G Y
T M M R A E Z L M W R
S B B G Z N A M R I F
M M B W D F D P L M L
```

Some _trust_ in _chariots_ and _some_
   in _horses_,
but we trust in the _name_ of the _Lord_
   our _God_.
They are _brought_ to their _knees_ and _fall_,
but we _rise_ up and _stand_ _firm_.

TRUST	BROUGHT
CHARIOTS	KNEES
SOME	FALL
HORSES	RISE
NAME	STAND
LORD	FIRM
GOD	

Psalm 22:19-21

```
R X N G Y X H C T A N S
S T R E N G T H R Y P J
E K Y L J A S D K Z Y M
Z R S A I A L G T M R M
H X A D T O W C O E R D
O K V P R S O S F D K W
R T E D S M W I N J N Q
N Y V Q E O L E V K R L
S V T R R Y X L Y P D N
R Y J D K O G X R Y J K
```

O _Lord,_ do not _stay_ far away!
You are my _strength; come_ quickly
  to my _aid!_
Save me from the _sword;_
spare my precious _life_ from these _dogs._
Snatch me from the lion's _jaws_
and from the _horns_ of these wild _oxen._

LORD	SPARE
STAY	LIFE
STRENGTH	DOGS
COME	SNATCH
AID	JAWS
SAVE	HORNS
SWORD	OXEN

Psalm 22:27-28

```
R B E L O N G S L R D
N E N R U T E X R R Y
E A M N O I N I M O D
N A T E L R U L E S L
D D R I M L X J P M K
S O M T O B O W K K V
N A W R H N E K G W X
F N D N Y L S R G P Q
```

All the <u>ends</u> of the <u>earth</u>
will <u>remember</u> and <u>turn</u> to the <u>Lord,</u>
and all the <u>families</u> of the <u>nations</u>
will <u>bow</u> <u>down</u> before him,
for <u>dominion</u> <u>belongs</u> to the Lord
and he <u>rules</u> over the nations.

ENDS	NATIONS
EARTH	BOW
REMEMBER	DOWN
TURN	DOMINION
LORD	BELONGS
FAMILIES	RULES

Psalm 23:1-4

```
R I G H T E O U S N E S S
S H E P H E R D H M L Y N
T F S T T L D T J H Q M R
R F V T L X E I T W A L K
O A P U I R Y E S W T Y D
F T O A O L D G A E E L R
M S B T S A L T J L B P Z
O L S H E T E M L N N W D
C E T L Z R U A K L D O R
R A R X S G V R M K Q L W
P Z V Z B P N Y E R R L J
N D D Q B P M Z J S M G V
```

The Lord is my <u>shepherd</u>; I shall
    not want.
He maketh me to lie down in green
    <u>pastures</u>: he <u>leadeth</u> me <u>beside</u>
    the <u>still</u> <u>waters</u>.
He <u>restoreth</u> my <u>soul</u>: he leadeth me
    in the <u>paths</u> of <u>righteousness</u> for
    his name's sake.
Yea, though I <u>walk</u> through the <u>valley</u> of
    the shadow of death, I will fear no evil:
    for thou art with me; thy <u>rod</u> and thy
    <u>staff</u> they <u>comfort</u> me.

SHEPHERD	PATHS
PASTURES	RIGHTEOUSNESS
LEADETH	WALK
BESIDE	VALLEY
STILL	ROD
WATERS	STAFF
RESTORETH	COMFORT
SOUL	

Psalm 24:1-2

```
G E L P O E P Q Z N
G N O L E B D G O Q
S O I L T L N I M E
H C B H R L T X A J
T E B O T A I R Q N
P A W L D Y T U S G
E N L N O H R A B N
D L U A D R E E J K
M O T M I S D D V Q
F J G L V D B W N E
```

The _earth_ is the _Lord_'s, and _everything_
   in it.
The _world_ and all its _people_ _belong_
   to him.
For he _laid_ the earth's _foundation_ on
   the _seas_
and _built_ it on the _ocean_ _depths_.

EARTH	LAID
LORD	FOUNDATION
EVERYTHING	SEAS
WORLD	BUILT
PEOPLE	OCEAN
BELONG	DEPTHS

Psalm 25:4-5

```
K T T L M X D L T B Z D
Z J O D D N L S F D A W
L N S J P D V O A O D G
G D M H R L L L R V O D
H Y R L O L W M B D E D
T T D I O W T N I O P S
D T A W G H L G B L Y E
M Q R P C H Y T Q X P X
J B T A D Q T R X O D L
R D E B R K Z U H L E K
M T G P O Y J T Z A G B
N Y R G L B D H D B G K
```

Show me the right path, O Lord;
point out the road for me to follow.
Lead me by your truth and teach me,
for you are the God who saves me.
All day long I put my hope in you.

SHOW	LEAD
RIGHT	TRUTH
PATH	TEACH
LORD	GOD
POINT	SAVES
ROAD	LONG
FOLLOW	HOPE

Psalm 25:14-15

```
R E S C U E S S Z
Z T T F W D E N N
A J N N R H R S Q
M L V A C I E O E
S G W A N I E Y L
R P E A M E E N N
A T A E Y S V T D
E Y N R Y S V O N
F E D W T Y D V C
```

The <u>Lord</u> is a <u>friend</u> to those who
  <u>fear</u> him.
He <u>teaches</u> them his <u>covenant</u>.
My <u>eyes</u> are <u>always</u> on the Lord,
for he <u>rescues</u> me from the <u>traps</u> of
  my <u>enemies</u>.

LORD	EYES
FRIEND	ALWAYS
FEAR	RESCUES
TEACHES	TRAPS
COVENANT	ENEMIES

Psalm 26:1-3

```
S S E N L U F H T I A F
E D E T S U R T Y B T Z
V R S Z A T Y T N S M Y
O O D E E C I R A W W D
R L T S Y R I F T A Y Z
P N T R G E D D V T T M
E M T E A A B E N T T X
D V T L E E R W N I X M
N N O T Y I H A T D V R
I X S L N G Y L T R M T
M W N G L M R K J Y T R
```

Vindicate me, O Lord,
for I have walked in my integrity,
and I have trusted in the Lord
*   without wavering.*
Prove me, O Lord, and try me;
test my heart and mind.
For your steadfast love is before
*   my eyes,*
and I walk in faithfulness to you.

VINDICATE
LORD
INTEGRITY
TRUSTED
WAVERING
PROVE
TRY
TEST

HEART
MIND
STEADFAST
LOVE
EYES
WALK
FAITHFULNESS

Psalm 27:13-14

```
S Y M M M D T G R J L
T E G A R U O C E Z R
R L K O S O G V Q Z J
O L L E D N E H D J M
N A E N I I E N W M D
G H E V L A A A L Z D
L S I E R L I T A K E
S L B T X T T Y R L Q
```

I <u>believe</u> that I <u>shall</u> <u>see</u> the <u>goodness</u>
  of the <u>Lord</u>
in the <u>land</u> of the <u>living</u>.
<u>Wait</u> for the Lord;
be <u>strong</u>, and let your <u>heart</u> <u>take</u>
  <u>courage</u>;
wait for the Lord!

BELIEVE	LIVING
SHALL	WAIT
SEE	STRONG
GOODNESS	HEART
LORD	TAKE
LAND	COURAGE

Psalm 28:8-9

```
N O I T A V L A S P I
A P B L E S S Y R N X
N E C Y B T G S H R S
O O A B J B H E F T R
I P R B M E R O R E W
N L R Y P I R E V Y N
T E Y H T T N E R V N
E J E A R G R L V P G
D R N E T O B L O A W
D C S H F D B W T R S
E S V X T B Q M K J D
```

The <u>Lord</u> is the <u>strength</u> of his <u>people</u>,
a <u>fortress</u> of <u>salvation</u> for his
   <u>anointed</u> one.
<u>Save</u> your people and <u>bless</u>
   your <u>inheritance</u>;
be their <u>shepherd</u> and <u>carry</u>
   them <u>forever</u>.

LORD	SAVE
STRENGTH	BLESS
PEOPLE	INHERITANCE
FORTRESS	SHEPHERD
SALVATION	CARRY
ANOINTED	FOREVER

Psalm 29:1-2

```
Y W V Z Y D V J L T
L O H D M R M S S G
N R V T T O P S S X
E S D L G L E G B E
V H X Z E N N Z B N
A I R N I I E I R G
E P D L E N R R L R
H O O B E C A O T L
R H T U S J R M W S
Y J D A R Y J B E M
```

Ascribe to the Lord, you heavenly
  beings,
ascribe to the Lord glory and strength.
Ascribe to the Lord the glory due
  his name;
worship the Lord in the splendor of
  his holiness.

ASCRIBE	DUE
LORD	NAME
HEAVENLY	WORSHIP
BEINGS	SPLENDOR
GLORY	HOLINESS
STRENGTH	

Psalm 30:4-5

```
E J M G R P Q K B W M R
T M N Y A O G L E P D R
P I I N L N V E J M B N
S R G T I D P A O L G N
L E A N E I O M F R D N
R H R I N F E G E M A N
J O J G S N I N I G H T
M L O Y T E K L O R D B
B Y Y K W N R N M Q L L
```

Sing to the Lord, all you godly ones!
Praise his holy name.
For his anger lasts only a moment,
but his favor lasts a lifetime!
Weeping may last through the night,
but joy comes with the morning.

SING	MOMENT
LORD	FAVOR
GODLY	LIFETIME
PRAISE	WEEPING
HOLY	NIGHT
NAME	JOY
ANGER	MORNING

Psalm 31:19

```
S T T L M T T T J
T Y N L D H A Z N
O W W A I T R K Q
R R O N D K W E E
E S G T T N G O J
D S I G S U U R H
T R O G F E A B W
D O Q E H E B Z A
D P R M F T L D K
```

How _abundant_ are the _good_ _things_
that you have _stored_ up for those who
  fear you,
that you _bestow_ in the _sight_ of _all_,
on those who _take_ _refuge_ in you.

HOW	BESTOW
ABUNDANT	SIGHT
GOOD	ALL
THINGS	TAKE
STORED	REFUGE
FEAR	

Psalm 32:1-2

```
S N O I S S E R G S N A R T
R E D N L L M R L T Q L D J
M V S E Q J M W K L R T Y Y
M I I L S C O V E R E D G Z
V G N Y P S A K T L B Y D J
C R S Z L G E I M V W B N J
K O R Z A T R L D E C E I T
T F U I Z I Z N B O G D R B
D L N N P R Q J N T R L T Q
P S X S T D M E Y K B D W V
T G X R N R W L R D Y R K Y
D T Z W Y O D Y T D P Z T J
D P N Y V L D P D D T T N N
```

Blessed is the <u>one</u>
whose <u>transgressions</u> are <u>forgiven</u>,
whose <u>sins</u> are <u>covered</u>.
Blessed is the one
whose sin the <u>Lord</u> does not <u>count</u>
  <u>against</u> them
and in whose <u>spirit</u> is no <u>deceit</u>.

BLESSED	LORD
ONE	COUNT
TRANSGRESSIONS	AGAINST
FORGIVEN	SPIRIT
SINS	DECEIT
COVERED	

Psalm 33:2-3

```
S G Y D P V J J R E G
T N R A W R N W K S G
R I V E L T A A K P Q
I S N P Y P M I Y N G
N Q P L R Y L O S N V
G J O D E L J X O E J
E R M J F C I S U M N
D T P U S H O U T Z P
G M L R T R L N N V G
R L Y B A V J D Z M B
Y M V G T H J Q V D G
```

Praise the *Lord* with the *harp;*
make *music* to him on the
    ten-*stringed* *lyre.*
Sing to him a *new* *song;*
play *skillfully,* and *shout* for *joy.*

PRAISE	SING
LORD	NEW
HARP	SONG
MAKE	PLAY
MUSIC	SKILLFULLY
STRINGED	SHOUT
LYRE	JOY

Psalm 33:10-11

```
S N O I T A R E N E G M P
P U R P O S E S N Y V R X
S R F A S S L A V Q N M L
T L L O T N T P E O P L E
R L I A R I A H R P Y P T
A D N O O E E L M M D J R
W D R N F A V R P Y Y W R
H M S O R Y I E K D G Z V
T B N T L F M M R T Q W K
```

The <u>Lord</u> <u>foils</u> the <u>plans</u> of the <u>nations</u>;
he <u>thwarts</u> the <u>purposes</u> of the <u>peoples</u>.
But the plans of the Lord <u>stand</u>
  <u>firm</u> <u>forever</u>,
the purposes of his <u>heart</u> through
  <u>all</u> <u>generations</u>.

LORD
FOILS
PLANS
NATIONS
THWARTS
PURPOSES
PEOPLE

STAND
FIRM
FOREVER
HEART
ALL
GENERATIONS

Psalm 34:12-14

```
L I E S M S T U R N D
K E E S Y E L R R P R
P T T A N T V L M N R
E E D R D E S I R E S
F L A Z E T Y L L P D
I I B C O V O N U R D
L P G N E V E R A G D
V S G N E X S O O M Z
B U X S R U Y O H T X
E R Q M E G D Q D W V
```

Whoever of you loves life
and desires to see many good days,
keep your tongue from evil
and your lips from telling lies.
Turn from evil and do good;
seek peace and pursue it.

WHOEVER	EVIL
LOVES	LIPS
LIFE	LIES
DESIRES	TURN
MANY	SEEK
GOOD	PEACE
DAYS	PURSUE
TONGUE	

Psalm 35:10

```
D Q V T R Z C E V Q Z
Z J Y J N O N R D H X
Z L Q T M O O R E N L
S B R P B O G L K B Q
T G A R P M P T P Y K
C R N T E L N R T Y R
E Y J O E S A N E J V
T L D S R I C V M R W
O O S O S T E U R O B
R R Q E B R S Z E G Q
P D D L Y Y M R Q S Q
```

With _every_ _bone_ in my _body_ I will
praise him:
"_Lord_, who can _compare_ with you?
Who else _rescues_ the _helpless_ from the
strong?
Who else _protects_ the helpless and _poor_
from those who _rob_ them?"

EVERY	RESCUES
BONE	HELPLESS
BODY	STRONG
PRAISE	PROTECTS
LORD	POOR
COMPARE	ROB

Psalm 36:5-6

```
S S E N S U O E T H G I R
S S E N L U F H T I A F M
H B L P Y O N J G S B S Q
S E J G C T U B N L D X M
E W A E N S H I L U T X M
H S A V T I A G O D R O L
C N H I E T L L I T T R Y
A Y C T N N C I S M R Q R
E E L U P D S A A R L N Z
R B O Z T E V Y N F T B J
J M V D N D D B Y Y N N Q
J M E W B M N B R R Y U V
```

Your <u>unfailing</u> <u>love</u>, O <u>Lord</u>, is as
<u>vast</u> as the <u>heavens</u>;
your <u>faithfulness</u> <u>reaches</u> beyond
the <u>clouds</u>.
Your <u>righteousness</u> is like the
<u>mighty</u> <u>mountains</u>,
your <u>justice</u> like the <u>ocean</u> <u>depths</u>.

UNFAILING	CLOUDS
LOVE	RIGHTEOUSNESS
LORD	MIGHTY
VAST	MOUNTAINS
HEAVENS	JUSTICE
FAITHFULNESS	OCEAN
REACHES	DEPTHS

Psalm 37:10-11

```
Y T I R E P S O R P
K Y J W F O U N D N
W O R M H X K I M E
I J Y L D I N O R Y
C N E M I H L O O B
K E T C E T M E B L
E N D R A E T N P Z
D T I N T E K L M W
V T B M A R P B E T
D K L R V L M N P M
```

A _little_ _while_, and the _wicked_ will be
    no _more_;
though you _look_ for them, they will not
    be _found_.
But the _meek_ will _inherit_ the _land_
and _enjoy_ _peace_ and _prosperity_.

LITTLE	MEEK
WHILE	INHERIT
WICKED	LAND
MORE	ENJOY
LOOK	PEACE
FOUND	PROSPERITY

Psalm 38:8b-9

```
S N Q D E S I R E L
I L O L Q Q N E L M
G L M I Q N R M J V
H A B Q T O A T G T
I H Y R F A R O R R
N N I E X A T W R L
G T B D E Y L I L G
D L L H D Y O O G K
M N T N B E R U M A
M B Y P D D N R N M
```

I _groan_ because of the _agitation_
   of my _heart_.
Lord, _all_ my _desire_ is _before_ _You_;
And my _sighing_ is not _hidden_ from You.

GROAN	DESIRE
AGITATION	BEFORE
HEART	YOU
LORD	SIGHING
ALL	HIDDEN

Psalm 40:5

```
W O N D E R S P J J J
D C V S Y V L N O N E
E R O N P A T S J Q R
C D A M N E G L L E T
L M E N P N A L J B Q
A D E E I A O K K N J
R D O H D R R D O N E
E V T G D S R E Z Y D
```

Many, Lord my God,
are the wonders you have done,
the things you planned for us.
None can compare with you;
were I to speak and tell of your deeds,
they would be too many to declare.

MANY	NONE
LORD	COMPARE
GOD	SPEAK
WONDERS	TELL
DONE	DEEDS
THINGS	DECLARE
PLANNED	

Psalm 40:9-10

```
S S E N L U F H T I A F J
R I G H T E O U S N E S S
H E A R T H I D E V S D Q
D L P N G T X R T P L X L
D N Y L R L V J E P J G D
Y L B M E S S A R C N S M
S L T D A H K O O I P Q Z
L T S N T B C N V I D J R
O K C E W L C A L L K T D
V Q Z A A E S R N N X X W
E D D I A L T J Y W B G J
R N M L B W Y T M Q Q R W
```

I <u>proclaim</u> your <u>saving</u> <u>acts</u> in the
   <u>great</u> <u>assembly</u>;
I do not <u>seal</u> my <u>lips</u>, Lord,
as you know.
I do not <u>hide</u> your <u>righteousness</u>
   in my <u>heart</u>;
I <u>speak</u> of your <u>faithfulness</u> and your
   saving <u>help</u>.
I do not <u>conceal</u> your <u>love</u> and
   your faithfulness
from the great assembly.

PROCLAIM	RIGHTEOUSNESS
SAVING	HEART
ACTS	SPEAK
GREAT	FAITHFULNESS
ASSEMBLY	HELP
SEAL	CONCEAL
LIPS	LOVE
HIDE	

Psalm 41:1-2

```
P E N E M I E S R L
P R R E V I L A P B
G O O L L M D R Z S
R I O S J B O R P R
Z E V R P T U E O D
W T S E E E E O N L
D Q D C S K R A R J
L N T Q U Z L I O T
Z S I D Z E Q Y T J
X R N K V D S T N Y
```

Oh, the joys of those who are kind
    to the poor!
The Lord rescues them when they are
    in trouble.
The Lord protects them
and keeps them alive.
He gives them prosperity in the land
and rescues them from their enemies.

JOYS	KEEPS
KIND	ALIVE
POOR	GIVES
LORD	PROSPERITY
RESCUES	LAND
TROUBLE	ENEMIES
PROTECTS	

Psalm 42:1-2

```
L I V I N G D D W
P T T G L X P P R
A E S H R E T A W
N E D M I W D X M
T M Y R A R H O V
S L E L B E S E G
G E U L B D R T N
D O N Y V D J T S
S M V J Y P J G S
```

As the <u>deer</u> <u>pants</u> for <u>streams</u> of <u>water</u>,
so my <u>soul</u> pants for you, my <u>God</u>.
My soul <u>thirsts</u> for God, for the
*   <u>living</u> God.*
<u>When</u> can I go and <u>meet</u> with God?

DEER	GOD
PANTS	THIRSTS
STREAMS	LIVING
WATER	WHEN
SOUL	MEET

Psalm 43:3-4

```
Q L G E R A C X N X
D M U A P B R I N G
P E T F D D A E L Q
R L L N H T E R Y L
A H E I N T L W D D
I S O U G I I W T Q
S J O L G H E A G G
E M O H Y L T O F P
Q M T Y L M D M N J
```

Send me your *light* and your
   faithful *care*,
let them *lead* me;
let them *bring* me to your *holy* *mountain*,
to the place where you *dwell*.
Then I will go to the *altar* of *God*,
to God, my *joy* and my *delight*.
I will *praise* you with the *lyre*,
O God, my God.

SEND	DWELL
LIGHT	ALTAR
FAITHFUL	GOD
CARE	JOY
LEAD	DELIGHT
BRING	PRAISE
HOLY	LYRE
MOUNTAIN	

Psalm 44:6-8

```
C O N T I N U A L L Y
T F N S E M A H S D T
H H O Y W D W G Y W N
A H A R L O B P B D W
T M A N E G R O V T N
E S W L K V A D S M G
E O E E E S E U N X R
B M V O T S R R Y P L
W A A E F T M N Q G Y
S X D N Z R M D P Y M
```

For not in my <u>bow</u> do I <u>trust</u>,
nor can my <u>sword</u> <u>save</u> me.
But you have saved us from our <u>foes</u>
and have put to <u>shame</u> those who
 <u>hate</u> us.
In <u>God</u> we have <u>boasted</u> <u>continually</u>,
and we will give <u>thanks</u> to your <u>name</u>
 <u>forever</u>. <u>Selah</u>

BOW	GOD
TRUST	BOASTED
SWORD	CONTINUALLY
SAVE	THANKS
FOES	NAME
SHAME	FOREVER
HATE	SELAH

Psalm 45:6-7a

```
R E T P E C S R R N R
F G N T T H G I R P U
D O N O R L G V K W K
E D R U R H J I N K L
K D O E T H N T D T Y
C Y E E V G T E D L M
I N O V D E T D G B Q
W U X O O A R R Q Q X
S T M V H L R N R R B
```

*Your throne, O God, is forever and ever.
The scepter of your kingdom is a scepter
of uprightness;
you have loved righteousness and hated
wickedness.*

YOUR
THRONE
GOD
FOREVER
SCEPTER
KINGDOM

UPRIGHT
LOVED
RIGHTEOUS
HATED
WICKED

Psalm 46:1-3

```
M F A L L X V T D B V
S O G N I G R U S R S
T R U Q P O E E L N D
R O X N U R G A I Y S
E A L B T U E A R R B
N R L R F A T S E T E
G E Y E F N I T E K H
T M R E U X A N A N Y
H B A O M W G U S Z T
P R M O P X Q P L E H
L R W D F M L B J D L
```

God is our <u>refuge</u> and <u>strength</u>,
an ever-<u>present</u> <u>help</u> in <u>trouble</u>.
Therefore we will not <u>fear</u>, though
*   the <u>earth</u> give way*
and the <u>mountains</u> <u>fall</u> into the heart
*   of the sea,*
though its <u>waters</u> <u>roar</u> and <u>foam</u>
and the <u>mountains</u> <u>quake</u> with their
*   <u>surging</u>.*

REFUGE
STRENGTH
PRESENT
HELP
TROUBLE
FEAR
EARTH
MOUNTAINS

FALL
WATERS
ROAR
FOAM
MOUNTAINS
QUAKE
SURGING

Psalm 46:10-11

```
A D W R L G D N M N B P
L F Q O N O A O T Y R J
M Z O O N T R J G Z Q D
I S M R I K L D M L T L
G A T O T E X A L T E D
H W N I H R J Z Q L P T
T S I T L A E X V K Q G
Y Q R T C L K S V N D N
W A R O H N G M S R W Z
E M B N D W W L Y B R R
```

He says, "Be _still_, and _know_ that
   I am _God_;
I will be _exalted_ _among_ the _nations_,
I will be exalted in the _earth_."
The _Lord_ _Almighty_ is _with_ us;
the God of _Jacob_ is our _fortress_.

STILL	EARTH
KNOW	LORD
GOD	ALMIGHTY
EXALTED	WITH
AMONG	JACOB
NATIONS	FORTRESS

Psalm 47:1-2

```
S H M M J L Y R D G
N A A O R E V O N B
O W G N S T G I J B
I E R Y D T K B B Y
T S E V D S L G Q Q
A O A S H O U T S E
N M T I P C B E A D
T E G N L N I R R N
P H X A R R T O L G
M W P X C H L Y R Q
```

Clap your hands, all you nations;
shout to God with cries of joy.
For the Lord Most High is awesome,
the great King over all the earth.

CLAP
HANDS
NATIONS
SHOUT
GOD
CRIES
JOY
LORD

MOST
HIGH
AWESOME
GREAT
KING
OVER
EARTH

Psalm 48:9-10

```
E H E J D G Z T U J K Y
D T M J O R J N L B S X
E R A D N H F P X E Q D
S A N T A A I I V R N G
I E R N I H E R L V W M
A Y D L S D E L T L Y Q
R G I R S S E H P R E J
P N O E E T G M O M S D
G W P D V I R T M D E N
K T Y M R O C O N R Z T
P J K T K I L E N N J
Y P X J V R L M B G X M
```

O _God_, we _meditate_ on your
  unfailing _love_
as we _worship_ in your _Temple_.
As your _name_ _deserves_, O God,
you will be _praised_ to the _ends_
  of the _earth_.
Your _strong_ _right_ _hand_ is _filled_
  with _victory_.

GOD	PRAISED
MEDITATE	ENDS
UNFAILING	EARTH
LOVE	STRONG
WORSHIP	RIGHT
TEMPLE	HAND
NAME	FILLED
DESERVES	VICTORY

Psalm 50:1-2

```
S S R N G R R L G L M
U T W B N I Y Z O O B
M E D J S T Y D Y R D
M S B I H W G G R Y D
O R N G P S P E A K S
N G I H H E Y Z S Y K
S M H I T T R V I U L
T Y N T U R D F L O N
L E R A R K A Y E P N
S M E B R O Q E X C W
X B Z B Z Z F N G Q T
```

The *Mighty* One, *God*, the *Lord*, *speaks* and *summons* the *earth* from the *rising* of the *sun* to where it *sets*.
From *Zion*, *perfect* in *beauty*, God *shines* *forth*.

MIGHTY	SUN
GOD	SETS
LORD	ZION
SPEAKS	PERFECT
SUMMONS	BEAUTY
EARTH	SHINES
RISING	FORTH

Psalm 51:1-2

```
T N Q Y D Z L T B X N V T J
G R T Y Y D Q V M X S N A L
G B A Y C R E M B T M B O M
Z G D N P L N R E R U V B Y
C P R N S P Y A V N E X T R
L Y R D G G D M D W A S H P
E D T V Y F R A G Y K D X R
A G P I A X N E D O G Q S D
N P M S U T X Y S G L I M V
S L T N M Q C L Y S N L Q L
E T Z D K R I W D Y I X Q V
W O J D E L G N M R X O R Q
D L B M D T M L I W Z L N J
P B P J W B Z M L Y P B D S
```

Have _mercy_ on me, O _God_,
according to your _steadfast_ _love_;
according to your _abundant_ _mercy_
blot out my _transgressions_.
Wash me thoroughly from
  my _iniquity_,
and _cleanse_ me from my _sin_.

MERCY
GOD
STEADFAST
LOVE
ABUNDANT
MERCY

BLOT
TRANSGRESSIONS
WASH
INIQUITY
CLEANSE
SIN

Psalm 51:10-12

```
E C N E S E R P S X
R E S T O R E P N Y
S G G L B C I O O H
U O T N L R I J E R
S D X E I T T A M C
T R A T A L R S R X
A N I V H T L E A W
I L L G J O A I E C
N A P X H T L N W P
S T P N E T G Y L W
```

Create in me a clean heart, O God,
and put a new and right spirit within me.
Do not cast me away from your
    presence,
and do not take your holy spirit from me.
Restore to me the joy of your salvation,
and sustain in me a willing spirit.

CREATE	PRESENCE
CLEAN	HOLY
HEART	RESTORE
GOD	JOY
NEW	SALVATION
RIGHT	SUSTAIN
SPIRIT	WILLING
CAST	

Psalm 52:8-9

```
M N G O D N X N W L D R G
I A X T L R D J U O S W B
A M W J R T V F O T G D P
L E T T D E H G E N K R G
C X J Y Z T E A B B E R N
O T Q J I Q D Y J S E P R
R G N A Y F B F E E J V Y
P T F Q A T O N N M L T D
E J S S B R C E T N H T O
N W T U E E Q P S A Y L G
O Z P V R L N L N U I V W
D R E J R T M K G V O Y R
Y R Q Y T B X Q E T X H M
```

But I am like a <u>green</u> <u>olive</u> <u>tree</u>
in the <u>house</u> of <u>God</u>.
I <u>trust</u> in the <u>steadfast</u> love of God
<u>forever</u> and ever.
I will <u>thank</u> you forever,
because of what you have <u>done</u>.
In the <u>presence</u> of the <u>faithful</u>
I will <u>proclaim</u> your <u>name</u>, for it is <u>good</u>.

GREEN THANK
OLIVE DONE
TREE PRESENCE
HOUSE FAITHFUL
GOD PROCLAIM
TRUST NAME
STEADFAST GOOD
FOREVER

Psalm 53:6

```
E C N A R E V I L E D
D B M F L E A R S I E
R E S T O R E S N L G
Z C K G G R M D P O Y
I I M N L P T O D C J
O O B R R A E U O V J
N J W O R P D M N L Y
K E D R C R E W T E M
Z R D R M A Y L Y T S
Y D Y M Y J J Y K D T
```

O that _deliverance_ for _Israel_ would _come_
  from _Zion!_
When _God_ _restores_ the _fortunes_ of
  his _people,_
Jacob will _rejoice;_ _Israel_ will be _glad._

DELIVERANCE	FORTUNES
ISRAEL	PEOPLE
COME	JACOB
ZION	REJOICE
GOD	GLAD
RESTORES	

Psalm 54:1-2

```
V T S E V I G D M
R I H D P T O L D
E Q N G R G N N J
Y B Y D I O A P Y
A H G T I M W O R
R S T R E C U G N
P N A U L R A P J
Z E J V O Y B T D
H N R G E M B Z E
```

*Save me, O God, by your name,
and vindicate me by your might.
Hear my prayer, O God;
give ear to the words of my mouth.*

SAVE
GOD
NAME
VINDICATE
YOUR
MIGHT

HEAR
PRAYER
GIVE
WORDS
MOUTH

Psalm 55:22

```
Y J T T T D Y J K R J G
O Z M B R J T N I Q N P
U X S O L N J G N Y W N
R D L H M G H N N M G P
U P O N A T W E Q R Z R
Z N Y T E K D T E G Y T
Q N I O K R E V Z R X N
R K U A U N E N A P X T
B S L B T N D L T S A C
B Q L M Y S L M L T T D
M B I B Z O U L Y B J Z
T B W R W T L S J W Q K
```

Cast your burden upon the Lord and He will sustain you;
He will never allow the righteous to be shaken.

CAST	SUSTAIN
YOUR	NEVER
BURDEN	ALLOW
UPON	RIGHTEOUS
LORD	SHAKEN
WILL	

Psalm 56:3-4

```
A F R A I D P D
N E L T E G M Q
E M S R R O O Y
H E E I R U X D
W M S T A D S P
Y P A O R R U T
M L L O H T P R
S G W V M W N T
```

When I am afraid, I put my trust in you.
In God, whose word I praise—
in God I trust and am not afraid.
What can mere mortals do to me?

WHEN	WHOSE
AFRAID	WORD
PUT	PRAISE
TRUST	MERE
GOD	MORTALS

Psalm 56:12-13

```
P H T A E D M N S D
R L I F E K T G E S
E I B D N E N R T Y
S G D A R I E U P W
E H H O R V M S J U
N T F E I B W G N Q
T E F L L O T D O K
B F E I V N E E L D
O D N R Z R N A E N
N G Q J V N W R G F
```

I am *under* *vows* to you, my *God*;
I will *present* my *thank* *offerings* to you.
For you have *delivered* me from *death*
and my *feet* from *stumbling*,
that I may *walk* *before* God
in the *light* of *life*.

UNDER	DEATH
VOWS	FEET
GOD	STUMBLING
PRESENT	WALK
THANK	BEFORE
OFFERINGS	LIGHT
DELIVERED	LIFE

Psalm 57:9-10

```
A V H R E A C H E S N S
M B B E Y S P M P J S K
O Z U G A R N E X E J S
N R G N A V O O N M D D
G P K I F P E L I U J R
J T S L L A U N O T D T
L E O E G F I L S R A L
S R K N H T C L K G O N
D L I T H V Q N I V R X
J S I G J R A R E N N Z
Q A I T N H W N Q M G T
F H B L T X J L B B B K
```

*I will <u>thank</u> you, <u>Lord</u>, <u>among</u> all
  the <u>people</u>.*
*I will <u>sing</u> your <u>praises</u> among
  the <u>nations</u>.*
*For your <u>unfailing</u> <u>love</u> is as <u>high</u> as the
  <u>heavens</u>.*
Your <u>faithfulness</u> <u>reaches</u> to the <u>clouds</u>.

THANK	UNFAILING
LORD	LOVE
AMONG	HIGH
PEOPLE	HEAVENS
SING	FAITHFULNESS
PRAISES	REACHES
NATIONS	CLOUDS

Psalm 59:16-17

```
S F D P Y J T J M L N D
T Z O K R I L O Y L E R
R R G R M A R J T R R L
E E O E T N I T J X K D
N G S U I R Q S Y O U R
G U Z N B G E L E L P G
T F G K N L O S K V N N
H E M I Q V E B S D Z Z
J R S D E L Q D B J L M
```

But I will <u>sing</u> of <u>your</u> <u>strength</u>,
in the <u>morning</u> I will sing of your <u>love</u>;
for you are my <u>fortress</u>,
my <u>refuge</u> in <u>times</u> of <u>trouble</u>.
You are my strength, I sing <u>praise</u> to you;
you, <u>God</u>, are my fortress,
my God on whom I can <u>rely</u>.

SING	REFUGE
YOUR	TIMES
STRENGTH	TROUBLE
MORNING	PRAISE
LOVE	GOD
FORTRESS	RELY

Psalm 61:2-3

```
H F A I N T O W E R
R I T G V Q E O H K
E D G J N N F E K L
F T Y H D O A B M Z
U E B S E R R G T R
G L A L T R M T Q W
E M E R L L A C S N
K A V T T R O C K N
D D L G B H N P T P
```

From the <u>ends</u> of the <u>earth</u> I <u>call</u> to you,
I call as my <u>heart</u> grows <u>faint</u>;
<u>lead</u> me to the <u>rock</u> that is <u>higher</u> than I.
For you have been my <u>refuge</u>,
a <u>strong</u> <u>tower</u> against the <u>foe</u>.

ENDS	ROCK
EARTH	HIGHER
CALL	REFUGE
HEART	STRONG
FAINT	TOWER
LEAD	FOE

Psalm 61:4-5

```
J M G Q X D R A E H X H W
R X J W D Y R T M T E X L
D W E L L E Q Y A R G V J
L N K X V W R E I K Y O Z
K Y R E Y I N T G S E R D
L G R R G N A B W U E R F
P O N Y T G P O M T F E V
F N Z O E S V R L N A E N
M V Z J L J T E J R A J R
Q J N R B E H L T L V M P
L R D Q N S M M Q T J M E
V N M T D R B D T R J T X
```

I *long* to *dwell* in your *tent* *forever*
and *take* *refuge* in the *shelter* of
   your *wings*.
For you, *God*, have *heard* my *vows*;
you have given me the *heritage* of those
   who *fear* your *name*.

LONG	WINGS
DWELL	GOD
TENT	HEARD
FOREVER	VOWS
TAKE	HERITAGE
REFUGE	FEAR
SHELTER	NAME

Psalm 62:1-2

```
N S A N L R L Y S
O S L J E J O I Y
I E O N R K L C C
T R N Q E E A O K
A T E W N V M H G
V R Y C A E E O S
L O E T S I D R B
A F L U O S T Y X
S B M V M L Y S N
```

For <u>God</u> <u>alone</u> my <u>soul</u> <u>waits</u> in <u>silence</u>; from him <u>comes</u> my <u>salvation</u>. He alone is my <u>rock</u> and my salvation, my <u>fortress</u>; I shall <u>never</u> be <u>shaken</u>.

GOD	SALVATION
ALONE	ROCK
SOUL	FORTRESS
WAITS	NEVER
SILENCE	SHAKEN
COMES	

Psalm 63:1

```
G R K D Y V M T K
X O E R T S D S P
F W D T O Y T M R
A E H U A S Z N T
I A L S R W N G G
N R S I E R E H W
T Y H E X L A N D
S T X Y E N F Y N
N B N M Y K M T P
```

O *God*, you are my God, I *seek* you,
my *soul* *thirsts* for you;
my *flesh* *faints* for you,
as in a *dry* and *weary* *land* *where* there
    is no *water*.

GOD
SEEK
SOUL
THIRSTS
FLESH
FAINTS

DRY
WEARY
LAND
WHERE
WATER

Psalm 63:3-4

```
T L O N G Y N Y P
S L D S S E L B S
A P O P P T Z D L
F R R V F G N L S
D A E I E A A P N
A I L T H C I A V
E S G I T L M M R
T E P M F E T N K
S N L J M E B R L
```

Because your <u>steadfast</u> <u>love</u> is <u>better</u>
   than <u>life</u>,
my <u>lips</u> will <u>praise</u> you.
So I will <u>bless</u> you as <u>long</u> as I live;
I will <u>lift</u> up my <u>hands</u> and <u>call</u> on
   your <u>name</u>.

STEADFAST	BLESS
LOVE	LONG
BETTER	LIFT
LIFE	HANDS
LIPS	CALL
PRAISE	NAME

Psalm 65:4

```
E S U O H R R T V T T R
D M M D P L B Y R B S B
S A T I S F I E D T Y Z
G O O D N E S S R G D P
B Y N Y V N J U V Y Y X
G E P E W N O X N Y C H
N L L P A C L B X H O B
I I N P A R B Y O L L Q
R V B N M H D O Y W N Y
B E X D N E S D R R B L
Z K Z Z Z E T R K B R N
```

*Happy are those whom you choose and
bring near
to live in your courts.
We shall be satisfied with the goodness
of your house,
your holy temple.*

HAPPY	SATISFIED
CHOOSE	GOODNESS
BRING	HOUSE
NEAR	HOLY
LIVE	TEMPLE
COURTS	

Psalm 65:5

```
M S F A R T H E S T E
Y N A R E W S N A C E
G O D L X J L R N N L
E N S G V N M A D M Q
W M L E T A R S H B B
H L O X A E T O K Y X
X T J S V S P I G P R
Y P R I E E D W O P Y
K D L A L W X E M N Y
R E T N E N A R E B R
D Q D L R N W N M D L
```

By <u>awesome</u> <u>deeds</u> you <u>answer</u> us
   with <u>deliverance</u>,
O <u>God</u> of our <u>salvation</u>;
you are the <u>hope</u> of all the <u>ends</u> of the
   <u>earth</u>
and of the <u>farthest</u> seas.

AWESOME	HOPE
DEEDS	ENDS
ANSWER	EARTH
DELIVERANCE	FARTHEST
GOD	SEAS
SALVATION	

Psalm 66:3-4

```
B X S D E E D T D S L Y
R P W M G L R N P B R R
M L T T J G C I A E L P
Y D Q R Y R H R W M E T
Q T T W L S Q O I M E S
M Z M Y R T P S O N E M
X N Q O A B E S E S G L
H J W E K L E M I G P E
V T R W A W I A S I N G
R G R H A E R G Y T Q Y
V L K A S P R L O J B V
L G R G E B Q Y R D M B
```

Say to _God_, "How _awesome_ are
   your _deeds_!
Because of your _great_ _power_, your
   enemies _cringe_ before you.
All the _earth_ _worships_ you;
they _sing_ _praises_ to you,
sing praises to your _name_." _Selah_

GOD	EARTH
AWESOME	WORSHIPS
DEEDS	SING
GREAT	PRAISES
POWER	NAME
ENEMIES	SELAH
CRINGE	

Psalm 67:1-3

```
G G M K M T E D L W P J
R S N A X A E S I A R P
A S K I R K N J P T Q D
C E K T V O N E N I H S
I L H D I A O O D J G V
O B O T E P S Y W P B D
U G A C L Y M V A N D T
S N A E P O W E R W T W
M F S Y L Z L Z L L W M
```

May <u>God</u> be <u>gracious</u> to us and <u>bless</u> us
and <u>make</u> his <u>face</u> to <u>shine</u> upon us,
  <u>Selah</u>
that your <u>way</u> may be <u>known</u> upon <u>earth</u>,
your <u>saving</u> <u>power</u> among all <u>nations</u>.
Let the <u>peoples</u> praise you, O God;
let all the peoples <u>praise</u> you.

GOD	KNOWN
GRACIOUS	EARTH
BLESS	SAVING
MAKE	POWER
FACE	NATIONS
SHINE	PEOPLES
WAY	PRAISE

Psalm 68:5-6a

```
P P R M H E L P J O Y Y L
D R Q E E O L L R Y Q L G
W S I R H A L E L S R B X
E W F S C T D Y E B R V J
L O T E O N A I R L X Y V
L D S D E N L F O T M M M
I I Y F S I E N G I V E S
N W E T M G E R L J M G M
G D E A O L B M S V L B Z
M S F D Y Q Z J M Y R K P
```

Father to the fatherless, *defender*
of *widows*—
this is *God*, whose *dwelling* is *holy*.
God *places* the *lonely* in *families*;
he *sets* the *prisoners* *free* and *gives*
them *joy*.

FATHER	LONELY
DEFENDER	FAMILIES
WIDOWS	SETS
GOD	PRISONERS
DWELLING	FREE
HOLY	GIVES
PLACES	JOY

Psalm 68:19-20

```
S  S  D  J  M  Z  J  D  E  A  T  H
B  O  N  Q  L  J  Z  V  D  Y  Q  Q
S  E  V  E  R  O  I  V  A  S  L  Z
E  E  A  E  D  E  S  C  A  P  E  D
V  S  M  R  R  R  D  L  D  M  R  W
A  D  I  O  S  E  U  A  T  X  D  J
S  R  G  A  C  B  I  B  N  G  T  J
P  O  N  T  R  L  Z  G  L  R  R  Z
D  L  M  M  Y  P  R  K  N  Y  R  R
```

Praise be to the _Lord_, to _God_ our _Savior_,
who _daily_ _bears_ our _burdens_.
Our God is a God who _saves_;
from the _Sovereign_ Lord _comes_ escape
   from _death_.

PRAISE	BURDENS
LORD	SAVES
GOD	SOVEREIGN
SAVIOR	COMES
DAILY	ESCAPE
BEARS	DEATH

Psalm 69:14-15a

```
F H L D D K N I S D
L A W A T E R S W L
U T K Z U N P O L Q
G E J C Q D L T D K
N D S T P L O E H J
E E T Z A E L O M S
R R Y W Q I E I L D
M L S B V D R D L F
B N J E W E K T Q J
B L R P T N G L V B
```

Rescue me from the mire,
do not let me sink;
deliver me from those who hate me,
from the deep waters.
Do not let the floodwaters engulf me
or the depths swallow me up.

RESCUE
MIRE
SINK
DELIVER
HATE
DEEP

WATERS
FLOOD
ENGULF
DEPTHS
SWALLOW

Psalm 69:32-33

```
D E S P I S E D B
P Z V T E V I L L
E V V E R S K C V
O N S S E A A N D
P D E E R P E R R
L A K E T A O H Y
E L D I D L E O R
W G V O J Y Q H R
Y E B B G Z D W Y
```

The <u>poor</u> will <u>see</u> and be <u>glad</u>—
you who <u>seek</u> <u>God</u>, may your <u>hearts</u> <u>live</u>!
The <u>Lord</u> <u>hears</u> the <u>needy</u>
and does not <u>despise</u> his <u>captive</u> people.

POOR	LORD
SEE	HEARS
GLAD	NEEDY
SEEK	DESPISE
GOD	CAPTIVE
HEARTS	PEOPLE
LIVE	

Psalm 70:1-2

```
N R E V I L E D D V
O J T G P T L I F E
I D O H S Z S M D L
S D E A G H M A K E
U S H N O I H Y S V
F H H N R E L E Y Q
N U O A L U E E M K
O R T P M K T L D B
C T Q L N E L T J Z
```

Make haste, O God, to deliver me!
O Lord, make haste to help me!
Let them be put to shame and confusion
who seek my life!
Let them be turned back and brought
  to dishonor
who delight in my hurt!

MAKE	SEEK
HASTE	LIFE
GOD	TURNED
DELIVER	DISHONOR
HELP	DELIGHT
SHAME	HURT
CONFUSION	

Psalm 71:14-15

```
S A L V A T I O N J T R G
Y L L A U N I T N O C W P
K N O W L E D G E P Y N R
E X D J T L D J K B M N B
S U O E T H G I R H M J R
I R E B M U N S T E P O H
A M L Z N N D U P A D N Y
R Z O L Z E O A C L V P T
P V Z R E M S T J Y B M J
D T B D E T S R Z B D R Y
```

But I will _hope_ _continually_
and will _praise_ you yet _more_ and more.
My _mouth_ will _tell_ of your _righteous_ _acts_,
of your _deeds_ of _salvation_ all the day,
for their _number_ is _past_ my _knowledge_.

HOPE	ACTS
CONTINUALLY	DEEDS
PRAISE	SALVATION
MORE	NUMBER
MOUTH	PAST
TELL	KNOWLEDGE
RIGHTEOUS	

Psalm 71:17-18

```
G E N E R A T I O N D M
S J R E J T Y N T L G M
Y U W T P G O V O W N E
M O O T Y Y U H Z T K M
P D L R M Y T B A A T G
R T T T D I H C S I R J
L M L V A N A R O A R M
M I G H T U O L Y M G S
S D E E D F G W C O E R
J G G T Y R R H D O W W
A D X V V W R R T B R B
R D N L W D N J B Y K P
```

O _God_, from my _youth_ you have
taught me,
and I still _proclaim_ your _wondrous_ _deeds_.
So even to _old_ _age_ and _gray_ _hairs_,
O God, do not _forsake_ me,
until I proclaim your _might_ to another
generation,
your _power_ to all those to _come_.

GOD	GRAY
YOUTH	HAIRS
TAUGHT	FORSAKE
PROCLAIM	MIGHT
WONDROUS	GENERATION
DEEDS	POWER
OLD	COME
AGE	

Psalm 73:23-25a

```
C A F T E R W A R D
D O E D I U G U D X
L A U J V L O G T R
O L K N O Y W A H J
H W W R S R K E Z L
A A Y H I E A Y T M
N Y N G O V L T M M
D S H L E M R J J M
Y T P N N V L P Y L
```

Yet I am <u>always</u> with you;
you <u>hold</u> me by my <u>right</u> <u>hand</u>.
You <u>guide</u> me with your <u>counsel</u>,
and <u>afterward</u> you will <u>take</u> me into <u>glory</u>.
<u>Whom</u> have I in <u>heaven</u> but <u>you</u>?

ALWAYS	AFTERWARD
HOLD	TAKE
RIGHT	GLORY
HAND	WHOM
GUIDE	HEAVEN
COUNSEL	YOU

Psalm 73:25b-26

```
N B P D F T L S N
J O W O R L T Q Y
R Y T A R R E B Z
Y E E H E T E S D
E H V N I S I E H
M A G E I N S O L
D T R D R I G I N
H O E T R O A K N
J S G E H F F M T
```

And <u>earth</u> has <u>nothing</u> I <u>desire</u>
  <u>besides</u> you.
My <u>flesh</u> and my <u>heart</u> may <u>fail</u>,
but <u>God</u> is the <u>strength</u> of my heart
and my <u>portion</u> <u>forever</u>.

EARTH
NOTHING
DESIRE
BESIDES
FLESH
HEART

FAIL
GOD
STRENGTH
PORTION
FOREVER

Psalm 74:16-17

```
E R P J Q P F M P H S Z
S E Y T D I A T T E P T
T M P D X D T R I N M Y
A M S E E Y A R X Y T Z
B U D T H E A V E N L Y
L S S N H D K W T J N M
I Y Z U N G I R P P J Q
S Z O U N N I J B W W T
H Y O U T B P L T N H J
E B Y E R Y A D K G D M
D T R B Q S W M I R J N
Z L Q G M R N N Q T L R
```

Yours is the day, yours also the night;
you have established the heavenly lights
*   and the sun.*
You have fixed all the boundaries of
*   the earth;*
you have made summer and winter.

YOURS	FIXED
DAY	BOUNDARIES
NIGHT	EARTH
ESTABLISHED	MADE
HEAVENLY	SUMMER
LIGHTS	WINTER
SUN	

Psalm 77:13-15a

```
D E M E E D E R
S W O R K S B D
L R U K A Y E V
M O E M N L A Q
Y I O D P O H W
A N G O N O W D
G R E H L O O N
N P M Y T G W Q
```

Your *way*, O *God*, is *holy*.
What god is *great* like our God?
You are the God who *works* *wonders*;
you have made *known* your *might* *among*
   the peoples.
You with your *arm* *redeemed* your *people*.

YOUR	KNOWN
WAY	MIGHT
GOD	AMONG
HOLY	ARM
WORKS	REDEEMED
WONDERS	PEOPLE

Psalm 77:19-20

```
L Y T R W X L Q Y P L Q H
S T N I R P T O O F Y A N
S P H Q W Y F L T N N A R
R E N R U L G Q A D R N W
E O D O O N V J E D R R Y
T P X C R U S B R P X O A
A L K T L A G E G M U E M
W E G D R V A H E R S O N
H T A P Q X X G V N S P M
D N V W Y K Z M T E J N L
L Z D G K X M P S N J X D
```

Your way was through the sea,
your path through the great waters;
yet your footprints were unseen.
You led your people like a flock
by the hand of Moses and Aaron.

YOUR	FOOTPRINTS
WAY	UNSEEN
THROUGH	PEOPLE
SEA	FLOCK
PATH	HAND
GREAT	MOSES
WATERS	AARON

Psalm 78:4

```
G E N E R A T I O N
G R S G D R Z C D W
Y L T R N Q H L M J
S Q O H E I L L E T
R D I R L D M L D R
L D E D I I N O J Y
E O R E G O N O C L
L E R H D E U Q W L
N Q T D N R Z S M R
```

We will not _hide_ them from their
   children,
but _tell_ to the _coming generation_
the _glorious_ _deeds_ of the _Lord,_ and
   his _might,_
and the _wonders_ that he has _done._

HIDE	DEEDS
CHILDREN	LORD
TELL	MIGHT
COMING	WONDERS
GENERATION	DONE
GLORIOUS	

Psalm 79:8b-9

```
M R N Y B R O U G H T A
N J E O L D Z N M L T M
E O N V I I D Y J O E D
M D I G I S D T N E D Y
O L O T L L S E T Q W N
C L L G A O E A E Y P X
L D E Q T V R D P P Y Z
Z D M S J L L Y D M S W
H W A N V J R A B M O X
R E N I M L G R S L T C
K L L S M T Q D M G D V
Z B M P G R Q R K M B L
```

Let your _compassion_ _come_ _speedily_ to
  meet us,
for we are _brought_ very _low_.
Help us, O _God_ of our _salvation_,
for the _glory_ of your _name_;
deliver us, and _atone_ for our _sins_,
for your name's sake!

COMPASSION	GOD
COME	SALVATION
SPEEDILY	GLORY
MEET	NAME
BROUGHT	DELIVER
LOW	ATONE
HELP	SINS

Psalm 80:8-9

```
P T V Y W R D L S
L P I L Q G A N T
A Y N R R N O H C
N G E O D I G L F
T E U R T U E I D
E N O A O A L E T
D V N R R L E O B
E N B E E P O V T
D R D D R R M G T
```

You <u>brought</u> a <u>vine</u> out of <u>Egypt</u>;
you <u>drove</u> out the <u>nations</u> and <u>planted</u> it.
You <u>cleared</u> the <u>ground</u> for it;
it took <u>deep</u> <u>root</u> and <u>filled</u> the <u>land</u>.

BROUGHT   CLEARED
VINE   GROUND
EGYPT   DEEP
DROVE   ROOT
NATIONS   FILLED
PLANTED   LAND

Psalm 81:1-2

```
X L J B D D B G N I S X T
S R D U Q Z L L Y L T A T
W O O N S Q K T M Z M E P
J L U H J A C O B B S S Z
A D O N T Y J J O I W G S
Q U K Z D D Y U A E O T B
T E R Y L H R R E D R D Z
V Q M R O I A T M E G J Y
Q B D Y N J V R N G L Z D
N G L E Y Q G G P N N B Y
W G X V D N T K T O K Y B
N D J T B H N J Z S W Q X
```

Sing aloud to God our strength;
shout for joy to the God of Jacob!
Raise a song; sound the tambourine,
the sweet lyre with the harp.

SING	RAISE
ALOUD	SONG
GOD	SOUND
STRENGTH	TAMBOURINE
SHOUT	SWEET
JOY	LYRE
JACOB	HARP

Psalm 84:1-2

```
G S T S O H N J S E B X Z
N G Y G L V J M C G T X C
I Y N B N O B A T L N O R
L M L S Y I L N G Z U O K
L H Y E T P V L O R D O L
E S R T V N N I T M D B S
W E D Q S O I S L D G P G
D L M I D Q L A T R A E H
L F N O J L L M F D J Q Y
X G G B G L X G Y R T N Y
```

*How <u>lovely</u> is your <u>dwelling</u> <u>place</u>,
O <u>Lord</u> of <u>hosts</u>!
My <u>soul</u> <u>longs</u>, yes, <u>faints</u>
for the <u>courts</u> of the Lord;
my <u>heart</u> and <u>flesh</u> sing for <u>joy</u>
to the living <u>God</u>.*

LOVELY	COURTS
DWELLING	HEART
PLACE	FLESH
LORD	SING
HOSTS	JOY
SOUL	LIVING
LONGS	GOD
FAINTS	

Psalm 84:3

```
S G G Y N S J N J X
D N B N R E S T T X
N I T A U P S L A Y
I K T L A O S T D N
F L O R N T Y D B N
A R R E S H O M E B
D O V O R G J P Y T
W E H B D R G V Z L
```

Even the sparrow finds a home,
and the swallow a nest for herself,
where she may lay her young,
at your altars, O Lord of hosts,
my King and my God.

EVEN   YOUNG

SPARROW   ALTARS

FINDS   LORD

HOME   HOSTS

NEST   KING

LAY   GOD

Psalm 84:10

```
B E T T E R B J M T J J Z
W Q K X L Q S P D L R B R
Y I Y W M T T B D Y D E Y
D A C Q N R N W K R P T T
L O D K A Y E T E E H M B
B N G T E L T L E O B N P
T Z H T L D S K U G N X R
R E T L C E R S R V D T P
R W B Z W O A E N M G Z Y
L B Z H O N U S B R X J
D W E D D G M R K U B J W
M R M R K V P Y T Y O V J
E Q Y Y P R W Y J S J H Z
```

*For a <u>day</u> in your <u>courts</u> is <u>better</u>
than a <u>thousand</u> <u>elsewhere</u>.
I would <u>rather</u> be a <u>doorkeeper</u> in the
   <u>house</u> of my <u>God</u>
than <u>dwell</u> in the <u>tents</u> of <u>wicked</u>ness.*

DAY	DOORKEEPER
COURTS	HOUSE
BETTER	GOD
THOUSAND	DWELL
ELSEWHERE	TENTS
RATHER	WICKED

Psalm 84:11-12

```
B W F A V O R Y U Z D L
E N I B S D V P L B L R
S T T T O H R V L M N N
T Q R O H I I E L H M J
O R G U G H S E O R L R
W T O H S S O S L S Y Y
S H T N E T T L U D N B
D I G D O S S N D R O L
O N T P Y H K L A W M V
G G Q W Z M J N P J Z P
```

For the <u>Lord</u> <u>God</u> is a <u>sun</u> and <u>shield</u>;
the Lord <u>bestows</u> <u>favor</u> and <u>honor</u>.
No <u>good</u> <u>thing</u> does he <u>withhold</u>
from those who <u>walk</u> <u>uprightly</u>.
O Lord of <u>hosts</u>,
<u>blessed</u> is the one who <u>trusts</u> in you!

LORD	THING
GOD	WITHHOLD
SUN	WALK
SHIELD	UPRIGHT
BESTOWS	HOSTS
FAVOR	BLESSED
HONOR	TRUSTS
GOOD	

Psalm 85:10-12

```
D R Y S S V E G S M E E T
F K I K G V N T Y I E L D
S A O G I N E R E D N A L
D O I G H A I S D E W T G
L N G T D T A R C X G D B
D T U F H E E A P E B Y Z
M O A O R F E O V S J Y Y
N S O C R P U O U K I S S
T V N G G G L L L S D N W
K I L L M B J R W P Z T X
```

Steadfast *love* and *faithfulness* *meet*;
righteousness and *peace* *kiss* each other.
Faithfulness *springs* up from the *ground*,
and *righteousness* *looks* down from
  the *sky*.
Yes, the Lord will *give* what is *good*,
and our *land* will *yield* its *increase*.

STEADFAST	GROUND
LOVE	LOOKS
FAITHFUL	SKY
MEET	GIVE
RIGHTEOUS	GOOD
PEACE	LAND
KISS	YIELD
SPRINGS	INCREASE

Psalm 86:1-2

```
D V T Y D E E N M E J V
Y E R N V Q R B N L J V
M G T A A R M I D N B D
V E S C E V L T L N X G
T W V X I C R O W Q G Z
R G W R N L R E Q M R N
U E O I E D F L S Y V M
S P W D P S T F S O U L
T G D S L Z E G A N V B
S K N T N Y R R J N L T
T K Y L L A P T P P J R
```

Incline Your ear, O Lord, and answer me;
For I am afflicted and needy.
Preserve my soul, for I am a godly man;
O You my God, _save_ Your _servant_ who
trusts in You.

INCLINE	PRESERVE
EAR	SOUL
LORD	GODLY
ANSWER	SAVE
AFFLICTED	SERVANT
NEEDY	TRUSTS

Psalm 86:4-5

```
T G D T B L N A E J V
N N K A O L B V Q M M
A I L R L U I L I F T
V V D A N G J D S G Z
R O C D R R O O R K Q
E L A O M E U O N B N
S N F Y A L A O D T T
T G G L K M P D J W G
V D D G E U X R Y T J
```

Make glad the soul of Your servant,
*   For to You, O Lord, I lift up my soul.*
For You, Lord, are good, and ready to
*   forgive,*
And abundant in lovingkindness to all
*   who call upon You.*

MAKE	READY
GLAD	FORGIVE
SOUL	ABUNDANT
SERVANT	LOVING
LORD	CALL
LIFT	UPON
GOOD	

Psalm 86:9-10

```
D G L D M E M A N N W
N L L Y M N R Y J W T
A S P O Z M R O K G D
W O N D R O U S F K M
P G D O Z I D Z R E B
I R O T I E F E N T B
H E G R E T A Y M Q W
S A B D E L A L K O Y
R T M D O B D N O T C
O V A R M T P R K N X
W M D T W R B Y Q J E
```

All nations whom You have made shall
  come and worship before You, O Lord,
And they shall glorify Your name.
For You are great and do wondrous deeds;
You alone are God.

ALL

NATIONS

MADE

COME

WORSHIP

BEFORE

LORD

GLORIFY

NAME

GREAT

WONDROUS

DEEDS

ALONE

GOD

Psalm 86:11-12

```
T W L Q M Y B X D Q L J
P T T T R A L W E K M R
R D B M H W E G R V W Z
N E M W Y A N M K J I Z
D K V Y K F N D A D L G
T H Y E T X I K V N O D
J B E R R H Y R S T R G
V L U A C O U Z O O Y F
W T Z A R P F N L L E D
H A E R J T Y B I A G Z
N T L Q Z Y D Z R T L G
D Y T K D V J G P D E L
```

Teach me Your way, O Lord;
I will walk in Your truth;
Unite my heart to fear Your name.
I will give thanks to You, O Lord my God,
  with all my heart,
And will glorify Your name forever.

TEACH	FEAR
WAY	NAME
LORD	GIVE
WALK	THANKS
TRUTH	GOD
UNITE	GLORIFY
HEART	FOREVER

Psalm 89:5-6

```
E L B A R A P M O C
F Y M I G H T Y S K
A S L S R E D N O W
I K P B B D E R Y X
T I S R M V R N J B
H E Q O A E H O L Y
F S K E N I S X L T
U J H R P S S S B Q
L K P G P M L E A J
```

The <u>heavens</u> will <u>praise</u> Your <u>wonders</u>,
  O <u>Lord;</u>
Your <u>faithful</u>ness also in the <u>assembly</u>
  of the <u>holy</u> ones.
For who in the <u>skies</u> is <u>comparable</u> to
  the Lord?
Who among the <u>sons</u> of the <u>mighty</u> is
  like the Lord?

HEAVENS HOLY
PRAISE SKIES
WONDERS COMPARABLE
LORD SONS
FAITHFUL MIGHTY
ASSEMBLY

Psalm 89:11-12

```
S N E V A E H N B T L P
Y H E R M O N R O B A T
W F H K A J L T Q N Y C
W O Z T O L U N N L O L
X U E Y U O L Y A N D S
B N A C H O T W T M R B
X D R S R Q S A O U E B
Y E T J Z E I Y O R H J
W D H J M N A Y R T L N
X T B Y S D B T R D R D
Y D M B V Z R O E Y T Y
B T J T M N N B Q D Q D
```

The _heavens_ are _Yours_, the _earth_ also
  is Yours;
The _world_ and _all_ it _contains_, You have
  founded them.
The _north_ and the _south_, You have
  created them;
Tabor and _Hermon_ _shout_ for _joy_ at
  Your _name_.

HEAVENS	SOUTH
YOURS	CREATED
EARTH	TABOR
WORLD	HERMON
ALL	SHOUT
CONTAINS	JOY
FOUNDED	NAME
NORTH	

Psalm 89:13-14

```
N O I T A D N U O F J R
E W S Y M T R E Y X L T
X E N T H Y C Y M M B J
A V N G R I Y I M B B L
L M I O T O G N I V O L
T R H S R H N Q B X M K
E A U A T H R G Y D K M
D J X Y N Z T R U T H Q
W X R Q Z D Z X D Q Z T
```

You have a <u>strong</u> <u>arm</u>;
Your <u>hand</u> is <u>mighty</u>, Your <u>right</u> hand
*   is <u>exalted</u>.*
Righteousness and <u>justice</u> are the
*   <u>foundation</u> of Your <u>throne</u>;*
Lovingkindness and <u>truth</u> go before You.

STRONG   JUSTICE
ARM   FOUNDATION
HAND   THRONE
MIGHTY   LOVING
RIGHT   TRUTH
EXALTED

Psalm 90:1-2

```
G Q B Y Q B V R Z X Y Z
D E V E R L A S T I N G
Q R N M O U N T A I N S
D J O E H T R I B E N D
B W T L R B L T A R J L
E O E L D A N R O B X D
F R L L P Z T B J Y Y N
O L D L L H V I P N Y P
R D A O J I W G O Y J Y
E C N Q G N N Y G N B D
E R R Z M L N G B Y S N
```

Lord, You have been our dwelling place
   in all generations.
Before the mountains were born
Or You gave birth to the earth and
   the world,
Even from everlasting to everlasting,
   You are God.

LORD	BORN
DWELLING	BIRTH
PLACE	EARTH
GENERATIONS	WORLD
BEFORE	EVERLASTING
MOUNTAINS	GOD

Psalm 91:1-2

```
R J R S L L E W D M P L R
E N Z T T J B P Y Z M J D
T P N T Y L X S H A D O W
L F V B M L J D T T J M E
E Y O N N D B R R T G G E
H D T R D Y Q D S L U D D
S W T H T W R O X F I W R
T Z N I G R M T E B N N L
M S N G Y I E R A Y Q O G
D T U H T T M S Z D R Z Z
J G L R B G T L S D D W L
W K D J T N M R A O V V R
N B W G D Y N G G T J P Y
```

He who <u>dwells</u> in the <u>shelter</u> of the
   <u>Most</u> <u>High</u>
Will <u>abide</u> in the <u>shadow</u> of the <u>Almighty</u>.
I will say to the <u>Lord</u>, "My <u>refuge</u> and
   my <u>fortress</u>,
My <u>God</u>, in whom I <u>trust!</u>"

DWELLS	ALMIGHTY
SHELTER	LORD
MOST	REFUGE
HIGH	FORTRESS
ABIDE	GOD
SHADOW	TRUST

Psalm 91:11-12

```
R J C O N C E R N I N G
D L N S H S V K D M M V
N T Y A L K T R I K T S
J A R E D R A U G R T X
W G G S E E P F P O T Q
E N G D B V O L N J R S
A K N N L O I E T B V X
G Z D A T L B G B Q T J
K T B H L B A V B D T J
```

For He will <u>give</u> His <u>angels</u> <u>charge</u> <u>concerning</u> you,
To <u>guard</u> you in <u>all</u> your <u>ways</u>.
They will <u>bear</u> you up in their <u>hands</u>,
That you do not <u>strike</u> your <u>foot</u> against
  a <u>stone</u>.

GIVE	WAYS
ANGELS	BEAR
CHARGE	HANDS
CONCERNING	STRIKE
GUARD	FOOT
ALL	STONE

Psalm 92:1-2

```
G L P B G K D P J Q T F
D N Y R M N T T T W A P
E J I T A H I M N I J Z
P V Z L A I I N T L D L
G M E N I A S H R N L H
I O K N L A F E L O I M
V S Y C I U F O S G M P
E T O D L N R N H Z L R
E R R N O D G W U G R T
P V E M D O M X N Z D G
Y S O Z V Z G I Y M R X
S Z V L K M S J N W R Y
```

It is <u>good</u> to <u>give</u> <u>thanks</u> to the <u>Lord</u>,
to <u>sing</u> <u>praises</u> to the <u>Most</u> <u>High</u>.
It is good to <u>proclaim</u> your <u>unfailing</u> <u>love</u>
*   in the <u>morning</u>,*
your <u>faithfulness</u> in the <u>evening</u>.

GOOD	HIGH
GIVE	PROCLAIM
THANKS	UNFAILING
LORD	LOVE
SING	MORNING
PRAISES	FAITHFULNESS
MOST	EVENING

Psalm 92:4-5

```
T B D Y B S P E E D
R H O R K B S V P R
L J O R O U N G J T
L D O U A L R Y X N
I W M C G E X E N N
R M E N A H N A L L
H B I T Y O T Z P D
T S D K D B P S Y V
```

You <u>thrill</u> me, <u>Lord</u>, with <u>all</u> you have
   <u>done</u> for me!
I <u>sing</u> for <u>joy</u> <u>because</u> of what you
   have done.
O Lord, what <u>great</u> <u>works</u> you do!
And how <u>deep</u> are your <u>thoughts</u>.

THRILL	BECAUSE
LORD	GREAT
ALL	WORKS
DONE	DEEP
SING	THOUGHTS
JOY	

Psalm 93:1

```
H G Y V D T B V B
D T N T T N N X W
E N G I S Z A O Q
E E R N K E R T D
D K O A E L J K S
N A B R D R O A M
I H E M J N T R M
J S D E B P I S D
W D P D Y F D Q K
```

The <u>Lord</u> is <u>king</u>! He is <u>robed</u> in <u>majesty</u>.
<u>Indeed</u>, the Lord is robed in majesty and
* <u>armed</u> with <u>strength</u>.*
The <u>world</u> <u>stands</u> <u>firm</u>
and cannot be <u>shaken</u>.

LORD
KING
ROBED
MAJESTY
INDEED
ARMED

STRENGTH
WORLD
STAND
FIRM
SHAKEN

Psalm 94:14-15

```
S  B  N  E  W  L  W  L  Y  N  P
U  F  D  G  E  K  A  S  R  O  F
O  O  M  A  N  M  T  U  G  T  L
E  L  L  T  J  O  T  R  H  L  E
T  L  D  I  P  E  D  G  A  C  R
H  O  L  R  R  E  I  N  I  E  L
G  W  R  E  B  R  O  T  A  O  H
I  R  R  H  P  Q  S  P  R  B  V
R  T  D  U  W  U  D  D  L  T  A
T  D  X  N  J  B  G  N  L  E  W
```

For the <u>Lord</u> will not <u>forsake</u> his <u>people</u>;
he will not <u>abandon</u> his <u>heritage</u>;
for <u>justice</u> will <u>return</u> to the <u>righteous</u>,
and <u>all</u> the <u>upright</u> in <u>heart</u> will <u>follow</u> it.

LORD	RETURN
FORSAKE	RIGHTEOUS
PEOPLE	ALL
ABANDON	UPRIGHT
HERITAGE	HEART
JUSTICE	FOLLOW

Psalm 94:18-19

```
S R R L G S O U L D K V T
W N S L I P P I N G R O E
J M O N T J N Z Q E O V V
T R L I R M Q N E F O X R
R S M G T N D H Y L X T N
L L A N H A C B N M V Q P
C L R F Z E L D A Q Q B J
A M P G D M A O M H L D L
R Q T N N A Y R S Z E O R
E M V W N R E T T N R L D
S G T T J M X T G D O X D
R X D G B L N W S L R C L
```

When I thought, "My _foot_ is _slipping_,"
your _steadfast_ love, O _Lord_, _held_
  me up.
When the _cares_ of my _heart_ are _many_,
your _consolations_ cheer my _soul_.

FOOT	CARES
SLIPPING	HEART
STEADFAST	MANY
LOVE	CONSOLATIONS
LORD	CHEER
HELD	SOUL

Psalm 95:4-5

```
S T H G I E H Y R D P
M O U N T A I N S D Z
S H T P E D E A R T H
J D X L Y E N Q D B V
P Q A M D M N A G B G
D N K A Q R T P H A W
D V Q D L O B G E T Y
M M Z E T F B S W T M
```

*In his <u>hand</u> are the <u>depths</u> of the <u>earth</u>;
the <u>heights</u> of the <u>mountains</u> are his also.
The <u>sea</u> is his, for he <u>made</u> it,
and the <u>dry</u> <u>land</u>, which his hands
    have <u>formed</u>.*

HAND	SEA
DEPTHS	MADE
EARTH	DRY
HEIGHTS	LAND
MOUNTAINS	FORMED

Psalm 95:6-7

```
M D R J W G G R J Y B D
L R M P B L T Z D Y K L
M O L P M P Z N P L K V
E L P O E P A E C Z T B
Q W W L B H E S K O E P
Q O M O J H Y N T F M M
B R W Z S R E D O U A E
T S N V Z E Z R P K R J
D H L W L N E M E Z D E
R I J D O G G R Y R P Q
B P G G V D P B T D T T
```

O <u>come</u>, let us <u>worship</u> and <u>bow</u> <u>down</u>,
let us <u>kneel</u> before the <u>Lord</u>, our <u>Maker</u>!
For he is our <u>God</u>,
and we are the <u>people</u> of his <u>pasture</u>,
and the <u>sheep</u> of his <u>hand</u>.

COME
WORSHIP
BOW
DOWN
KNEEL
BEFORE
LORD

MAKER
GOD
PEOPLE
PASTURE
SHEEP
HAND

Psalm 96:2-3

```
N S N O I T A N M B
O P E D E C L A R E
I S Y L D T R N L P
T M S R P V E L L Z
A Y O E E O W L S Y
V L R L L O E I L V
L Y O O R B N P Y K
A U A K L G N A M E
S D S D V G B T L J
```

Sing to the Lord, bless his name;
tell of his salvation from day to day.
Declare his glory among the nations,
his marvelous works among all the peoples.

SING	DECLARE
LORD	GLORY
BLESS	NATIONS
NAME	MARVELOUS
TELL	WORKS
SALVATION	PEOPLES
DAY	

Psalm 96:8-9

```
N O F F E R I N G D E Y A
A V Z B E L Y N D L Y S J
M J X A O L J J B S C G T
E V R R O Y P M P R J C D
G T D H Z I E L I B O J Y
H L N S H R E B G M J Q B
P Z O S T N E M E N R N V
Y N R R D R L G Y L I Q D
M O Y O Y Z U N B L M R G
W R R V Z Q N O N N Y M B
X T Y R K V P Y C T Y K G
```

Ascribe to the Lord the glory due
*   his name;*
bring an offering, and come into
*   his courts.*
Worship the Lord in holy splendor;
tremble before him, all the earth.

ASCRIBE	COURTS
LORD	WORSHIP
GLORY	HOLY
NAME	SPLENDOR
BRING	TREMBLE
OFFERING	EARTH
COME	

Psalm 96:10

```
S F R E V E N L T L D W D
N I M X Q G O T E J D J D
O R L Q B R B G R E X E P
I M T K D R D D V Y H V R
T L Q X B U X O W S G L M
A Y V J J M M B I N D L W
N Y P J Q T Q L O M W K C
R T D E L J B M G Q D T M
B I Y T O A A N Y L N D T
R U Z A T P I X R B K T Q
T Q Q S S K L O W Z R Q P
W E E W W J W E T B J W D
```

Say among the nations, "The Lord is king!
The world is firmly established; it shall
never be moved.
He will judge the peoples with equity."

SAY	ESTABLISHED
AMONG	NEVER
NATIONS	MOVED
LORD	JUDGE
KING	PEOPLE
WORLD	EQUITY
FIRMLY	

Psalm 97:10

```
S E U C S E R F P Q
W D J L L Z A X J R
I W R I O I J L N Y
C S V A T R O Q Z D
K E E H U V D N A H
E T F V E G N Z B Q
D U X S I H A T E W
L T L T T L Y D T K
```

The <u>Lord</u> <u>loves</u> those who <u>hate</u> <u>evil</u>;
he <u>guards</u> the <u>lives</u> of his <u>faithful</u>;
he <u>rescues</u> them from the <u>hand</u> of
the <u>wicked</u>.

LORD	LIVES
LOVES	FAITHFUL
HATE	RESCUES
EVIL	HAND
GUARDS	WICKED

Psalm 98:8b-9

```
R L E P E O P L E S D W K
I N Y C B Y L J D D L M Y
G R B N N J Y U B P T R G
H G E B N E V D L L K N Y
T N H H V Y S G M J R K N
E I D T T R E N Z T G L
O M H L R E T K R R T N
U O G I R A G V B P R R Y
S C W M L O E O K D B T X
S M Q X R L W J T Y I Y T
N I N B D Y S P D U Y T V
D L N R Y T W W Q B Y O R
V T N G R K K E N V L N J
```

Let the <u>hills</u> <u>sing</u> <u>together</u> for <u>joy</u>
at the <u>presence</u> of the <u>Lord</u>, for he
  is <u>coming</u>
to <u>judge</u> the <u>earth</u>.
He will judge the <u>world</u> with <u>righteousness</u>,
and the <u>peoples</u> with <u>equity</u>.

HILLS	JUDGE
SING	EARTH
TOGETHER	WORLD
JOY	RIGHTEOUS
PRESENCE	PEOPLES
LORD	EQUITY
COMING	

Psalm 99:1-2

```
P G R E A T L K M E Z
E Z I O N N Y I L M D
O N P L W Y B B H N N
P D T W D U M T R P N
L R Q H R E R Q Q R L
E O M E R A T U B L T
S L H T E O A L K L N
T C T Z V K N I A T D
I N M E E N N E G X Y
S Y R V J G R W D M E
```

The <u>Lord</u> is <u>king</u>; let the <u>peoples</u> <u>tremble</u>!
He <u>sits</u> <u>enthroned</u> upon the <u>cherubim</u>;
* let the <u>earth</u> <u>quake</u>!*
The Lord is <u>great</u> in <u>Zion</u>;
he is <u>exalted</u> <u>over</u> all the peoples.

LORD	EARTH
KING	QUAKE
PEOPLES	GREAT
TREMBLE	ZION
SITS	EXALTED
ENTHRONED	OVER
CHERUBIM	

Psalm 100:1-2

```
G E A R T H E M O C
W L P I H S R O W L
S L A X R E G T Q J
M O J D R L U K N B
V O N O N O O V X T
Y Y F G H E G R L Y
L E W S S Y S L D L
B D M T B R A S P R
```

Shout for _joy_ to the _Lord_, _all_ the _earth_.
Worship the Lord with _gladness_;
come _before_ him with joyful _songs_.

SHOUT	WORSHIP
JOY	GLADNESS
LORD	COME
ALL	BEFORE
EARTH	SONGS

Psalm 101:3b-4

```
P H Q L L Q T T F
E K E I L R T A L
O S V A A A I D G
P E R P R T H N K
L F P E H T I S Z
E Q A L V H Q T M
L T E R T R A D W
T S A O Q H E J B
S N N H W Y M P R
```

I <u>hate</u> what <u>faithless</u> <u>people</u> do;
I will have no <u>part</u> in it.
The <u>perverse</u> of <u>heart</u> <u>shall</u> be <u>far</u>
from me;
I will have <u>nothing</u> to do with <u>what</u> is <u>evil</u>.

HATE	SHALL
FAITHLESS	FAR
PEOPLE	NOTHING
PART	WHAT
PERVERSE	EVIL
HEART	

Psalm 102:15-16

```
E E F S N O I T A N
R A E J R R D G D B
E R A K A L L O R D
V T R E I O R N L D
E H P U R N A X Z X
R P B Y O M G B B J
A E J I E D T S T Q
R T Z T W L D Z G K
```

The <u>nations</u> will <u>fear</u> the <u>name</u> of the <u>Lord</u>,
all the <u>kings</u> of the <u>earth</u> will <u>revere</u>
   your <u>glory</u>.
For the Lord will <u>rebuild</u> <u>Zion</u>
   and <u>appear</u> in his glory.

NATIONS	REVERE
FEAR	GLORY
NAME	REBUILD
LORD	ZION
KINGS	APPEAR
EARTH	

Psalm 103:8-10

```
C O M P A S S I O N A T E
A L R R X J R Y S T T D K
B J N M J Y K D Q I E I M
O S U O I C A R G S N Q L
U R T Z J E T V E I Y S X
N E G N R A S R Q H L M Q
D G X P E M V U A Y B T N
I N J R L E I R C N M Z X
N A T O W T B L E C X V Q
G J R L I O N N O P A P K
L D N E R R L Y L V A X V
W M S M N M N S B D E Y W
```

The <u>Lord</u> is <u>compassionate</u> and <u>gracious</u>,
<u>slow</u> to <u>anger</u>, <u>abounding</u> in <u>love</u>.
He will not always <u>accuse</u>,
nor will he <u>harbor</u> his anger forever;
he does not <u>treat</u> us as our <u>sins</u> <u>deserve</u>
or <u>repay</u> us according to our <u>iniquities</u>.

LORD	ACCUSE
COMPASSIONATE	HARBOR
GRACIOUS	TREAT
SLOW	SINS
ANGER	DESERVE
ABOUNDING	REPAY
LOVE	INIQUITIES

Psalm 103:11-12

```
T R A N S G R E S S I O N S
S N E V A E H R L Y T X B T
D B X N L H X M K P R D M T
T E W V F I T S A E G D M R
P D V E D G E R J W M Q T D
Y V A O A H Q A N T Z Y P P
T R D B M N T B R D G L Y X
T Z O B T E J L T T D L Z W
Q V T A T T R R O X H B V W
E M E T S E W A K V N M P W
M R Q B Q V Z F R V E D T G
G L D T D D J Y X L V Y Z M
```

For as _high_ as the _heavens_ are _above_
  the _earth_,
so _great_ is his _love_ for those who
  fear him;
as _far_ as the _east_ is from the _west_,
so far has he _removed_ our _transgressions_
  from us.

HIGH	FEAR
HEAVENS	FAR
ABOVE	EAST
EARTH	WEST
GREAT	REMOVED
LOVE	TRANSGRESSIONS

Psalm 104:2-3

```
S T R I D E S C S T T W
N L N W Q D H T T Z T J
E O D E U A R O S Y M G
V R B O M E I R W G N R
A D L B T R E R E P P U
E C E C A T A T H G I L
H R H H A P S G N I W B
S E C W S B E A M S D B
S T E N T D N I W R D M
```

The _Lord_ _wraps_ himself in _light_ as
    with a _garment_;
he _stretches_ out the _heavens_ like a _tent_
and lays the _beams_ of his _upper_
    chambers on their _waters_.
He makes the _clouds_ his _chariot_
and rides on the _wings_ of the _wind_.

LORD	UPPER
WRAPS	CHAMBERS
LIGHT	WATERS
GARMENT	CLOUDS
STRETCHES	CHARIOT
HEAVENS	RIDES
TENT	WINGS
BEAMS	WIND

Psalm 104:33-34

```
M R G R K T L G D R X Y
E Q N V P W P R K N J Y
D V I L Q R O A M N V R
I Z S X J L L Y L V Z Y
T B A R P L P V Z R Z M
A G E V E R G J Y D V K
T T L N G J A N L I V E
I T P N R G O I I D K M
O E O R O T W I S S R L
N L F D X B T Y C E T B
N X B I L W X K T E J Q
G R Y R L R R R B D K V
```

I will <u>sing</u> to the <u>Lord</u> <u>all</u> my <u>life</u>;
I will sing <u>praise</u> to my <u>God</u> as <u>long</u>
  as I <u>live</u>.
May my <u>meditation</u> be <u>pleasing</u> to him,
as I <u>rejoice</u> in the Lord.

SING	LONG
LORD	LIVE
ALL	MEDITATION
LIFE	PLEASING
PRAISE	REJOICE
GOD	

Psalm 105:8-9

```
G E N E R A T I O N S
M A H A R B A C S T W
Q S T N Q L O R H C G
F W A L N V E O A E N
R O O R E B U A S Z D
B R R N M S S I X T Z
T E A E A I M T L J R
Y N M N V O X A D L X
T E D V R E Y V D M D
R M Z P L Z R M V E P
```

He remembers his covenant forever,
the promise he made, for a thousand
   generations,
the covenant he made with Abraham,
the oath he swore to Isaac.

REMEMBERS   GENERATIONS
COVENANT   ABRAHAM
FOREVER   OATH
PROMISE   SWORE
MADE   ISAAC
THOUSAND

Psalm 106:47

```
E  G  N  O  M  A  E  R  B  N  J
V  X  G  N  T  S  X  N  Y  J  M
I  S  G  L  I  G  A  V  D  Q  B
G  L  K  A  O  T  D  L  L  L  D
A  R  R  N  I  R  O  N  A  M  E
T  P  E  O  A  R  Y  H  R  D  B
H  D  N  V  D  H  O  N  L  Q  Z
E  S  O  P  A  L  T  W  R  Q  T
R  Y  Y  G  Y  S  Q  Y  B  L  L
```

Save us, O Lord our God,
and gather us from among the nations,
that we may give thanks to your
   holy name
and glory in your praise.

SAVE	GIVE
LORD	THANKS
GOD	HOLY
GATHER	NAME
AMONG	GLORY
NATIONS	PRAISE

Psalm 107:8-9

```
Y J R Z L B X R T J D B V T
H D D R S T Y W H Y L D M L
D U G W Y E P J I S N Q T D
P Y M R O M I J N X L S N M
D W Z A G N M F G G A L L L
T R O D N X D T S F O G I B
Y H O R R K H E D I K O G F
R D I L K A I A R Q T M D L
G R D R N S E N Y F B A N N
N L B K S T M Q D M U Y S Z
U Y T J S T L O V E X L M Y
H M T M L L Y B D Q B M V M
```

Let them _thank_ the _Lord_ for his
   steadfast _love_,
for his _wonderful_ _works_ to _humankind_.
For he _satisfies_ the _thirsty_,
and the _hungry_ he _fills_ with _good_ _things_.

THANK	SATISFIES
LORD	THIRSTY
STEADFAST	HUNGRY
LOVE	FILLS
WONDERFUL	GOOD
WORKS	THINGS
HUMANKIND	

Psalm 107:28-29

```
V R Y L M D R R A W L D
D R X J J R B R Q E E K
E I E L B U O R T I S M
H Y S Y Y R L T R G B Z
S L B T J W O C S X K T
U T Y R R X L U M A D E
H D W S Q E R N G Y V L
Z J D T E T S J D H O T
W M V I V V Q S W R T B
M B R L W B A N D B T Y
X J N L D D D W G M N Z
```

Then they *cried* to the *Lord* in
their *trouble*,
and he *brought* them out from
their *distress*;
he *made* the *storm* be *still*,
and the *waves* of the *sea* were *hushed*.

CRIED	STORM
LORD	STILL
TROUBLE	WAVES
BROUGHT	SEA
DISTRESS	HUSHED
MADE	

Psalm 108:5-6

```
T P R G S N E V A E H R P
X W X H O R B D A B O V E
Y E T T D D M P R V T J K
G N X R L Y R I N D L L M
L W M A B L G E N D Q V W
O D Y E L H R A W Y M D J
R Y K D T T H E R S R N T
Y J L T R Y E O S E N V L
E V I G W E T D V C P A T
K W P G N C V O Y N U Q N
N R Q B I X L O N N J E B
R L Z V D L L D M Z N Q D
```

Be _exalted_, O _God_, _above_ the _heavens_,
and let your _glory_ be _over_ all the _earth_.
Give _victory_ with your _right_ _hand_, and
    answer me,
so that those whom you _love_ may be
    rescued.

EXALTED	GIVE
GOD	VICTORY
ABOVE	RIGHT
HEAVENS	HAND
GLORY	ANSWER
OVER	LOVE
EARTH	RESCUED

Psalm 109:21-22

```
P P K D A N D N S P G
O I J C X E Y T L W Y
O E T K L N E E D Y L
R R H I T A Y T D M V
N C V E D F L A H E B
Y E E F A D W D Q J P
R D A V R R O L R W Q
G S J O O O T S A K E
T M L V G L Y B X M Y
```

But you, O *Lord* my Lord,
act on my *behalf* for your name's *sake*;
because your *steadfast* *love* is *good*,
   deliver me.
For I am *poor* and *needy*,
and my *heart* is *pierced* within me.

LORD	GOOD
ACT	DELIVER
BEHALF	POOR
SAKE	NEEDY
STEADFAST	HEART
LOVE	PIERCED

Psalm 111:2-3

```
R R S D F R D X Z M W L N R
I B J E V O T S Y X Z M Y Q
G N Z N R Q R T T N A T X Z
H Q L B D U H E V U S L W D
T T G M B G D B V E D B L L
E W T D I G L N J E R I Z W
O D Z L L X R A E J R N E L
U N E M L M M E W O R K S D
S D R O N O H F A L O R D R
N L K M R K U Y K T R D R Q
E K K L P L Q D P N K Q Y J
S J N K L V T Y L L N X M Y
S R D J X T Z Z M W M P N J
```

Great are the *works* of the *Lord*,
studied by *all* who *delight* in them.
Full of *honor* and *majesty* is his work,
and his *righteousness* *endures* *forever*.

GREAT	FULL
WORKS	HONOR
LORD	MAJESTY
STUDIED	RIGHTEOUSNESS
ALL	ENDURES
DELIGHT	FOREVER

Psalm 111:9-10a

```
U N D E R S T A N D I N G
N E C I T C A R P D W B L
T O Y L O H B P E I E P X
N N I Q R B J D S G E V K
A R E T Y Q N D I O R N W
N Q E S P A O N P E X D M
E A N V M M N L M L R G M
V N M M E I E O F O J L D
O D O E N R S D L E X G T
C C O G D E O J E T A J V
R M G O W P Y F T R D R M
P B Q A G Z D V G N J Y M
```

He _sent_ _redemption_ to his _people_;
   he has _commanded_ his _covenant_
forever.
Holy and _awesome_ is his _name_.
The _fear_ of the _Lord is the beginning_
   of _wisdom_;
all those who _practice_ it have a _good_
understanding.

SENT	NAME
REDEMPTION	FEAR
PEOPLE	LORD
COMMANDED	BEGINNING
COVENANT	WISDOM
FOREVER	PRACTICE
HOLY	GOOD
AWESOME	UNDERSTANDING

Psalm 112:1b-2

```
U P R I G H T D W L Y Y R L
V W N J Q N G R L Y X G X J
T S N Z N N M O V M E D C M
Q Z T L D I Y L M N D O Y M
G X T N G K Z T E R M P Y R
R P F H A P L R Y M P P T T
E D T E N D A V A A R Y D R
A Y B J A T N N H B K E M L
T J N L I R D E K Y L D A L
L N P O E M X J C I G N R X
Y Y N G E S K Y G S D Y K Y
D Z T N W M S H K D E V X B
B K T P G R T E T Q N D Z B
P S Q T N Y K N D Y W M D W
```

Happy are those who *fear* the *Lord*,
who *greatly* *delight* in his
commandments.
Their *descendants* will be *mighty*
in the *land*;
the *generation* of the *upright* will
be *blessed*.

HAPPY
FEAR
LORD
GREATLY
DELIGHT
COMMANDMENTS

DESCENDANTS
MIGHTY
LAND
GENERATION
UPRIGHT
BLESSED

Psalm 113:2-3

```
E R O M R E V E R O F
V G R J T G D T I M E
P M N I R E M V Q M J
Y R B I S N A M E Z M
S Q A S T I G Y D R V
U I E I D T N Y T B R
N L H R S T E G Q Y Z
B V O T Y E G S Y L M
N L B X M L D Q B J M
```

Blessed be the name of the Lord from this time on and forevermore. From the rising of the sun to its setting the name of the Lord is to be praised.

BLESSED	FOREVERMORE
NAME	RISING
LORD	SUN
THIS	SETTING
TIME	PRAISED

Psalm 113:7-8

```
T W M A K E B Q
S E S I A R T K
S E C N I R P Z
T G Y T P E B T
F R I D O A S N
I S O P E U E A
L D L O D E S H
N E Z D P H N L
```

He raises the poor from the dust,
and lifts the needy from the ash heap,
to make them sit with princes,
with the princes of his people.

RAISES	HEAP
POOR	MAKE
DUST	SIT
LIFTS	PRINCES
NEEDY	PEOPLE
ASH	

Psalm 114:7-8

```
T T E L O R D E M
R N R A D G C W J
E I O R R N O A Y
M L C B E T C D S
B F K S S O H P W
L L E N B G R A P
E R R Z R I T O B
P U Y T N E O D Y
T J D G R L R V L
```

Tremble, O *earth*, at the *presence*
   of the *Lord*,
at the presence of the *God* of *Jacob*,
who *turns* the *rock* into a *pool* of *water*,
the *flint* into a *spring* of water.

TREMBLE	TURNS
EARTH	ROCK
PRESENCE	POOL
LORD	WATER
GOD	FLINT
JACOB	SPRING

Psalm 115:1-2

```
E F Y T B P D J P Y K T Y
R R A J D Y J P W M N D W
E L R I T S N O I T A N N
H L T Q T S L O R D R L M
W W Z B D H A N N T G S J
Y T J E L K F F P N A O B
R B M V L R X U D Y X K D
Y A N I D D Y W L A Q K Y
N R R G S A K E O N E R Y
T B O R J Z M Y V T E T Y
L N Z L W N R P E N Q S S
Z Q V L G R Y W Z M Q P S
```

Not to us, O Lord, not to us, but to your
   name give glory,
for the sake of your steadfast love and
   your faithfulness.
Why should the nations say,
"Where is their God?"

LORD	LOVE
NAME	FAITHFULNESS
GIVE	NATIONS
GLORY	SAY
SAKE	WHERE
STEADFAST	GOD

Psalm 116:1-2

```
S U P P L I C A T I O N S
J W K B Y Z N E E C I O V
T Q D N N P D Y V B P D Q
E R O F E R E H T I R J J
I N C L I N E D L O L P N
G P D L B N V O L J T T T
H N W T B Z V G W P M G T
B E O L Y E L T C Q L L Z
B R A L J Y P A T D K P Z
G N B R P T L Z B G Z L T
Z N W P D L V T R X V N L
```

*I love the Lord, because he has heard
my voice and my supplications.
Because he inclined his ear to me,
therefore I will call on him as long as
I live.*

LOVE	INCLINED
LORD	THEREFORE
HEARD	CALL
VOICE	LONG
SUPPLICATIONS	LIVE

Psalm 116:12-14

```
Y  Q  Q  K  M  P  B  B  M  N  T  E
B  B  C  U  P  P  J  J  M  V  C  W
N  O  I  T  A  V  L  A  S  N  T  Y
R  U  J  P  L  O  R  D  E  W  A  Y
U  N  C  Y  E  T  W  S  T  P  O  E
T  T  W  A  B  O  E  Y  L  M  M  V
E  Y  T  Q  L  R  P  I  J  A  D  L
R  N  J  X  P  L  F  L  N  Y  J  B
B  L  K  N  G  T  G  N  E  R  M  L
```

What shall I return to the Lord
for all his bounty to me?
I will lift up the cup of salvation
and call on the name of the Lord,
I will pay my vows to the Lord
in the presence of all his people.

RETURN   CALL
LORD   NAME
BOUNTY   PAY
LIFT   VOWS
CUP   PRESENCE
SALVATION   PEOPLE

Psalm 117

```
S S P Y W Q V D T K P V D
E T N Q T R D S Q E P F D
R A L O V E A Q O L A T J
U E F T I F D P G I T L X
D R O P D T L E T X N L X
N G R A G E A H S W Y R N
E N E T S Y F N N I J D Y
T T V K E U D X R D A W L
S W E Y L X J L R T Q R B
P M R N V M T O V T G J P
B M E B L N L O G D R R N
N S J M D L D N L L T M W
S N T T W V N D L R Z N Q
```

Praise the Lord, all you nations!
Extol him, all you peoples!
For great is his steadfast love toward us,
and the faithfulness of the Lord endures
forever.
Praise the Lord!

PRAISE	STEADFAST
LORD	LOVE
NATIONS	FAITHFULNESS
EXTOL	ENDURES
PEOPLES	FOREVER
GREAT	

Psalm 118:5-6

```
S L A T R O M M D L Q
D E D R P L T E V D V
R I T E O L R S I D E
B T S R L E A N M B P
B R D T W L R C L Y K
O Q O S R A A Z E B L
P U N A E E R C J T Y
P A T F D J S J W L D
T V G G K K V S Z R M
```

Out of my *distress* I *called* on the *Lord*;
the Lord *answered* me and *set* me in a
    broad *place*.
With the Lord on my *side* I do not *fear*.
What can *mortals* do to me?

OUT	BROAD
DISTRESS	PLACE
CALLED	SIDE
LORD	FEAR
ANSWERED	MORTALS
SET	

Psalm 118:22-23

```
E Y E S Q Q T P V J Z R
S C O R N E R S T O N E
R U G L R R E R F Y L W
E G O L Z M E E K L X T
D X Y L O J I L D J M W
L B R C E H L O D S D N
I Y E C C V I O T N N P
U B T T T N R O R D J T
B E M J G Z N A R D X J
D T X L Q E V R M Y G L
```

The <u>stone</u> that the <u>builders</u> <u>rejected</u>
has <u>become</u> the <u>chief</u> cornerstone.
This is the <u>Lord</u>'s <u>doing</u>;
it is <u>marvelous</u> in our <u>eyes</u>.

STONE	CORNERSTONE
BUILDERS	LORD
REJECTED	DOING
BECOME	MARVELOUS
CHIEF	EYES

Psalm 119:1-3

```
S N V J G P V K G D N
S V H V G L N J L W V
E S E E R C E D H A W
L H G J A Z P O N A W
E A G N B R L E Y J R
M P K N P E T L E J T
A P R K O G L Z W K B
L Y E J Q R D D X X Q
B E L A W Z W R R D K
S T J K N X N Z O Q Y
R M J J R Q Q N M L T
```

Happy are those whose way is
    blameless,
who walk in the law of the Lord.
Happy are those who keep his decrees,
who seek him with their whole heart,
who also do no wrong,
but walk in his ways.

HAPPY	KEEP
WAY	DECREES
BLAMELESS	SEEK
WALK	WHOLE
LAW	HEART
LORD	WRONG

Psalm 119:54-55

```
S W H E R E V E R Z J
T S G N O S Y D M Z G
A H Z R E M E M B E R
T T G M L H K E E P Y
U B A I O O M Y W Z L
T K X M N A R W A L V
E T E T N Y N D J N V
S J J Q Z B P K B L B
```

Your <u>statutes</u> have been my <u>songs</u>
<u>wherever</u> I <u>make</u> my <u>home</u>.
I <u>remember</u> your <u>name</u> in the <u>night</u>,
  O <u>Lord</u>,
and <u>keep</u> your <u>law</u>.

STATUTES	NAME
SONGS	NIGHT
WHEREVER	LORD
MAKE	KEEP
HOME	LAW
REMEMBER	

Psalm 119:75-76

```
S S E N L U F H T I A F
D E S I M O R P J R M N
S E R V A N T U S R E T
T W L J P X D T B V R B
T B J B N G E W O L R G
Z R Y V M A T L O K P X
M Q O E D U J H R N D X
Y T N F Q D H M G R K B
L T A P M R L Q G I L D
S S Q P W O W Z B M R N
T G R B X L C B L Z Q Z
```

I know, O Lord, that your judgments
   are right,
and that in faithfulness you have
   humbled me.
Let your steadfast love become
   my comfort
according to your promise to your
   servant.

KNOW   STEADFAST
LORD   LOVE
JUDGMENTS   COMFORT
RIGHT   PROMISE
FAITHFULNESS SERVANT
HUMBLED

Psalm 121:1-2

```
Z E F T E D Q H T J
B R S R W M E J Y V
S E E N O A O T Y J
L H Y A V M T C N D
L W E E R F W H Z X
I O N D I T E D A M
H N R L L L H L M Z
L X B D P Y D V V T
```

I lift up my eyes to the hills—
from where will my help come?
My help comes from the Lord,
who made heaven and earth.

LIFT   COME
EYES   LORD
HILLS   MADE
FROM   HEAVEN
WHERE   EARTH
HELP

Psalm 121:5-6

```
S  T  H  G  I  N  M  K  Y
T  D  K  E  E  P  E  R  R
R  N  L  R  L  M  N  I  P
I  A  M  O  O  Y  G  U  D
K  H  R  O  S  H  D  A  S
E  D  N  D  T  H  Y  M  W
J  T  R  V  Z  J  A  X  Q
M  Z  T  Y  K  K  L  D  R
Z  Y  L  K  M  T  L  K  E
```

The Lord is your keeper;
the Lord is your shade at your
* right hand.*
The sun shall not strike you by day,
nor the moon by night.

LORD	SUN
KEEPER	STRIKE
SHADE	DAY
RIGHT	MOON
HAND	NIGHT

Psalm 125:1-2

```
E R O M R E V E R O F X
S M M Q W T F Q S G R Q
E V E R P O S U M M X W
D M X L R E R U O W R B
I X O E A R O U R T W T
B L V V O S N P Z T R M
A E R U E T U I L O R D
R W N T L D O R T E J K
D D Q K J N B T E M I T
K Y W J R M D L V J L Y
```

Those who <u>trust</u> in the <u>Lord</u> are like
<u>Mount</u> <u>Zion</u>,
which cannot be <u>moved</u>, but <u>abides</u>
<u>forever</u>.
As the mountains <u>surround</u> <u>Jerusalem</u>,
so the Lord surrounds his <u>people</u>,
from this <u>time</u> on and <u>forevermore</u>.

TRUST	FOREVER
LORD	SURROUND
MOUNT	JERUSALEM
ZION	PEOPLE
MOVED	TIME
ABIDES	FOREVERMORE

Psalm 126:5-6

```
S H E A V E S W Y R Q D
S G Q X S O E O D Y N L
H G N O W E J P E M O H
O P H I P G N I R A E B
U T A I Y S J S N B J B
T C N E R R H Q S W G T
S G O A R A R E Z M R Y
G Q E M L Y E A Y B D M
N T N L E D Y T C T Y R
```

*May those who sow in tears
reap with shouts of joy.
Those who go out weeping,
bearing the seed for sowing,
shall come home with shouts of joy,
carrying their sheaves.*

THOSE	BEARING
SOW	SEED
TEARS	SHALL
REAP	COME
SHOUTS	HOME
JOY	CARRYING
WEEPING	SHEAVES

Psalm 127:1

```
S S V A I N Y T I C
S H D K L Z P J P W
E C S R E L D E Z M
L T D D A E S J W V
N A R B L U P L M K
U W O M O I G S D B
R R L H Y M U L Z M
V M M B G V T B P W
```

Unless the Lord builds the house,
those who build it labor in vain.
Unless the Lord guards the city,
the guard keeps watch in vain.

UNLESS	VAIN
LORD	GUARDS
BUILDS	CITY
HOUSE	KEEPS
LABOR	WATCH

Psalm 130:3-4

```
S S E N E V I G R O F
S E I T I U Q I N I Z
D M D M M D M A R K J
L N R E L X S W W M D
O X A U R H W I T P B
R M O T O E T H T M M
D C G U S H V M O M Z
L L L T P J B E B T W
L D P N M M L G R T D
```

If you, O <u>Lord</u>, <u>should</u> <u>mark</u> <u>iniquities</u>,
Lord, <u>who</u> <u>could</u> <u>stand</u>?
But there is <u>forgiveness</u> <u>with</u> you,
so that you may be <u>revered</u>.

LORD	COULD
SHOULD	STAND
MARK	FORGIVENESS
INIQUITIES	WITH
WHO	REVERED

Psalm 131:1b-2a

```
M A R V E L O U S D B B
S K Y D R G Z D X Z Q B
G D D G E T R T L B Q Y
N E W E H R G E V I P D
I M E M T V N G A U H G
H L A D O E T M C T M C
T A N P M V I C L U O S
Y C E Q W K O U R D J R
B P D J L K M M Q Y M Q
```

*I do not <u>occupy</u> myself with <u>things</u>
too <u>great</u> and too <u>marvelous</u> for me.
But I have <u>calmed</u> and <u>quieted</u> my <u>soul</u>,
like a <u>weaned</u> <u>child</u> with its <u>mother</u>.*

OCCUPY	QUIETED
THINGS	SOUL
GREAT	WEANED
MARVELOUS	CHILD
CALMED	MOTHER

Psalm 132:8-9

```
S S E N S U O E T H G I R
F Q Y W D B V S R Z R D P
A Y K B K W T M T E T Q Y
I E O K D S I U S Y N T X
T S Q J E G O T E C A L P
H I L I H H I N M P Q G B
F R R T S N C L O T H E D
U P K G G L X M O D M D D
L R Z W R T G P D R W J Z
A B Q T M N J G Q N D D J
```

Rise up, O Lord, and go to your
resting place,
you and the ark of your might.
Let your priests be clothed with
righteousness,
and let your faithful shout for joy.

RISE	PRIESTS
LORD	CLOTHED
RESTING	RIGHTEOUSNESS
PLACE	FAITHFUL
ARK	SHOUT
MIGHT	JOY

Psalm 133:1-2

```
S U O I C E R P H E A D
Z B Q D D D Z N O T T R
T N A S A E L P R I R T
K I N D R E D E R A L Q
G Y B W A U H R L Y K X
O K T A O T N L A R Z J
O Y R I E D O N O E E Y
D O K G N C X B I V B T
N Y O Y Q U E T I N M T
D T Y J D S D L P V G W
```

How very <u>good</u> and <u>pleasant</u> it is
when <u>kindred</u> <u>live</u> <u>together</u> in <u>unity</u>!
It is like the <u>precious</u> <u>oil</u> on the <u>head</u>,
<u>running</u> <u>down</u> upon the <u>beard</u>,
on the beard of <u>Aaron</u>,
running down over the <u>collar</u> of his <u>robes</u>.

GOOD
PLEASANT
KINDRED
LIVE
TOGETHER
UNITY
PRECIOUS
OIL

HEAD
RUNNING
DOWN
BEARD
AARON
COLLAR
ROBES

Psalm 134:1-2

```
S Y J Q Q S M X K C
E L V X D R R R O D
R O D N A T S M R R
V H A L Y Z E O D Y
A H T N I N L V R W
N D S T E F Z N E A
T G T S H Q T C L D
S J U R E G A L X L
N O X X D L I M L V
H R D P P P B N K N
```

*Come, bless the Lord, all you servants of
   the Lord,
who stand by night in the house of
   the Lord!
Lift up your hands to the holy place,
and bless the Lord.*

COME	NIGHT
BLESS	HOUSE
LORD	LIFT
ALL	HANDS
SERVANTS	HOLY
STAND	PLACE

Psalm 135:5-6

```
R L H E A R T H
E D N E D R O L
V P L E A S E S
E T V Y P V E D
T G A E K V E S
A O E E O N A N
H D N B R E O L
W S A Y S G T W
```

For I <u>know</u> that the <u>Lord</u> is <u>great</u>;
our Lord is <u>above</u> all <u>gods</u>.
<u>Whatever</u> the Lord <u>pleases</u> he does,
in <u>heaven</u> and on <u>earth</u>,
in the <u>seas</u> and all <u>deeps</u>.

KNOW	PLEASES
LORD	HEAVEN
GREAT	EARTH
ABOVE	SEAS
GODS	DEEPS
WHATEVER	

Psalm 135:13-14

```
C T V I N D I C A T E
S O J R E M A N U R J
E G M L E J N O L S R
R R Q P M V H S E G A
U W E J A G E R R P D
D D T N U S V R E N V
N D R O O A S O O Y Q
E R R O N W P I B F N
T H D T L L N G O P D
T G S Z E V R D B N T
```

Your <u>name</u>, O <u>Lord</u>, <u>endures</u> <u>forever</u>,
your <u>renown</u>, O Lord, <u>throughout</u>
  all <u>ages</u>.
For the Lord will <u>vindicate</u> his <u>people</u>,
and have <u>compassion</u> on his <u>servants</u>.

NAME	AGES
LORD	VINDICATE
ENDURES	PEOPLE
FOREVER	COMPASSION
RENOWN	SERVANTS
THROUGHOUT	

Psalm 136:3-4

```
S K N A H T R V S
E R S D E E W T R
B N O R V N E R E
T E D E E A O V Y
S T R U D D I L E
L O A F R G N V A
F O A E R E O O Y
B S R W R L S D W
T D M D R G Z Y T
```

O *give* *thanks* to the *Lord* of lords,
for his *steadfast* *love* *endures* *forever*;
who *alone* *does* *great* *wonders*,
for his steadfast love endures forever.

GIVE	FOREVER
THANKS	ALONE
LORD	DOES
STEADFAST	GREAT
LOVE	WONDERS
ENDURES	

Psalm 137:6

```
R J E R U S A L E M N
G E K Y E X H T U O M
N N M T Y I V E D N R
I W T E G D U T J N N
L L J H M G A B O V E
C J E V N B R O O F Y
G S O O V Y E B T M Y
T J T Y X W G R M R B
```

Let my <u>tongue</u> <u>cling</u> to the <u>roof</u> of
  my <u>mouth</u>,
if I do not <u>remember</u> you,
if I do not <u>set</u> Jerusalem
<u>above</u> my <u>highest</u> joy.

TONGUE	SET
CLING	JERUSALEM
ROOF	ABOVE
MOUTH	HIGHEST
REMEMBER	JOY

Psalm 138:4-5

```
P R A I S E G A M T
D B W H T G B N L X
R L X O T A N B I L
A Z L D R U E I D S
E Y R R S D O R K V
H O R Y R E S M G B
L V A O A W R T X G
L W Y R L T X J R J
T J T B N G N W K Z
R H Y B B G Y B Y N
```

All the *kings* of the *earth* shall *praise*
    you, O *Lord*,
for they have *heard* the *words* of
    your *mouth*.
They shall *sing* of the *ways* of the Lord,
for *great* is the *glory* of the Lord.

ALL	WORDS
KINGS	MOUTH
EARTH	SING
PRAISE	WAYS
LORD	GREAT
HEARD	GLORY

Psalm 138:7

```
M P J N H R S X S Z
I R R A H T I R N E
D Q N E R G E G L G
S D E E S V U B H T
T W T N I E U O S T
B C A L E O R N H W
H R E L R M I V R T
L D M T K A I A E N
D Z P Z G D T E R Z
G K D A R H R Q S V
```

Though I walk in the midst of trouble,
you preserve me against the wrath of
*   my enemies;*
you stretch out your hand,
and your right hand delivers me.

THOUGH	WRATH
WALK	ENEMIES
MIDST	STRETCH
TROUBLE	HAND
PRESERVE	RIGHT
AGAINST	DELIVERS

Psalm 139:1-3

```
T L R M L N D H R L R B L
D E T N I A U Q C A O Y X
S T N T W T V V Y R I R L
K I R W N L H Z T N A Q D
D R T K O R B O G Q R E D
N E Q J W N E D U X A L S
K N H T A P K C B G F N K
R B J C X N J M S T H V B
R I M P R Y V J L I X T S
P Q S R R A M B P Z D Y S
R R R E X R E Y G Y A T G
M V G K P X J S N W L P R
```

O _Lord_, you have _searched_ me and
   known me.
You know when I _sit_ down and when
   I _rise_ up;
you _discern_ my _thoughts_ from _far_ away.
You _search_ out my _path_ and my _lying_
   down,
and are _acquainted_ with all my _ways_.

LORD	FAR
SEARCHED	SEARCH
KNOWN	PATH
SIT	LYING
RISE	ACQUAINTED
DISCERN	WAYS
THOUGHTS	

Psalm 139:7-8

```
S H E A V E N P L L
A P V T K E R E H W
S E I A H E Y L M Y
C E M R S E O D E B
E L T E I E R M Y B
N F N M H T T E K R
D C K S N G D M M T
E D R G T M Q Z Z Q
```

Where can I go from your spirit?
Or where can I flee from your presence?
If I ascend to heaven, you are there;
if I make my bed in Sheol, you are there.

WHERE	HEAVEN
SPIRIT	THERE
FLEE	MAKE
PRESENCE	BED
ASCEND	SHEOL

Psalm 139:14-15

```
Y S H T P E D X R Z B P G Q
L K W Y R L T R G W W I R P
L D R O Q R J J L R N T R L
U G X Z V D R S T T J A L J
F Z N J P E K T R T I U L D
R N T B T R N I E S F G Y Q
A Z D M O E C R E R K N O W
E X A W A A C V E M H P N X
F D B R T E V D L I A T J G
E J T E S P N G D W D R Z X
D H L D T O N D G E B P F R
V Y D N W B E L J L Q T N M
R D Y R R N D Y L L W Z V L
```

I _praise_ you, for I am _fearfully_ and
    wonderfully _made_.
Wonderful are your _works_;
that I _know_ very _well_.
My _frame_ was not _hidden_ from you,
when I was being made in _secret_,
intricately _woven_ in the _depths_ of
    the _earth_.

PRAISE	FRAME
FEARFULLY	HIDDEN
MADE	SECRET
WONDERFUL	INTRICATELY
WORKS	WOVEN
KNOW	DEPTHS
WELL	EARTH

Psalm 139:23-24

```
Z G R L N G D D S V J M
Y J N Y W L L E T M Z M
K P L I J B A V S G T L
T Y A W R T T K P N Y
R V R N C S H G K T D N
A Q T H T G A N G E D G
E G P E U L O L K D M B
H X S O G W E C R L B G
K T H S E E I A L E O Y
Q T T D Q W K M D D V Z
L R N M Y P B R K R X E
```

Search me, O God, and know my heart;
test me and know my thoughts.
See if there is any wicked way in me,
and lead me in the way everlasting.

SEARCH   SEE
GOD   WICKED
KNOW   WAY
HEART   LEAD
TEST   EVERLASTING
THOUGHTS

Psalm 140:12-13

```
M E S U A C R U P S
A E M E D Y P O U D
I V C M T R D O O E
N I G N I U E E C P
T G P G E T C I E S
A K H M H S T E K N
I T A G K S E N X D
N N I N U V A R R E
S R O J I H V O P L
D W D L T K L J Z T
```

I <u>know</u> that the <u>Lord</u> <u>maintains</u> the <u>cause</u>
   of the <u>needy</u>,
and <u>executes</u> <u>justice</u> for the <u>poor</u>.
Surely the <u>righteous</u> shall <u>give</u> <u>thanks</u> to
   your <u>name</u>;
the <u>upright</u> shall <u>live</u> in your <u>presence</u>.

KNOW
LORD
MAINTAINS
CAUSE
NEEDY
EXECUTES
JUSTICE
POOR

RIGHTEOUS
GIVE
THANKS
NAME
UPRIGHT
LIVE
PRESENCE

Psalm 141:1-2

```
E M V B T B R H T T D D Y B
V Y Q R N J J L A X D R Z M
E B R R X K Z Q L N E R M L
N V A R D Y D D I V D L B D
I E T P L B P N I B I S R S
N E C I O V C G J F C O A N
G T T C K E Y R T A L C C Z
Q N O J N L E I L Q R O T V
L M R S K Y N L B I U Z D G
E Z E C A G M J F N B R L Q
Z G I R V P J I T M Q V W T
W U P N K G C E D N D J B L
Q K J L K E D V W L K D L L
```

I <u>call</u> upon you, O <u>Lord</u>; <u>come</u> <u>quickly</u>
to me;
give <u>ear</u> to my <u>voice</u> when I call to you.
Let my <u>prayer</u> be <u>counted</u> as <u>incense</u>
before you,
and the <u>lifting</u> up of my <u>hands</u> as an
<u>evening</u> <u>sacrifice</u>.

CALL	PRAYER
LORD	COUNTED
COME	INCENSE
QUICKLY	LIFTING
GIVE	HANDS
EAR	EVENING
VOICE	SACRIFICE

Psalm 143:5-6

```
R M P L U O S N D V
D E E A T T T D L O
E S M D R H A N D S
E D K E I C I Y R D
D W T R M T H N D N
S C S D O B A E K Q
H T V N A W E T D X
S B N A Z Y R E N
D D Y L R X S N J D
```

I *remember* the *days* of *old*,
I *think* about all your *deeds*,
I *meditate* on the *works* of your *hands*.
I *stretch* out my hands to you;
my *soul* *thirsts* for you like a *parched*
    land.   *Selah*

REMEMBER	HANDS
DAYS	STRETCH
OLD	SOUL
THINK	THIRSTS
DEEDS	PARCHED
MEDITATE	LAND
WORKS	

Psalm 145:8-9

```
C O M P A S S I O N D B
A B S A N G E R N S Y D
L B T U D L S A T J J M
U L O R O L O E L O V R
F L O U O I A V V L K T
I L Y W N D C E E R R M
C R W M F D R A G O O D
R L D A N R I J R W L L
E T S E D A M N N G M Y
M T L W J K M Y G T J T
```

The <u>Lord</u> is <u>gracious</u> and <u>merciful</u>,
<u>slow</u> to <u>anger</u> and <u>abounding</u> in
<u>steadfast</u> love.
The Lord is <u>good</u> to <u>all</u>,
and his <u>compassion</u> is <u>over</u> all that he
has <u>made</u>.

LORD	LOVE
GRACIOUS	GOOD
MERCIFUL	ALL
SLOW	COMPASSION
ANGER	OVER
ABOUNDING	MADE
STEADFAST	

Psalm 147:4-5

```
U N D E R S T A N D I N G
A J Q E N R X Z B M Y R J
R B Q Y T B V Q Y E G S Q
E G U W V E R G R M R L L
B I N N B R U Y A V R V
M V B Y D D S M T Q G R Z
U E Y R N A G S I D Z M D
N S X O E R N P K N S L N
N D Y M E N O T Q E E Q B
V E R A D W N Q M W D S M
B K T O E D L A Y W M Q N
Q R Z R L V N Q L J L M T
```

He _determines_ the _number_ of the _stars_;
he _gives_ to all of them their _names_.
Great is our _Lord_, and _abundant_
   in _power_;
his _understanding_ is _beyond_ _measure_.

DETERMINES	LORD
NUMBER	ABUNDANT
STARS	POWER
GIVES	UNDERSTANDING
NAMES	BEYOND
GREAT	MEASURE

Psalm 150:3-6a

```
P D N U O S C E P E E K L
R L U T E Y W R C V P G V
A J M L M D A J E N N I E
I T G B B I M R G I A N P
S T A N S K Y G H L I D B
E L R E I T Y S J R O R P
S L G U H G A Y U G E R S
H Z M I M L N O N A R G D
A W N L C P B A T B N P R
R G R R J M E H L I T N V
P D M Q A J E T R C B M Q
N Y K T Y S J T Q G J J M
T Z Q D P L S Y D P Y N M
```

Praise him with trumpet sound;
praise him with lute and harp!
Praise him with tambourine and dance;
praise him with strings and pipe!
Praise him with clanging cymbals;
praise him with loud clashing cymbals!
Let everything that breathes praise
  the Lord!

PRAISE	PIPE
TRUMPET	CLANGING
SOUND	CYMBALS
LUTE	CLASHING
HARP	EVERYTHING
TAMBOURINE	BREATHES
DANCE	PRAISE
STRINGS	LORD

ANSWER KEY

Psalm 1:1-2

```
B W N N M S S S L O R D   D Q
D B B B X T E B K Y R T Z   Y
M W L Q A C G T N L H D B   D
K W I N V G O J A G A N   V R
B N D C T S R U I T S W B   B
T S I D K T I L N R I W D   Y
N Q B G Q E E N E S P D J   D
S W N Y H D D F N B E B E   Y
D E M Y L T F G J E L L M   M
A K A B L O D J G E R W D   M
Y G Y T C Z D V S R A S W   L
W Y Y S W V Y S T L M W Z   D
Y V N T J T E J R N T R M
P B N G X D R Q G Z M T Y N
```

Psalm 2:10-11

```
N T K E C I O J E R
T H E R E F O R E B
T R E M B L I N G N
W D S M E S O H M M
E A N G R V T R R Z
S D R E N R R A D X
I R L N A I E E J J
W U V E E F K W S Q
R Q K Q D D J D L T
```

Psalm 3:3-4

```
S Y S N P L M A Z T
H R M T L B N B R N
I O N A F S G D G Y
E L C I W I R R L P
L G A E A O L O M W
D D R R L T H G I H
Z S Q Y O E N D M P
M B R D A U Y U D W
K L Q D L N N R O N
V Z B N L T T D N M
```

Psalm 4:6-8

```
Y D R E T T E B B B
E S R E P S W W T
Q C T O T E A N L L
X S A S L A A F N
T M N F E D E C E
Y I R I N V W R E
O L M U A O R N G
J E B E H R I A R
N A J S S W G J H
```

Psalm 5:11-12

```
R E J O I C E S X Y T T
D A E R P S U K W M B L
R X Q W N R M G G D N J
L R Z R R B B F R O O W N
P R K O L G E I I D P P
J D U E Q F F T L R L L
Y N S T U O C E A L B Y
O S D G R E I I S N E L
B B E E T H S Z P I O D
P D V O S E Y Y Z V N J
D E R M S T W N E N O G
R P M Z M M R L X Y G K
```

Psalm 6:2-4

```
G B R L W K T N M M
N O S E O F A I N T
I N O G V R N R U T
L E U P L I D B H D
I S L O L M L S L X
A E N Y E X I E Y Y
F G V R H U G N D E
N B C A G E O N V Y
U Y T N S G A O X P
N W A W A L L L L D
```

Psalm 7:9

```
X R B S M I N D S M J T
T Y D U N R T Z O Y X E
T V I O L E N C E G R Z
P W S E W E K A M U K G
R N X T Y I V J C D N M
O V Q H R R C E D I L M
B W G G D A S K R N W N
E D R I P R E B E L E P
S P Y R M R D H J D Q M
```

Psalm 8:3-5

```
Q Y L A J L K Y F Z T J
R H D W N R L I E R A C
D E L D O G N H U M A N
E A D W N G E V R Y K R
N V X I E I T L R V B M
W E S R S R K O S R N Y
O N S T E N L N O P T B
R S M W A G O N A M R D
C N O O M R O C D M B X
D L M J X H S D X D T R
```

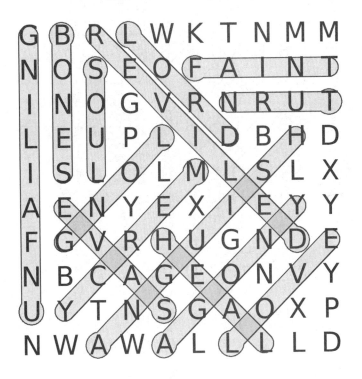

Psalm 9:9-10

```
B Z D T I M E S T G R B
X N E N W N R R G E B N
K W S P M T U R V D E Y
T N S D B S R E L K D R
N D E Z T M N O A K B Q
K D R O L G H S U M J X
D Z P N W G R N K B M Q
K R P T N O B E A E L P
T M O O F V N V F M E E
R R R D W N Z K N U E S
P T B M Z K G N Y D G N
S X Y B Z R L T N N K E
```

Psalm 10:14

```
M W V G B O C Z N K A J B
B S Y I O Y T M F R C J
E W S M C Y M F R O R T
K A T M E G T L T N D H J
A I R R L I S Z E B V
T K I O C R I M L G D L
W E S T U D E P S N T Q
F E E L E B E H A N Y G
E D L R P R L H T D O G
Y D P V T B R E R A P K
L R D J T B D Z X L F D
```

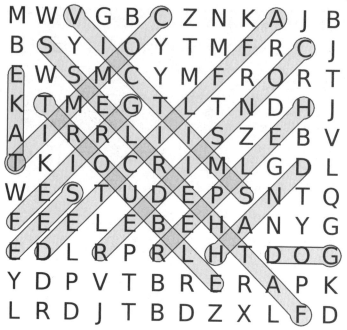

Psalm 12:5-6

```
D B S R B Q T V G T K Z K
K Q O E T R I E U C S E R
X O Z S S O E C A N R U F
P B R S L I G F D Z B T L
B K Y E D D M R I R T M V
Z W N L T E R O O N O Q D
L C Y P L T G A R A E L Q
E S I L V E R N E P N D K
R B D E P R N K O H K S R
B R L H I U P Y Q L J V K
L M N S D Y R J D Z V D D
G P E T J M G E W G W T R
```

Psalm 13:5-6

```
U S E C I O J E R L
P N O I T A V L A S
R R F M D S R R Y R
A U M A L L U J T G
I O D O I H B R G T
S Y V D E L G N T K
E E R A T O I G D Q
P O R M O S B N V G
L T L D R M X Y G D
```

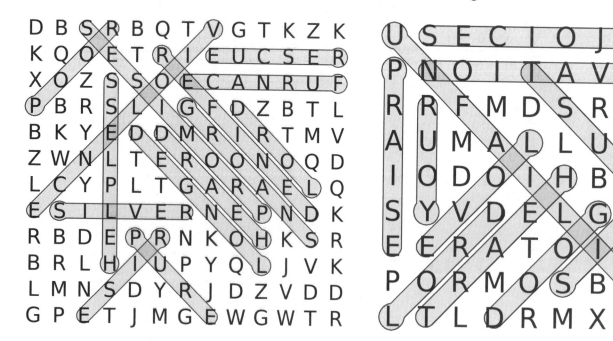

172   Peace of Mind Bible Word Search

Psalm 16:9-11

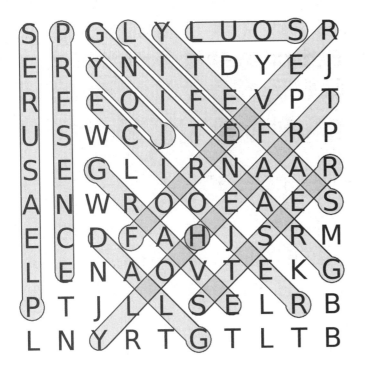

```
S P G L Y L U O S R
E R Y N I T D Y E J
R E E O I F E V P T
U S W C J T E F R P
S E G L I R N A A R
A N W R O O E A E S
A C D F A H J S R M
E E N A O V T E K G
L T J L L S E L R B
L N Y R T G T L T B
```

Psalm 17:6-7

```
J P V X U N N M P N J T R D
Y A Y M W N Y L D N L G R K
L R N E Z Y F N B N D Y D T
G U V S N V E A V V Q R Y B
M O F Y W B G N I Y A R P S
L R D R T E D E B L M J H N
E L R V E H R B G Y I O T V
W N D E Z D G Q L U W N N Z
Y V E W S W N I T P F T G Y
M T M M V C S O M D O E N B
K W D X I T U M W J J Y W R V
B O Q T E E R E R Q T R E R
G V N N Q S Q D B T Z Q R
```

Psalm 18:1-3

```
S A L V A T I O N D L M P J
E T L D D Y S S E R T R O F
I L R L L R D L Z S D L L K
M W Z O Q E I D T R O C K T
E R O B N V I R E G U F E R
N S M R E G E H P R A I S E
E L A R T N H T S L O V E L
Q O E V G H D O Z D L N M X
T R B T E X Y X L N R B R M
D D H B G D R W X D R R R V
```

Psalm 18:35-36

```
T E E F M N B X J
S U P P O R T S G
V I C T O R Y N T
D G G M R H I R H
L R I R R P E A M
E E K V P I N L P
I A D I E D G A P
H T L I D N T H V
S S Y V W H Q L T
```

Psalm 19:9a-11

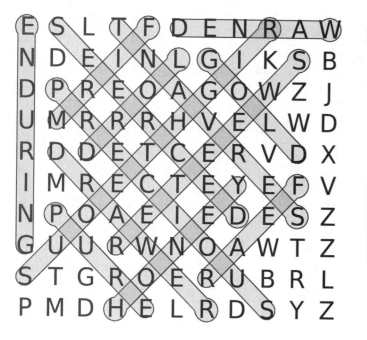

```
E S L T F D E N R A W
N D E I N L G I K S B
D P R E O A G O W Z J
U M R R R H V E L W D
R D D E T C E R V D X
I M R E C T E Y E F V
N P O A E I E D E S Z
G U U R W N O A W T Z
S T G R O E R U B R L
P M D H E L R D S Y Z
```

Psalm 20:7-8

```
C H K R X D R K D B P
H O M T S I N G T P P
A R V O S E G H L Q W
R S M E E U G O N Y D
I E S S D U R A D L L
O S J T O D M T L G Y
T M M R A E Z L M W R
S B B G Z N A M R I F
M M B W D F D P L M L
```

Psalm 22:19-21

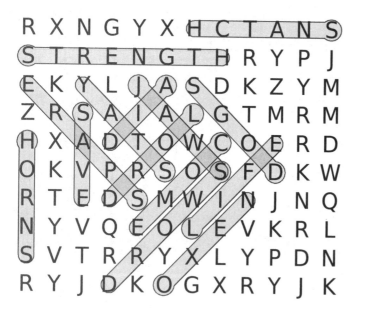

```
R X N G Y X H C T A N S
S T R E N G T H R Y P J
E K Y L J A S D K Z Y M
Z R S A I A L G T M R M
H X A D T O W C O E R D
O K V P R S O S F D K W
R T E D S M W I N J N Q
N Y V Q E O L E V K R L
S V T R R Y X L Y P D L
R Y J D K O G X R Y J K
```

Psalm 22:27-28

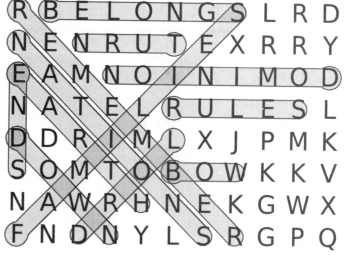

```
R B E L O N G S L R D
N E N R U T E X R R Y
E A M N O I N I M O D
N A T E L R U L E S L
D D R I M L X J P M K
S O M T O B O W K K V
N A W R H N E K G W X
F N D N Y L S R G P Q
```

Psalm 23:1-4

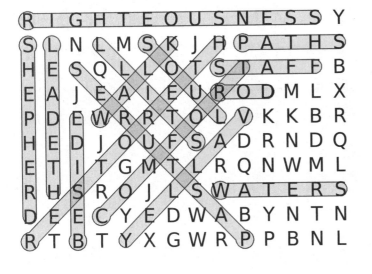

```
R I G H T E O U S N E S S Y
S L N L M S K J H P A T H S
H E S Q L L O T S T A F F B
E A J E A I E U R O D M L X
P D E W R R T O L V K K B R
H E D J O U F S A D R N D Q
E T I T G M T L R Q N W M L
R H S R O J L S W A T E R S
D E E C Y E D W A B Y N T N
R T B T Y X G W R P P B N L
```

Psalm 24:1-2

```
G E L P O E P P Q Z N
G N O L E B D G O Q
S O I L T L N I M E
H C B H R L T X A J
T E B O T A I R Q N
P A W L D Y T U S G
E N L N O H R A B N
D L U A D R E E J K
M O T M I S D D V Q
F J G L V D B W N E
```

Psalm 25:4-5

```
K T T L M X D L T B Z D
Z J O D D N L S F D A W
L N S J P D V O A O D G
G D M H R L L L R V O D
H Y R L O L W M B D E D
T T D I O W T N I O P S
D T A W G H L G B L Y E
M Q R P C H Y T Q X P X
J B T A D Q T R X O D L
R D E B R K Z U H L E K
M T G P O Y J T Z A G B
N Y R G L B D H D B G K
```

Psalm 25:14-15

```
R E S C U E S S Z
Z T T F W D E N N
A J N N R H R S Q
M L V A C I E O E
S G W A N I E Y L
R P E A M E E N N
A T A E Y S V T D
E Y N R Y S V O N
F E D W T Y D V C
```

Psalm 26:1-3

```
S S E N L U F H T I A F
E E D E T S U R T Y B T Z
V R S Z A T Y T N S M Y
O O D E E C I R A W W D
R L T S Y R I F T A Y Z
P N T R G E D D V T T M
E M T E A A B E N T T X
D V T L E E R W N I X M
N N O T Y I H A T D V R
I X S L N G Y L T R M T
M W N G L M R K J Y T R
```

Psalm 27:13-14

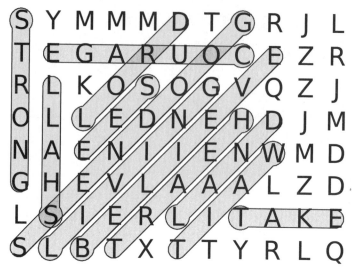

```
S Y M M M D T G R J L
T E G A R U O C E Z R
R L K O S O G V Q Z J
O L L E D N E H D J M
N A E N I I E N W M D
G H E V L A A A L Z D
L S I E R L I T A K E
S L B T X T T Y R L Q
```

Psalm 28:8-9

```
N O I T T A V L A S P I
A P B L E S S Y R N X
N E C Y B T G S H R S
O O A B J B H E F T R
I L R B M E R O R E W
N E R R Y P I R E V Y N
T E Y H T T N E R V N
E J E A R G R L V P G
D R N E T O B L O A W
D C S H F D B W T R S
E S V X T B Q M K J D
```

Psalm 29:1-2

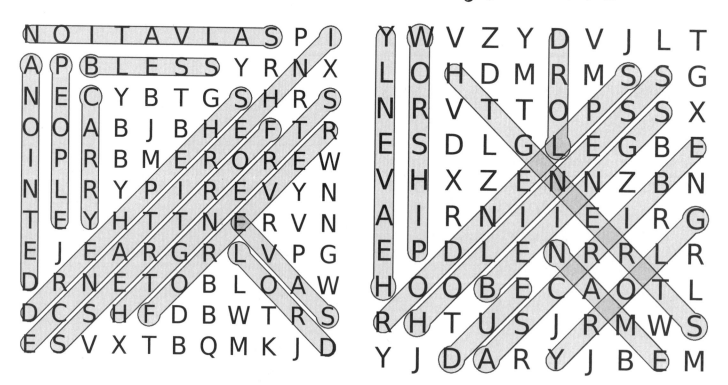

```
Y W V Z Y D V J L T
L O H D M R M S S G
N R V T T O P S S X
E S D L G L E G B
V H X Z E N N Z B N
A I R N I I E I R G
E P D L E N R R L R
H O O B E C A O T L
R H T U S J R M W S
Y J D A R Y J B E M
```

Psalm 30:4-5

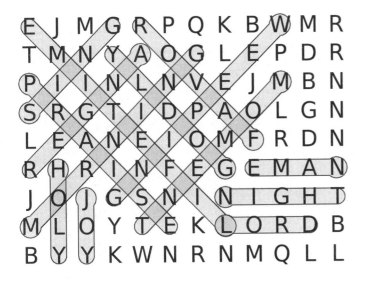

```
E J M G R P Q K B W M R
T M N Y A O G L E P D R
P I I N L N V E J M B N
S R G T I D P A O L G N
L E A N E I O M F R D N
R H R I N F E G E M A N
J O J G S N I N I G H T
M L O Y T E K L O R D B
B Y Y K W N R N M Q L L
```

Psalm 31:19

```
S T T L M T T T J
T Y N L D H A Z N
O W W A I T R K Q
R R R O N D K W E E
E S G T T N G O J
D S I G S U U R H
T R O G F E A B W
D O Q E H E B Z A
D P R M F T L D K
```

Psalm 32:1-2

```
S N O I S S E R G S N A R T
R E D N L L M R L T Q L D J
M V S E Q J M W K L R T Y Y
M I I L S C O V E R E D G Z
V G N Y P S A K T L B Y D J
C R S Z L G E I M V W B N J
K O R Z A T R L D E C E I T
T F U I Z I Z N B O G D R B
D L N M P R Q J N T R L T Q
P S X S T D M E Y K B D W V
T G X R N R W L R D Y R K Y
D T Z W Y O D Y T D P Z T J
D P N Y V L D P D D T T N N
```

Psalm 33:2-3

```
S G Y D P V J J R E G
T N R A W R N W K S G
R I V E L T A A K P Q
I S N P Y P M I Y N G
N Q P L R Y L O S N V
G J O D E L J X O E J
E R M J F C I S U M N
D T P U S H O U T Z P
G M L R T R L N V G G
R L Y B A V J D Z M B
Y M V G T H J Q V D G
```

Psalm 33:10-11

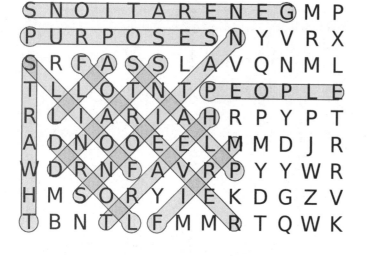

```
S N O I T A R E N E G M P
P U R P O S E S N Y V R X
S R F A S S L A V Q N M L
T L L O T N T P E O P L E
R L I A R I A H R P Y P T
A D N O O E E L M M D J R
W O R N F A V R P Y Y W R
H M S O R Y I E K D G Z V
T B N T L F M M R T Q W K
```

Psalm 34:12-14

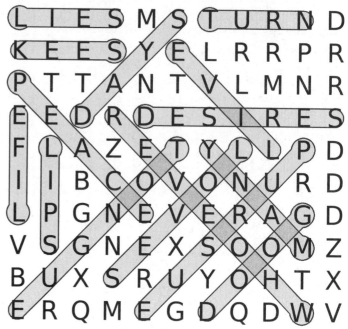

```
L I E S M S T U R N D
K E E S Y E L R R P R
P T T A N T V L M N R
E E D R D E S I R E S
F L A Z E T Y L L P D
I I B C O V O N U R D
L P G N E V E R A G D
V S G N E X S O O M Z
B U X S R U Y O H T X
E R Q M E G D Q D W V
```

Psalm 35:10

```
D Q V T R Z C E V Q Z
Z J Y J N O N R D H X
Z L Q T M O O R E N L
S B R P B O G L K B Q
T G A R P M P T P Y K
C R N T E L N R T Y R
E Y J O E S A N E J V
T L D S R I C V M R W
O O S O S T E U R O B
R R Q E B R S Z E G Q
P D D L Y Y M R Q S Q
```

Psalm 36:5-6

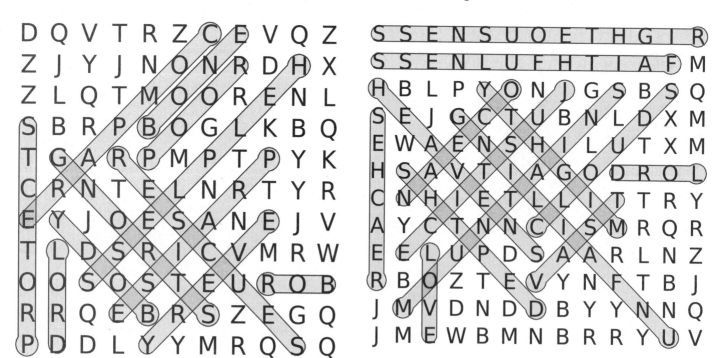

```
S S E N S U O E T H G I R
S S E N L U F H T I A F M
H B L P Y O N J G S B S Q
S E J G C T U B N L D X M
E W A E N S H I L U T X M
H S A V T I A G O D R O L
C N H I E T L L I T T R Y
A Y C T N N C I S M R Q R
E E L U P D S A A R L N Z
R B O Z T E V Y N F T B J
J M V D N D D B Y Y N N Q
J M E W B M N B R R U V
```

Psalm 37:10-11

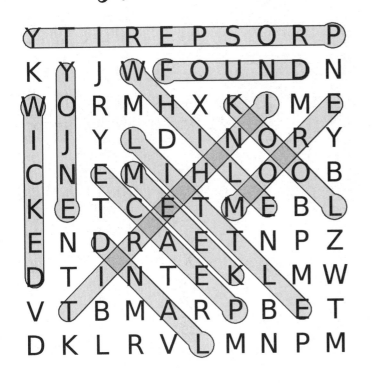

Psalm 38:8b-9

Psalm 40:5

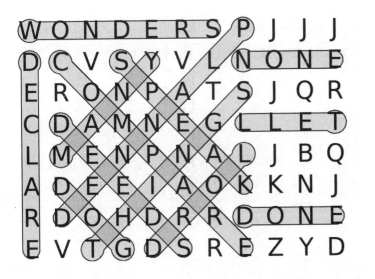

Psalm 40:9-10

Psalm 41:1-2

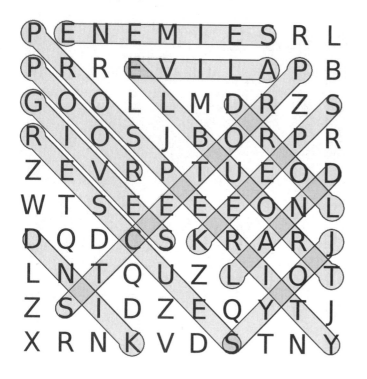

```
P E N E M I E S R L
P R R E V I L A P B
G O O L L M D R Z S
R I O S J B O R P R
Z E V R P T U E O D
W T S E E E E O N L
D Q D C S K R A R J
L N T Q U Z L I O T
Z S I D Z E Q Y T J
X R N K V D S T N Y
```

Psalm 42:1-2

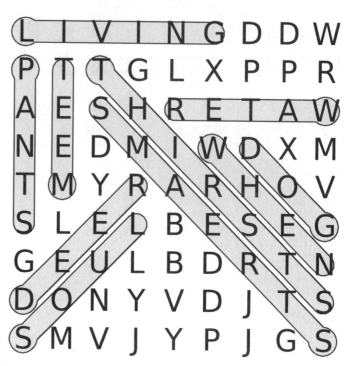

```
L I V I N G D D W
P T T G L X P P R
A E S H R E T A W
N E D M I W D X M
T M Y R A R H O V
S L E L B E S E G
G E U L B D R T N
D O N Y V D J T S
M V J Y P J G S
```

Psalm 43:3-4

```
Q L G E R A C X N X
D M U A P B R I N G
P E T F D D A E L Q
R L L N H T E R Y L
A H E I N T L W D D
I S O U G I I W T Q
S J O L G H E A G G
E M O H Y L T O F P
Q M T Y L M D M N J
```

Psalm 44:6-8

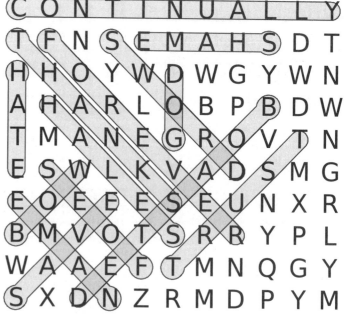

```
C O N T I N U A L L Y
T F N S E M A H S D T
H H O Y W D W G Y W N
A H A R L O B P B D W
T M A N E G R O V T N
E S W L K V A D S M G
E O E E E S E U N X R
B M V O T S R R Y P L
W A A E F T M N Q G Y
S X D N Z R M D P Y M
```

Psalm 45:6-7a

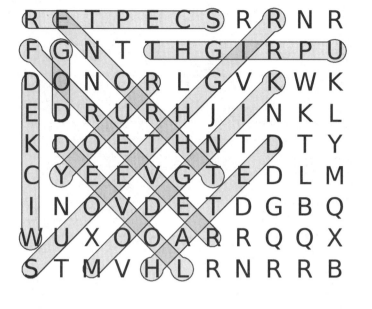

Psalm 46:1-3

Psalm 46:10-11

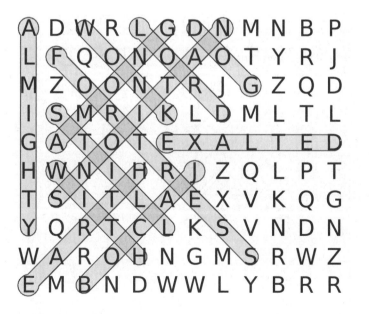

Psalm 47:1-2

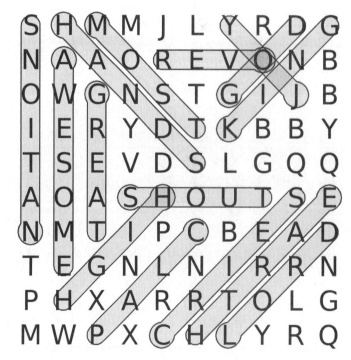

Psalm 48:9-10

```
E H E J D G Z T U J K Y
D T M J O R J N L B S X
E R A D N H F P X E Q D
S A N T A A I I V R N G
I E R N I H E R L V W M
A Y D L S D E L T L Y Q
R G I R S S E H P R E J
P N O E E T G M O M S D
G W P D V I R T M D E N
K T Y M R O C O N R Z T
P J K T K I L E N N N J
Y P X J V R L M B G X M
```

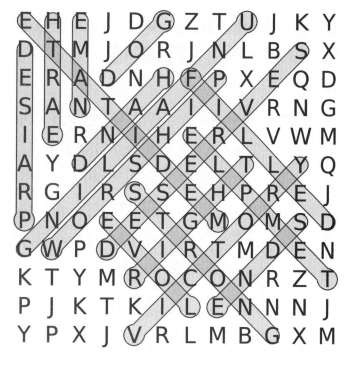

Psalm 50:1-2

```
S S R N G R R L G L M M
U T W B N I Y Z O O B
M E D J S T Y D Y R D
M S B I H W G G R Y D
O R N G P S P E A K S
N G I H H E Y Z S Y K
S M H I T T R V I U L
T Y N T U R D F L O N
L E R A R K A Y E P N
S M E B R O Q E X C W
X B Z B Z Z F N G Q T
```

Psalm 51:1-2

```
T N Q Y D Z L T B X N V T J
G R T Y Y D Q V M X S N A L
G B A Y C R E M B T M B O M
Z G D N P L N R E R U V B Y
C P R N S P Y A V N E X T R
L Y R D G G D M D W A S H P
E D T V Y F R A G Y K D X R
A G P I A X N E D O G Q S D
N P M S U T X Y S G L I M V
S L T N M Q C L Y S N L Q L
E T Z D K R I W D Y I X Q V
W O J D E L G N M R X O R Q
D L B M D T M L I W Z L N J
P B P J W B Z M L Y P B D S
```

Psalm 51:10-12

```
E C N E S E R P S X
R E S T O R E P N Y
S G G L B C I O O H
U O T N L R I J E R
S D X E I T T A M C
T R A T A L R S R X
A N I V H T L E A W
I L L G J O A I E C
N A P X H T L N W P
S T P N E T G Y L W
```

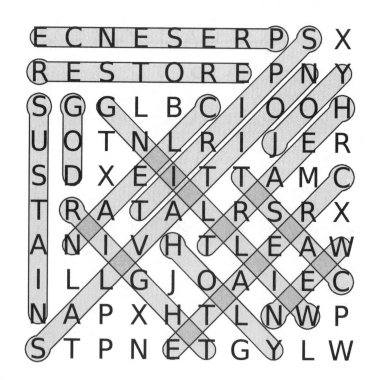
```
```

Psalm 52:8-9

Psalm 53:6

Psalm 54:1-2

Psalm 55:22

Psalm 56:3-4

```
A F R A I D P D
N E L T E G M Q
E M S R R O O Y
H E E I R U X D
W M S T A D S P
Y P A O R R U T
M L L O H T P R
S G W V M W N T
```

Psalm 56:12-13

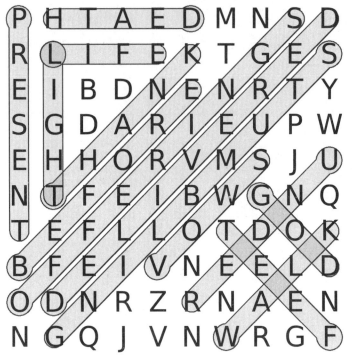

```
P H T A E D M N S D
R L I F E K T G E S
E I B D N E N R T Y
S G D A R I E U P W
E H H O R V M S J U
N T F E I B W G N Q
T E F L L O T D O K
B F E I V N E E L D
O D N R Z B N A E N
N G Q J V N W R G F
```

Psalm 57:9-10

```
A V H R E A C H E S N S
M B B E Y S P M P J S K
O Z U G A R N E X E J S
N R G N A V O O N M D D
G P K I F P E L I U J R
J T S L L A U N O T D T
L E O E G F I L S R A L
S R K N H T C L K G O N
D L I T H V Q N I V R X
J S I G J R A R E N N Z
Q A I T N H W N Q M G T
F H B L T X J L B B B K
```

Psalm 59:16-17

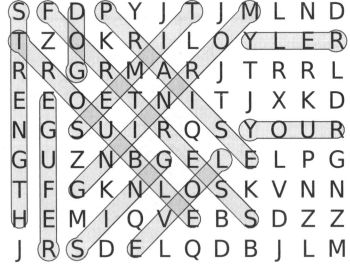

```
S F D P Y J T J M L N D
T Z O K R I L O Y L E R
R R G R M A R J T R R L
E E O E T N I T J X K D
N G S U I R Q S Y O U R
G U Z N B G E L E L P G
T F G K N L O S K V N N
H E M I Q V E B S D Z Z
J R S D E L Q D B J L M
```

Psalm 61:2-3

```
H F A I N T O W E R
R I T G V Q E O H K
E D G J N N F E K L
F T Y H D O A B M Z
U E B S E R R G T R
G L A L T R M T Q W
E E M E R L L A C S N
K A V T T R O C K N
D D L G B H N P T P
```

Psalm 61:4-5

```
J M G Q X D R A E H X H W
R X J W D Y R T M T E X L
D W E L L E Q Y A R G V J
L N K X V W R E I K Y O Z
K Y R E Y I N T G S E R D
L G R R G N A B W U E R F
P O N Y T G P O M T F E V
F N Z O E S V R L N A E N
M V Z J L J T E J R A J R
Q J N R B E H L T L V M P
L R D Q N S M M Q T J M E
V N M T D R B D T R J T X
```

Psalm 62:1-2

```
N S A N L R L Y S
O S L J E J O I Y
I E O N R K L C C
T R N Q E E A O K
A T E W N V M H G
V R Y C A E E O S
L O E T S I D R B
A F L U O S T Y X
S B M V M L Y S N
```

Psalm 63:1

```
G R K D Y V M T K
X O E R T S D S P
F W D T O Y T M R
A E H U A S Z N T
I A L S R W N G G
N R S I E R E H W
T Y H E X L A N D
S T X Y E N F Y N
N B N M Y K M T P
```

Psalm 63:3-4

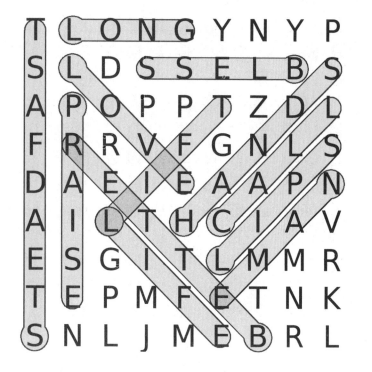

Psalm 65:4

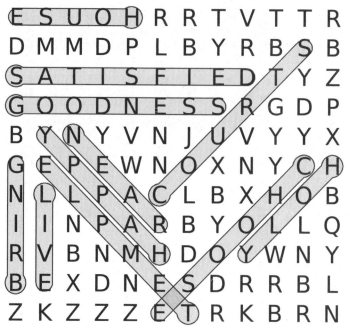

Psalm 65:5

Psalm 66:3-4

Psalm 67:1-3

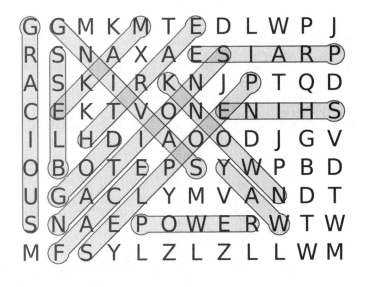

Psalm 68:5-6a

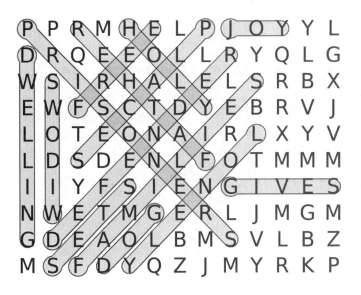

Psalm 68:19-20

Psalm 69:14-15a

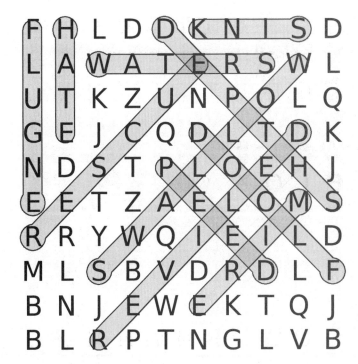

Psalm 69:32-33

Psalm 70:1-2

Psalm 71:14-15

Psalm 71:17-18

Psalm 73:23-25a

Psalm 73:25b-26

Psalm 74:16-17

Psalm 77:13-15a

Psalm 77:19-20

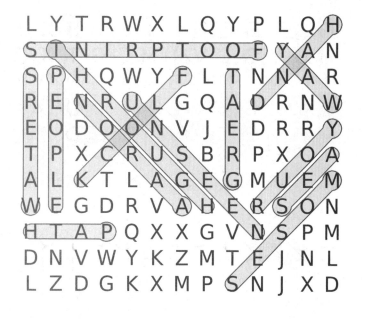

```
L Y T R W X L Q Y P L Q H
S T N I R P T O O F Y A N
S P H Q W Y F L T N N A R
R E N R U L G Q A D R N W
E O D O O N V J E D R R Y
T P X C R U S B R P X O A
A L K T L A G E G M U E M
W E G D R V A H E R S O N
H T A P Q X X G V N S P M
D N V W Y K Z M T E J N L
L Z D G K X M P S N J X D
```

Psalm 78:4

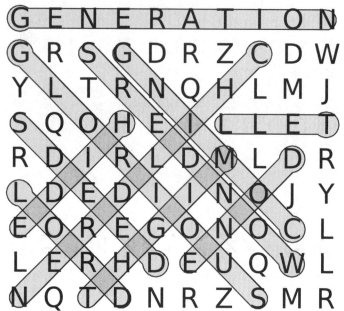

```
G E N E R A T I O N
G R S G D R Z C D W
Y L T R N Q H L M J
S Q O H E I L L E T
R D I R L D M L D R
L D E D I I N O J Y
E O R E G O N O C L
L E R H D E U Q W L
N Q T D N R Z S M R
```

Psalm 79:8b-9

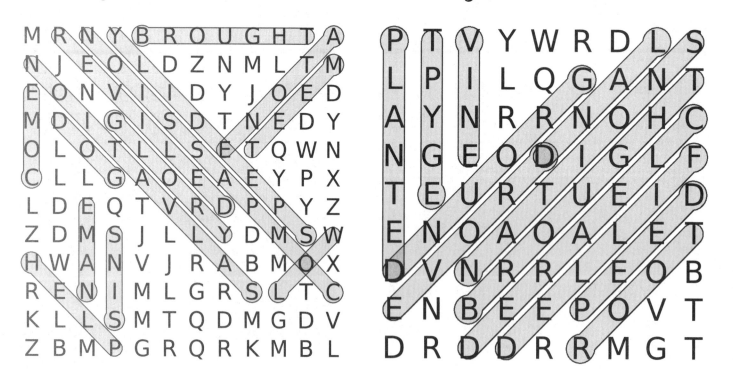

```
M R N Y B R O U G H T A
N J E O L D Z N M L T M
E O N V I I D Y J O E D
M D I G I S D T N E D Y
O L O T L L S E T Q W N
C L L G A O E A E Y P X
L D E Q T V R D P P Y Z
Z D M S J L L Y D M S W
H W A N V J R A B M O X
R E N I M L G R S L T C
K L L S M T Q D M G D V
Z B M P G R Q R K M B L
```

Psalm 80:8-9

```
P T V Y W R D L S
L P I L Q G A N T
A Y N R R N O H C
N G E O D I G L F
T E U R T U E I D
E N O A O A L E T
D V N R R L E O B
E N B E E P O V T
D R D D R R M G T
```

Psalm 81:1-2

Psalm 84:1-2

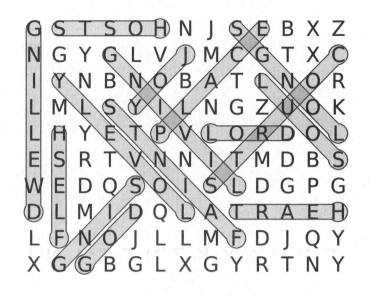

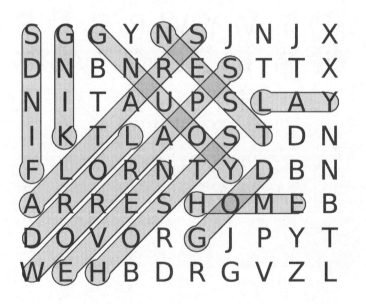

Psalm 84:3

Psalm 84:10

Psalm 84:11-12

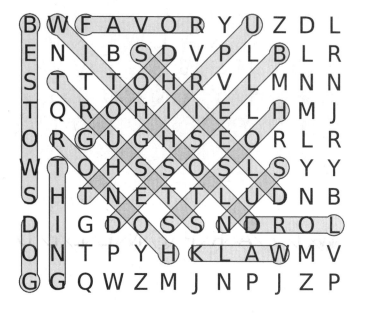

```
B W F A V O R Y U Z D L
E N I B S D V P L B L R
S T T O H R V L M N N
T Q R O H I I E L H M J
O R G U G H S E O R L R
W T O H S S O S L S Y Y
S H I T N E T T L U D N B
D I G D O S S N D R O L
O N T P Y H K L A W M V
G G Q W Z M J N P J Z P
```

Psalm 85:10-12

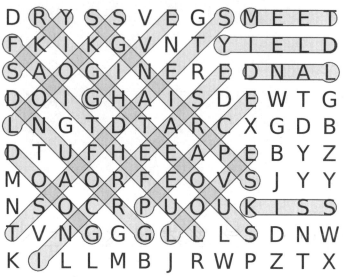

```
D R Y S S V E G S M E E T
F K I K G V N T Y I E L D
S A O G I N E R E D N A L
D O I G H A I S D E W T G
L N G T D T A R C X G D B
D T U F H E E A P E B Y Z
M O A O R F E O V S J Y Y
N S O C R P U O U K I S S
T V N G G G L L L S D N W
K I L L M B J R W P Z T X
```

Psalm 86:1-2

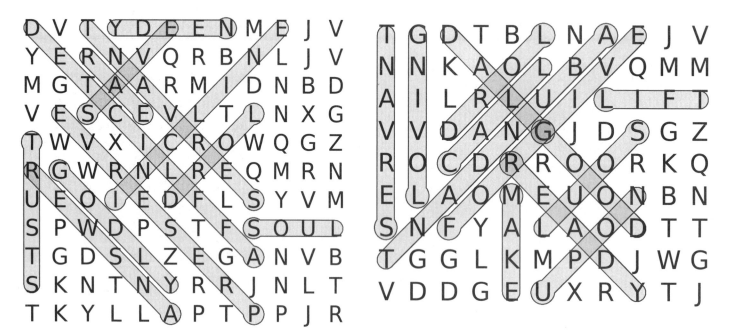

```
D V T Y D E E N M E J V
Y E R N V Q R B N L J V
M G T A A R M I D N B D
V E S C E V L T L N X G
T W V X I C R O W Q G Z
R G W R N L R E Q M R N
U E O I E D F L S Y V M
S P W D P S T F S O U L
S T G D S L Z E G A N V B
S K N T N Y R R J N L T
T K Y L L A P T P P J R
```

Psalm 86:4-5

```
T G D T B L N A E E J V
N N K A O L B V Q M M
A I L R L U I L I F T
V V D A N G J D S G Z
R O C D R R O O R K Q
E L A O M E U O N B N
S N F Y A L A O D T T
T G G L K M P D J W G
V D D G E U X R Y T J
```

Psalm 86:9-10

```
D G L D M E M A N N W
N L L Y M N R Y J W T
A S P O Z M R O K G D
W O N D R O U S F K M
P G D O Z I D Z R E B
I R O T I E F E N T B
H E G R E T A Y M Q W
S A B D E L A L K O Y
R T M D O B D N O T C
O V A R M T P R K N X
W M D T W R B Y Q J E
```

Psalm 86:11-12

```
T W L Q M Y B X D Q L J
P T T R A L W E K M R
R D B M H W E G R V W Z
N E M W Y A N M K J I Z
D K V Y K F N D A D L G
T H Y E T X I K V N O D
J B E R R H Y R S T R G
V L U A C O U Z O O Y F
W T Z A R P F N L L E D
H A E R J T Y B I A G Z
N T L Q Z Y D Z R T L G
D Y T K D V J G P D E L
```

Psalm 89:5-6

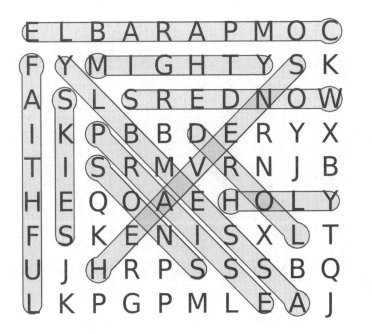

```
E L B A R A P M O C
F Y M I G H T Y S K
A S L S R E D N O W
I K P B B D E R Y X
T I S R M V R N J B
H E Q O A E H O L Y
F S K E N I S X L T
U J H R P S S S B Q
L K P G P M L E A J
```

Psalm 89:11-12

```
S N E V A E H N B T L P
Y H E R M O N R O B A T
W F H K A J L T Q N Y C
W O Z T O L U N N L O L
X U E Y U O L Y A N D S
B N A C H O T W T M R B
X D R S R Q S A O U E B
Y E T J Z E I Y O R H J
W D H J M N A Y R T L N
X T B Y S D B T R D R D
Y D M B V Z R O E Y T Y
B T J T M N N B Q D Q D
```

Psalm 89:13-14

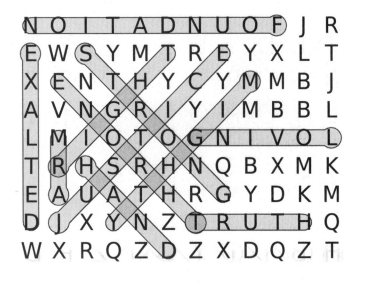

```
N O I T A D N U O F J R
E W S Y M T R E Y X L T
X E N T H Y C Y M M B J
A V N G R I Y I M B B L
L M I O T O G N I V O L
T R H S R H N Q B X M K
E A U A T H R G Y D K M
D J X Y N Z T R U T H Q
W X R Q Z D Z X D Q Z T
```

Psalm 90:1-2

```
G Q B Y Q B V R Z X Y Z
D E V E R L A S T I N G
Q R N M O U N T A I N S
D J O E H T R I B E N D
B W T L R B L T A R J L
E O E L D A N R O B X D
F R L L P Z T B J Y Y N
O L D L L H V I P N Y P
R D A O J I W G O Y J Y
E C N Q G N N Y G N B D
E R R Z M L N G B Y S N
```

Psalm 91:1-2

```
R J R S L L E W D M P L R
E N Z T T J B P Y Z M J D
T P N T Y L X S H A D O W
L F V B M L J D T T J M E
E Y O N N D B R R T G G E
H D T R D Y Q D S L U D D
S W T H T W R O X F I W R
T Z N I G R M T E B N N L
M S N G Y I E R A Y Q O G
D T U H T T M S Z D R Z Z
J G L R B G T L S D D W L
W K D J T N M R A O V V R
N B W G D Y N G G T J P Y
```

Psalm 91:11-12

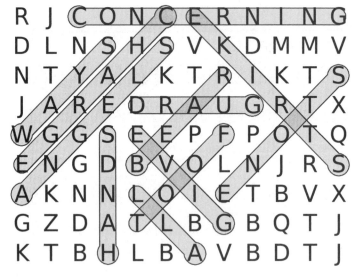

```
R J C O N C E R N I N G
D L N S H S V K D M M V
N T Y A L K T R I K T S
J A R E D R A U G R T X
W G G S E E P F P O T Q
E N G D B V O L N J R S
A K N N L O I E T B V X
G Z D A T L B G B Q T J
K T B H L B A V B D T J
```

Psalm 92:1-2

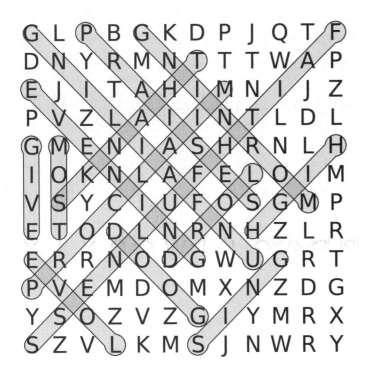

Psalm 92:4-5

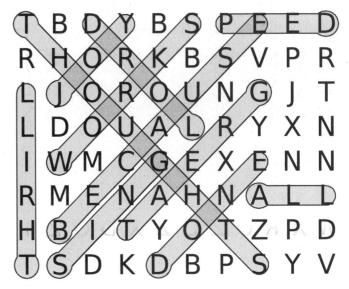

Psalm 93:1

Psalm 94:14-15

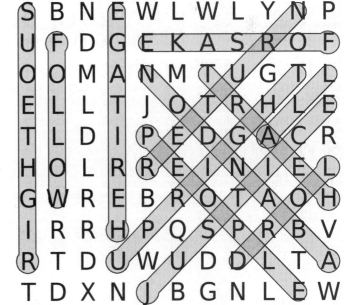

Psalm 94:18-19

```
S R R L G S O U L D K V T
W N S L I P P I N G R O E
J M O N T J N Z Q E O V V
T R L I R M Q N E F O X R
R S M G T N D H Y L X T N
L L A N H A C B N M V Q P
C L R F Z E L D A Q Q B J
A M P G D M A O M H L D L
R Q T N N A Y R S Z E O R
E M V W N R E T T N R L D
S G T T J M X T G D O X D
R X D G B L N W S L R C L
```

Psalm 95:4-5

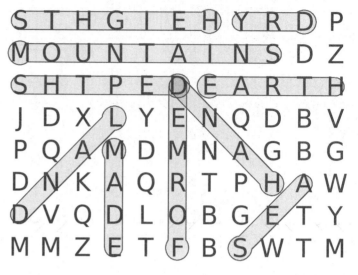

```
S T H G I E H Y R D P
M O U N T A I N S D Z
S H T P E D E A R T H
J D X L Y E N Q D B V
P Q A M D M N A G B G
D N K A Q R T P H A W
D V Q D L O B G E T Y
M M Z E T F B S W T M
```

Psalm 95:6-7

```
M D R J W G G R J Y B D
L R M P B L T Z D Y K L
M O L P M P Z N P L K V
E L P O E P A E C Z T B
Q W W L B H E S K O E P
Q O M O J H Y N T F M M
B R W Z S R E D O U A E
T S N V Z E Z R P K R J
D H L W L N E M E Z D E
R I J D O G G R Y R P Q
B P G G V D P B T D T T
```

Psalm 96:2-3

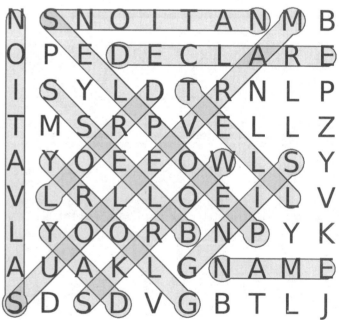

```
N S N O I T A N M B
O P E D E C L A R E
I S Y L D T R N L P
T M S R P V E L L Z
A Y O E E O W L S Y
V L R L L O E I L V
L Y O O R B N P Y K
A U A K L G N A M E
S D S D V G B T L J
```

Psalm 96:8-9

Psalm 96:10

Psalm 97:10

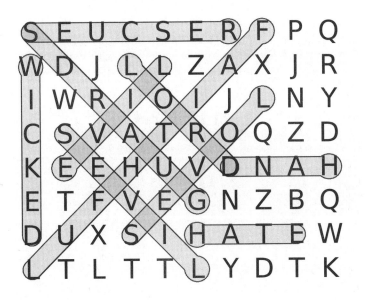

Psalm 98:8b-9

Psalm 99:1-2

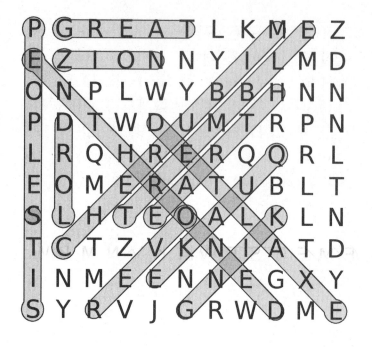

Psalm 100:1-2

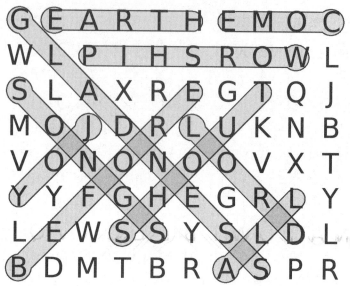

Psalm 101:3b-4

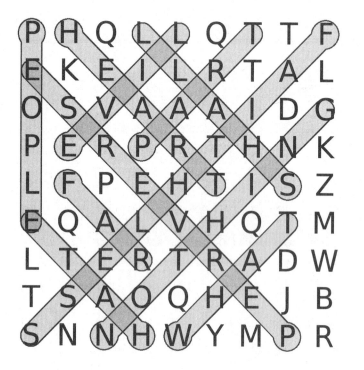

Psalm 102:15-16

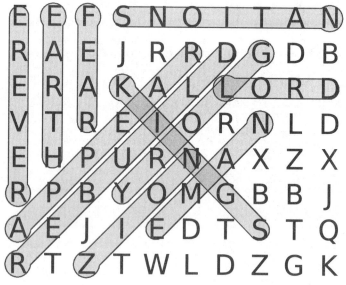

Psalm 103:8-10

```
C O M P A S S I O N A T E
A L R R X J R Y S T T D K
B J N M J Y K D Q I E I M
O S U O I C A R G S N Q L
U R T Z J E T V E I Y S X
N E G N R A S R Q H L M Q
D G X P E M V U A Y B T N
I N J R L E I R C N M Z S
N A T O W T B L E C X V Q
G J R L I O N N O P A P K
L D N E R R L Y L V A X V
W M S M N M N S B D E Y W
```

Psalm 103:11-12

```
T R A N S G R E S S I O N S
S N E V A E H R L Y T X B T
D B X N L H X M K P R D M T
T E W V F I T S A E G D M R
P D V E D G E R J W M Q T D
Y V A O A H Q A N Z Y P P
T R D B M N T B R D G L Y X
T Z O B T E J L T T D L Z W
Q V T A T T R R O X H B V W
E M E T S E W A K V M P W
M R Q B Q V Z F R V E D T G
G L D T D D J Y X L V Y Z M
```

Psalm 104:2-3

```
S T R I D E S C S T T W
N L N W Q D H T T Z T J
E O D E U A R O S Y M G
V R B O M E I R W G N R
A D L B T R E R E P P U
E C E C A T A T H G I L
H R H H A P S G N I W B
S E C W S B E A M S D B
S T E N T O N I W R D M
```

Psalm 104:33-34

```
M R G R K T L G D R X Y
E Q N V P W P R K N J Y
D V I L Q R O A M N V R
I Z S X J L L Y L V Z Y
T B A R P L P V Z R Z M
A G E V E R G J Y D V K
T T L N G J A N L I V E
I T P N R G O I I D K M
O E O R O T W I S S R L
N L F D X B T Y C E T B
N X B I L W X K T E J Q
G R Y R L R R R R B D K V
```

Psalm 105:8-9

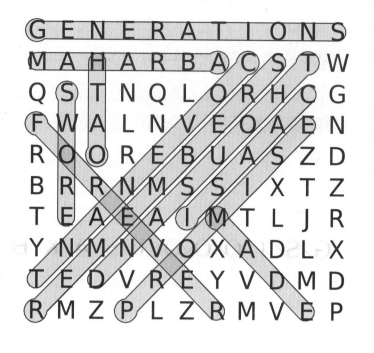

Psalm 106:47

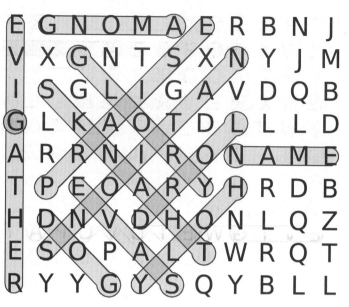

Psalm 107:8-9

Psalm 107:28-29

Psalm 108:5-6

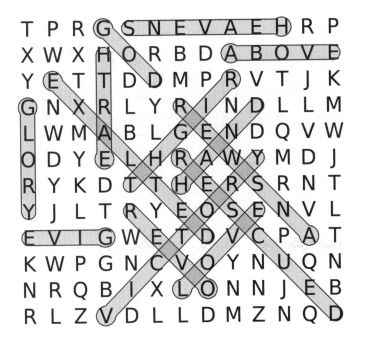

```
T P R G S N E V A E H R P
X W X H O R B D A B O V E
X Y E T T D D M P R V T J K
G N X R L Y R I N D L L M
L W M A B L G E N D Q V W
O D Y E L H R A W Y M D J
R Y K D T T H E R S R N T
Y J L T R Y E O S E N V L
E V I G W E T D V C P A T
K W P G N C V O Y N U Q N
N R Q B I X L O N N J E B
R L Z V D L L D M Z N Q D
```

Psalm 109:21-22

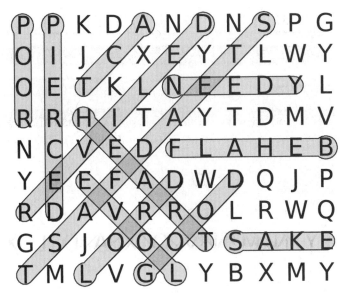

```
P P K D A N D N S P G
O I J C X E Y T L W Y
O E T K L N E E D Y L
R H I T A Y T D M V
N C V E D F L A H E B
Y E E F A D W D Q J P
R D A V R R O L R W Q
G S J O O O T S A K E
T M L V G L Y B X M Y
```

Psalm 111:2-3

```
R R S D F R D X Z M W L N R
I B J E V O T S Y X Z M Y Q
G N Z N R Q R T T N A T X Z
H Q L B D U H E V U S L W D
T G M B G D B V E D B L L
E W T D I G L N J E R I Z W
O D Z L L X R A E J R N E L
U N E M L M M E W O R K S D
S D R O N O H F A L O R D R
N L K M R K U Y K T R D R Q
E K K L P L Q D P N K Q Y J
S J N K L V T Y L L N X M Y
S R D J X T Z Z M W M P N J
```

Psalm 111:9-10a

```
U N D E R S T A N D I N G
N E C I T C A R P D W B L
T O Y L O H B P E I E P X
N N I Q R B J D S G E V K
A R E T Y Q N D I O R N W
N Q E S P A O N P E X D M
E A N V M M N L M L R G M
V N M M E I E O F O J L D
O D O E N R S D L E X G T
C C O G D E O J E T A J P
R M G O W P Y F T R D R M
P B Q A G Z D V G N J Y M
```

Psalm 112:1b-2

```
U P R I G H T D W L Y Y R L
V W N J Q N G R L Y X G X I
T S N Z N N M O V M E D O M
Q Z T L D I Y L M N D O Y M
G X T N G K Z T E R M P Y R
R P F H A P L R Y M P P T T
E D T E N D A V A A R Y D R
A T B J A T N N H B K E M L
T J N L I B D E K Y L D A L
L N P O E M X J C I G N R X
Y Y N G E S K Y G S D Y K Y
D Z T N W M S H K D E V X B
B K T P G R T E T Q N D Z B
P S Q T N Y K N D Y W M D W
```

Psalm 113:2-3

```
E R O M R E V E R O F
V G R J T G D T I M E
P M N I R E M V Q M J
Y R B I S N A M E Z M
S Q A S T I G Y D R V
U I E I D T N Y T B R
N L H R S T E G Q Y Z
B V O T Y E G S Y L M
N L B X M L D Q B J M
```

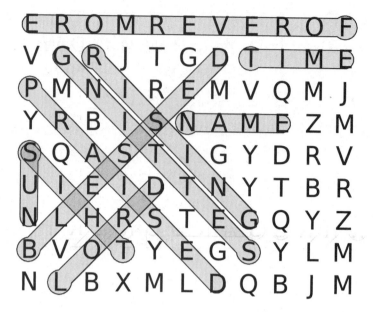

Psalm 113:7-8

```
T W M A K E B Q
S E S I A R T K
S E C N I R P Z
T G Y T P E B T
F R I D O A S N
I S O P E U E A
L D L O D E S H
N E Z D P H N L
```

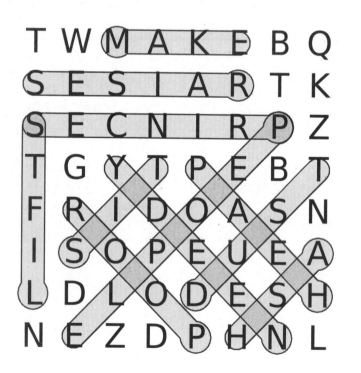

Psalm 114:7-8

```
T T E L O R D E M
R N R A D G C W J
E I O R R N O A Y
M L C B E T C D S
B F K S S O H P W
L L E N B G R A P
E R R Z R I T O B
P U Y T N E O D Y
T J D G R L R V L
```

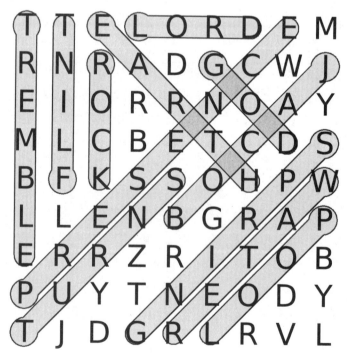

Psalm 115:1-2

```
E F Y T B P D J J P Y K T Y
E R R A J D Y J P W M N D W
R E L R I T S N O I T A N N
E H L T Q T S L O R D R L M
H W W Z B D H A N N T G S J
T Y T J E L K F F P N A O B
R B M V L R X U D Y X K D
Y A N I D D Y W L A Q K Y
N R R G S A K E O N E R Y
T B O R J Z M Y V T E T Y
L N Z L W N R P E N Q S S
Z Q V L G R Y W Z M Q P S
```

Psalm 116:1-2

```
S U P P L I C A T I O N S
J W K B Y Z N E E C I O V
T Q D N N P D Y V B P D Q
E R O F E R E H T I R J J
I N C L I N E D L O L P N
G P D L B N V O L J T T T
H N W T B Z V G W P M G T
B E O L Y E L T C Q L L Z
B R A L J Y P A T D K P Z
G N B R P T L Z B G Z L T
Z N W P D L V T R X V N L
```

Psalm 116:12-14

```
Y Q Q K M P B B B M N T E
B B C U P P J J M V C W
N O I T A V L A S N T Y
R U J P L O R D E W A Y
E N C Y E T W S T P O E
T T W A B O E Y L M M V
E Y T Q L R P I J A D L
R N J X P L F L N Y J B
B L K N G T G N E R M L
```

Psalm 117

```
S S P Y W Q V D T K P V D
E T N Q T R D S Q E P F D
R A L O V E A Q O L A T J
U E F T I F D P G I T L X
D R O P D T L E T X N L X
N G R A G E A H S W Y R N
E N E T S Y F N N I J D Y
T V K E U D X R D A W L
S W E Y L X J L R T Q R B
P M R N V M T O V T G J P
B M E B L N L O G D R R N
N S J M D L D N L L T M W
S N T T W V N D L R Z N Q
```

Psalm 118:5-6

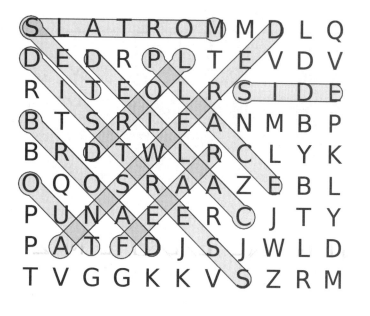

Psalm 118:22-23

Psalm 119:1-3

Psalm 119:54-55

Psalm 119:75-76

Psalm 121:1-2

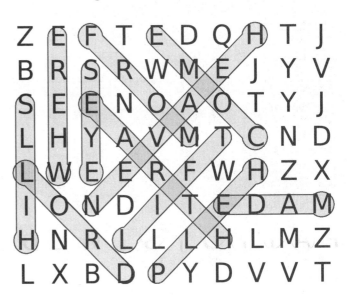

Psalm 121:5-6

Psalm 125:1-2

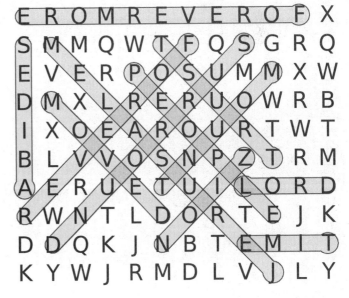

Psalm 126:5-6

```
S H E A V E S W Y R Q D
S G Q X S O E O D Y N L
H G N O W E J P E M O H
O P H I P G N I R A E B
U T A I Y S J S N B J B
T C N E R R H Q S W G T
S G O A R A R E Z M R Y
G Q E M L Y E A Y B D M
N T N L E D Y T C T Y R
```

Psalm 127:1

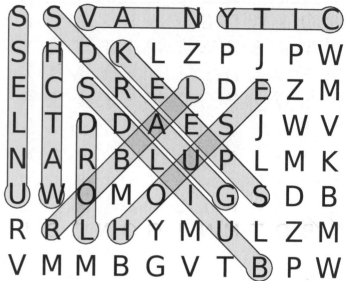

```
S S V A I N Y T I C
S H D K L Z P J P W
E C S R E L D E Z M
L T D D A E S J W V
N A R B L U P L M K
U W O M O I G S D B
R R L H Y M U L Z M
V M M B G V T B P W
```

Psalm 130:3-4

```
S S E N E V I G R O F
S E I T I U Q I N I Z
D M D M M D M A R K J
L N R E L X S W W M D
O X A U R H W I T P B
R M O T O E T H T M M
D C G U S H V M O M Z
L L L T P J B E B T W
L D P N M M L G R T D
```

Psalm 131:1b-2a

```
M A R V E L O U S D B B
S K Y D R G Z D X Z Q B
G D D G E T R T L B Q Y
N E W E H R G E V I P D
I M E M T V N G A U H G
H L A D O E T M C T M C
T A N P M V I C L U O S
Y C E Q W K O U R D J R
B P D J L K M M O Y M Q
```

Psalm 132:8-9

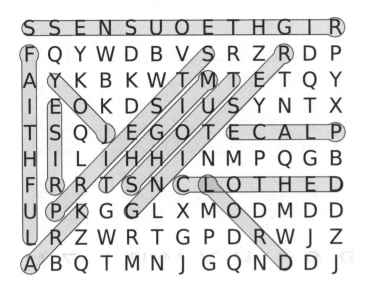

Psalm 133:1-2

Psalm 134:1-2

Psalm 135:5-6

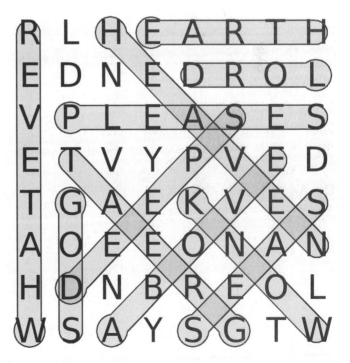

Psalm 135:13-14

Psalm 136:3-4

Psalm 137:6

Psalm 138:4-5

Psalm 138:7

```
M P J N H R S X S Z
I R R A H T I R N E
D Q N E R G E G L G
S D E E S V U B H T
T W T N I E U O S T
B C A L E O R N H W
H R E L R M I V R T
L D M T K A I A E N
D Z P Z G D T E R Z
G K D A R H R Q S V
```

Psalm 139:1-3

```
T L R M L N D H R L R B L
D E T N I A U Q C A O Y X
S T N T W T V V Y R I R L
K I R W N L H Z T N A Q D
D R T K O R B O G Q R E D
N E Q J W N E D U X A L S
K N H T A P K C B G F N K
R B J C X N J M S T H V B
R I M P R Y V J L I X T S
P Q S R R A M B P Z D Y S
R R R E X R E Y G Y A T G
M V G K P X J S N W L P R
```

Psalm 139:7-8

```
S H E A V E N P L L
A P V T K E R E H W
S E I A H E Y L M Y
C E M R S E O D E B
E L T E I E R M Y B
N F N M H T T E K R
D C K S N G D M M T
E D R G T M Q Z Z Q
```

Psalm 139:14-15

```
Y S H T P E D X R Z B P G Q
L K W Y R L T R G W W I R P
L D R O Q R J J L R N T R L
U G X Z V D R S T T J A D J
F Z N J P E K T R T I U L D
R N T B T R N I E S F G Y Q
A Z D M O E C R E R K N O W
E X A W A A C V E M H P N X
F D B R T E V D L I A T J G
E J T E S P N G D W D R Z X
D H L D T O N D G E B P F R
V Y D N W B E L J L Q T N M
R D Y R R N D Y L U W Z V L
```

Psalm 139:23-24

```
Z G R L N G D D S V J M
Y J N Y W L L E T M Z M
K P L I J B A V S G T L
T Y A W T R T T K P N Y
R V R N C S H G K T D N
A Q T H T G A N G E D G
E G P E U L O L K D M B
H X S O G W E C R L B G
K T H S E E I A L E O Y
Q T T D Q W K M D D V Z
L R N M Y P B R K R X E
```

Psalm 140:12-13

```
M E S U A C R U P S
A E M E D Y P O U D
I V C M T R D O O E
N I G N I U E E C P
T G P G E T C I E S
A K H M H S T E K N
I T A G K S E N X D
N N I N U V A R R E
S R O J I H V O P L
D W D L T K L J Z T
```

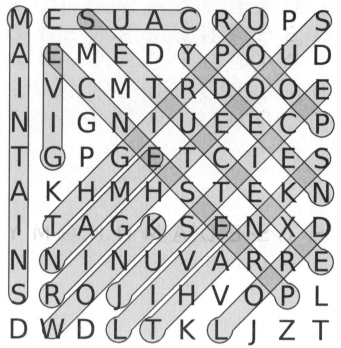

Psalm 141:1-2

```
E M V B T B R H T T D D Y B
V Y Q R N J J L A X D R Z M
E B R R X K Z Q L N E R M L
N V A R D Y D D I V D L B D
I E T P L B P N I B I S R S
N E C I O V C G J F C O A N
G T T C K E Y R T A L C O Z
Q N O J N L E I L Q R O T V
L M R S K Y N L B I U Z D G
E Z E C A G M J F N B R L Q
Z G I R V P J I T M Q V W T
W U P N K G C E D N D J B L
Q K J L K E D V W L K D L L
```

Psalm 143:5-6

```
R M P L U O S N D V
D E E A T T T D L O
E S M D R H A N D S
E D K E I C I Y R D
D W T R M T H N D N
S C S D O B A E K Q
H T V N A W E T D X
S B N A Z Y Z R E N
D D Y L R X S N J D
```

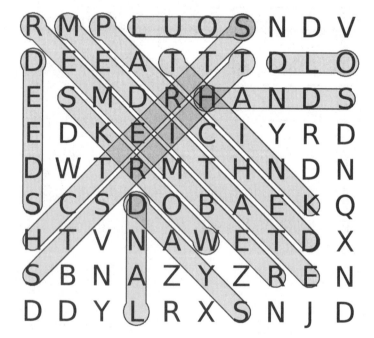

Psalm 145:8-9

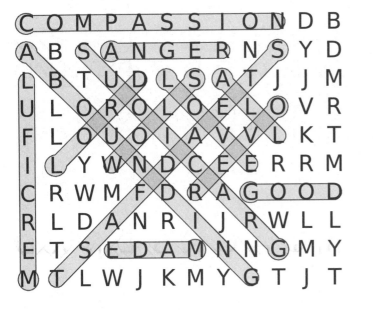

Psalm 147:4-5

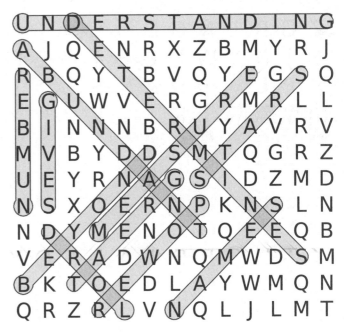

Psalm 150:3-6a

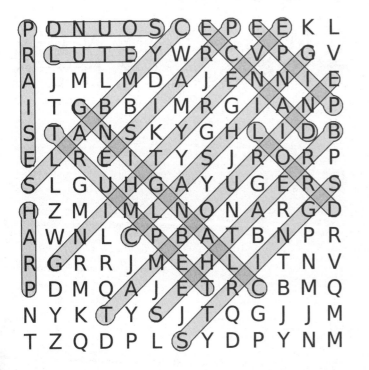

Organic Fruits and Vegetables

Growing Healthy and Delicious Food at Home

By Teo Gómez
with Quico Barranco

Translated by Elizabeth Watson

Skyhorse Publishing

"If you want to be happy for a day, drink.
If you want to be happy for a month, travel.
If you want to be happy for a year, get married.
If you want to be happy for life, become a farmer."

CHINESE PROVERB

* * *

DEDICATED TO SERAFIN SANJUAN AND ALVARO ALTES, PIONEERS OF ECOLOGICAL AGRICULTURE.

Editor's Note: The advice in this book is based on a temperate climate.
Refer to your seed packets or a gardening professional if you're located
outside temperate zones. Although every effort has been made to ensure that the
information in this book was correct at press time, the author and publisher hereby
disclaim any liability to any party for any loss, injury, damage, or disruption caused by
errors or omissions. Please note that any advice contained herein may not be suitable
for every individual.

Original title: TU HUERTO Y JARDÍN ECOLÓGICOS
© 2007 EDITORIAL OCÉANO, S.L.
(BARCELONA, SPAIN)

All rights reserved. No part of this book may be reproduced or stored in a retrieval system or transmitted in any form or by any means,
whether electronic, mechanical, photocopying, recording or other kind, without the prior permission in writing of the owners.

Photos: Corbis, Getty, Océano archives; Illustrations: Xavier Bou

English translation © 2016 by Skyhorse Publishing

All rights reserved. No part of this book may be reproduced in any manner without the express written consent of the publisher, except in the case of
brief excerpts in critical reviews or articles. All inquiries should be addressed to Skyhorse Publishing, 307 West 36th Street, 11th Floor, New York, NY 10018.

Skyhorse Publishing books may be purchased in bulk at special discounts for sales promotion, corporate gifts, fund-raising, or educational purposes.
Special editions can also be created to specifications. For details, contact the Special Sales Department, Skyhorse Publishing,
307 West 36th Street, 11th Floor, New York, NY 10018 or HYPERLINK "mailto:info@skyhorsepublishing.com" info@skyhorsepublishing.com.

Skyhorse® and Skyhorse Publishing® are registered trademarks of Skyhorse Publishing, Inc.®, a Delaware corporation.

Visit our website at www.skyhorsepublishing.com.

10 9 8 7 6 5 4 3 2 1

Library of Congress Cataloging-in-Publication Data is available on file.

Cover design by Qualcom
Cover photo credit Thinkstock

ISBN: 978-1-63450-347-1
Ebook ISBN: 978-1-63450-908-4
Printed in China

Contents

Introduction: Why ecological agriculture?

In a not-so-distant future, producers will have to opt for organic crops, products free from chemicals, in the face of increasing demand.

Any agricultural practice that doesn't contaminate the environment and consumes a reasonable amount of energy—including manual labor, the use of machines, and the consumption of fertilizers—can be considered ecological.

Therefore, ecological agriculture should eliminate as much as possible the use of fertilizers and pesticides on plants. In the case of animals, it should avoid growth regulators in general, including steroids, and the use of medications and dietary supplements.

You could say that the agriculture practiced in ancient times was ecological, since they did not use fertilizers or chemical products to fight plagues or diseases in the plants. However, when we go beyond the regions where agriculture fostered civilizations, it becomes clear that the agriculture that we are going to practice is *more* ecological than that practiced by, for example, the Sumerians.

Agriculture began in the Near East, in the deltas of the Tigris, Euphrates, and Nile rivers. The young land, formed by sedimentary material washed down from the mountains, had an extraordinary yield because it had never been utilized before.

Land formed in this way produces abundant harvests without needing fertilizer for many years, and then begins to lack essential components that have all been absorbed by the plants. In the Nile, the annual floods brought fertile soil from the mountains of Ethiopia and deposited it across the valley, on both sides of the river, renewing the nutrients each year. In Mesopotamia something similar happened, although the expansion of farming into higher areas forced them to fertilize with the manure of livestock in order to use the soil continually. The ingenious irrigation systems of the Sumerians and Babylonians did not account for the fact that when the water evaporated in the channels, the salt stayed behind and accumulated on the surface and, over time, left the land barren.

The myths of industrial agriculture

Agricultural engineers, chemists, and politicians in general defend industrial agriculture as the only option to end world hunger. Why? Because of the scarce yield of organic agriculture, which requires a greater amount of manual labor and produces less.

First myth

Industrial agriculture will produce food for everyone. In poor countries, many farmers have been dispossessed of their lands, from which they obtained subsistence foods, in order to produce industrial foods such as tobacco and cotton, which only benefit landowners and the government. In Latin America and Africa there are still vast expanses of uncultivated land that could feed millions of people. In the Amazon, they transform immense tracts of jungle into poor pasture land to

This windmill is the cleanest way to bring up ground water without polluting the environment. Unfortunately, they have almost completely disappeared from the landscape, to be replaced by electric pumps that depend on the burning of fuel in a power plant.

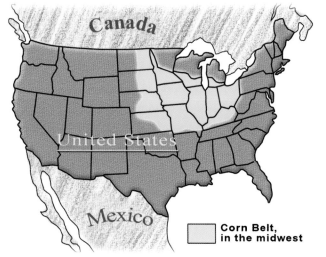

Corn Belt,
in the midwest

produce hamburgers destined for North Americans. In many parts of Africa, it would only take some irrigation to convert hundreds of thousands of hectares of arid and unused lands into worthwhile crop land.

Second myth

Industrial foodstuffs are healthy and nutritious. It is enough to just mention the pesticides, insecticides, and genetic modification, which could cause cancer in the long term and which damage the environment.

Third myth

They are cheaper. The social and environmental cost of products created in laboratories is very high, and that's not to mention the dependency created around them. They expel small farmers from their lands, and pollute the atmosphere and soil. It is not true that industrial agriculture produces higher yields, since it has been demonstrated that small parcels cultivated intensely, as is done in Japan and Italy, produce a much higher yield in all aspects. The myth that genetically modified plants are more resistant to disease is also false, since, as we will see, they require specific pesticides and insecticides and make farmers dependent, as well as replacing more flavorful and nutritious species.

In this map, observe the Corn Belt in the Midwestern United States, very rich tracts of land where they have applied the most efficient technology in fertilization and genetic engineering. Government subsidies make the production so inexpensive that corn grown in this way is cheaper on the global market than that grown the traditional way in Mexico, where manual labor is much cheaper. The result is that more and more people are abandoning systems of production that are hundreds of years old, an extraordinary genetic diversity is being lost, and a good part of the farming community is going broke.

The cosmetic value of fruits and vegetables is becoming increasingly more important than other aspects, such as flavor and nutritive value. For this reason they apply harmful wax to oranges, for example.

Mechanization

It is normal to think that the mechanization of agriculture is a notable improvement and should stimulate production. Well, this is a superficial conclusion, and in many cases is the result of propaganda from those who profit from it. It does not benefit the rural community, which ends up in poverty, unemployed, or in the city, but rather the consumer who can squander more. This happens not because the citizens are organized, but because the farmers are not and the corporations are, due to the small size of our country and researchers paid by them. Mechanization must be cut back because it is responsible for rural depopulation, the reduction of the quality of products, and enslavement to the anonymous societies in possession of the technological arsenal. These failures indicate that mechanization is ineffective and uneconomical.

Let's look at a real case: Recently, the University of Florida developed, for mechanical harvest, a salad tomato whose characteristics make it optimal for the harvester: thick lining, hard pulp, and skin that does not break. This is perhaps a little tough for the consumer, but you can't please everyone. The use of this tomato will eliminate thousands of jobs in Florida alone, but in some ways that is an advantage, since machines don't create the same conflicts.

It is designed to be harvested green and ripen while stored by applying ethylene gas. It has been demonstrated that this gas reduces the quantities of vitamins A and C, the flavor, and the consistency in tomatoes, but the South Carolina Agricultural Experiment Station has demonstrated that treating tomatoes with red fluorescent light increases their red color, and the taste and consistency become similar to those ripened on the vine. The University of Ohio confirms that tomatoes peeled chemically with moisturizing agents and caustic lye reduce the work by 75 percent and increase the final output. Did anyone ask what the consumer thinks of this? Is it guaranteed that those who make the machines, control the gas and oil, make the herbicides and fertilizers, process, store, and distribute, will not extort the mechanical grower? And who wants to know what has happened to the vitamins?

The legacy of chemical pesticides left by World War II, selective cross breeding, and cultural improvements increased crop production in California from 60 tons per hectare, to 100. But one enemy emerged: the people. It's an enormous industry that is almost entirely manual. The fluctuation in the workforce was more or less manageable, but the order from Washington was that no more dollars were to leave the country: the migrant workers had to stay in their country. Although the industry did not collapse because it already had machines and the tomato had already been "improved" to suit the use of machines.

At the University of California, Hanna, a geneticist, was looking for a tomato that grew like a conifer, with the fruits on a conical surface, which all ripened at the same time and had a good dose of pectins to give them consistency. The plant had to weigh half as much as the average plant. She crossed appropriate varieties and selected the Red Top variety, with its satisfactory architecture, to cross with the Tiny Tom, with fruits the size of a cherry.

The cultivation of the new tomato and its mechanical harvesting require more irrigation (because they are superficial plants), perfect fields, meticulous weed "control" so they don't obstruct the machines, and a course in the use

Growth hormone, which is given to livestock despite being carcinogenic for humans, earned almost three million dollars in 1998 for its discoverers and promoters: the University of Iowa. And the sales by distributors reached seventy million. Something similar occurred with the use of antibiotics as pesticides, prohibited in Europe because of the danger of resistant pathogenic microbes, but which continues to be used in the United States because of business interests.

and maintenance of the machines. But all this inconvenience is small when it comes to saving an industry. So, for the last fifteen years we have had excellent reddened tomatoes: small and dense, and probably sprayed with varnish to improve their outer appearance, since cosmetic research is common for fruits, including apples, peaches, citrus, and tomatoes. Chickens are also given xanthophylls so that their skin has a "pleasant yellow tint."

They have done and are conducting studies on consumer behavior and their preconceived ideas about the appearance of foods. The idea is to make people think that the food is "good." In this way, the University of Kansas Extension, by confirming that apples sell by the criteria of outer appearance more than nutrition, urges growers to produce a more attractive product, and that they beautify the displays in stores with mirrors and lights. The University of Iowa has studied the wrappers of foods, and it found that the color of ham was better conserved by vacuum packing or CO_2, thus attracting more consumers.

Alvaro Altés, biologist

Agrarian Systems

Agrarian systems and eco-friendly
alternatives

Intensive agriculture has only one goal—economic gain—and disregards the health of the planet entirely

Agriculture for life

Where do we want to end up? And where do we come from? Agriculture began ten thousand years ago in the Middle East, to the north of the Euphrates River or in the desert kites (see textbox). From there, it extended across the globe, although keep in mind that other areas have their own history. At the beginning, agriculture was extensive: they would plant one area until the yield diminished and then moved on to a new place, because there was enough space. It is similar to the slash-and-burn method still practiced in jungle regions today. To this type of agriculture, they added organic fertilizers that allowed the land to be used for many years. The fields were small, since they were tended by hand and required a lot of manual labor. The yields were reduced but enough to maintain a modest population.

The growth of the population and the needs of businesses gave rise to industrial agriculture, which uses large tracts of land to plant a single crop and fertilizes the land with chemical products to obtain maximum yields. It also introduces pesticides and herbicides to prevent the growth of weeds and insecticides to prevent insects from attacking the crops; it selects varieties with the highest yield per hectare, and uses machines to plant and harvest. The process suffers an adaptation period, since the first industrial crops were harvested by cheap manual labor: the combines in Europe and slaves in America.

Genetic engineering introduces species that are more resistant to drought, cold, heat, wet, altitude, and attacks by certain funguses or insects. These crops need chemical accessories that are only sold by the same company that makes the seed.

The desert kites

Many years ago, humans built traps out of stone in the shape of huge kites in the deserts of Syria and Jordan. Gazelles were trapped in large numbers during their migratory period, and they were slaughtered and conserved in salt, allowing the people to be at leisure the rest of the year. In this region, wild wheat and barley grew, and sheep grazed, not yet domesticated. It's not hard to believe that in this region under these circumstances, agriculture and livestock raising began and changed the life of humankind.

Modern agriculture is pushing out natural systems and causing the progressive poisoning of nature.

Monocropping, which consists of sowing a single species to make it most profitable, is associated with intensive agriculture. In some countries, monocropping coincides with the national needs, as happens in Thailand.

But, they have a high yield per hectare and are easy to harvest, store, conserve, and ripen.

Monocropping, which consists of sowing a single species to make it most profitable, is associated with intensive agriculture. In some countries, monocropping coincides with the national needs, as happens in Thailand with rice, but in others, the interests are those of a minority, such as in Ghana or Guinea with cacao (although, due to the high need for manual labor, a large part of the population benefits minimally).

In the face of this agriculture of profits, we find traditional agriculture practiced on a small scale, which applies modern knowledge to traditional methods, but without additives, herbicides, and insecticides that could be harmful to our health, based on the goal of obtaining a quality product that is, above all, healthier.

Industrial crops

In the case of some African countries in which there are food shortages, such as Ethiopia, they opt to dedicate great expanses of land to industrial crops and exports, such as sugar, cotton, or cacao. This deprives the people not only of the land they need to survive, but also the benefits of this type of agriculture. These are the most scandalous cases in modern agriculture.

The case of Japan

Japan is a super-populated country that needs to import the majority of its foods. It is small and mountainous, and only 14 percent of the land is suitable for agriculture. Thanks to its wet climate, half of its crops are flood crops and almost exclusively rice, a staple in all of southeast Asia. The rest are small plantations of soy, grains for humans (not animals), and fruit trees.

The average parcel is a hectare, but the majority are small parcels that the inhabitants use to plant vegetables part of the time. During the dry season, many rice paddies become rich vegetable gardens. In one such garden, Masanobu Fukuoka made his discoveries. This system of agriculture, based on quality products for direct consumption, is not very important to the Japanese economy.

The case of Guatemala

In the Cuchumatanes mountains, in the town of Todos Santos, not so long ago they grew corn, helped by an excellent climate and fertile lands. Between the corn stalks, they grew beans and squash. The harvest was abundant, although since the parcels were small, it was basically subsistence. They complemented this by trading corn for potatoes or coffee from the valley.

All this changed recently, when industrial agriculture appeared with the introduction of broccoli for exportation; farmers took out loans to buy seeds, irrigation systems, and pesticides. In exchange, they earned money to buy what they previously got from trading, and also clothing, radios, and televisions. The system put the population into debt, created unhappiness, and ended in failure.

Conventional agriculture

Conventional agriculture is essentially a polluter and a homogenizer, since it values quantity over quality and does not think twice about eliminating plagues or epidemics, unless there is a social outcry.

Conventional agriculture is also known as intensive agriculture. Its objective is to increase production at a lower cost. Until recently, the methods used were mainly genetic selection and hybridization through crossing different varieties to obtain more productive and resistant seeds.

In this type of agriculture, the use of herbicides and pesticides is the norm. The poisons used are increasingly more powerful and poisonous for the environment because plagues become resistant and need to be fought each year with more aggressive substances. There are specific ones that target a certain insect, or there are generic ones that, in order to kill a harmful fly, also kill off butterflies and dragonflies.

Recently and with the presumption of reducing the use of pesticides, genetic engineering has developed genetically modified products, which create plants resistant to diseases and plagues, but which carry other risks, such as the dependence of the grower on the company that produces the seeds. They are required to sign exclusivity contracts so that, in addition to the seeds, they get all the related products they need from the same company.

The great dilemma is: at what point do the advantages outweigh the disadvantages? On a large scale, the development of industrial agriculture produces ever increasing yields, and in improbable places. On the contrary, defenders of biological agriculture maintain that you can produce the same amount through natural means, without contaminating the atmosphere or soil. A basic list of the main problems caused by conventional agriculture is:

Requires continual fertilization of the fields, which ends up polluting the soil and groundwater, especially with nitrates, which could come from inorganic fertilizers or the compounds produced on farms. There are already entire regions where it is inadvisable to drink the well water because of this.

The use of herbicides and pesticides that are stronger every year to eliminate weeds, poisons the environment and kills off numerous wild plants, useful insects, and even the birds and mammals that feed on them.

In addition to breaking the ecological balance, the use of pesticides causes, through natural selection, the survival of the most resistant weeds and harmful insects.

Genetically modified organisms

Theoretically, the businesses that produce seeds and chemical products for the fields are seeking alternatives that allow them to pollute less and increase production, without forgetting about the dependence of the growers on the crops. The result: genetically modified organisms, which are by definition living organisms artificially created by the introduction of genes of another being (virus, bacteria, plant, animal, or human). The result of this cross undoubtedly produces improved seeds, which, in addition to resisting plagues

Traditional corn, like that found in any province of Mexico or Guatemala, was cultivated by the indigenous people. Today, they are trying to save these varieties, which are better adapted to the environment, more resistant and, above all, self-sufficient. The seeds gathered each year by the farmers are enough to sow the following year, something impossible to do with genetically modified corn. (photo by Tiara)

and inclement weather, can grow in extreme conditions, which guarantees harvests and optimizes yields.

What are the inconveniences? In the first place, the dependence on the company that produces the seeds and the pesticides and herbicides, which are specific for the product and are applied on a smaller scale. As a result, we see the same effects on the environment that we saw before, to which we can add the issue of genetic erosion. But even more important, in the mid- and long-term, is the harm it can cause people: we're talking about allergies, antibiotic resistance, and the appearance of tumors from the accumulation of toxins.

In any case, genetic modification is a Pandora's box that, once opened, could bring about major alterations to the environment.

According to a report by the European Environmental Agency, there is no sure way to completely isolate genetically modified crops from others.

The isolation zones established—a distance of six meters between the crops and nearby vegetation, or barriers of different species—can't prevent extreme atmospheric conditions from dispersing the pollen long distances.

In Mexico, genetically modified contamination of corn has been confirmed to be the result of North American imports. In 2006, Greenpeace presented a document in Barcelona that demonstrated the impossibility of coexistence of genetically modified and traditional crops. It showed that the local contamination had already covered Aragon and Catalunya.

In 2005, in Australia, a group of genetically modified peas were developed, and fortunately not commercialized, that produced major changes in the immune systems of lab rats, causing them to develop allergies to the peas and other substances.

Genetically modified products

- **The varieties resistant to herbicides**, which allow the use of stronger poisons that destroy the environment and harm people.

- **Insecticidal plants**, agricultural crops modified to resist insects. The majority come from the bacteria, *Bacillus thuringiensis*, which is found in the soil. This bacteria causes disease in the harmful insects that ingest it, via a protein that is toxic to them. The genes of the bacteria responsible for producing the toxin are transferred to the plant and thus, a genetically modified plant is created.

- Genetically modified species also have the nickname of **terminator** because they are sterile and must always be bought from the same company.

Cross pollination

In the United States they tested a genetically modified grass for the greens of a golf course that was resistant to herbicides. In this way, they could eliminate all the weeds except that grass that was supposed to carpet around the hole. Afterward, it was demonstrated that cross pollination was very high within a radius of two kilometers of the grass, but its effects were even found in a sample more than twenty kilometers away.

Genetic erosion

In the year 2002, genetically modified organisms already made up 16 percent of the crops worldwide, in this order: soy, corn, and cotton, followed by wheat and sunflowers. The United States cultivates more than 80 percent and it invades the rest of the world from there. There's no way to be rid of them; flours made from GMO products are used in the production of 80 percent of prepared foods, from baby foods to cookies, and, above all, in the feeds given to the livestock that give us milk, meat, and eggs.

The list of those to blame is getting long. These companies have names: Monsato, Novartis, Aventis, DuPont, Bayer, Hi-Breed, and Astra-Zeneca. Monsato has been fined for their activity in many countries, and one type of genetically modified corn is prohibited in the United States.

The garden

They now produce genetically modified tomatoes, potatoes, and carrots, and probably peaches, lettuce, cucumbers, and apples. We can defend ourselves from products bought in the store, by choosing to plant our own gardens. If we want to be certain that our seeds won't be affected, we must confirm that there are no genetically modified crops in a radius of several kilometers. Otherwise, cross pollination is a risk for our garden, as are the pesticides and plagues that have genetically mutated to resist traditional methods of control. Some insects and bacteria have mutated once their natural enemies were killed off and have become dangerous, even for humans.

Safety in Using Genetically Engineered Food and Food Products

According to the FDA website, "Food and food ingredients derived from GE plants must adhere to the same safety requirements under the Federal Food, Drug, and Cosmetic (FD&C) Act that apply to food and food ingredients derived from traditionally bred plants.

"FDA encourages developers of GE plants to consult with the agency before marketing their products. Although the consultation is voluntary, [the director of the FDA's Office of Food Additive Safety, Dennis] Keefe says developers find it helpful in determining the steps necessary to ensure that food products made from their plants are safe and otherwise lawful.

"The developer produces a safety assessment, which includes the identification of distinguishing attributes of new genetic traits, whether any new material in food made from the GE plant could be toxic or allergenic when eaten, and a comparison of the levels of nutrients in the GE plant to traditionally bred plants."

"FDA scientists evaluate the safety assessment and also review relevant data and information that are publicly available in published scientific literature and the agency's own records.

"As of May 2013, FDA has completed 96 consultations on genetically engineered crops. A complete list of all completed consultations and our responses are available at www.fda.gov/bioconinventorywww.fda.gov/bioconinventory."

Because of this, it is important to have seed banks, to save your own seeds and to get new ones from other organic gardeners. Experience shows us that the yield can be even greater by practicing biologic agriculture, and, of course, the produce obtained is much more flavorful and healthy for the earth and you.

Subsidies

One problem associated with conventional agriculture is related to subsidies. Producing a ton of wheat does not cost the same in a wealthy country as it does in a poor country. Farmers need to earn a lot more money in the first world, and if the market worked freely, industries would buy from poor countries where the price is much lower. Subsidies (and the conventional agrarian methods that value quantity over

Genetically modified crops that have the highest risk of cross-pollination are the three most common: rapeseed, corn, and beets. The risk is lower in the case of barley, potatoes, and wheat.

GMOs and the problem of hunger

And how to solve the problem of hunger . . . Although they want to convince us otherwise, the problem of world hunger is not a matter of scarcity of food, but rather a matter of distribution, and access to land and seeds. A simple increase in production, promised by the biotech revolution (a mirage very far off, as the reality of developed GMO crops demonstrates) does not feed the most needy populations, but does dispossess them of their lands, their seeds, and more.

The prohibitive costs of new biotechnologies and the patents make them inaccessible to public research programs, favoring a worrisome amount of control over the sector by a handful of multinational agrochemical companies, whose only pursuit is to control the world markets and increase their profits.

The high price of patented seeds and the herbicides that go with them, and the characteristics of new varieties that are advantageous for large, fully mechanized operations, increases the marginalization of small local farmers. This will not solve the problem of hunger, but rather will endanger the means of subsistence for about half the world's population, which still lives off of agriculture. It also puts global biodiversity at risk and aggravates the problem of access to food for the poorest. Far from contributing to solving the problems of hunger, therefore, genetically modified crops and the monopoly on seeds via patents are a threat to sustainable agriculture, our health, and food security for many populations.

Ecologists in Action

quality) make it so that corn produced in the United States ends up being cheaper on the international market than that produced in Mexico, for example. This policy is bankrupting many Mexican farmers and blocks the development of agriculture in poorer countries. On the other hand, doing away with subsidies would abandon many growers in Europe and North America, which are major exporters of foods, and could produce problems in poor regions that are net importers, such as India. Governmental intervention that regulates the price of basic products, and the corporations that determine the price of industrial products such as cacao and coffee, have made agriculture an abused sector of the economy, from which only the owners benefit.

An alternative

The disappearance of subsidies would leave growers with only one alternative: the production of quality, organic products. Consumers are increasingly more health-conscious and aware of the dangers of manipulated foods. Industrial agriculture has no qualms about the use of herbicides and pesticides. What's more, it sets up shop in countries where the legislation gives more freedom in this regard. The future of agriculture must move toward recovering species that were cast aside for their lower productivity or incompatibility with machinery. The agriculture of the future must focus on quality and diversity. In this book, we will show that these qualities are not mutually exclusive with quantity and profits, as European wine and cheese produces have demonstrated.

An ecological prince

The Prince of Wales—who has distinguished himself for attacking English architects, in defense of an aesthetic in harmony with reason—published an article in the *Daily Telegraph* (1998) titled "The Seeds of Disaster." This positioned him alongside defenders of eco-friendly agriculture and, obviously, on our side. Unfortunately, the tabloid press in his country did not allow him to get more deeply involved in this cause, but his words remain. Below is an excerpt:

"I have always believed that agriculture should proceed in harmony with nature, recognising that there are natural limits to our ambitions. That is why, some 12 years ago, I decided to farm organically—without artificial pesticides or fertilisers. From my own experience I am clear that the organic system can be economically viable, that it provides a wide range of environmental and social benefits, and, most importantly, that it enables consumers to make a choice about the food they eat.

"(...) The fundamental difference between traditional and genetically modified plant breeding is that, in the latter, genetic material from one species of plant, bacteria, virus, animal or fish is literally inserted into another species, with which they could never naturally breed. The use of these techniques raises, it seems to me, crucial ethical and practical considerations.

I happen to believe that this kind of genetic modification takes mankind into realms that belong to God, and to God alone. Apart from certain highly beneficial and specific medical applications, do we have the right to experiment with, and commercialise, the building blocks of life? We live in an age of rights—it seems to me that it is time our Creator had some rights too.

"(...) We are told that GM crops will require less use of agro-chemicals. Even if this is true, it is certainly not the whole story. What it fails to take into account is the total ecological and social impact of the farming system. For example, most of the GM plants marketed so far contain genes from bacteria which make them resistant to a broad spectrum weedkiller available from the same manufacturer. When the crop is sprayed with this weedkiller, every other plant in the field is killed. The result is an essentially sterile field, providing neither food nor habitat for wildlife. These GM crop plants are capable of interbreeding with their wild relatives, creating new weeds with built-in resistance to the weedkiller, and of contaminating other crops. Modified genes from a crop of GM rape were found to have spread into a conventional crop more than a mile away. The result is that both conventional and organic crops are under threat, and the threat is one-way.

"(...) Once genetic material has been released into the environment it cannot be recalled. The likelihood of a major problem may, as some people suggest, be slight, but if something does go badly wrong we will be faced with the problem of clearing up a kind of pollution which is self-perpetuating. I am not convinced that anyone has the first idea of how this could be done, or indeed who would have to pay."

Prince of Wales

In the year 2004, the Chinese government approved the importation of genetically modified soy, cotton, and corn, adding themselves to the list of countries who have come to depend directly on American corporations.

Biodynamic agriculture

Rudolf Steiner (1861-1925) is the founder of biodynamic agriculture.

Biodynamic agriculture follows the principles set forth by **Rudolf Steiner,** the father of anthroposophy, in 1924, during a course given in Koberwitz. According to his teachings, there is an interrelation between matter and the cosmic forces of the universe.

Biodynamic agriculture, therefore, comes from the cooperation between the earth and mankind, maintaining a balance between the principles of matter and the immaterial world present in nature. All the processes of the fields—the preparation of the soil, the sowing, the rotation of crops, the harvest—should bear in mind the cosmic forces, that is to say, the stars, sun, moon, and planets, and the terrestrial forces, water, and mineral elements.

In order to make the soil and plants more receptive to these forces, one must use some special biodynamic preparations.

These preparations are made by a special composting technique, which puts new energy into organic compounds, to then mix them with the soil.

The principles of biodynamic agriculture

You must start with balanced soil, that is to say, it must be analyzed and its nutritive deficiencies corrected, for example, trace elements and an excess or lack of acidity.

The compost and biofertilizers used are simply vehicles for the biodynamic substances, herbs or homeopathic preparations of micronutrients that accelerate the decomposition of compost, will benefit the good microorganisms, and accelerate the growth of the plants.

The soil should be considered a living organism that has its own structure. You should avoid subsoiling too deeply, which breaks this structure, and use direct sowing. But leaving a poor-quality soil to its own devices does not help much either, so it should be prepared appropriately, as the previous points indicated. Also add in the presence of beneficial species, like some types of trees.

The grower should diversify the species to the maximum, in the forest, in the garden, or in the fields. The creation of new ecosystems always favors the proliferation of life and a greater quantity of biomass that gets recycled in the soil. You should favor rotation or succession of ecosystems, and experimentation.

Another important factor is the planning of the garden or fields: the paths, the tool shed, the silo, the fruit trees—basically, the distribution of elements.

Don't discard economic viability. At the end of the day, you want to benefit, whether in the form of food, or, in the case of a farm, a sufficient yield to sustain the experience.

And there is a spiritual aspect to biodynamic farming that must not be forgotten. The land should be considered a part of ourselves, that is, a part of the universe that we understand, although others prefer to consider it the body of Christ, and therefore, as something sacred. Its products are also sacred and should

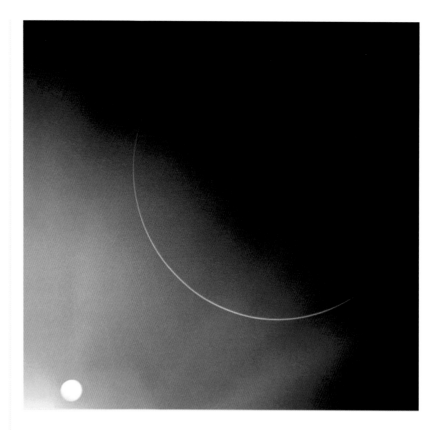

Extract of horsetail

This consists of boiling 50 grams in three liters of water for an hour. Strain and dilute in 20 liters. With this liquid, water the earth several times a year, especially in spring and fall. The water of horsetail harmonizes the earth and combats certain diseases, like mold and mildew.

be seen in this way. It is a way of giving importance to that which we make and to lend it part of our spiritual energy.

In order for all this to produce results, you should keep in mind the dynamic of the Cosmos, which is reflected in the biodynamic calendar—which is different every year, as it depends on the position of the stars. The stars indicate when to perform different tasks.

The most well-known calendar for planting is that of Maria Thun, a German farmer who has followed the principles of biodynamic farming for over fifty years. Maria confirmed that crops develop differently depending on the day they were planted, according to the position of the celestial bodies.

Finally, there are the biodynamic preparations, mediators between the earth and the Cosmos, which are vegetable, animal, and mineral extracts, usually fermented, dynamized by shaking, and then diluted before application.

The use of biodynamic preparations can cause an increase in infestations and diseases for the first year, but it has been shown to reduce these with continued use.

Biodynamic preparations

There can be two kinds: preparations of medicinal herbs introduced by Steiner, which harmonize the soil-plant-cosmos relationship, and preparations from compost, extracts of humic acids that prepare the plant to take advantage of cosmic influences. Although the dosage is not calculated mathematically, they can be bought commercially and there are a series of methods that must be done with certain precision. The plants used in these preparations are as common as chamomile, fennel, dill, nettle, or horsetail.

Basic preparations

The basic preparations are divided into two kinds: those that are sprayed on the ground and plants, and those that inoculate the compost or other organic marinades as biofertilizers.

The preparations are numbered from 500 to 508. The first two, 500 and 501, are preparations of manure and silica. Preparation 500 of silica is made by burying the horn of a cow filled with manure, medicinal plants, and even pulverized quartz, for the entire summer. Then it is dug up, diluted with a large quantity of water, and distributed over the earth in a fine mist, providing it with a large quantity of microorganisms. In this way, there is no need to fight plagues because we give the earth the means to fight them itself.

The Moon

After Rudolf Steiner described the influences of the stars on the lives of plants, others began to investigate the influence of the moon.

The result is that in order to have a good harvest, you should keep in mind the position of the moon with respect to the zodiac constellations, before which it remains for two days.

- **Leafy plants** should be planted during a water zodiac sign: Cancer, Scorpio, or Pisces.

- **Seed plants and fruits** should be planted in a fire sign: Aries, Leo, or Sagittarius.

- **Root plants** require an earth constellation: Taurus, Virgo, or Capricorn.

- **And flowers should be planted** with an air constellation: Gemini, Libra, or Aquarius.

In any case, you must also keep in mind the phases of the moon. If it is waxing and the energy is in full swing, it is a good time to graft and plant rapidly germinating plants, but you shouldn't prune the trees. **If the moon is waning**, it is a good time to prune and work the soil deeply.

Preparations for the compost

These are made from six plants: yarrow, chamomile, nettle, oak, dandelion, and valerian. These represent the digestive processes of nature, so for their production they are placed in the peritoneum, intestine, or bladder of an animal, where they are left to age for at least a winter.

The theory is that the manure has captured the astral forces upon passing through the intestine of the animal, and the buried horn preserves these forces and strengthens them. There could be a lot of biology in all this, since the horn when buried at certain depths causes an increase in microbial activity where previously there was none. This preparation is also called the "Preparation of Light," since it attracts the effects of the sun, favoring the root system.

The next six preparations, yarrow (502), chamomile (503), nettle (504), oak (505), dandelion (506), and valerian (507) serve as complements to compost, manure, or biofertilizer.

To make the preparation from chamomile (503), the flowers are picked and dried in the summer, dampened with chamomile extract, and placed in the small intestine of a cow, where they are left all winter to be used in the spring.

The preparation from oak (505) consists of putting the bark of the tree in the skull of a cow or sheep, putting it in a hole or a barrel, and letting it soak with rain water. The preparation of yarrow (502) requires putting the flowers of this plant in the urinary bladder of a deer.

Dynamization

This is the final phase. When a biodynamic preparation is diluted in water, it should be stirred rhythmically in a circular motion, which will transfer the powers of the preparation into the water. The water is stirred by hand or by a special machine, in one direction. This will create a vortex or whirlpool in the mixture, representative of a determined order. Suddenly, this order should be reversed, stirring in the opposite direction. The chaos created will transmit the forces from the preparation to the water. There are other conditions, such as that the water must be 37 degrees Celsius. You should use a container made of natural materials and not stainless steel. The vortex should reach 85 percent of the maximum height of the container, and the rotation should last an

In Europe, it is common to add a mixture of basalt dust and crushed eggshells to the manure used in the preparations.

hour, without timing it. It should never be done with more than 250 liters of water, so the water entraps the life.

Animal infestations

Biodynamic agriculture has diverse options for combating plagues and infestations. If they are from insects or snails, begin by burning some in a wood fire during the appropriate constellation. The ash that is left should be ground for an hour in a mortar and pestle. Of this ash, dilute one gram in nine grams of water and shake for three minutes, obtaining a D1 dilution. This action should be performed eight times, until you reach a D8 dilution. Then, this liquid should be sprayed over the crops three afternoons in a row, to end the infestation.

The plants and the cosmos

Influence of the celestial bodies on the growth of plants

BODY	FAVORS
Sun	Orange, saffron, sunflower, cinnamon, chamomile, dandelion, rosemary, marigold, olive, passionflower, and mistletoe.
Moon	Irises, willow, honeysuckle, watercress, chard, melons, and cucumbers.
Mercury	Anise, parsley, fennel, and lavender.
Mars	Thistle, roses, blackberries, raspberries, peppers, carrots, garlic, mustard, basil, hawthorn, aloe, nettle, arnica, tobacco, and geraniums.
Venus	Irises, apples, poppies, orchids, violets, elder, lemongrass, thyme, birch, yarrow, alder tree, and primrose.
Jupiter	Cabbage, cauliflower, grapes, figs, olives, blackberries, acorns, nuts, oregano, jasmine, and lemon balm.
Saturn	Horsetail, hemlock, deadly nightshade, holly, plantain, valerian, onion, mosses, potatoes, and eggplant.

Alfredo Luis Pepi (buenasiembra.com.ar)

Permaculture

Permaculture is the design of sustainable human habitats, following Nature's guide.

It was developed in 1970 by two Australian ecologists, Bill Mollison and David Holmgren, to offer an alternative to industrial agriculture and the destruction of nature, which was occurring in their country at a shocking rate. The three basic principles of permaculture are:

Integrate care for the land, the care of people, and the exact yield in an ethical manner. That is, grow only what is necessary, in a way that is appropriate for you, keeping in mind the needs of the land.

Use the ecologic principles derived from the observation of natural systems.

The use of tools and processes in a way that requires the minimum use of resources for its implementation and maintenance.

Ethical principles

The ethics of caring for the earth is possibly the most difficult principle to understand. Therefore, many have sought a way to explain it. One of the simplest can be found at the Permaculture Association of Aldehuela, in Spain. Summarized, its main points are the following:

Care for the earth, keeping in mind sustainability, fertility, and the use of natural energy such as the sun; planning on the small scale and recycling.

Care for people, stimulating mutual help between individuals and communities

Redefine necessities and sow a possible future, according to the equation: Population x lifestyle = required load capacity.

Principles of design

Permaculture focuses a lot on the harmony of the garden with Nature. For these purposes, it upholds the following principles:

Work in favor of nature, not against it.

Everything is part of the garden, including the slugs, which can help us clean up the lettuce patch.

The limits of the harvest are in your imagination, since everything can help increase its yield. What's more, that which is or isn't beneficial is in your way of looking at things.

All that we use has its positive and negative side, its advantages and disadvantages, and the way you utilize it will determine your ability to obtain maximum yield.

You should carefully observe nature to make the minimum changes (or minimum intervention) in order to obtain maximum yield.

In addition to these elemental principles, the permaculturist should bear in mind that the garden contains diverse microclimates, since the presence of a tree or a slope have a notable influence on the plants. You must also remember the limits of the garden; protect against plagues and external factors in many ways at once; consider the relationship between the plants and arrange them so that they benefit from each other; value diversity; and, above all, think on the small scale, even if the garden is large.

A way to achieve ecological sustainability of the planet

Permaculture is a system of design for the creation of sustainable human environments. The objective is to create systems that are ecologically sustainable and economically viable, that satisfy needs, that don't exploit or pollute, and that are self-sufficient in the long term. Permaculture deals with plants, animals, construction, and infrastructure (water, energy, communications), not just as elements in and of themselves, but in relation to each other. The basis is the observation of natural ecosystems, along with the ancestral wisdom of primitive peoples and scientific knowledge. It tries to use the inherent qualities of the plants and animals combined with the natural characteristics of the land and structures in order to produce a system that supports life in the city or country, using as little space as possible. It tries to work with Nature and not against it.

Permacultura-es.org: Bill Mollison, Introduction to Permaculture

The basic principle of permaculture is to "work for" or "in favor of," not "against," nature.

Since 1980, permaculture has spread across the globe, thanks to a group of volunteer students who learned from its creators. A country like Zimbabwe has more than fifty specialized schools on the science.

Bioenergetic plots

The Hartmann net is like a net of square mesh, most evident from a bird's eye view of the crops.

Hartmann lines and trees

Isidoro Zudaire, an ecological grower in Guadalajara, has proved that:

Firs, acacias, chestnuts, holm oaks, rubber plants, ash, oaks, and elder trees **resist** negative zones.

Hazelnuts, fig trees, plum trees, black poplars, mulberries, and grape vines **tolerate** them.

Cherries, peach trees, walnuts, elms, pear trees, bananas, lime trees, and arborvitae **do not resist** negative zones.

The Earth is crossed continuously by a series of subtle energies that have a notable effect on living beings. The main one is an electromagnetic field, which converts the planet into a gigantic magnet crisscrossed by magnetic lines between the North and South poles, and which, among other things, can contribute to the orientation of migratory birds.

There are other natural forces, which have to do with the rocky substratum, geologic faults, or currents of subterranean water. The energy given off by one of these phenomena can be more or less intense, and can be positive or negative. In ancient times, geomancers determined if a place was favorable to construct a house or not, and even today it is practiced in places like Germany. Remember that nomadic groups like the gypsies only camped in places that the dogs chose to lie down to rest, since these animals always avoid places with negative energy.

Hartmann lines

Among the natural energies that influence the growth of plants are those called Hartmann lines, discovered by the German doctor of the same name and by Manfred Curry. These are an invisible energy that covers the whole planet in the form of a screen. Doctor Peyre, who formed the hypothesis of its existence, defined it thusly:

"This deals with a north-south radiation, apparently magnetic and caused by the magnetism of the earth, and an east-west radiation, perpendicular to the other and of an electric appearance. They are rectilinear radiations, so they cannot be a result of different terrestrial influences, like the composition of the soil or the presence of faults in the subsoil or subterranean water flow, which are always winding and cut through the earth's crust along a variable path, accidents of the soil. They cover our sphere in a net that demarcates

square neutral zones, compartmentalizing the soil and extending into the air, crossing over in the north-south and east-west direction . . ."

Peyre even demonstrated that there was a certain relationship between these lines or bands, which cover the entire planet, and cancer. But the one who truly developed the theory was doctor Hartmann: "The earth is covered with a global network of fixed waves that seem to be produced by terrestrial radiation coming from the interior of the planet which are ordered in a mesh-like shape when going through the layers of the earth's crust."

The dangerous spots are those where the energetic lines cross. The bands of energy go up as high as two thousand meters, are about 25 centimeters thick, and are arranged parallel every two and a half meters when oriented north to south, and every two meters east to west. These bands can be wider in the case of disturbances such as earthquakes, and undulate following the terrain. The intersections of these lines are harmful to humans, the lines alone less so, and the spaces in the squares are harmless.

Animals have a special sensitivity to detect these places. For example, dogs will flee from them, while cows, hens, and horses suffer illnesses if they are forced to stay in these places, and even bees produce less honey if the hive is placed where it shouldn't be. Only cats, among domesticated animals (and ants, among other animals) are able to benefit from these energies, which indicates that you shouldn't choose a cat's resting spot for yourself or your plants, since the energies don't harm the cats.

Energetic networks and the garden

You must keep in mind that we are talking about a complementary system, which adds control over a series of energies to the necessary organic practices in order to obtain a better yield from our garden. The energies to keep in mind are: the cosmic energies (of

Our own negative influences

Over time, human beings have added negative energies to nature, whether they **are crosses in the Hartmann lines, geologic faults, radioactive beds, water currents, or our own unnatural** energies. Televisions, computers, microwaves, mobile phones, and electric wires add countless lines of energy to the atmosphere, which disturb the normal functioning of the delicate energetic balance between living beings. We would love to be able to add a chart on the plants that are affected by these forces and how much, but we can only suggest you do your own experiments, beyond geomancy, to determine how much a nearby phone tower can affect your tomatoes.

the stars) and earthly energies, among which are the Hartmann net, and those caused by faults, caves, gases, or underground water currents. These energies influence the plants and animals that act on them.

Furrows

Our relationship with the energetic lines starts and ends in the design of the garden, and in this respect, the arrangement of the plants, that is to say, the furrows. These should be dug from north to south, between the Hartmann lines, which are wider in this direction, and you should make two or three furrows in the two and a half meters between the lines. It is best to measure them with a pendulum to be certain of the width. The Hartmann lines from east to west don't have as much influence on plants, but Isidoro Zudaire of Salamanca, Spain recommends you plant cover crops like clover, alfalfa, or legumes in rotation with grains in the areas where the lines cross. These crops, once cut, will serve to cover and fertilize the furrows with organic material. The negative zones of the Hartmann lines are favorable for the growth of weeds, fungus, and bacteria, mineral deficiencies, and plagues.

The Fukuoka Method

We must sow and sow if we want to offer a future to our descendants.

Masanobu Fukuoka

Fukuoka inspiration

Inspiration came to Fukuoka one day when, passing through the countryside, he discovered some rice plants flourishing in an abandoned field. He decided that he had to sow his plants when the seeds naturally fell to the ground, in autumn, rather than spring, as tradition dictates. He would avoid weeds with a cover crop of clover and he would interfere as little as possible with the natural process of the soil.

The method

This method, widespread in Japan, manages to obtain two harvests, one of rice in the summer and one of grains, wheat or barley, in the winter. The extraordinary part of this is that it does not require fertilizer or preparation of the land, but rather that the land be respected as is and enriched each year. The yield is equal to that of chemical agriculture and the system has a natural philosophical compo-nent that adapts perfectly to the climate fluctuations of the area. The rainy season, dominated by monsoons, allows for the cultivation of rice in a short period of time. The rest of the year, with generous rain, Fukuoka uses a series of tricks which he has taught all across the country and has developed for many years. For example, the substrata of the base is formed by a layer of clover that protects the land from erosion and gives natural fertilizer, since it is a good assimilator of nitrogen. The clover dies off during the flooding, allowing for the sowing of rice, but it re-sprouts every year.

The seeds of the rice, barley, and wheat are mixed with clay and wet until they form little balls, which are placed on top of a layer of decomposing straw in the autumn. Then, you add another layer of grass and straw harvested the same year as the rice and grain. With the damp earth added, the seeds sprout and go through the straw underneath to reach the soil. The clover will sprout again when the grain is already tall enough to not be affected, and then the clover helps hold moisture. The rye and barley sprout quickly and are harvested in May, but the rice waits until spring. The wheat and barley straw is left to dry on the ground, then it is a collected, and, once the grain is separated, the straw is ground and laid out once more on the ground as a cushioning. The monsoon floods of June weaken the grass and then the rice grows.

The philosophy of doing nothing

This is the name given to Fukuoka's philosophy, whose fundamental principle involves the idea that purifying the spirit and healing the earth are the same process. One has to wonder what would happen if one did nothing. And the conclusion is that you should not plow the soil, you should not use chemical fertilizers or prepared composts, you shouldn't remove weeds with herbicides and, in general, you shouldn't use chemical products for no reason.

Fukuoka's five principles

1 **No working the land**

2 **No fertilizers**

3 **No pesticides**

4 **No weeding**

5 **No pruning**

In Japan, the spirit of permaculture has manifested in the extraordinary personality, Masanobu Fukuoka, through the publication of his book, *One Straw Revolution.* In the images, Fukuoka during a famous course in Ibiza.

Nendo dango

Nendo dango is the Japanese name for the balls of clay that Fukuoka has discovered to be the most efficient way to plant seeds. The seeds are covered in a layer of clay, the thickness of which depends on the size of the seed. This is left on the ground in the fall, well before germination.

The clay prevents the seeds from being eaten by birds or rodents, and when it rains, the clay absorbs moisture.

There are two ways to make these: manually, one by one, and mechanically, using a cement mixer with the blades removed. Fukuoka travels the world teaching his method to recover desert regions that should

not be considered deserts, such as the southeast of Spain, which he considers a rocky desert. In this case, one must select at least a hundred different seeds, including those of wild trees and fruit trees, grains, legumes, and vegetables in order to get a two percent germination—ten times higher than in conventional sowing—and recuperate the land.

Synergetic agriculture

The idea of **synthesizing** the most advanced methods of alternative agriculture is thrilling.

Emilia Hazelip

The four principles of synergy

1 Don't plow the land

2 Don't fertilize. The self-fertilizing of the land is enough.

3 Don't use chemical products.

4 Don't compress the soil.

This is a model of production so that the land fertilizes itself, based on the natural agriculture without the labor of Masanobu Fukuoka, created and developed by Emilia Hazelip around the year 1987. She synthesized the methods of Ruth Stout (cultivating without working the land), the plots of Alan Chatwick, the work of Fukuoka, and permaculture.

In Emilia's words: "Personally, I believe that having to deconstruct the soil and keep it fertile artificially, fattening it up with fertilizers, compost, etc. is a mistake that has been repeated since the beginning of agriculture, and it's time to correct this practice which is responsible for so much erosion of the planet."

Her system notably accelerates the start-up process of a garden; it takes barely ten days to start one, but one must follow her methods for at least three years to obtain the desired yield. Synergy is, by definition, "the action of two or more causes that produce one effect that is superior to the sum of the individual effects." It deals with maintaining coherence between all the elements that make up the garden: the soil, the plants and animals, and the interaction between them all will produce the desired result.

The garden

Make patches that are 48 inches wide and 20 inches high, with 32 inches between them. Cover them with a cushion that will serve as a protective filter between the surface of the soil and the atmosphere, which will protect from the drying of the sun and prevent compaction caused by rain. You can use straw or dry grass, but also wool or cardboard, or any other organic scrap that protects and favors the existence of beneficial living things, such as earthworms. The only area of soil that is left clean is a small margin around the crops. Except for root crops like potatoes and carrots, everything else should be left to rot in the soil, so that it contributes to creating a permanent humus layer on the soil. This is why it takes at least three years.

Patience is one of the necessary virtues for ecological gardening if you want to become self-sufficient.

Biointensive organic agriculture

Biointensive agriculture allows you to obtain a very high yield from a small parcel of land, since it takes advantage of all the layers of soil and light with plants that grow and take root to different heights.

This is a technique that has begun to be applied in third-world countries. The reason is in its definition: a system of food production on the small scale, centered on the unity of family production, with the use of available resources and an intensive use of manual labor over capital.

The method

First of all, it uses narrow, elevated beds which should not be walked on, and which are dug twice as deep as normal—that is, about 20 to 24 inches (which is known as *double bêchage* in French, or *double dug* in English).

Secondly, it uses compost abundantly and a large quantity of organic material. But it does not use inorganic fertilizers or those derived from petroleum, which have been proven to deteriorate the soil and pollute the earth.

Third of all, you must plant intensively, so that the soil is always protected from solar radiation by a layer of plants. This increases the yield. The leaves of the plants should touch, and they should all be at different heights. The microclimate created retains moisture, protects microscopic fauna of the soil, and the plants don't mature too quickly.

Fourth, it uses a combination of other species that benefit mutually from each other's company, like green beans and strawberries, for example. Always sow local plants and varieties that are resistant to plagues and disease.

It is necessary to rotate between types of plants: tubers, leafy greens, fruits, legumes, etc.

The system is an accelerated producer of organic material that will be used for compost.

The planting of tubers makes this system a high source of calories. To do so, 30 percent of the land should be occupied by potatoes, garlic, or parsnips.

This favors free pollination between all the plants; modified species are not necessary, genetic diversity is conserved, and the grower does not have to buy prepared seeds every year.

Finally, one should plant every type of plant in the garden each year, although in different places.

The Soil Association

In England there are many associations devoted to nature conservation. Some even buy land to conserve it as nature dictates. Their enthusiasm went as far as to buy alpine meadows in Switzerland after World War I so that their beauty was not disturbed, but they made the mistake of not allowing cows to graze there. Soon those rocky hillsides were taken over by new, emergent forests, since their green perfection had been maintained by those underrated ruminants.

But we learn from our mistakes, and since then many years have passed. The Soil Association was founded in 1946 to find an alternative to the industrialization of agricultural production. Its starting point was the soil erosion caused by modern methods. Because of this, the land loses nutrients and its health deteriorates.

The goal of the Soil Association is to combine the best of the old ways with the new, and return the land to its natural richness. Based on the experiences of Albert Howard with the Indians, and his disciple Eve Balfour, they developed a system that is based on two techniques: composting and soil rotation.

A biointensive planting would be one that combines corn, green beans, and pumpkins. The beans climb the corn stalks, while the pumpkins sprawl across the ground between the corn rows, taking maximum advantage of the space.

Compost

Composting is the basis of the biologic farm, and its function is to recycle. It takes into account all the elements that form part of the soil: nutrients, worms, beetles, fungus, bacteria, microorganisms, minerals, water, and air.

Rotation

If we grow the same species in the same plot of land each year, the least abundant minerals will be used up and the health of the soil and plants will decline. For the Soil Association, rotation is the spirit of biologic agriculture. The important thing is to return to the soil that which we have taken from it the previous year, by growing different species.

Enemies of the soil

The main enemy of the soil is agrochemical products, that is, fertilizers and pesticides. These worsen the condition of the soil, are needed in higher quantities each year, and their effects are more harmful each time, causing a vicious cycle.

Inorganic fertilizers only give the soil nitrogen, phosphorus, and potassium, and their production consumes petroleum. They are easily washed into rivers and pollute the and adjacent lands, as we already know.

Genetically modified plants are developed to combat the degradation of the soil, caused by fertilizers and pesticides. Their effects on our health remain unknown, the environmental contamination caused by cross pollination with wild species is also unknown, and in any case, irreversible and uncontrollable. As if that weren't enough, these types of crops create dependency among farmers, which makes them poorer. All of these aspects are widely addressed in other parts of this book.

Vegetable-flower garden

The *acequia*, from the Arab word **al-saqiya** (irrigation channel), is the channel through which water is distributed from the reservoir to the garden. The precious liquid flows downhill to the furrows, where it is filtered and absorbed by the plants.

The expression defines itself: The garden should contemplate forms and be not just a source of healthy and natural foods, but also a way to satisfy our spirit and give the beauty that all of us need around us to feel good.

If you let yourself follow your tastes, you will probably obtain the desired effect, but a little help to achieve the proper balance would not hurt. Given that the majority of ornamental plants have an edible component, it should not be hard to find the combination of medicinal and aromatic herbs, vegetables, and fruits that will bring beauty to your vegetable-flower garden on the balcony, in the terrace, or in the country, using the space you have reserved for it. The parcel of land should not exceed ten or fifteen square meters per person it will feed.

The Muslim vegetable-flower garden

In the ancient Islamic Spain, the garden was more than a simple esthetic arrangement of plants. It contained aromatic plants, fruit trees, and horticultural products, all connected by an ingenious distribution of water.

There is a work in Arabic titled *The Book of Agriculture*, written in verse so it could be easily remembered, which contains basic instructions: the garden should be divided in plots separated by paths or aisles covered with vines. At its head, there will be a reservoir from which you water the garden. Next to it, in one of the plots, are the aromatic plants, then the flower beds and fruit trees, the vines and fig trees, and finally the biggest trees, such as cherries and plums, on the north face, to protect the garden from wind.

In the Arabic garden, three elements are singularly important: the waterwheel, the reservoir, and the irrigation channel.

The *nuria* (na'ura) (waterwheel)

Even in modern times, we shouldn't discount the use of a waterwheel if we find ourselves close to a water current. In this way, we could do without electricity. The waterwheel is a wheel whose base is situated in running water. The wheel is made up of buckets that fill with water when they pass the bottom and empty at the top, into channels that direct the water into a reservoir or irrigation channel. In places where the water does not have enough force to push the wheel, such as in ponds or wells, they used water wheels powered by animals, generally donkeys. This same system can be implemented with wind power.

The *alberca* (al-birka) (reservoir)

This is an important element of this vegetable-flower garden, since in addition to allowing for calm, measured watering, it also is an esthetic element. You can grow water lentils or keep fish, and it is a refreshing element of the garden, around which the cherries and fig trees grow, and the farmer can rest and eat in the shade.

The *acequia* (al-saqiya) (irrigation channel)

This is the basis of the irrigation system, the channels through which water is distributed from the reservoir, a dam, a waterwheel, or sometimes a pump. This name encompasses both the major channels, that can be observed on the banks of the Nile River to water the fields of grains, and the minor ones, which go through the fields and branch out. In a small family garden, it will be enough to have one channel that crosses the garden and a series of temporary ones, opened and closed with a hoe when necessary.

This process constitutes one of the most pleasurable moments of the work day, in which the water, the source of life, floods clean furrows and feeds your plants.

The Arabic orchard

The vision of a garden in medieval, Arabic Spain was very different from that which we have now. Without tomatoes and potatoes, they instead had date palms. These are still the staple of Egyptian gardens (there are over two hundred species), where it is easy to find dates of all colors drying in the sun in September. Other trees that decorate the garden were peach, lemon, orange, cherry, quince, and pomegranate trees. If the land was favorable, they grew a large fig tree, and if not, some trellises with vines.

On the ground, melons, watermelons, eggplants, beans, spinach, carrots, artichokes, lettuce, kidney beans, cabbages, chickpeas, peas, lentils, garlic, onions, and countless useful plants grew; everything except the American products that had not yet come to Europe, such as corn, potatoes, tomatoes, sunflowers, cacao, and tobacco grew. Some aromatic plants were found in the country and considered poor people's foods, such as oregano, thyme, and basil. As far as nuts, they ate almonds, hazelnuts, walnuts, and pine nuts that were harvested in the country. But they also grew olives, which produced oil, processed at home or at a local mill.

Arabic cooking

They say that you can live for three weeks on a single date, but perhaps **if we bring some sweet biscuits, made from honey, hazelnuts, almonds, cinnamon, anise, cloves** (brought by the Arabs in the Middle Ages from the Maluku Islands), cilantro, sesame, sugar, and flour, without modern eggs and milk, **we could survive much longer**. Arabic cooking, because of its long tradition, is incredibly rich and includes lemon preserves, pickled green olives, eggplant pâté, mint and cucumber soup, hummus, falafel, lentil soup, and many other things. And that's not even getting into the couscous.

Basic rule for organic agriculture from IFOAM

The base for plant production

Gardening, agriculture, or the forest systems should take into account the structure and fertility of the surrounding ecosystem, and with this knowledge, strive for maximum diversity of species and minimal loss of nutrients. To do so, utilize:

● **A rotation of versatile crops**, including legumes.

● **An appropriate ground cover during as much of the year as possible**, and with maximum diversity of plant species.

The IFOAM, International Federation of Organic Agriculture Movements, has published a small manual to establish conditions that organic agriculture must meet:

● Produce foods with high nutritive quality and in sufficient quantities.
● Interact constructively with the natural systems and cycles.
● Keep in mind the wide social and ecological impact of the organic production and processing systems.
● Promote and intensify the biologic cycles within the agrarian system, which involves an understanding of microorganisms, the flora and fauna of the soil, plants, and animals.
● Develop a valuable and sustainable aquatic ecosystem.
● Maintain and increase the fertility of the soil in the long term.
● Maintain genetic diversity in the productive system and its surroundings, including the protection of habitats for wild plants and animals.

● Promote the careful use and appropriate care of water, aquatic resources, and the life they sustain.
● Employ, as much as possible, renewable resources in locally organized agrarian systems.
● Create a harmonic balance between agricultural production and livestock.
● Provide livestock with living conditions that take into account their basic functions and innate behaviors.
● Minimize all forms of possible pollution.
● Process organic products using renewable resources.
● Produce ecological products that are completely biodegradable.
● Allow all those involved in the agricultural production and processing to lead a life that will cover their basic needs and allow them to obtain adequate income and satisfaction from their work, including a safe work environment. Progress toward a chain of production, processing, and distribution that is socially sustainable.

Fertilization

One must return sufficient quantities of biodegradable microbial, vegetable, or animal material to the soil, to improve or at least maintain the fertility and biologic activity.

The base of fertilization programs should be made up of biodegradable material of microbial, vegetable, or animal origin, produced on organic farms.

To do so, they recommend:

● The handling of fertilization should minimize the loss of nutrients.

● One should prevent the accumulation of heavy metals and other contaminants.

● Non-synthetic mineral fertilizers and biologic fertilizers brought to the farm should be considered supplements, and not a replacement for the recycling of nutrients.

● One should maintain adequate pH levels in the soil.

Disease control

Systems of organic agriculture should be managed in a way that minimizes losses caused by plagues, diseases, and weeds. You should prioritize the use of crops and varieties adapted to the environment, a balanced fertilization program, fertile soils with intense biologic activity, adequate rotation, association of crops, green manure, etc. The growth and development should occur naturally.

Weeds, plagues, and diseases should be controlled with different preventative cultural techniques that limit their development, for example, adequate rotation, green manure, a balanced fertilization program, early preparation of the land and pre-sowing, covering the soil (mulch), mechanical control, and interference in the life cycle of infestations. The natural enemies of plagues and diseases should be protected and encouraged, through appropriate management of the habitat to provide them places to live and nest.

Management of infestations must come from knowing and inferring the ecological necessities for them to flourish.

Genetic engineering

There is no place for genetic engineering in organic agriculture and processing. **Genetic engineering is a group of techniques of molecular biology** (such as recombinant DNA) through which the genetic material of plants, animals, microorganisms, cells, and other biologic units can be altered in ways or with results that could not be obtained through natural processes of reproduction or crossing.

Chilean nitrate and all synthetic nitrogenous fertilizers, including urea, are prohibited.

AGRARIAN SYSTEMS AND ECOLOGIC ALTERNATIVES

Conventional agriculture and GMO crops

Industrial crops and mono crops of rice, sugar, cotton, coffee, cacao, bananas, tea, vegetables, and grains, mainly to feed livestock, use more and more GMO seeds and chemical products. Fertilizers with excess nitrogen pollute water sources.

Integrated agriculture

Differentiated from conventional agriculture in that the use of chemical products is reduced by nearly half, and elements of organic agriculture are introduced. Requires a higher technical element, for example, soil analysis to add the necessary chemical fertilizers, without saturating the ground with harmful elements.

Permaculture

Developed by Bill Mollison and David Holmgren in Australia, it mainly supports the design and distribution of spaces around the house so that plants and animals help each other grow in harmony, for example, protecting the garden from north winds with a barrier of fruit trees, and these with bigger trees.

Bioenergetic plots

As the name indicates, this is biologic or organic because it does not use chemical products, and it is energetic due to the use of cosmic and terrestrial energies. The former come from the moon and stars, and the latter from the different forces that go through the earth and influence the growth and health of plants.

Biodynamic agriculture

Introduced in 1924 by Rudolf Steiner, the father of anthroposophy, in a famous conference in Koberwitz, this is the basis of the entire alternative movement and has given way to numerous branches. It was Albert Howard who put this into practice in India. It is based in composting, biodynamic preparations, and cosmic influences.

Ecologic agriculture

Rejects the use of chemical products and opts for maintaining the richness of the soil through crop rotation, avoiding erosion, and using biological systems to combat infestations. Developed in the five continents, there are different methods associated with different masters or cultures.

Biointensive agriculture

The objective is to make a self-sufficient garden using only organic methods and manual tools, with a high yield and a low consumption of energy. It was created by Alan Chatwick to combine the biodynamic and intensive horticulture systems, with high and soft beds. It is called the "edible landscape."

Natural agriculture according to the Fukuoka method

Developed by the Japanese master Masanobu Fukuoka, it emphasizes the respect for the land, sowing appropriate plants in the proper moment without plowing the land at all. Its starting point is in the question: Is doing this necessary? and his philosophy is summed up as the method of doing nothing.

Vegetable-flower garden

This is a garden in which the aesthetic aspect is important, so it combines vegetable plants with ornamental plants that are helpful in controlling plagues or attracting useful insects, and thus favor the growth of crops.

Get to know
the soil

Nature and in-depth preparation of the soil

The best soils in the world are found in volcanic zones of the Caribbean, but if you put your mind to it, you can have better soil in your garden.

Soil covered in plants is protected from erosion. When you remove a layer of vegetation in order to plant or to eliminate a forest, the earth is easily washed away by rain. This would not happen if the soil was mixed with stubble of past crops, or if selective logging was used.

The composition and structure of the soil are important factors in the growth of plants. If you are trying to have a small balcony garden, the problem of composition decreases because you will buy conditioned soil, with all the elements that it needs to help plants grow well. But if you have a plot of land from which you want to obtain a good yield, it is best to know its characteristics before you begin working. The nature of the soil you are dealing with depends on the climate that has eroded and modified it, and the historic use of the area.

Fertility

The most fertile soils in the world are found in volcanic regions, and the most productive are those that also receive abundant rainfall; this is the case of the volcanic chain that traverses the western part of the America continent, the Ring of Fire that goes around the oceans and includes Japan, the Philippines, Hawaii, the Azores, and the Canary Islands.

If you are lucky enough to live in one of these places, or in Jamaica or Costa Rica, you can use the soil just as you find it.

The poorest soils are found in very rainy places formed from ancient soils, granite above all, which have been washed away for thousands of years by precipitation that took with it all the essential components. Large areas of the Amazon have very infertile soils that, once cleared of the vegetation that feeds it, becomes compact, rusty, and hard, and in turn absolutely unproductive because they are formed from just a single chemical compound.

In Venezuela, under the Roraima ridge, there are huge extensions of the sandy terrain that are only capable of producing grasslands, in a place where abundant rainfall and high annual temperatures should sustain tropical jungles. In Spain, the poorest regions are found in Galicia, where

The water cycle

The lack of vegetation makes it so that only part of the water soaks into the soil; the majority is lost in runoff, and, what's worse, takes away fertile soil with it, provoking soil erosion.

The ground heats up faster, and more intensely than vegetation. In places with bare soil, heat is greater and the evaporation of water more intense. The soil cracks and the capillarization makes the water disappear more quickly.

The function of trees is varied: not only do they protect the ground from the sun, but the fallen leaves give a humid layer that enriches it. On the other hand, wooded areas attract rain, retain water in the damp soil, and prevent erosion.

Evapotranspiration of the trees puts a large quantity of moisture into the air. Water goes up from the roots and evaporates from the leaves, while these perform their chlorophyllic function and trap CO_2 from the atmosphere.

---

the granitic soil is frequently washed by rain. This same type of soil in Extremadura, Spain, which has more moderate rainfall, is much richer. In the Iberian Peninsula, where the richest soils are found in the flat lands along rivers, erosion caused by deforestation and intensive use of the land for thousands of years has caused a major loss of fertile soil, as well as practically the entire moist layer.

Historic wear

The historic wear on the soil is an important factor, especially in Europe, where they have practiced agriculture for thousands of years. In America, the majority of the land has remained untouched until relatively recently, and are notably productive (except for natural disasters such as droughts, floods, or cold spells), but in Europe the soil has been cultivated continuously for hundreds of generations, especially on the Mediterranean coast. This soil is spent; that is, it lacks trace elements and organic material. And on top of this excessive use is the erosion, which long ago took off the organic horizon and the top layers of soil. In these zones, the only useable soil that does not require fertilizer is found along rivers and in recently cleared forested areas. The rest of the land requires extensive fertilization each year.

The nature of the soil

Kneel down and pick up a handful of earth. You will probably have to use a small spade. Observe if the soil is sandy or very fine, like dust. Sandy soils, which are formed from granite, do not retain moisture well and lack many necessary elements to feed plants, as is the case with the sands on the beach or the banks of mountain rivers. Clay soils, which form from the decomposition of slate or limestone, can be more or less fine. Since all extremes are bad, very fine clay soil has the opposite problem:

The size of the particles

According to their diameter, types of earth are classified as:

- **Rocks and gravels,** which depend on bedrock and which do not form part of usable soil for plants, except to aerate it.

- **Sands,** which measure between 2mm and 50 micrometers (thousandths of a millimeter).

- **Silt,** between 50 and 2 micrometers, and a very fine fraction, of less than 2 micrometers, called clay.

they retain moisture for a long time and not all plants can thrive in this; what's more, when they dry they become very hard and impede the growth of roots.

In greater or lesser proportion, soil is composed of the following elements:

● **Sand**, formed by the decomposition of the parent rock, granite, gneiss, or slate. Granite is formed by grains of quartz and mica cemented with feldspar. When this dissolves with the movement of water, the grains of quartz and mica are freed and carried off by rivers, deposited along their beds, or accumulated on beaches, where later they will mix with other sediments to create fertile soil.

● **Siliceous clay**, formed from the decomposition of silicates in the parent rock, for example, the feldspar from granite. They are typically aluminum silicates and follow the same process as sands, although since they are finer and can dissolve in water, they often go farther.

● **Limestones**, generally calcium carbonate, come from the decomposition of the parent rock, dissolve, and are carried off by rivers to lakes or oceans, where they are deposited on the bottom and harden into limestone rock. When they decompose in the environment, they form part of the soil.

● **Iron oxide**. Come from the decomposition of mica and certain iron silicates, and give the soil a red or yellow color.

● **Salts**. In addition to silicates and carbonates, in the soil there are phosphates, nitrates, and sulfates that come from the decomposition of organic material or that are put in the soil by bacteria activity, like the mycorrhizas of legumes. The phosphorous, nitrogen, and sulfur that plants use comes from these salts, although sulfur is only necessary in very small quantities and excess is harmful. The chlorides that come from the sedimentation of saltwaters are not usually useful to plants.

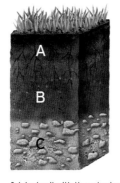

Original soil with three horizons, A, B, and C.

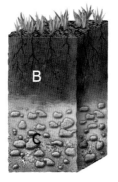

Eroded soil without the organic horizon.

Ideal soil with a composted organic horizon.

In the top drawing, you can observe the three classic horizons, or layers, of soil: an organic A horizon, a transitional B horizon, formed by inorganic materials, and a C horizon, which is composed of parent rock. In the center image, you can observe an eroded soil, without an organic layer, and in the lower image, ideal soil with a deep horizon of compost.

● **Humus**. Comes from the decomposition of organic material, and we will talk at length about its composition in the following sections.

Formation

A virgin soil covered by forest or jungle is formed by a series of well-defined layers, which are divided into an organic part (horizon A) and a mineral part (horizon B), on top of a rocky substratum (horizon C). If you observe a terrain that is recently formed (after an eruption or due to a change in a river's course), you can see how the soil is formed in situ: if the soil is not extremely resistant, it will break up or crack and the first plants will grow in these cracks. **Little by little, in a process that can take years, the soil will grow thicker as an organic layer made up of decomposed plants and the growth** of new ones develops. In flat areas, the soil is usually brought by rivers, which deposit a layer of soil washed down from higher ground, especially at the bottom of the rivers, which, when they change their course, leave fertile grounds uncovered.

If you want the soil of your garden to give you its best, you should add compost or manure regularly.

Texture

Take a handful of soil in your palm, add a little bit of water, and knead it, trying to form a ball. If the ball falls apart, your soil is too sandy. From here, you can determine the grade of the texture of the soil according to your own scale, by trying to roll it out in the shape of a spindle. Continue to roll it into the shape of a fine wafer. If you can do so, you have a clay soil. The four basic types of soil are:

● **Sandy**: The soil will be well aerated and easy to work, but is bad at retaining water and nutrients.
● **Silty**: This is a very fine soil, which compacts easily and can only be penetrated by certain plants. This can be improved by adding a lot of organic material.
● **Clay**: This is a secondary soil, rich in nutrients but excessively impermeable and which, when dry, hardens and impedes the growth of roots. Retains a lot of water and is difficult to work, but can be improved by adding manure or humus.
● **Loamy soils, or balanced**: These are the best and are formed by 20 to 25 percent clay, 30 to 35 percent silt, and 40 to 45 percent sand.

Layers

The soil of our garden, once it has matured and is ready to give yield, will be formed by a mixture of the different horizons that make up virgin soil:

Horizon A formed from organic materials in different stages of decomposition, as we will see shortly.

Horizon B is below the organic material. It is made up partially of primary minerals, in the form of gravel or sand, and secondary minerals, in the form of silt or clay. The secondary minerals, except for humus, have already been mentioned: quartz, silicates (among which is silica), micas, and feldspars (if they come from

Loamy soils have a dark brown color and are extraordinarily fertile: however, industrial agriculture still adds chemical fertilizers, which should be prohibited in our organic garden.

hard rocks such as granite), the elements that form clay (which come from sedimentary rocks like limestone, chalk, or sandstone), and iron or aluminum hydroxides, whose importance is relative until you consider the soils of the Amazon. There, the predominance of iron hydroxides makes the soil harden too much and impede the growth of plants.

Horizon C, which is only of interest if your garden is in the country, or if the soil is shallow enough that you reach it easily, is made up of parent rock. It could be granite, slate, sandstone, limestone, or basalt, among other types. Depending on its nature it will retain more or less moisture and will provide primary minerals. If it is granite, you will have quartz, feldspar, and mica in relatively large grains. Depending on these primary materials, you will find secondary minerals, which form from the biochemical alteration of primary minerals and produce clays and free oxides.

The extracting capacity of plants

The roots of plants function like water pumps. They do not all have the same capillary strength, defined by the ability to take advantage of moisture. **There are plants and trees that need water periodically and in abundance, and prefer sandy, well saturated soils** (where water can be seen). This is the case of the silver fir (*Abies alba*), which needs a lot of water, but also periods of dry soil. **On the other hand, there are species that need water constantly**, like the weeping willow, and which also have a great capacity to extract water from silty (extremely fine) soils,

which retain water for a long time (in the form of invisible molecules) but don't allow all plants to use it. Weeping willows (usually on the bank of a river or lake) grow better in dry places with silty soil, where they can get water every day, than in wet areas with sandy soil, which dries out between rains.

Horizon A

This is made up of fresh organic material, which comes from dead plants and leaves in different stages of decomposition, the final one being humus, which is useable to plants. The process to get to this point is called humification.

Humus is most abundantly formed in temperate forests, where the leaves fall each year. Humification can be more or less active, depending on the climate, which determines the types of bacteria, fungi, and animals present to accelerate decomposition. In forest soils, humus accumulates year after year depending on the amount of fallen leaves, and thus, depending on the type of forest. Beeches are sometimes called the mothers of the earth, because they grow easily and rapidly increase the depth of the soil, but other trees such as oaks, ash, chestnuts, or bananas also have the same effect. In the Mediterranean climate, the holm oak produces excellent humic soils, but decomposition is very slow due to the lack of moisture. Depending on the type of trees, the soil can be acidic or basic, or even unusable, like that created under a eucalyptus.

Humus can be of many different classifications: there are less active and active ones, rapidly formed, divided into acids, carbonates and andics, over volcanic ash, or deeply formed. In all types you will find humic compounds which carry out the decomposition.

Living organisms in the soil
From smallest to largest:

● **Bacteria**: Unicellular organisms that live in soils with a lot of nitrogen and low acidity, around the roots of grasses and legumes, and especially in the rhizosphere. These break down cellulose and sugars and oxidize ammonia into useable nitrates; some are nitrogen-fixing

This is the percentage of holes over the total volume of soil, which gives the volume of air and water that the soil can absorb.

The gaseous exchanges that occur in the soil between oxygen and carbon dioxide (oxidation-reduction) are what make the soil useable for plants and allow the roots to breathe. If there is no oxygen, there is no life.

Some willows and purple moor grass are able to survive a lack of oxygen by taking it in through the leaves, and sending it to the roots.

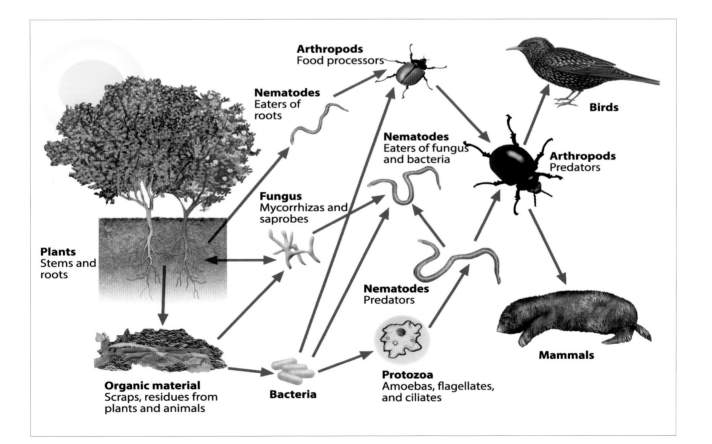

Fungi are extremely varied and contribute notably to humification.

Humification

In the prairies or in the tundra, the soils are formed from the decomposition of roots, which thanks to cold winters, renew each year, producing very deep humic soils that are sold for use in gardens and flower pots. **In agricultural soils, humification depends on human intervention**, with the addition of manure, compounds, straw, grass, dead leaves, compost, etc. which is precisely what you are going to prepare at home.

and others live in the rhizomes of legumes. In swampy areas, there are anaerobic bacteria that provoke methane fermentation.

● Fungi: These are parasitic plants that live on decomposing organic material. They are characterized by mycelia, a system of branching filaments with which they nourish themselves. They resist acidity and drought better than bacteria. There are many varieties. They decompose fresh organic material and cellulose, and hydrolyze lignins, so their action is a necessary step to humification.

● Fauna: This group is composed of the microfauna, including protozoa and nematodes that attack microbial flora; mesofauna, up to 1 cm in size and includes smaller arthropods such as mites; and macrofauna, larger than 1 cm, especially earthworms, but also insect larvae and larger arthropods, especially in acidic soil. The mechanical

labor of ants is also very important, since it carries soil to the surface. Termites, on the other hand, interfere with biochemical processes.

Depth

Soil that is less than 32 inches deep before hitting bedrock is considered rather shallow. In Spain, except for in the flat lands, deltas, and some coastal zones, the majority of soils do not reach this depth and the parent rock is easily found. Soils that are deeper are more fertile, and this is observed especially in trees, which grow much higher. If you buy a lot on rocky soil and you want to add some, you must be sure to get alluvial topsoil, although this means we are robbing Peter to pay Paul. Soil that is more than 20 inches below the surface is poor quality and lacks life. You will have to fertilize it, and it will take a while to get a good yield from it.

Natural cycles

The chemical elements essential for life are nitrogen, phosphorous, and potassium, and each one has its own natural cycle.

The nitrogen cycle

Nitrogen is found in the atmosphere in gas form. Symbiotic bacteria that live in the roots of certain plants (legumes, algae, lichens) introduce it to the food chain. The bacteria live on these plants and provide them with useable nitrogen (in the form of nitrates), which transform into vegetable proteins and feed animals. When plants and animals die, the nitrogen returns to the soil in the form of ammoniacal nitrogen. In this way, it is used over again by plants, nitrified by certain organisms (also to be used by plants), or washed into rivers and lakes by rain, where it returns to the atmosphere and the cycle begins again.

The phosphorous cycle

This mineral is found in nature in the form of phosphates, whether it is calcium, magnesium, iron, or aluminum, and gets into the soil through the decomposition of rocks or volcanic eruptions. The phosphate ion is absorbed by plants, which use it to complete photosynthesis. Animals

Loss of nitrates in cultivated soil

In cultivated soils, excess nitrogen, which is not absorbed by plants in the form of **nitrate ions**, tends to react with basic minerals in the soil, such as **calcium, magnesium, and potassium**. Then it becomes soluble and is easily washed away by rainwater and watering. **The land, by losing these basic ions, becomes acidic very easily,** and the water sources with an excess of nitrates are not suitable for human consumption.

absorb it through plants and when they die, return it to the soil, where it can be washed into lakes or oceans, or returned to the atmosphere as dust, where it will fall again with rain.

The potassium cycle

This element is essential for photosynthesis and for cells. It is found in clay soils, from which it is washed out by rain. It also passes from the soil to plants, and from plants to animals, and returns to the soil from both. Another necessary element in soil is sulfur, whose cycle has been well studied and is similar to potassium, sulfur appears in nature in the form of sulfates, after having been oxidized from volcanic eruptions. Plants take it up, pass it to animals, and when those die, microorganisms return it to the soil, where it oxidizes and becomes sulfate again.

Trace elements

These are a series of minerals that are only necessary in trace amounts, but are of utmost importance to the health of the soil. These are boron, molybdenum, iron, copper, zinc, and magnesium. They appear as impurities in silicates, hydroxides, or the parent rock.

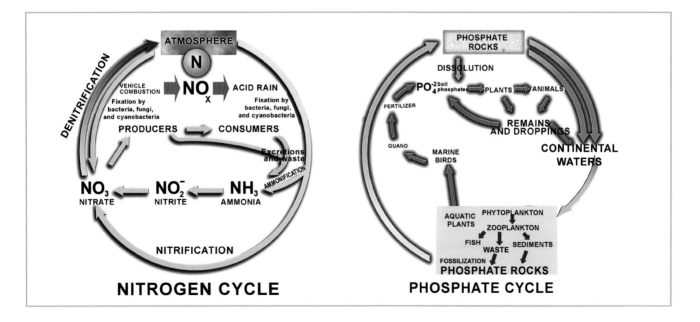

NITROGEN CYCLE

PHOSPHATE CYCLE

Soils that are frequently washed by rain are usually deficient in water-soluble compounds.

Lack and excess

The lack of minerals, shown in the table below, cause growth deficits, weak plants, and defective fruits. This can happen due to the insolubility of the compounds that contain these minerals, so that even if they are abundant in the soil, they cannot be used. It is possible that you will have to add one of

Lack of nutrients

NUTRIENT	DEFICIENCY
Nitrogen	The leaves will yellow, although there are infestations that give the same symptoms. Its excess will cause rapid growth and weakening.
Phosphorous	The leaves become pale and the edges dry and turn brown. Bears little fruit.
Potassium	Old leaves get reddish, young leaves have yellow or brown borders. Potassium gives the plant resilience. It is often lacking in sandy soils with a lot of rain.
Magnesium	Yellow areas appear between the veins on young leaves, which later affects new leaves. The leaves fall.
Sulfur	Symptoms similar to the lack of nitrogen.
Iron	Like the lack of magnesium, but the yellow stains between green veins appear first on the newest leaves. Often occurs in silty soils.
Zinc	The space between the branches becomes shorter and groups of yellow leaves appear. The old leaves turn golden and fall.
Manganese	Like iron deficiency, but with a green halo around the nerve.
Copper	Yellow stains appear on the leaves.
Molybdenum	Like nitrogen, older leaves turn yellow.
Boron	The plant struggles to grow.

these minerals to your garden to improve its health. The effects of excess minerals are the same. For example, the leaves of the fir that grows on granite of the Vosges Mountains accumulate magnesium, which impedes reproduction because it is toxic to the seedlings. An excess of copper can also occur as a result of sulfation.

How to adjust acidity

The acidity or basicity of the soil depends on the concentration of acidic or basic ions that it contains—in other words, its capacity for oxidation or reduction. A neutral soil, with balanced positive and negative ions, is not reactive and is acceptable to the majority of plants.

pH is measured on a scale from 0 to 14. A pH of 7 equals a neutral substance in which the acids and alkalines are balanced. A pH between 0 and 7 is acidic. To give some perspective, the pH of stomach acid, which dissolves foods, is 1.1, and that of Coca Cola is 1.5—enough to dissolve a piece of meat and surely any plant, since plants can't live in a pH lower than 4 or 4.5. A pH between 7 and 14 is alkaline. On the extreme end

Charlemagne and rotation

During the Roman Empire biennial cultivation was the commonly practiced method. The land was divided in two parts. The first one was cultivated and the other one was idle. The following year the assignment was inverted. **Population growth and careless practice of this system wore out the land in the late Middle Ages**. To avoid this, Charlemagne introduced the triennial rotation, which consisted of two years of cultivation and then an idle time for the third one. Thus, cultivation took up ⅔ of the properties: one year was devoted to cereal, the following legumes, and the third the land was allowed to rest.

Another way of looking at pH

Pour vinegar or diluted hydrochloric acid over a soil sample in a glass and observe what happens:

● **If a strong effervescence occurs, the soil is alkaline and has a pH higher than 7.5.** You should take measures to neutralize it. Copper, iron, manganese, and zinc will be hard for plants to assimilate in these conditions. Add iron sulfate to the soil along with some iron chelate to lower the pH and ease the iron chlorosis in the plants.

● **If it produces light effervescence**, with very small bubbles, the soil is neutral.

● **If it does not cause any bubbling**, the soil is acidic and does not react. It will be difficult for the plants to assimilate calcium, magnesium, molybdenum, and phosphorous. Raise the pH by adding lime.

Hydrangeas are a good indicator of soil acidity. In acid soil, their flowers are blue and in basic soil, they are pink.

of basicity is concentrated caustic soda (lye). Be careful with the bleach, sodium chloride, which can dissolve dirt and plants but can't live with a pH higher than 8. It is natural for plants to have preferences, since there are those that prefer acidic soils, such as rosemary, azalea, and hydrangea, and those that prefer alkaline soils, such as thyme, marigold, or petunia. To test the acidity of the soil, you must buy pH testing paper in a drug store or lab supply store. Dilute a sample in tap water, shake well, and insert a strip of test paper. The pH is then shown by comparing the color that appears on the paper with the sample card. Generally, the papers are tinted with phenolphthalein, which turns blue or green in basic soil, or red in acidic soil. Basic soils are those that are high in limestone content—calcium carbonate—with a pH higher than 7. It begins to be dangerous when the pH is greater than 8.5.

Acidic soils are those in which the pH is very low, between 3 and 5. These lack calcium, do not absorb nutrients well, and

do not decompose organic material. They form on slate or granite bases, and in forests with pines or eucalyptus, due to the decomposition of the leaves. It is easily corrected by adding lime until you reach an appropriate pH. In the high regions of the Venezuelan Amazon, some rivers have a pH of 3–3.5 and the water is clear and lifeless.

The life of plants in a vegetable-flower garden develops in soils with a pH between 4.5 and 8. In general, the best range is between 6 and 6.9.

Deficiencies and pH

Alkaline soils tend to lack iron, manganese, copper, boron, and zinc, so many plants such as hydrangeas or oranges will display yellowed leaves. To lower the acidity, you can add acidic peat or powdered sulfur and mix it with the earth. You can also add iron sulfate or iron chelates if you grow acid-loving plants. If the soil is acidic, it will have a deficit of calcium, magnesium, phosphorous, molybdenum, and boron, but an abundance of iron, manganese, and zinc. Correcting this is easy, since all you have to do is add lime.

Chelates

Chelates are used in agriculture to provide trace elements or micronutrients when the soil is lacking. Although it's unlikely that you will use them on a small-scale garden, it's always useful to know the products that are used in horticulture to balance overused soils or ones that are too alkaline.

On the market you can find chelates of iron, boron, magnesium, manganese, molybdenum, copper, and zinc for the garden, but also chelates of amino acids of the same elements that are fit for human or animal consumption, to make these essential elements easier to absorb. Chelates are made with a chelating agent, that is a Ethylenediaminetetraacetic acid (EDTA) that makes the nutrient more easily absorbed by the plant. And not just this, but it also makes the element present in

The difference between sulfate and chelate

Sometimes, in order to promote the absorption of iron from the soil, it is not necessary to add a chelate, which can be very expensive. **If the problem is that the soil is too alkaline**, adding an iron sulfate is sufficient to reduce the pH in the soil.

Iron sulfate is sold in powders. It should be diluted at a ratio of 3 grams per liter of water and sprayed on the ground. This will be sufficient.

the soil more easily assimilable. These compounds, which are sold in vials that should be diluted in water, can be applied to the roots, by spraying the ground, or directly to the leaves, and are notably effective when the plants show early signs of iron chlorosis—yellowing of the leaves while the veins remain green.

A well composted soil does not need any chemical additives to be fertile.

Lowering the pH on the balcony

If you are growing in flower pots or planters, **forget about chelates and even iron sulfates**, since it is unnecessary and, if you mistake the dosage, could make the situation worse.

Normally you would start with a base with a balanced pH, but if you need to lower it because you want to plant hydrangeas in the pot with tomatoes, add citric acid to the water. It is sold in drugstores and looks like sugar. **Another more expensive option is to use vinegar.** In any case, proceed with caution. An option for medium-sized gardens is to use sulfur, or less ecological peat, which has a pH of 3.5.

Care of the Garden

What you need to know about
caring for your garden

Here you face the gardener's most important task: the preparation of the ground and how to maintain its fertility.

Long before any known human civilization existed, since humans discovered or invented agriculture, they trusted the productivity of the land in the hands of a goddess of fertility.

In the beginning, the fertility of the land was one with feminine fertility; this is the idea behind the tiny goddesses with round bellies that our ancestors buried in the ground to ensure a good harvest.

The disappearance of the matriarchy corresponds with the appearance of masculine gods, such as the Egyptian Osiris, that assume, among other things, the fertility of nature. Amulets representing these gods were also buried in the soil.

The Greeks, who are our cultural ancestors, worshiped Demeter, goddess of the fertility of the earth. She was sad because her daughter had to descend to the underworld for four months of the year, and thus is the cause of winter and of rain with her tears.

We don't believe in agrarian gods, because our civilization stopped believing in divine intervention, but we believe in the pleasure obtained from a job done well.

The fertile soil that you want

When you visit an old garden and see the soil, crumbly and dark, which sinks when you walk on it (although you shouldn't do this unless you are working or picking), you hope that your future garden will be just the same, that you will merely have to bend

over and bury the seeds or plant the seedlings, add a little water, and wait for them to grow.

You don't think about the work that is behind that soil, or of the gardener who has been digging, fertilizing, cleaning, mulching, sowing, weeding and picking the fruits and dry plants to return them to the soil in the form of compost.

And if you think, do you do this for the pleasure of the feel of the earth, the pleasure of using the correct tools, of creating a work of art with furrows and rows, in sowing as you should, and the immense pleasure of knowing that "in this soil, two inches deep is enough," in knowing how much water to use and how many days to wait?

Because, is there any greater pleasure than coming to the garden in the morning to find the bright skin of the tomatoes, peppers like mirrors, radishes like fists, and carrots so big that even the rabbits wouldn't attempt it? Stop dreaming and keep reading.

The nature of the soil you are dealing with depends on the climate that has eroded and modified it, and the use it has had previously.

The tools

Although you only need a few tools to maintain a small garden, the simple sight of a series of garden tools, clean, organized, and lined up ready to use, can be an inspiration or motive to get to work. At least you should know which tools you can count on.

The mattock

The size of the mattock that you will use will depend on the size of your garden. For a balcony, you will only need a handheld two- or three-pronged weeding hoe, a small rake, and a spade. You will also need a gardening broom, which looks like a small rake with the teeth separated like fingers.

There are kinds of mattocks and hoes that have two prongs instead of a blade, in case the ground is harder. This will help dig the soil in a small garden, but if you have a larger garden planned, you will need a wheel hoe, which consists of an interchangeable plow applied to a wheel, with handlebars to guide and push it. Of course you could use an old-fashioned plow pulled by a horse, ox, or cow, but this type of plow is beyond expectations for an affordable garden that does not require too much work.

The proposed mattock has a series of blades that can be combined, like a plow, to turn the earth, a scraper to remove the

The basic tools

● **Mattock**: Instrument formed by an iron blade on one side with a sharpened edge on the other, affixed to a pole. It is used to dig and gouge the soil.

● **Hoe**: Similar to the mattock, but it only has a blade on the end of the pole. It is used to pull and push the earth.

● **Rake**: Formed by a long arm with a row of points like teeth. Functions to collect grass and dead leaves, or to smooth the ground after it's been dug up.

● **Pitchfork**: This is a long pole that ends in two or more long spikes that is used to move straw or, in most cases, to turn the soil.

● **Wheelbarrow**: This is a small cart with a bucket to transport a load, with a wheel in front, two handlebars to steer it, and two feet in the back to hold it upright.

● **Watering can**: This is a container made up of a reservoir with a tube and a mouth with numerous small holes, to water plants or freshly sown seeds. You must use this generously.

● **Pruning shears**: These are small, strong scissors that are used to prune trees and strong stems, or, for example, cut the stakes that hold the tomatoes.

Getting home in the afternoon and going out, armed with gloves and a tool, to clear your garden of weeds.

grass between the rows of crops or cover the seeds, to break up the earth and soften it before sowing, and also to bury the seeds, all consisting of a variety of iron spikes that are arranged one after the other at various distances apart.

It would also be a good idea to have a harrow, to open up the furrows to plant seedlings, or to irrigate.

The two-handled pitchfork

As the name indicates, this is a pitchfork with two handles. It functions to aerate and loosen the earth with minimal effort, since it can be forced in with your foot and moved back and forth with your hands to soften the ground. It can be used after the wheel hoe, to soften up the soil where you walked, or simply to aerate it. And in order to get maximum benefit, it should be made of unpainted iron.

Good advice

"In reality, once you've dug the plots or readied the pots, you don't need many tools to work and maintain the garden, maybe a small hoe, a trowel for transplanting, a weeding hoe, a rake, and not much else, since the ground will remain soft since you are not walking on it, and most work can be done simply by hand, which allows for greater contact with nature and life."

Mariano Bueno

The rototiller

The use of a gas rototiller is not recommended for an organic garden. It makes the work easier, but it also pollutes the environment, from both the exhaust fumes and the noise. A gardener who prides himself in his work does not want to find oil stains in his garden.

For the terrace

If you don't have a lot of space, or have a bad back, a good solution is to build work tables with borders a hands-width high. Once filled with soil, you can use them as a nursery, although there are people who use them as a garden, because of how easy it is to water. You can find on the market planting tables of galvanized steel, with a drip irrigation system installed.

Weed whackers and rototillers

There are those who have a yard as well as a garden and buy a weed whacker, one of those tools with a gas motor, an arm that is about 5 feet long, and a disc or nylon cord that turns to cut weeds. It serves to maintain small patches of grass, clean weeds from the edge of the woods, and to cut the grass in corners, along fences, or along walls where you would otherwise have to use pruning shears. It has the serious downside of the noise and pollution it produces. Another thing is the rototiller, which also pollutes and makes a deafening noise. It works well for the small gardener with too much land to dig up by hand, but be careful, because these tools should not be necessary for an ecological garden.

Machines that use gasoline should never enter into your organic garden.

Fertilizer

Guano

This is the oldest natural fertilizer in the world. It is obtained from the excrement of thousands of marine birds, or bats, dried in the sun. **Once clean and refined, it is used in biologic gardening and horticulture.** Before they began to manufacture nitrates industrially, it was the only known fertilizer, and the Chilean coast was its principal producer, thanks to the gulls that deposit their excrement on the rocks. **Guano is organic**, both in origin and due to its low phosphate content, it favors the creation of humus, and reinforces the plants' defenses against diseases and infestations. It can be applied with a spoon around the plant, in moderation.

There are fertile soils that barely need fertilizers, such as the loamy soils of the American Corn Belt, or the volcanic soils, but even these, which produce abundant harvests year after year, need to be supplemented. The plants grow at the expense of the soil and the nutrients they extract from it, making it poorer in quality. So there is no other option than to replace them.

On the other hand, a well fertilized land will be spongy, retain moisture in the right amount, and requires little work to handle it.

Plants take the basic components of their nutrition—carbon, nitrogen, oxygen, and other bioelements—from the air and the soil. In nature, these are replaced when the plants die and decompose. But in the garden, the majority of the dead vegetation is removed to make compost, or because it is diseased. The biogardener should replace these elements by incorporating nutrients into the soil. There are various ways to do so, with organic and inorganic fertilizers.

Inorganic fertilizers

Organic agriculture rarely considers this option. Inorganic fertilizers are synthetic chemical products far from the natural state of the soil, that in the best-case scenario, produce plant growth similar to overwatering—lacking in flavor—and then leech into the ground water. However, we can't ignore learning about them.

They are divided into nitrogenous, phosphorus, and potassium, and can be solids or liquids. They are assimilated immediately by the plant, unlike organic fertilizers that need processing. There are even some foliage fertilizers, which are applied directly to the leaves after a frost to help them recover.

Even still, there are a few inorganic fertilizers that ecological agriculture allows: natural phosphates (like those obtained in the mines of Buchra, in the Sahara), siliceous rock, which are used to compensate for a lack of acidity, potassium chloride (obtained in old salt mines), dolomite (calcium and magnesium carbonate), magnesite, and magnesium sulfate (these last two like dolomite).

Organic fertilizers

Can be one of three kinds: compounded, surface, or green.

Compounded fertilizers are formed from a mixture of organic waste from the kitchen, waste from the garden, straw, etc. and soil. This is a homemade fertilizer that we will study in detail under compost. We will use all the waste from the garden and home to make it, but we won't use many of the things that ordinarily appear on the lists of ecological products, such as meat meal, blood, or fish. This would be permitted but they are difficult to obtain and would have to be from organically raised animals, that is, our own, if we had a farm instead of a garden.

Surface fertilizers are the organic waste products that you put directly on the soil around the plants, or on the surface that you want to fertilize or protect from freezing or washout. We will see more on this in the section on mulch.

Green manure is any plant that is buried in the ground to improve its fertility. Normally, one plants a mixture of legumes, such as alfalfa, and grasses, like oats or barley, in a plot and after some weeks, before they flower, bury them.

Prepare a plot of land, plow it, aerate it, and smooth it with a rake. Then plant the seeds, either scattering them, or burying them a few centimeters. **The seeds should be rapid-growing legumes**, with more leaves than stem—for example alfalfa, broad beans, green beans, or peas—or a grass such as oats or barley, or any other plant that has the desired characteristics.

After a few weeks, at least four although eight is better, or when half the plants are flowering, dig a furrow along the edge, cut them to the root, and bury them in the furrow at a depth of about 6 to 12 inches. **The soil should be moist.** You have to wait between one and four weeks to use the plot.

Compost

To make compost

- Grass, without seeds if possible
- Ground-up branches and dead leaves
- Vegetable scraps
- Fruit scraps
- Dead flowers
- Soil used in flower pots and gardens
- Kitchen scraps (see box on page 65)
- Coffee grounds or tea leaves
- Hair
- Hair from the dog's brush
- Damp paper napkins
- Damp newspapers
- Damp cardboard
- Damp sawdust
- Medicinal plants
- Old wool
- Brush and shrubs from the forest
- Manure from farm animals
- Dry grass
- Freshwater algaes

Compost is the fertilizer of an organic garden, since it digests and transforms the "scraps" that the biogardener accumulates during the year. If you incorporated a sufficient quantity of compost in the soil, the plants will look fresher and healthier.

Making compost is an art. Dead leaves, the remains of plants that have already completed their cycle, tree trimmings, potato skins, pea pods, tomato cuttings, and the organic kitchen waste all become humus, thanks to natural decomposition by bacteria and fungi. We can help this cycle occur more quickly and efficiently.

Humification includes a series of chemical reactions that transform organic material into a reusable element for plants. In collaboration with microbes, fungi, and bacteria transform these raw materials into a biologically nutritious substance for plant roots. They absorb nitrogen from the air, combine small particles from the soil, and produce a spongy substance with a dark color and a high capacity to retain mineral elements: a light, airy soil, capable of absorbing and retaining rain. Rain will not harden it or flood it, and humus combined with clay in the soil forms the essential humic-clay compounds. Humus has a negative charge, which acts like a magnet to attract mineral elements—which tend to have a positive charge—and then pass them to the plants.

What we try to do in making compost is to imitate nature and return to the earth that which it so generously offered us.

Difference between compost and manure

Manure has long held a prime position among fertilizers used in agriculture. But from a biological perspective, it's important to point out that manure only enriches the soil when used appropriately. Manures have a cycle of maturation. It is not the same when fresh as it is when mature, or semimature, and its application has different uses. The gardener tends to spread manure from cows, horses, birds, or pigs on their garden, believing it will enrich the soil. What many don't realize is that, buried without oxygen, it will not decompose and its components will not be released; it will just rot and not fertilize. Fresh manure is recognizable by its strong ammonia odor; you can tell it is sterile because nothing grows on fresh manure until it has reached adequate maturity.

Unlike manure, compost has a much more appropriate use in the practice of biologic gardening, whether you have extensive croplands, a modest garden, or a microgarden in the city, such as balcony gardens, flower pots, flower beds, and rooftop gardens, etc.

How to make compost

It is important to choose the location carefully, so that it is favorable to the growth of microorganisms. Compost needs moderate heat and moisture. A spot that is partially shaded by trees will protect it from excess sun and keep it fresh.

It is important to protect the compost from atmospheric extremes, such as heat, cold, and wind.

To block the wind, you can use a fence, ornamental bushes, sunflowers, or corn. If you use a metal fence, you can plant lavender and nasturtium around it, which repel ants and look nice as well. The size of the corner you will dedicate to compost must be in accordance with the area you have available and your fertilizer needs.

Humus mineralizes (becomes usable to plants) more quickly in sandy soils and more slowly in clay soils; heat, working the soil, and organic contributions also help.

Prevent ants from infesting the compost

During the cycle of decomposition, **biocomposters are a very attractive place for ants due to the quantity of nutrients and heat that they generate.** To prevent them from moving in, it is good to plant nasturtium and lavender around. It is a natural repellant.

On the rooftop or balcony, you can use barrels, bags, or sacks with slots or openings that allow air to circulate, although you can also make a small silo out of wood. It is best to have at least two containers, to put fresh scraps in one while the other container ripens, and thus have compost in different stages of decomposition. Once you've chosen a spot, it's best not to change it, since the process gives life to all sorts of living creatures, which inoculate the new compost with bacteria and fungi.

Ideal plants for compost

At first, you can add all the weeds you pull to the compost, but there are two that are especially good for it: **nettle and comfrey**—the nettle because of its richness in nitrogen and in enzymes that support microbiotic life, and comfrey for its richness in minerals, nitrogen, and potassium. Both can be used to make a very useful compound for spraying on the soil.

Natural humus

In the country, humus forms from the fallen leaves and animal droppings. The top layer of dead leaves, branches, and fresh organic material cover the lower layers and accumulate. In the second layer, or layer of decomposition, bacteria and fungi begin to act by attacking the cellulose and lignins of the hard parts—aided by slugs, snails, beetles, mites, and springtails. In this layer, the humus begins to appear; it has a brown color and crumbles in your fingers. The third layer is in contact with the soil and this is the humus itself. Here fungi and bacteria flourish, and it is the territory of the earthworms. You can no longer distinguish the elements of the forest and it has a dark brown or black color.

The carbon-nitrogen balance

Compost needs an adequate mixture of both elements, since an excess of nitrogen accelerates decomposition but produces little humus, and an excess of carbon produces the opposite effect. High levels of nitrogen are found in chicken manure, nettle purine, grass, legumes, coffee grounds, and kitchen scraps. High levels of carbon are found in sawdust, straw, peat, branches, and leaves. Fresh nettles, sheep or horse manure with straw, leaves of fruit trees, and small branches cut in spring help maintain a good balance.

The Four Seasons of Compost

Summer
Work on filling the compost bin. Cover each layer of scraps with leaves and already decomposed material. Dig and stir the pile often.

Fall
Gather the finished compost. Use it as a cover for your flowers or garden.

MATERIALS RICH IN CARBON
Dry leaves
Wood shavings
Sawdust
Branches

MATERIALS RICH IN NITROGEN
Plant, fruit, and vegetable scraps
Animal manure
Egg shells
Tea leaves
Coffee grounds

Spring
Time to start again. Empty the finished compost into the garden and start a new pile.

Winter
Continue making the compost in the cold months. Add kitchen scraps to the compost bin.

Aeration and watering

The majority of microbes need oxygen to survive and carry out their functions. For a compost to develop properly, it needs to take in oxygen and let out carbon dioxide. Therefore, you should choose a place for your compost that is well ventilated, and this depends on the volume of compost. In a terrace, it may be enough to put holes in the bag or drum. In a small garden, use slightly separated boards or wire mesh, and monitor the moisture, which is another important aspect of good compost development. If it dries out too much from too much ventilation, you must compact it, or cover it with a tarp or plastic. If you have a large mass, you can air it out with a compost aerator, pushing it in and moving it back and forth.

The moisture depends on the components. Manure typically doesn't need help, kitchen scraps and plant remains sometimes need straw to prevent excess moisture, but leaves and branches may need watering—in the case of branches, you can even soak them in water before adding them to the pile.

Heat and acidity

Although the small compost piles on terraces or balconies barely see an increase in temperature, if you make a pile of more than a cubic meter, which happens if you have a garden with a lot of trees, the temperature can reach more than 122°F after the second day, and remain at about 140°F for two weeks. At this temperature, the thermophilic microbes work and parasites and undesirable seeds die. If it does not heat up, it's because it lacks volume, it is too dry or too wet, or the carbon-nitrogen balance is off.

As far as acidity, on average it should be more basic so that the fermentation is adequate: between 6 and 8 pH. If it is more acidic—that is, if there are too many dry pine needles, for example—the bacteria

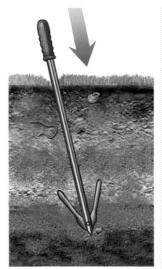

A compost aerator is a tool that is used to introduce air in the compost and thus speed up its decomposition.

Kitchen scraps

Your starting point is important and it is in the kitchen: there you should have two containers, **one for organic material and one for inorganic**, and each will follow its own path to recycling.

The more varied the mixture is, the more nutritious the compost will be. **And if you grind the material, the decomposition will be more efficient**. For example, you can add fruit and potato peels, ground egg shells, coffee grounds, vegetable skins, dry bread, etc, **although be careful not to use too much of:**

- **meat scraps, bones, or grease**
- **citric peels like lemon or orange**
- **rotted or sprouted potatoes**
- **ash from the fireplace—a little bit, dampened**
- **sawdust—a little bit, dampened**
- **paper and cardboard, without ink**
- **cloths and rags, as long as they are natural fibers**

al any which way; it's best to have a plan. It's better to have a spot reserved for pre-compost, where you will separately accumulate the fresher elements, such as grass clippings, garden waste such as rotten tomatoes or bean plants, and kitchen scraps, and another to put drier elements, such as clipped branches, straw, or dried weeds. If you have a lot of trees, you will need a third space to collect dry leaves. The pile should be about five feet wide and about the same height, although it can be as big as you want. First of all, you have to create an aerated space for the base, so it's best to use woody materials, such as branches, corn stalks, or dry grass, all ground or crumbled. If the pile is very large, it is good to put aeration tubes in horizontally, or rolled wire mesh forming tubes up and down.

and earthworms will not appear. In a balanced and slightly basic compost, when fermentation happens it releases organic acids that acidify it slightly. However, the final maturation of the compost produces a final alkalinization, leaving you with humus with a pH of 7.5.

The addition of rock dust

In unbalanced soils, either excessively lime-filled or siliceous, it may help to add rock dust to compensate the acidity or alkalinity. But instead of adding it directly to the soil, you should add it to the compost. For example, limestone soil can be corrected with compost of clay or loam, and clay or acidic soils can be corrected with limestone rock dusts, like dolomite, lime, or natural phosphates.

Ways to make compost

There are two ways to get a good compost for a small garden: the pile and the container. The compost pile is the easiest to prepare, because you just need a space to accumulate the waste.

Experience shows, however, that it's not enough to just accumulate the materi-

The progressive pile

In many cases, a small garden does not allow you to make huge compost piles which produce decomposition with an elevated temperature. They are progressive piles, to which the gardener adds scraps continuously as they come. In this case, one should mix them with a pitchfork every time new material is added.

Compost bins

It's a personal choice, but **if you keep in mind that the compost bin should last a few years, and dedicate an appropriate amount of space**, it is best to make it from brick or cement, with an open front and some lateral slots in which to put boards to close it as it fills. **But that's not to say you can't make it from wood, with pallets, or even wire mesh in a circle.** And if you only have a balcony, you can use a simple drum with a plastic bag. You can even buy plastic ones that are pre-made.

From there, alternate layers of about 8 inches thick of fresh, fine materials with thick, dry materials, and between each layer, put a layer of old compost, manure, or previously fertilized soil from the garden. Between each layer you can also add powdered ash, rock dust, dolomite, or whatever element is necessary to correct the deficiencies of the soil.

Each time you add a layer, you should mix the previous ones with a pitchfork. If the climate is dry, you can water it whenever you water the garden, or do so when it has not rained in a while, but it's good to always maintain consistent moisture. It can also be sprayed down with a compound of nettle or comfrey.

When the pile is finished, cover it with a layer of soil and straw, and water it until it becomes compacted. But you can also use other materials, such as tarps or plastic sheets, as long as the sides are uncovered.

Ripening

The compost is at its peak when it has transformed into a brown humus that smells like the forest. If it has been made on top of soil, you will be surprised to see that once they completed their mission, the earthworms disappeared.

To test the level of moisture, dryness, and ripeness, stick a broom handle or cane into the center of the compost. If it comes out black and greasy, this is a sign that it is too wet and could rot. You should aerate it and turn it as soon as possible. If it collapses, it is too dry and could mold. You need to spray it with warm water. If it is ripe, it will have the moisture of a wrung-out sponge.

At the end of a month, in any case, it is good to dig it with a pitchfork to give it a little life. Experts recommend you make compost and stir it when there is a full or waning moon. As we've seen, the temperature will rise to about 140°F for a few weeks, then cool down.

Two or three months later, it may already be useable as fresh compost, to mulch, not bury, as long as it does not touch the plants.

Five or six months later, it is ripe compost and can be used to fertilize the soil, and after a year it becomes humus and will no longer evolve any further. This is a good time to make new beds.

Compost containers

In general, these are used when you don't have enough waste to make a pile as we proposed previously. So, you can use compost bins, barrels with holes, or bags in which the organic material is added to the top and the decomposed material is collected from the bottom through an opening.

With a certain quantity of compost but not so much space, you can take advantage of a wall or build large boxes, in which you will add compost as previously described. It is best to have two boxes made with boards or bricks, which get higher as the pile grows. In one, you will deposit fresh organic scraps, and in the other you will collect decomposed compost. If you have space, you can prepare three boxes to have compost at different stages of decomposition, but this depends on

The decomposition of leaves

It is faster if the leaves come from fruit trees, maple trees, ash trees, lime trees, banana trees, or chestnut trees. **It is very slow if they are hard leaves such as those from beech, poplar, oak, or walnut—these should be ground before adding them to compost.** Pine needles require special treatment: one week in water, three weeks of fermentation, and three months of ripening before they can be used.

Bokashi

This is a Japanese compost that is being used a lot in Latin America, and has the advantage of fermenting in as little as 15 days, after which it is ready to use. Its essential components are:

- chicken manure
- carbon
- rice hulls and ground rice
- cane molasses
- yeast or humus from the forest, or already made compost
- soil
- calcium carbonate or lime
- water

Manure tea

The name is ironic, but it is made in Ecuador and is a good fertilizer for plants. **Take 22 pounds of manure and put it in a bag of strong cloth, along with 9 pounds of legume leaves, 9 pounds of muriate of potash, and a 10-pound rock.** Close the bag and tie it. Put it in a 50-gallon container and fill it with water. Cover and let ferment for two weeks. Squeeze out the bag and what's left is the tea, which you should dilute to half strength before spraying it on the leaves of the plants as fertilizer.

the preferences of each gardener. Don't forget to make it the same as a pile on the ground, alternating layers, mixing, watering, and adding mature compost or manure.

Manure

The traditional fertilizer that has been used since the beginning of gardening. When a small landowner or someone who has just bought a farm decides to make a garden, the first thing he will do is ask the nearest farmer for a load of manure. By adding this every year, the soil will never wear out.

In regions with poor soil, watering with purines, which are nothing more than diluted manure, maintain fertility indefinitely; however, its excessive use in areas with lots of livestock, especially pigs, is common and this pollutes wells and rivers, and the rain washes the excess nitrates into the groundwater.

It's not always possible to choose the type of manure you want, since it depends on what is available. If you have the choice, in a dry climate, sheep or goat is best, and in a wet climate, cow manure is best.

Sheep and goat manure

This is very concentrated and its direct application can burn the plants; however, it's good for making a balanced compost. In any case, it's best to let it age a year, like chicken manure.

Cow manure

Ideal for wet soils, this can be used directly or in compost, although you have to watch it because it tends to have a high water content.

Pig manure

This is widely used on large tracts of land in the form of purines. By itself, it is very thick and tends to harden. It is not good, however, because it usually contains antibiotics and other chemical substances used to treat the pigs, or to fatten them.

Horse manure

Considered very good, although it is weak for making compost, since it decomposes quickly. It tends to have a lot of cellulose because it comes mixed with straw from the stables, and once it has fermented it loses its odor. It is used in starter pots and seedling beds.

Rabbit manure

This is too strong and acidic to use directly. It should be mixed with compost and complemented with lime or dolomite to cut its acidity.

Chicken manure

This is the manure of any domestic birds. It is too strong to use directly, since its components pass rapidly to the plants. It is not unusual to find a hobby gardener who has burned her plants with chicken manure applied directly to the soil. If you do so, you will have to wait until the next year to get a good yield, although it's best to add it to compost or prepare with the bokashi that is shown on the previous page.

Dead leaves

If your house has a path lined with deciduous trees, you will collect a huge quantity of leaves in the fall. These leaves, rich in carbon, decompose slowly, and if they accumulate on their own, they quickly compact and ferment. It is good to mix them with other waste, such as ground branches or kitchen scraps, and make a separate pile to make a good peat to add to the compost after winter.

A good way to store them is in a ring of wire mesh, staked to the ground. This way they will be aerated and under control, for example, from the wind.

Biodynamic compost

One of the most prestigious organic farmers in Spain, Mariano Bueno, author of the excellent book on compost titled *Como hacer un buen compost (How to Make a Good Compost)*, tells us: "In biodynamics, one adds different preparations to the compost, the manures, and the liquid manures, to increase their effect on the plants and the soil," since, "the goal is not just to activate the world of the microorganisms, such as bacteria, but primarily to concentrate the vital forces . . . "

In this type of agriculture, cow manure is "the noblest material," and therefore it can be used separately or mixed with vegetable compost.

Fruit fertilizer

In a five-gallon bucket, put two pounds of fruit and two pounds of molasses or honey, in alternating layers. Finally, cover it with wood, or put a heavy weight on top to press it. **After 8 days, filter the liquid obtained and put it in bottles.**

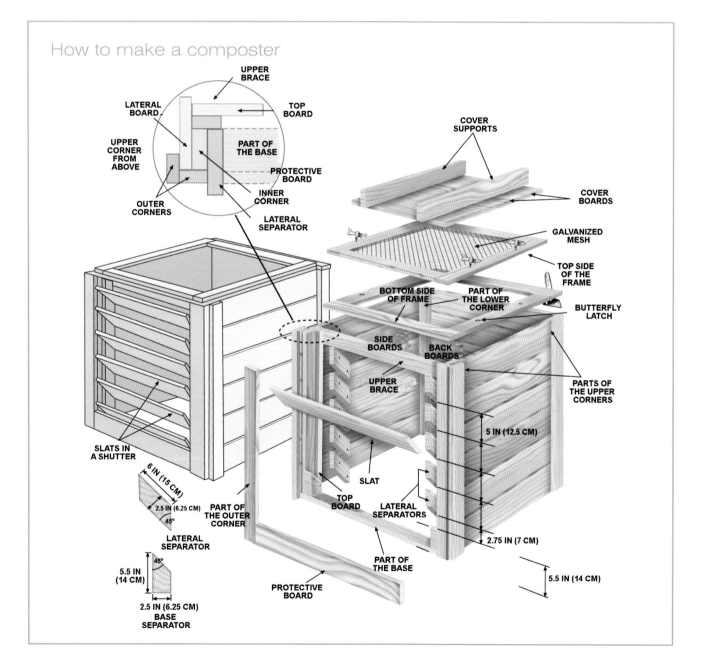

How to make a composter

> Compost is a gardener's best friend; you must be generous with it but not abuse it.

"To dynamize means to create, to liberate forces." There are six preparations to add to fertilizers, two of which are powdered. They were explained in the section on biodynamic agriculture. The compounds are added to compost as injections, in holes about 12 inches deep in the damp compost or manure, with a spoon. Add the five semi-solid preparations (yarrow, chamomile, nettle, oak bark, and dandelion) to both sides, each in a different hole, and that of nettle in the middle. The preparation of valerian is diluted in five liters of water and sprayed on top. The other two preparations are those called preparation 500, made with cow manure, and preparation 501, with crystallized silica, that is, powdered quartz. Then, cover the whole thing with two inches of soil. The resulting compost should be used when it has a lumpy, colloidal consistency, after three to six months, depending on the season, after the fourth phase of maturation. This is the phase of the earthworms (after the thermal phase, the fungal and bacterial phase, and the microfauna phase). After that, the compost is no longer useful.

Other fertilizers

All types of fertilizers have been developed around the world from unwanted organic material. Every culture and region has its methods, as we have seen in the aside about manure tea or fruit fertilizer. Other interesting fertilizers are: urine from farm animals—which often forms part of purines—separating it and letting it sit for a week, or orujo compost, which is made from leftover wine fermented in the open air. It improves the structure and aeration of the soil, and retains water that the plants absorb little by little, as if it were a drip irrigation system.

Comfrey purine

Comfrey (*Symphytum oficinalis*) is a plant with many virtues. It grows easily and, when mixed with alfalfa, is a good livestock feed. It is an excellent healing plant and due to its potassium content, it is a good fertilizer. To make a purine, prepare a barrel with water in which you will place two and a half pounds of comfrey leaves for every two and a half gallons of water. Let the leaves rot for a month and a half, covering the container with mosquito netting. Strain the remaining liquid and use it to water the plants, especially those that need potassium.

Compost can be improved with the help of seaweed, which is rich in nitrates, when mixed with good soil and ripe manure will help invigorate the compost. Ashes can also be utilized, but not as they are, and not those from charcoal, which contains sulfur. Ash from vegetable residues contains valuable potash and will help keep the soil loose, and in the best conditions, conserve moisture for a long time.

Soot from the chimney is very rich in potassic salts and is a useful fertilizer. It also contains carbon, which enables nitrification and has disinfectant properties. This is added to manures.

Nettle marinade

This fertilizer is one of the easiest to make at home, and will be very useful, since the dreaded nettles should not be totally eliminated from the garden. In order to make a nettle marinade, use fresh plants (without seeds). The plants should be cut in spring and early summer, chopped into pieces as small as possible, and put in a 50-gallon barrel. Fill this with rain water, not quite to the top, and cover with mesh to prevent small animals or birds from getting in, while still allowing airflow.

The barrel, which preferably should be made of wood, should be in a sunny place.

Once a day, mix the contents of the entire container well to introduce oxygen into the decomposition process. The level of liquid content will increase due to the formation of foam. To avoid bad odors, add a handful of rock dust on the surface or extract of valerian leaves. Twenty days later, the liquid will get dark and the foam will disappear. Then it is ready to use with the watering can, diluted at a proportion of one to twenty.

The majority of plants and the earthworms like this fertilizer, and the insects do not like it so much. But be careful, it is not good for beans, peas, onions, or garlic.

Vermicomposting bins

These serve to speed up the decomposition of organic material from your kitchen. There are two kinds: vertical and horizontal. The vertical ones are made by stacking various containers on top of each other: they can be flower pots (not one inside of the other, but on top), drawers, or round plastic ones that are sold commercially. The bottom drawer collects the liquid byproducts of the processes in the upper drawers. The next one up contains a colony of earthworms, a thousand to start, separated by a mesh from the drawers above, which will contain the kitchen scraps. Instead of throwing away vegetable scraps, put them in the drawer that is above the worms. They will go up through the holes in the mesh and eat the scraps, consuming the equivalent of about their own body weight every two days.

A thousand worms will transform about a pound of trash into compost. When the drawer is full, continue with the one above it. The drawers are interchangeable. You will place an adequate substrate, based on coconut fiber, in the drawer where the worms live. The ideal worm is the red wriggler or tiger worm (*Eisenia fetida*). As the compost forms, add it to the garden, and with the liquid waste, water your flower pots.

We can use this in the following ways:

● **Burying 4 to 6 tablespoons** around the roots in small flower pots, or up to 12 tablespoons if the pots are more than 16 inches in diameter, every three months.

● **If you change pots**, add 15 percent humus to the soil.

● **As mulch**, spread a layer about a centimeter thick around the plants.

● **In the soil**, you can put about 7 to 14 ounces per square meter and mix before planting.

The red wriggler (*Eisenia fetida*) is easily distinguished by the red band it has in the middle of its body.

Raw materials and their contribution to the compost

● **Leftovers from the harvest**	Organic material rich in nitrogen
● **Green manure**	Carbon/nitrogen balance
● **Grass clippings**	Rich in nitrogen (mix with straw)
● **Fruit tree clippings**	Use ground-up version; good, but slow
● **Leaves**	Slow, decompose apart; rich in humus
● **Weeds, without seeds**	Rich in moisture
● **Nettles**	Favor decomposition/balance
● **Kitchen scraps**	Rich in nitrogen/poor in carbon (mix with straw)
● **Chicken manure**	Provides nitrogen, use at 10–20%
● **Cow manure**	Excellent dry raw material
● **Horse manure**	Accelerates fermentation/helps heat
● **Sheep manure**	Rich in nitrogen/use in moderation

● **Mineral complements. Apply directly to the compost**

Natural phosphates, rocks rich in potassium and trace elements, and ground siliceous rocks.

● A fine rock dust or clay dust eliminates bad odors, since they combine with the ammonia that forms with decomposition. **In this way, the odor doesn't bother the neighbors and flies stay away.**

Mulch

In soil that is rich in humus and well planted, using mulch shouldn't be necessary. But in a newer garden, it is good to do so with grass clippings and the plants themselves, which protect the soil when they dry.

Mulching serves to protect the soil around plants from the rigors of rain, drought, and extended cold spells with a protective layer of organic material or plastic.

Of course, ecological mulch is made from organic material. The use of plastic, as we will see further on, has commercial purposes.

Organic mulch

In fact, in a well established organic garden, in which all the plants provide coverage, mulch is not necessary. But we'll suppose that you are in a hurry and don't entertain yourself by combining plants; you make plots of a single species and want to avoid weeds and keep the soil from drying out.

Get your hands on a large basket or wheelbarrow. In the case of the latter, you will also need a shovel, and in both cases, a rake or simple spade to spread the mulch, which can be made of peat, compost, leaf mold, dry grass, plants, straw, and many more things, as we will see later on. Sawdust is not ideal, unless it is more than two years old, because it will absorb nitrogen from the soil and steal it from the plants. And you don't want to have to add a nitrogen fertilizer.

Mulch prevents the loss of moisture from the soil, provides nutrients (especially if it is compost), maintains and improves the soil quality, and prevents weeds from growing (although, it also prevents good plants from growing, so you must only put it down when the plant is already a few inches tall). Put it down in spring and summer, depending on the state of the seedlings, and it must be at least two inches thick.

Plastic mulch

As we already said, this is usually done out of commercial interest. Of course, the use of plastic derived from petroleum is not ecological, but it is good to know about it, since many so-called organic crops are grown with this system.

There are three kinds of plastics: white, black, and transparent. The white ones are used to reflect light onto the plants that need it to ripen, such as tomatoes and melons, although black plastic is also used in these cases to prevent weeds and heat the air around the plants. Transparent plastics are used to heat the ground in the spring.

In any case, their purpose is to: maintain moisture, increase the ground temperature, accelerate the life cycle of the plant, heat the plant with absorption and reflection of light, keep the plant clean of soil splatter, and prevent soil erosion.

Unlike organic mulch, plastic is placed on the furrows when the seeds are planted. In this way, it speeds up germination (especially transparent plastics). It is fastened onto fences or buried at the edges. Black plastic is used more often, since it impedes the sun from reaching the soil and accelerates growth much more. If the seed has already been planted, make an x-shaped cut where the plant will sprout. Of course, this is accompanied by drip irrigation, and

The problem with plastic is that in full sunlight, they degrade each year and have to be thrown away, as they only last one harvest. The pollution produced from this is enormous.

the only thing left to worry about are slugs, which hide under the plastic.

The plastic used is polyethylene, but we prefer organic material, although it will require more attention to what is going on in the soil.

Experience shows that each plant requires a different mulch, for example, an experimental plantation proved that broccoli grew faster and better with white mulch, cabbage with an opaque black mulch, and cauliflower with transparent mulch, which provides a higher temperature.

Materials for mulch

- **Leftovers from pruning trees**, after being passed through a wood chipper.

- **Dried grass or straw**, which can come from the remains of grains.

- **Plants**, although still green, that are not useful, and especially without seeds.

- **Tree bark**, shredded, especially from pines.

- **Scraps of wool**, not fibers.

- **Egg cartons**, since they are made of cardboard they will decompose quickly.

- **Newspapers**, but be careful with too much ink.

- **Cardboard**

- **Wood shavings and** coconut fiber (sold in bags). Sawdust is used in parks to keep grass from growing, and is not recommended.

- **Wrapping paper**

Solarization

It is recommended every three or four years. It eliminates fungus, nematodes, worms, weeds, and bacteria through heat and asphyxiation. It is not a very humane method, but it works.

This is a technique to disinfect the soil. You must have room in the garden, it requires very little work, it eliminates seeds, roots, and parasites from the soil, and it consists of heating damp soil, using solar radiation, by covering it with a sheet of polyethylene that retains and accumulates heat.

Method

It must be done in the summer, between early July and mid-August, and the steps are:

Deep excavation of the soil—if it is done with a rototiller, adding the subsoiler and then the rototiller, to break up all the clumps.

Measure the width of the plastic sheets and dig furrows at the right distance to bury the edges. If you are using several, you will have to bury the edges in the same trench.

Abundantly water the soil, at least 16 inches deep.

To improve solarization, add fresh manure, which will ferment in the heat and add more heat.

Cover the soil with plastic, so that it is taut and in contact with the soil. If the solarization is done with a tunnel of plastic, it is called double-layered, and will reach even higher temperatures.

The thickness of the plastic depends on the wind, but it should be between 100 and 200 gauge thicknesses.

Leave for 30 to 45 days in full sun. The soil will reach temperatures above 122°F.

Problems

You must keep in mind that the effectiveness is less at the edges, within at

The goal of solarization is to avoid the use of insecticides and pesticides, so sometimes the use of plastic can be justified in a medium or large farm.

Pasteurization

Solarization forms part of a group of techniques to heat the soil to temperatures that will prevent the spread of diseases. The techniques are mulching, solarization, and pasteurization, eliminating all traces of life in the soil.

least a meter, so it is useless to do this with very small parcels. It is a technique used by growers with a relatively large area of land, possibly near a wild area where animals will tend to confuse the plastic with water and could tear it. In this case, you would have to fence it with a few strands of wire, even to prevent cats, dogs, and chickens from getting in. If you have a tractor, do not drive over the plastic, as the effect will not be the same.

Irrigation

Watering is one of the gardener's pleasures, so never deprive yourself of watching the furrows as water flows through them and reaches the plants, wetting their roots.

In very few climates can you go without watering the land. In the Mayan mountains, for example, seasonal rains occur during the growth cycle on a daily basis, then stop when it's time to harvest. Corn, green beans, and squash are perfectly adapted for this cycle.

This type of planting could also be done in our climates and we will almost certainly get a good harvest, as long as we protect ourselves from the climate change.

Irrigation in dry climates allows you to obtain maximum yield from your crops, but you must be careful to avoid excess water. Some plagues and diseases develop because of excess water and in many cases, you will have to take measures to aerate the soil.

Methods of irrigation

Probably, the first irrigation system was done by flooding, as they still do today in Egypt, where the water is pumped from the channels of the Nile River and poured directly onto the fields. This option requires a huge quantity of available water, and flat fields, but over time produces salinization of the soil. Unless you have a good drainage system, the water accumulates on the surface and evaporates, depositing salts that will turn the soil unproductive. If you don't have that much water available, the best option is furrow irrigation. The plants are planted on ridges separated by furrows that can be opened or closed with a hoe. Since the water can go as far as you want from the main channel, it is possible to irrigate on slopes by making terraces.

All you have to do is open or close the furrows to water the plants that need it and when they need it. The same way, the furrows can be lined with a hose connected to the water source or siphoned from a pond. A more sophisticated system of irrigation is by sprinkler, installing a hose and sprinkler that can be turned on when needed. This system, similar to watering with a hose from the edge of the garden, is good for onions, leeks, and carrots, or other types of crops on flat ground, without furrows. However, there is the risk of wetting the leaves too much, which favors the growth of fungi.

Drip irrigation requires an initial investment that, in the case of industrial plantations, is amply compensated through the conservation of water in areas where it is scarce.

Drip irrigation

The best option that is currently out there is drip irrigation. This system, however, is a huge step back from our idea of a self-sufficient garden that requires very few tools. It is most advisable to water with channels or, if you have a pond nearby, by channeling the water through furrows, although it requires daily work. Drip irrigation is designed for large gardens or those in which the farmer is frequently absent. If you have a weekend garden, this system is suitable, but first you must be willing to make the initial investment, and maintain it.

The eternal watering can

Never forget this tool, which is so useful for watering seed beds and seedlings that have just been transplanted. It is the best option for small tomatoes, peppers, eggplants, etc. And you can always decorate the watering can to your taste.

Filling the watering can in late afternoon and sprinkling the beds, making sure the watering is homogenous and does not damage the fragile, newly sprouted plants is one of the best ways to get in touch with nature.

For larger areas, it's better to use a hose and even the hoe and irrigation channel, to let the water run and feed that which will be your sustenance the next morning, when the peppers and lettuce are ready for the healthiest, most delicious salad you can imagine.

The system

Drip irrigation consists of a system of hoses that goes through the whole garden with a small hole next to each plant for water to come out. The irrigation is programmed and, in each section, the garden should have an electric valve that opens and closes when the programmer decides; this way, we can program different routines for tomatoes and eggplants, for example, without leaving home.

Ideally this water would come from a source positioned so that the pressure is always the same. If it comes directly from the faucet, before the electric valves you should install pressure regulators and filters to avoid obstructions. In the holes of the hose, put drip emitters, which can be of different kinds. You will also need elbow, 4-way, and T-tube fittings to connect sections of the hose. If the hose if very long, you will need auto compensators to maintain the water flow at the same pressure.

The average flow for drip irrigation is one gallon per hour. Under each plant there will form what is called a wetted zone—narrow and deep in sandy soil, and wide and shallow in clay soil.

Frequency and problems

Obviously these plans are not applicable to all plants, but fruit trees, for example, should be watered according to this plan: in spring, three or four times a week, for about 20 minutes with a flow of one gallon per hour; in summer, daily, for at least half an hour; in fall, five to ten minutes two or three times a week; in winter, depending on the rain. As you have seen, this system is good for fruit trees and flower gardens especially, although it is also used in large gardens where the ridges are covered with plastic. The system is ecological at first, but anyone who has seen these types of crops, with the plastic hoses (made from petroleum) piled up each year at the end of harvest, with hundreds of meters of broken tubes or those destroyed by pollutants, will not be too attracted to this method. It

Climate change is causing shortages of rainfall in many areas where not so long ago, it was common. Although alterations to the climate are normal throughout history, the increase of carbon dioxide causes a more precipitous change. One way to avoid it is by planting trees, since forests favor rain and prevent excessive heating of the soil.

certainly saves a lot of water, but that is not the idea we have of a garden. Watering should be done depending on the needs of the plants. And you have to be there to see with your own eyes and to feel with your own senses.

The forest and the microclimate

Advice for watering

- **Water in the early morning** or at sundown.

- **Avoid the hours of most intense sun**, although if it is cloudy and cool you can water then.

- **Don't use water that is too salty**, since except for tomatoes, all plants will weaken quickly. If the water you have is too salty, use tap water.

- **Make sure the water is not too hot or too cold**. The ideal is that the irrigation channel, if you have one, is well shaded by trees.

- **Keep in mind that the wind dries the soil** and that, if you have

a wall to protect it from the wind, the sun will still dry it. Each garden and each parcel has a different history, and finding that out is one of the pleasures of gardening.

- Tomatoes, peppers, green beans, squash, peas, and cucumbers **need more water when they start to flower**.

- **Root plants**, such as carrots and beets or radishes, need more water when the roots are forming.

- **Leafy plants**, such as lettuce and spinach, must be watered frequently before they ripen. Otherwise, they will bolt quickly.

Excess watering

If you waste water in the garden, the only thing you will achieve is causing moisture that attracts fungi and other diseases, as well as causing the fruit to lose flavor. Tomatoes and carrots that are overwatered become bland, and then you can't complain. Some people are too impatient, or enjoy watering so much they want to do it every day; sometimes you must contain yourself.

Plants should be watered when they need it, and if possible, you should distribute the plants to fully take advantage of the water. You must also keep in mind that plants need more water when they are young, and when it is almost time to harvest, you should stop watering, so they get more flavor. You must also consider that root crops, such as potatoes, when overwatered, produce a very tall plant (as when it rains too much) and very few tubers, which is not what you want.

The best yield

To not waste water, it is best to make sure the soil is conditioned to retain it, without puddling. Sandy soils, for example, retain very little water, and are good for certain species like ash, which want to have water only when they are thirsty. On the other side of the spectrum, clay soils retain a lot of water and rarely get muddy, but when water is scarce they do not give it up to the plants and only some, such as the weeping willow, are able to extract it from the capillaries of the earth. To avoid these problems, we use organic material, which contain water and oxygen together. But you already know that a good fertilizer solves these problems.

The emitters

The hoses used for drip irrigation will have holes every 12 to 16 inches in which there are drip emitters, through which the water comes out. These can be button emitters, which are stuck into the hose and can be taken out, or integrated, which remain fixed along the hose. You can also use a drip irrigation tape or even a hose with holes.

In flower gardens, the hose is often buried, so you have to install some microtubes from the hole to the surface, where you will attach the emitters.

One foreseeable problem involves the lime in the water, which ends up obstructing the emitters. Experience teaches us that the best emitters are those that can be removed to be cleaned. Cleaning is done by sticking a needle in the holes to open them, or with diluted nitric acid, taking necessary precautions.

Proper sowing

The importance of
proper sowing

The first and most important thing that the self-sufficient gardener must do is obtain the proper seeds, and then treat them with care.

Let's not fool ourselves, without good seeds, there is no worthwhile garden. The majority of the seeds that our grandparents used have disappeared from the market, and only exist in the hands and cupboards of a few old gardeners and lovers of good food, who guard them like a great treasure. So in order to begin, we must behave like detectives, and then we will learn to use them.

Seeds

Plants reproduce through seeds. The embryo of the new plant, its form and characteristics, are all contained inside a seed. The job of the gardener is to select the best seeds, from the best plants or fruits, so that the new generations are better each time. It is always said that you should save the best tomato from the first crop for seeds. That is how your biologic garden should work: with your own seeds, selected each year, at least for the majority of the plants, although it's not always possible.

Many of the seeds that are available commercially are hybrids; that is, the companies that produce them have crossed incompatible plants through force so that they are more resistant and have a greater production. The seeds obtained from these plants are not the same and will not work for the next year's seedlings. So, if you buy them, you have to be very sure that they are not hybrids.

The selection of good traditional seeds, in the face of the surge of genetic technology by the agro-industrial companies, has become a real battle. It even feels somewhat radical.

In just a few days, all the plants in your seedbed will have sprouted. Then you will have to thin them, so that they don't get in the way of each other, and get rid of the weakest. If you take a little dirt with them when you transplant them, it will be easier for them to take root, although if you have them too close together you won't be able to. In some cases it is even good to air them out a little, such as with lettuce and onions. Want to know a trick? Mix the seeds of radishes and carrots. The radishes grow more quickly and save you from thinning out the carrots.

The largest known seed is that of the Sea Coconut, *Lodoicea maldivica*, and weighs 44 pounds (20 kilograms). The smallest belong to the epiphytic orchids, and there are almost a thousand million in a single gram.

Let's experiment

Some schools ask children to perform the following experiment with vegetable seeds: disinfect them with diluted bleach and put them in boxes with cotton and pieces of damp cloth, keep in the dark, and wait for germination, which will have occurred in most of the seeds at the end of a week. Start with the fastest, the radishes, and continue with squash and pumpkins, onions, spinach, peas, green beans, cucumbers, leeks, chard, eggplants, peppers, tomatoes, and carrots. As soon as the plants have sprouted, they should be transplanted to pots or other containers in which there is potting soil, not soil from the garden.

Some specialists recommend covering the container (open milk cartons, cups, pots, or whatever) with transparent plastic. This way, they maintain heat and speed up germination.

When the seeds have sprouted, you have to thin them carefully, and when they are two or three fingers high they can be transplanted to bigger containers, although many gardeners prefer to leave them in the original container until they are big enough to transplant outside.

The method can be great if you have children, because it allows you to observe germination and note the time each species takes, but be careful: this is not the best method to grow seeds that you are going to plant in the garden. Those should develop from the start in a layer of soil, and if they are going to be transplanted, it should be done as close as possible to the final location, so they adapt. For this, instead of wet cotton, you can use potting soil in pots and then place them directly in the spot they will grow. Don't use peat, since a cubic meter takes five hundred years to develop, and it's a resource that has been excessively plundered.

The quality of the seeds

Experience will teach you which are the most useful seeds, but to start, use those produced by the best fruits from the first crop, and let them dry on a paper in the shade.

If you buy seeds in envelopes, keep in mind the following factors that should appear on the back of the package: the germinating power (as a percentage)—that is, how many of the seeds from the package will germinate; **the longevity, which indicates how long the seeds will have germinating power** (remember that once exposed to air, some will not last more than a year); and the purity, which indicates the proportion of seeds in the contents of the envelope.

Onion seeds have the shortest germinating power; they cannot be kept for more than a year. After them are **parsnips, dandelion,** **spring onions, sweet corn, peas, leeks, green beans, lima beans, and parsley,** which barely last two years. The rest begin to weaken after the fourth year, up until the ten years that endives and cucumbers can last. Don't trust any seeds that have been in an envelope for more than five years. In order to lengthen the duration of the fertile state of the seeds, put them in a tightly sealed glass jar and keep in a dark place.

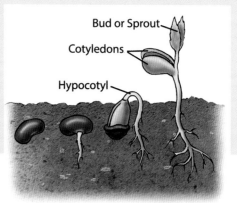

Bud or Sprout

Cotyledons

Hypocotyl

Forms of reproduction

Reproduction through seeds is just one of the ways that plants have to propagate themselves; for example, no one ever thinks of planting potatoes this way. Here we see some of the possibilities.

Seeds

This is the universal method. The plants grow, flower, and the flowers transform into fruits that contain seeds. Some, like cacao, have a germinating power of a few days, while others, like baobab, have a germinating power of a few years. The seeds of gymnosperms are very resistant and can wait long periods of time on the ground. The sequoia needs fire to open the seed, while other species need to be soaked for several days. In general, (moderate) heat and moisture are enough to cause germination.

Cuttings

Some plants, such as rose bushes or many fruit trees, can reproduce by cutting a young branch and planting it in the ground. In Guatemala, I have seen walls built by cuttings that sprouted in the spring, producing colorful flowers. In general, this occurs with species of softwoods, in which the sap runs close to the surface and can flow with a small scratch. Cuttings are also sometimes called slips.

Suckers

Similar to the previous case, but these are branches that grow very close to the ground and have their own roots, such as with olives. This system is used with artichokes in the garden.

Runners

Some plants project horizontal stems a specific distance and, once in contact with the ground, these grow their own roots, and from there sprout leaves and a new plant, which can be separated from the mother plant and transplanted to another place. The most common example of the use of this method is with strawberries, but water reeds also reproduce this way.

Bulbs

Some species, like garlic and onion, or tulips, form bulbs at the base of the stems in which they store nutrients that help them sprout again the following year. **To use them, separate the shoots from the original bulb, store in a dry place, and plant them separately the next season.** This does not mean that they don't grow from seeds, but by using the bulb you will avoid having to plant in a seed bed and wait more than a year, except in the case of onions, since the bulb does not last that long.

Layering

Like the previous case, but forced. There are two main types: air layering—in which you make a cut in a branch, cover it with peat, and wrap it in plastic until it grows roots—and ground layering, in which you bend a branch and bury part of it underground, tying the part that comes out to a stake, like with a vine. Once the branch has sprouted and grown roots, it is separated from the mother plant and transplanted. (See Fruit trees).

Tubers

These are roots that store reserve substances and form enlarged bulbs, from which a new plant will emerge, as occurs with potatoes, sweet potatoes, yuca, begonias, and dahlias. The way to use them is to cut them in pieces and plant them separately. With flowering plants, the reproduction of tuberous plants is better done with cuttings. As is the case with bulbs, reproduction through seeds does not allow you to maintain uniformity of the species as using the roots does.

Rhizomes

These are underground stems that grow horizontally and put out shoots, which allows us to separate them to reproduce the plant. This occurs in canes, bamboos, ferns, and water hyacinth.

Grafts

This consists of joining part of one plant to another. Then it begins to grow and you have a new plant formed from two different ones. It is a curious form of reproduction widely used in fruit trees.

Sowing

We've reached the point that we can say confidently, although not as much as in pruning fruit trees, that every master has their manual. We find ourselves facing one of the joys of the garden, along with watering and harvesting, since it allows us to come in direct contact with the soil after all the prior work to dig and fertilize it. The different methods used are forms of direct sowing—either broadcast sowing, or hand sowing in the soil itself; or sowing in seedbeds, which implies posterior transplanting.

Direct sowing

This is done when the soil is perfectly dug, fertilized, loosened, and softened, and above all, free of weeds. There are two methods:

Broadcast sowing—scattering the seeds from the air, as was done in ancient times with grains on large fields, and is done in the garden with very small seeds, like those of carrots in the soil, or those of onions in the seedbed. This is a technique that requires experience and thinning of the plants once they have sprouted.

Hand sowing in the soil—making a small hole in which you introduce one or more seeds. The depth depends on the size of the seeds, from a couple millimeters for those plants that you would plant through broadcast sowing, and which are then covered with a layer of mulch or compost, to 1.5 to 2 inches with large seeds, such as green beans, lima beans, or chickpeas.

If the seeds are very small and you are going to plant them in plots without furrows, or even if they are bigger, it's a good idea to use a string to mark the lines. Stick a post in each end of the row to hold the string. If the seeds are very small, you can make a furrow with your spade or the corner of a hoe and sprinkle them by hand.

If the seeds are large, you should make holes at regular distances, which you can measure with a stick made for this purpose, and on which you can even make notch marks for different species. The distances you will find in the chapter dedicated to vegetables.

A few tricks

Some gardeners put their seeds in water a day before so that they are warned that it's time to grow. Others put them under a lamp, so the heat simulates the start of spring.

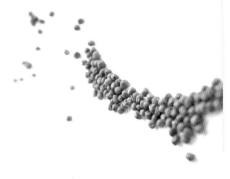

Sowing in seedbeds or starter pots

This system is useful to speed up the growth of the vegetables, or simply to allow yourself a seedbed from which to choose the best plants. It can be covered or uncovered.

The starting point is the same: wood or plastic drawers, pots, or any other container, although I recommend the prettiest option, built in a corner of the garden or against a wall. It's enough to just enclose a bit of land with small walls of stone or brick about 8 inches high and of a size that suits the size of the garden. From here, you can cover it with a roof that is high enough to allow you to work under it. It can be wood or corrugated plastic, tile, or a strong glass. Keep in mind that it must allow enough light. The one I built has four stone pillars and the roof is made of tiles and opaque glass. If it is very small, a glass cover that can be removed, or a transparent plastic tied to stakes is enough.

Now the important part is to lay down a good organic substratum, and then you have a small greenhouse where you can plant your onions, lettuce, and tomatoes while waiting for good weather.

Hybrid seeds

All kinds of hybrid seeds are sold commercially, **developed for greenhouse crops or hydroponic crops**, so the principal advantage of the hybrid is its long life, as happens with tomatoes and melons, seedless watermelons, peppers, cucumbers, onions, and all kinds of flowers. On the envelopes you will find symbols like **F1** or **F2** (Fusarium 1 or 2) or **TMV** (Tobacco mosaic virus), which mean these are varieties that are resistant to certain viruses and tobacco mosaic, which attack greenhouses. Keep in mind that, if you use them, you can't consider yourself an organic gardener.

The organic substratum

Ecological agriculture does not recommend using peat for organic substratum. The peat that is sold in bags in nurseries, and which is great for making the ground spongy, has been extracted from the north of Europe or Canada and is the protective layer formed over thousands of years in the tundra, from the grass that dies each winter on which a new layer grows each spring. The lower layers rot and the land rises little by little, producing a layer of humus or peat many meters thick, which is cut in blocks and sold in sacks. **Its use implies the destruction of an ecosystem and because of this, you should prepare your organic substratum yourself**, although to start you will need a little help. This is a mixture of three parts of well composted compost, and one part river sand. As you see, it's impossible not to damage some small corner of nature in order for humans to get theirs. It's best if the sand is perlite or vermiculite, which are very porous minerals that favor bacteria, and one part of the compost can also be coconut fiber to improve the mix. **In summary: two parts compost, one of coconut fiber and the other of perlite or vermiculite. No chemical products, and perhaps a little liquid manure (purine) to enrich the mix.**

Method of sowing

- **Roots or shoots**: garlic, artichoke, sweet potato, potato, rhubarb

- **Direct sowing**: chard, celery, pea, beet, green onion, cilantro, endives, spinach, bean, fennel, lettuce, corn, melon, turnip, cucumber, parsley, green bean, radish, watermelon.

- **Seedbed and transplant**: chili pepper, artichoke, celery, eggplant, watercress, broccoli, onion, cauliflower, asparagus, lettuce, pepper, leek, cabbage, tomato.

Uncovered seedbed

In gentle climates, where frost is rare, such as on the Mediterranean coast, you can sow directly into the soil. The first condition is that you've prepared a small parcel of land with the best soil possible: the organic substratum that you've prepared.

In some gardens, it's not unusual to find even old buckets in which there is a mess of disorganized tomato and pepper plants growing, which the gardener will use to substitute those that die off. So an open air seedbed can be made on the ground, in boxes, in buckets, in a wheelbarrow, in pots, or in beds. In the same place that you already did the protected sowing, it is common to sow an uncovered bed later to replace the losses.

Protected seedbed

Any of the previously mentioned forms of constructing a seedbed can serve as a starting point. It is enough to just cover it with plastic, which will heat the ground and accelerate germination. If it is on the ground, put stakes in the four corners to hold up the plastic, and if you have planted in rows, you can put metal hoops and make a greenhouse tunnel, although I'm not fond of this industrial option since the use of plastic implies pollution. You can also put

What can we plant in the seedbed?

Although depending on the climate, you can plant in a covered or uncovered seedbed, the plants that need to spend some time in protected soil free of weeds and parasites are **celery, eggplants, onions, cabbage, lettuce, pepper, leeks, and tomatoes**. In greenhouses, they also do this with melons, cucumbers, and watermelons.

resistant glass over it, which can be taken off easily, or put the pot on the windowsill or simply put it on your porch.

The hotbed

This is a seedbed with its own heat source, which accelerates germination and protects the plants from the cold. It is made by forming a series of layers in the seedbed: the first serves as drainage and is mainly gravel; the second formed by manure, mainly horse manure since that is the one that produces the most heat; a third of old compost; and a fourth of humus, in which you will plant the seeds. All of this goes under a roof. The manure should be moist and compact, although not too much or it will not ferment properly. If you do not have horse manure, make a mixture of sheep and cow manure. A simple pile of dry leaves, buried more than two feet deep, begins to heat up quickly. With manure, it does not need to be more than 8 inches deep.

In ten or twelve days, the temperature in the bed will be 140 or 160°F, but you must wait until it goes down to 75°F on the surface before sowing. You don't want to exterminate your own seeds.

Planting in containers

In this modality, the seeds are placed in small containers such as those sold in the market or in greenhouses for transplanting. If you do this at home, anything works, from an egg carton to ice cream boxes or ice cube trays. Fill the container with a mixture of sand and compost, wet it, and make a hole with your finger or a small stick, and put a seed in each hole—a couple if they are very small. Cover with glass or transparent plastic to retain heat and keep in a warm place (for example, on top of the fridge). The next step is to leave one plant per section, when they have two or three leaves, or separate them about two inches if you are using a wide container.

Repotting

This is done when the plants have two leaves. Prepare another tray with one part organic substratum, one part mulch, and one part sand. If you don't have a tray with containers but just a flat one, it's a good idea to make a board with nails distributed at regular intervals which you can place on top of the substratum to mark the spots where you will put the new plants. Stick a sharp pencil or stick into the place where you are going to transplant and insert the plant, without bending the stem. There are wooden gadgets you can buy in the shape of a 'V' to avoid touching the plant with your fingers, although a fork works as well. With the same pencil, pat down the soil around the plant.

Water the soil generously, without wetting the leaves, keep in the shade for a day, and then put in a place with abundant light, but out of direct sun.

Some advice

If you are worried about birds or insects attacking the newly transplanted plants, do as you would with direct sowing: cut a plastic bottle in half and place it over the plant, being careful that the excess heat doesn't roast it.

Don't bury the transplanted seedlings with the roots folded and the ends facing up. This will make the plant do unnecessary work and they will take longer to grow.

Direct thinning

Some people consider thinning to be moving the plants directly to the ground. But if you let them grow a little more, until they have four or five leaves, then we can talk about transplanting.

Transplanting

This is the definitive move of the plant into the ground of the garden. Once the plant has grown to the appropriate size, you will have a root ball—that is, the plant with the soil that accompanies the roots. In this case, we can talk about moving the root ball to the garden. If you used containers with individual plants, you will just have to turn them upside down and gently loosen the root ball. Then place each one in the hole you have made in the ground and water abundantly. This is the correct method for tomatoes, peppers, and eggplants, for example. If you do not have individual plant containers, and you have to pull the plant out with the roots and minimal soil—such would be the case for a tray of plants you bought at a store or perhaps a bucket of tomato plants—you will have to move as quickly as possible to minimize the time the plant is exposed, and you will plant it just like those plants that are transplanted with naked roots. It is better to do this with plants such as lettuce, onions, celery, and leeks because this will make them stronger. Place them in holes made with a stick, taking care not to fold the roots.

The influence of the moon

It has always been believed that the moon has a certain influence on plants, and so old gardeners keep this in mind when it comes time to plant. There is no doubt that the attraction the moon exerts on the earth has a certain influence on all the phenomena of the biosphere, most notably the tides. Plants clearly reflect the action of gravity, since this determines the direction that they must grow in. It has been shown that plants that grow without gravity do so randomly, in no particular direction, and tend to self-destruct.

We must observe the moon from two different points of view. In one, we consider the lunar phase: whether it is waxing, full, new, or waning. In the other, we consider if it is ascending or descending on the horizon, since during the period of time when we see it in the sky, which lasts 28 days, it appears at first higher in the sky each night, and then, lower each time.

These two phenomena must not be confused, since sometimes there is a waning moon that is ascending at the same time. The moon is ascending when it is moving to the north toward the constellations Aries or Taurus. And it is descending when it is moving south, each time lower in the sky, and gets nearer to Libra and Scorpio. The cycle lasts about 27 days.

The phases of the moon, on their part, last a little more than 29 days, depending on the illumination. It is waning when it appears like a C and waxing when it appears like a D.

Ascending and descending moon

The ascending moon favors activities with the aerial parts of plants, such as grafting or picking fruit, which will be much juicier. It is unfavorable to pruning, as it will spill too much sap, or planting garlic.

The descending moon means the majority of activity is transferred to the ground. This is the time to work the soil, fertilize, and harvest roots such as potatoes, carrots, onions, or garlic. It is also the time to prune, since there is less sap, and to perform other tasks related to the ground, such as transplanting and planting cuttings, since they will take root better. It is also a good idea to chop firewood, as it will dry quicker.

Waxing and waning

When the moon is waxing, the vitality of the plants diminishes, and if the moon is ascending at the same time, it's the ideal time for grafting. The grape and olive harvest is best done during the waning moon, since it is said that the grapes are sweeter and the oil is better. This period is also a good time to plant roots and tubers. The legend that garlic comes out of the ground if it is sown in the waxing quarter is well known, so you should do the opposite.

The full moon, favors the planting of lettuce and the pruning of hardwood trees. On the other hand, they say it is best to harvest aerial crops in the waxing moon and roots and tubers in the waning quarter, except for garlic and onions, which prefer the waxing moon.

Pumpkins and squash must be harvested during the waxing moon, although the truth is that with the oil in the hot pan and the fruit fully ripe, I would not wait too long. Another aspect to keep in mind is **the apogee and perigee of the moon**, that is, the closeness of the satellite

To close the cycle of sowing

A small commentary on **hydroponic crops**, which don't fit in a biologic garden, but it's important to know about them to understand why the fruits obtained this way are bland: **plants that are cultivated without soil, on a substratum of coconut fiber that holds the roots and through which is passed a nutritious solution with all the elements that the plants need to grow**: sulfur, boron, calcium, carbon, copper, phosphorous, hydrogen, iron, magnesium, manganese, nitrogen, oxygen, potassium, and zinc under strict control of pH and temperature.

On the left, a **waning moon**, and in the center, a **waxing moon**.

in its revolution around the Earth. It is said that during the perigee, when the moon is closest, it is not good to work in the garden, since its influence is greater. The plant is more sensitive, potatoes sprout eyes easily, etc.

And the planets

The moon has its favorite plants. According to cosmobiology, chard, watercress, melons, and cucumbers are lunar plants. Each planet has its own influences: Mercury prefers plants with fine stems and small flowers, such as anise, parsley, and fennel; Mars prefers conical roots, like garlic, mustard, or nettles; Venus, the most beautiful plants with white flowers, like orchids or thyme; Jupiter, the big aromatic fruits, like cabbage, grapes, figs, or olives, and nutmeg, oregano, and jasmine; Saturn likes trees that live for many years and ancient, slow-growing plants like horsetail, hemlock, holly, plantain, onion, and potatoes. The sun, obviously, prefers plants that reproduce its color and shape, like oranges and sunflowers.

Good and bad
company

Good and bad
company

There are many ways to get rid of plagues that attack the garden without harming the environment or contaminating the foods with chemical products.

Weeds

The gardener's first problem is the problem of weeds, the so-called "bad plants" that for us are simply "annoying." Especially for weekend gardeners, who stay away for five days and come back to find the garden invaded by weeds, there is no other choice than to pull them. There are two types of plants that threaten our gardens:

Annual plants

These are born from seeds and only live a few months, such as the poppy, dandelion, and wild oats. These are easy to eliminate with a hoe, spade, trowel, or by hand, pulling them out when the soil is damp so the roots come out more easily.

Perennial plants

These reproduce by rhizomes, such as Bermuda grass, nettles, bindweed, and Java grass. These require more work, since even if you pull them, pieces of root will still be left behind and sprout again at the first opportunity. But don't despair, keep pulling them and each year they will be weaker, until they disappear. After several years of fighting, I have been able to completely exterminate nettle stalks that seemed invincible, simply by cutting them with a weed whacker over and over again. However, don't let your guard down, since the seeds can always come back on the wind.

Harmful insects

The majority of insects end up being beneficial to the crops, mainly through pollination but also from the aeration of the soil by ants, for example, and the contribution to forming humus and converting certain chemical elements into useable form for plants.

There are, however, a percentage of insects that are harmful because they eat the crops, whether as adults or larvae. Or because they attack the roots and kill the plant. And this population of harmful

Controlling weeds

The best way to get rid of annoying weeds is to not let them grow, by laying good mulch around the crops, which can be straw or wood chips from fruit trees.

But if they are already there, you have to face them. If they are tall, you will have to grab them by the stem, as close to the ground as possible, and pull them out in one go to eliminate the aerial part and as much of the roots as possible.

It's not a good idea to take drastic measures like salting the pathways or the cracks in the pavement. The best thing is mulch, or if not that, proper weeding.

Useful insects destroy 80 percent of harmful insects. The grower only has to worry about the other 20 percent.

A seven-spotted ladybug can devour up to 250 aphids a day.

Earthworms

Earthworms are one of the most cherished species of gardeners and agriculturists, since they allow the soil to stay aerated, and form a layer of humus that enriches it.

Their activity of swallowing and digesting the earth is very productive, since the organic material that they excrete allows for the accumulation of high-quality humus.

Shake a juniper branch in autumn: a few ladybugs that have not yet gone dormant will certainly fall out, and hurry to get back on.

plants proliferates from year to year due to the use of insecticides that leave only the most resistant ones alive—which must then be combated with even more destructive pesticides.

It is certain that science is working toward the creation of more specific insecticides, which only destroy the species, but recent events show that these do not actually work. When they fumigated areas such as the Ebro River Delta to kill off an infestation of insects, even the butterflies ended up suffering. The destruction of harmful and beneficial insects alters the balance of nature, and anyone who has an organic garden must keep in mind that if the garden is near large farms or even pine forests that suffer from processionary moths, it's very likely that large-scale fumigations affect all the insects in the area.

We propose an alternative idea that can be beneficial for all: the creation of an

island of beneficial insects, where they can safely take shelter and reproduce.

The beneficials

Beneficial insects are the predatory ones, that is, those that eat other insects. Among them, a standout is the hoverfly, those flies with yellow and black stripes on the abdomen that hover around flowers. Their larvae are big consumers of aphids.

Ladybugs are efficient predators; the two-spotted ones hunt in trees and the seven-spotted ones do so in the lower vegetation, and thus are the ones we see more frequently.

Some species of bedbugs are also beneficial because they capture and kill harmful insects such as red spiders and some butterfly eggs, which hatch into leaf-devouring larvae. Lacewings, with their four transparent wings, are big aphid and mite hunters. Hunting wasps—not all of them sting!—are also useful for plants. Finally, there are the parasitic insects that live inside other insects, such as some worms that—and this is not safe for kids—eat away at their victim but leave the nervous system intact so that it lives to the last moment.

Good plants

These useful insects will look for food and protection in the plants you have put in your garden. As for food, it could come from the sap or molasses of some plants, and for protection, hollow stems can work well, from species such as blackberry, elder, raspberry, or reeds. Wasps engineer those clever hanging houses that cause us so much panic, and will sometimes make them in tubes or even in the keyhole of seldom used doors. The plants that we are going to propose have diverse functions, as nectariferous plants or as refuges for the insects, but they are also decorative and can be wind blocks for us.

Plants don't just serve to attract beneficial insects, but they also repel harmful ones or serve for hanging traps. For example, **garden nasturtium** is used at the base of fruit trees to fight aphids; **cabbage, turnips, and radishes between tomatoes** repel various beetles; **hemp and rosemary** scare off cabbage moths; **Jimson weed** repels moles and **elder branches** stuck in the ground will scare them off; and **parsley** at the foot of rose bushes eliminates green aphids.

Juniper has many uses, since it protects beneficial ladybugs and gives us gin, and is an excellent wood for making kitchen utensils or pipes.

The disappearance of insects is not only due to the use of insecticides: it is largely due to the removal of the vegetation that allows them to survive. A controversy erupted in northern France because of the disappearance of numerous species of birds. **The cause of the disaster was due to the liquidation of the bocage,** which is an agricultural system of small fields separated by strips of vegetation covering the slopes on uneven terrain or separating the plots of different land owners. In these green lines, which when seen from above give the landscape the appearance of a chessboard, some farmers planted fruit trees and medicinal and aromatic plants, particularly in Mediterranean areas. Others simply let the weeds and brambles take over and burned them off every year. Still others grew the trees and shrubs that birds and beneficial insects need to live. Modern agriculture, based above all on performance, and the use of large machines, required the removal of these margins, and the leveling and transformation of the fields in large desolate expanse. This open field system facilitates farming but removes vegetation and the associated wildlife that lives on the margins.

Beneficial plants

Most plants that are mentioned in this paragraph can be found in large nurseries or sold in catalogs, but for small plants, I would just get a good guide and go look for them in the forest. We can always transplant some. Sometimes it is also good to just observe. Maybe the area in which you live has some plants that are especially attractive to certain insects, like some big thistles that attract many beneficial insects.

Wormwood

(*Artemisia absinthium*, above) This is a tall plant, with silky, silvery leaves, with small buds. Artemisia comes from the fierce Greek goddess of the hunt, and *absinthium* for its active component, absinthe. Prohibited in some countries for its toxicity, it grows in dry, sandy soils, in hot climates. It attracts hoverflies and, because of its bad odor, it is sliced and used to repel harmful insects such as moths.

Goldenrod

(*Solidago virga-aurea*) This is valuable for its melliferous

quality, because it attracts insects, and is used as a diuretic.

Umbelliferae

These are among the most appetizing for insects. The best are angelica (*Angelica archangelica*) (photo below), *Heracleum Giganteum* from Caucasus, more than two meters tall, and dill (*Anethum graveolens*).

Elder

(*Sambucus nigra*) A good-sized bush that produces edible black berries. Helps with the decomposition of compost and allows useful insects to live inside it, due to its soft pith. Inside

its branches live beneficial wasps, which flourished in the area around Paris after these trees were planted by French gardeners for this very purpose. It is part of the family of pithy bushes that give shelter to rubicola insects, from *rubus*, the family of plants that includes blackberries.

Pastinaca or parsnip

(*Pastinaca sativa*) It is cultivated for its root, and attracts useful insects. For this purpose, it is planted frequently in Russia.

Ivy

(*Hedera helix*) This is well known for its climbing ability, although many people try to get rid of it because it holds moisture in the walls and soil. Precisely because of this, it supports a lot of useful insects. It should be planted on north-facing walls.

Phacelia

(*Phacelia tanacetifolia*) Nourishes bees if you plant it throughout the garden. Other melliferous plants are buckwheat, mustard, honeysuckle, sweet clover, heliotropes, and wild thyme.

Juniper

(*Juniperus communis*) This is a small, perennial tree that supports ladybugs. Its berries are used to make gin.

Cherry laurel

(*Prunus laurocerasus*) This is a small tree whose stems are rich in sap which nourishes insects.

Marigold or calendula (*Calendula officinalis*).

Animals and hedgerows

If you have a garden near a forest, you will certainly have unexpected visitors, in the worst-case scenario, wild boars. In this case, the only way to protect your garden is by fencing it in. But if you want to attract your friends—insects such as dragonflies, and insectivorous birds such as swallows, robins, goldfinches, finches, blackbirds, thrushes, or nightingales—you will have to make a hedgerow to shelter them, whether you are near a forest or not. Although it's true that swallows and bee eaters perch on telephone wires, the majority prefer a good shelter in a hedgerow, made up of box-wood, holly, yew, tamarind, or hazelnuts, depending on how much space you have.

Wooden nest box, which is easy to obtain or even make, and will attract beneficial species to your garden.

Gardeners advise these clean techniques to get rid of weeds:

- **Pull the weeds,** stolons, bulbs, and rhizomes, digging up the soil before beginning.

- On the ground where you are not going to plant crops, **place a weed barrier**, nailed down, and put a layer of gravel or pine chips over the top.

- **Plant a cover crop** that prevents the germination of seeds in areas you are not planting.

- **Don't water bare ground**, to prevent weeds from growing.

- **Mulch around the plants**: this can be done with chipped, pruned branches; pine bark; dry leaves or grass clippings; peat or compost; or straw or rubber mats. You can decide for yourself which is most ecological.

Toads and frogs are insect-eaters. Don't disregard them, no matter how unattractive they may seem to you.

Prevent and fight

A garden in Asturias

The soil is clay and the climate is very wet. To improve the soil, they add ripe manure, which is called *cucho*, to make the soil spongier and keep it from compacting too much. To fight acidity, they add lime each year, and to ensure the peas have enough potassium, they add ash from wood fires.

Plagues, the prevention

Begin by choosing the best plants. You can start with your own seeds, but in many cases you will buy them in a nursery or market from other farmer. Don't buy ten tomato plants to plant ten tomato plants; buy a few more and select the healthiest ones after planting them. If you plant one that appears sick, is yellowed, or has few roots, you will most likely have to replace it.

Select the species

Think about the climate and soil in your garden. It's not the same to have a garden in one region of the country as it is in another, or in a tropical country. Peaches, cabbages, and onions need cold; tomatoes need heat. If your garden is at a high elevation, the growing cycle will be shorter and later. Potatoes will flower later. There are some species of tomatoes that grow well at 1500 meters above sea level in the Pyrenees. In this case, it's best to buy your seedlings in a local nursery or market, or grow your own from the first and best specimens of the previous year. If you buy seeds in a different city, do your research. Another important question is the soil in your garden. If it is well conditioned, you can plant anything, but if it is new land, you will have to factor in the acidity and salinity, as well as the consistency. Peanuts require very loose soil, and chickpeas don't care as much. Root plants also need loose soil to grow well. Salinity may be caused by excessive watering or being close to the coast. Look at the tables included in the chapter on soil to see how well different plants resist acidity.

Condition the soil properly, as we explained in the section on soil, with the pH within a healthy range and the necessary drainage. Avoid contaminated soil. You can also disinfect it via solarization with a layer of coconut fiber.

Don't forget about rotation

To avoid wearing out the soil, you know that you can't plant chard in the same place for at least two years. Keep in mind that every garden has areas with better sun or more wind, and this depends on the trees, walls, or buildings that are around it. There are species that don't tolerate wind and need to be sheltered. Try to give the tomatoes full sun. Green beans don't need as much light, although they still need some. Cucumbers and squash wrinkle with too much heat and are fine if they get shade in the mid-afternoon. Your own experience will teach you the assets of your garden. Try to space out the plants and form combinations that will help each other mutually.

Biologic warfare

Biological plague control consists of the use of the natural enemies of the infestations to finish them off. The use of chemical products such as pesticides, herbicides, and fungicides is prohibited. The pollution they cause is well known, as well as the appearance of resistant species and the harm to human health caused by the consumption of chemically treated foods.

Biologic warfare that is practiced in greenhouses or large plantations follows these steps:

- Identify the attacking species.
- Figure out what its natural enemy is.
- Quantify the damage caused or calculate the population of the attackers.
- Calculate how many specimens of the natural enemy you will need.
- Obtain the natural enemy and encourage it to intervene.
- Test the effectiveness of the method, without losing sight of which is the attacker and the attackee.

These methods are not as fast as chemical products, and require more hours of work. The use of natural enemies is also delicate.

In our small garden, we don't have the luxury of these methods, although it's not a bad idea to learn about them. Ours will be a team fight. We will plant the proper plants, use our hands, and water the plants with mixtures that you will see shortly. This is the time to meet the enemy.

Surround the garden with aromatic plants, such as lavender, rosemary, salvia, and thyme, which help to avoid insect invasions and can always be used to make soup or tea.

Bad company

The majority of these **unwelcome visitors** are found habitually in any garden, although you shouldn't consider them invincible or too destructive if you give them proper attention.

Birds

At one time, sparrows and corvids were considered plagues, since they descended upon recently sown fields of grain in vast flocks and devastated the fields. They can be fought off with scarecrows, nets, shiny paper, plastics, or CDs that are hung to move in the wind.

Cats vs. Dogs

Depends on how they are trained. **Both dig, urinate, and defecate.** Cats are more predictable: they like to roll around in freshly dug earth, in which they also do their business, digging up and disturbing the seeds. If they are young, they will play among the lettuce, cabbages, and seedlings, breaking anything in their path. But they also protect the garden from birds and moles. You must evaluate the pros and cons, but in general, cats are not your enemy. There's also not much you can do, since as soon as you are not looking, they will go back to what they were doing. However, some people recommend transparent water bottles, since the reflections of the sun seem to scare them off. Dogs are more particular, since there are many different breeds and characteristics. **In general, small dogs are as annoying as cats and barely scare the birds.** Big dogs might squash plants, but you can train them not to go certain places or dig, and that is enough. You can also give them a sandpile for them to do their business, and teach them to do it there.

Rabbits and mice

- If you have your garden near a forest, you will be visited by rabbits that eat carrots and all sorts of green plants if you don't put a three-foot fence around your garden. Since cats eat the baby rabbits, they are effective for controlling the rabbit population.
- Mice are easily combated with a cat or with traps (do as you like, but we don't endorse kill traps).

Moles

If you have moles in the garden that dig up your fields, feed a cat. Felines are very patient. They like to sit and wait for hours for a mole to appear that they can hunt and play with. Remember that jimson weed also repels them, and if you pierce their tunnels with elder sticks, they will leave your dominion. Some use traps, ingeniously engineered from wire, at the entrances to their tunnels, or hang balls with camphor to scare them off. Voles, which are smaller, feed on bulbs and roots. Place camphor or mothballs in their tunnels. Ultrasounds also work, and they sell traps that don't harm them. Moles are more abundant in wet years, since very dry earth is difficult to tunnel in.

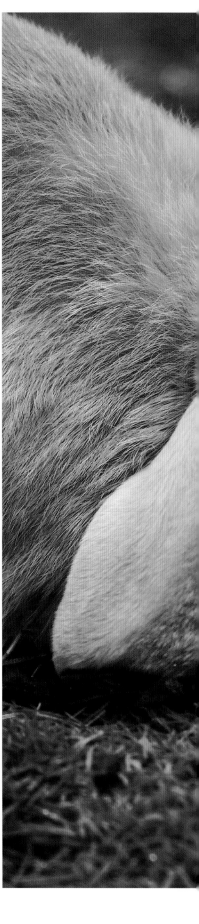

Snails and slugs

Both flourish in wet areas. In rainy years, they are a good food source. All you have to do is get up early and collect them before they eat the tender leaves of newly sprouted plants.

When there begins to be too many, you will have to resort to other methods. Among the ecological options are:

● Place bricks or up-side-down containers to give the snails and slugs a place to hide from the sun. If you also include orange peels, it will be easier to catch them in the morning.

● Place a plate or tray, filled with beer up to the rim, so that the snails climb in and drown. Some people attract them with lettuce leaves or slices of potato.

● Scatter shavings or ashes around the plants so that the snails don't pass over them. When they get wet, you have to replace them.

● A cruel method consists of breaking up eggshells and sprinkling them around plants. They catch the slugs and snails and they die.

● Snails also have predators—toads, ducks, geese, and hedgehogs—which can be your good friends in this sense.

As a method of prevention, only work the soil superficially, since slugs take shelter in deep soil; don't spread out compost but mound it, and don't leave the soil in clumps since they also like that. In winter, you must dig up the eggs so that they freeze.

On the other hand, some species of slugs are useful for the decomposition of vegetable scraps.

Ants

The ant should not be the enemy of the organic gardener. In fact, lately they are in decline, as if they were one of the insects harmed by mass fumigation or climate change. However, ants bother us because they favor aphids. They carry them up the shoots and collect the nectar that they secrete. They are often found on rose bushes.

They also gnaw away at recently sprouted plants and steal small seeds. It is not surprising that the carrots disappear before sprouting. Ants are, in general, beneficial, since they attack the caterpillars in trees. But if you don't want them to get out of hand, you can make a funnel from paper and fasten it around the tree. The ants, while ascending, will have to go down and this will throw them off. If you also place cotton balls with a sticky substance, you will end their plans.

Other possible systems are: put salt in their path, put soapy water at the entrance of their holes, spray a nicotine solution (not recommended anymore), trap them with honey or sponges soaked in sugar water, or use lemon juice, which they don't like.

It is also common to lime the trees, grease them, put a circle of cotton strung on a wire, or put sulfur around the base.

Finally, it is possible to plant a series of plants that repel them, such as lavender, mint, thyme, marjoram, marigolds, etc. And in the garden, they also dislike lettuce, so look for similar plants.

Worms

There are many types: the click beetle worm (Agriotes lineatus), and white worms (Anoxia villosa) are found by digging up the soil with a knife to find the damage to roots. Cutworms (Agrotis segetum) eat the base of the stems.

- Click beetle worms are attracted by fresh manure and can be trapped by burying slices of carrot or potato. Once captured, cut them in half.
- Cutworms attack the stems and leaves of new plants. They are found by digging up around the plants that you find wilted each morning, or looking for them with a flashlight at night, although the best way to eliminate them is to dig them up in winter.
- White worms are the larvae of the violet carpenter bee, and they attack strawberries, lettuce, and artichokes. They should be fought by finding them in the soil or following the method described for cabbage moth caterpillars.

Above: the click beetle **worm** (*Agriotes lineatus*), fierce attacker of roots, is the larvae of this inoffensive-looking beetle.
Below: root of lettuce attacked by **nematodes**. In bio-gardening, it's common to plant certain species that repel them, such as *Targetes patula*, *Schkuhria seneciodes*, *Ambrosia trifidus*, and hybrids of helenium and gaillardia.

Nematodes

Nematodes are very small worms, less than 0.2 millimeters. They live underground and attack bulbs and roots, and the only way to discover them would be to send them to a laboratory. They like sandy soils, heat, and humidity.

The most common variety leaves small lumps on the roots that can be detected by pulling them up. The plant gets weak or wilts little by little. The fight against these worms is complicated, but in ecological agriculture you shouldn't bother with them too much. In any case, if you begin with a soil infested with nematodes, the best way to get rid of them is solarization.

Potato beetle

Mole cricket

They are 1.5 to 2 inches long and they cut the roots of plants when they are still young and tender. The name of the mole cricket comes from its digging legs, similar to those of moles, which feed on these insects.

You must defeat them by catching them, and the best way to do so is to bury empty pots level with the soil so that they fall in. Another system is to make holes and fill them with manure in winter to trap them little by little.

In summer, they can be discovered when you dig up the earth and find the tunnels they make as they go along. You can flood the tunnels, or poison them with rotenone. Some people place a mixture of two tablespoons of coffee, a few oleander leaves, and a few cigarette butts diluted in water at the entrance of the tunnels.

The best way to get rid of beetles is by picking them off one by one by hand, but not everyone has time for this, and it's not reasonable if you have a lot of land. Chamomile planted between the potatoes will repel the potato bug and it is a lot less work.

Its origin is in the United States, to the east of the Rockies, where two centuries ago they devoured all kinds of thistle and barely bothered the potatoes that grew wild in the mountains. Once the extensive cultivation of potatoes with inorganic fertilizers began, the beetles began to attack them. But the real problem began when, in the mid-nineteenth century, North American farmers began to spray the potatoes with lead arsenate, the first known broad spectrum insecticide.

Instead of eliminating the beetles, it made them stronger and eliminated the rest of the fauna, among them, another predator beetle, and bees and birds that fed on them. In the mid-twentieth century, the potato bug was already a worldwide plague. Today, the only biological way to fight them is picking them by hand or planting chamomile.

In the search for a biological remedy that can be sprayed on the fields, they are studying species such as *Bacillus Thuringiensis*, of the subspecies Thenebrionis, which has proven effective in the control of the beetle, but with the danger that resistant larvae will emerge, making the cure worse than the disease.

At the time this book was written, they were attempting to isolate the toxin that this bacillus contains that kills the beetle larvae, to incorporate it in the genetic fabric of the potatoes, and create a dangerous genetically modified product with toxins incorporated.

Aphids

This is one of the most common plagues. There are many varieties and they attack almost all plants. Plant louse, as they are also called, can be seen with the naked eye, because the leaves of the plant appear curled up, or from the yellow stains that their bites leave. The black aphid is accompanied by ants that graze on it, collecting drops of honeydew that the aphids excrete, formed from the sap that they suck from the leaves.

The apparition of the insect

Aphids are born fully formed, since they are viviparous. The females may have wings and are the ones that spread to other plants. They can transmit diseases if they bite a sick plant and then a healthy one. They are very adaptable and mutations can occur in a single season.

They often appear due to a poor management of the garden. Above all, it is a surprise if they go a week or two without showing up. When you fertilize too much or add nitrogen to the soil, it increases the sugars in the sap and the plant oozes or bleeds, attracting aphids, which will reproduce quickly.

The remedy

● **First of all**, keep the garden clean between the plants. When there are weeds, they propagate. As soon as the aphids appear, you must remove the affected leaves. Gardeners suggest using a toothbrush on plants with flowers to clean them.

● **You must attract the natural enemies** of the aphids: ladybugs and wasps, or parasitic wasps that increase vegetable diversity. Earwigs are a natural enemy that you can help with a few tricks (see the section on earwigs).

Signs of the presence of aphids

● **They are visible to the eye.**

● **The leaves curl at the tips.**

● **Yellowish bite marks appear on the leaves.**

● **Sooty mold, a fungus, appears, which can be fought with copper oxychloride.**

Rose bushes can be attacked by green or yellow aphids. If you don't want to get rid of them by shaking the leaves, you can use a solution of pyrethrin every fifteen days, a natural insecticide obtained from the chrysanthemum flower.

Natural enemies of aphids

In the biologic warfare that greenhouses use to fight aphids, you will find two parasitic wasps (*Aphidius ervi and Aphidius abdominalis*), **a midge larvae** (*aphidoletes aphidimyza*), **and a lacewing** (*Chrysoperia carnea*). The **wasps** lay eggs inside the aphids and the larvae eat them from inside. The **midge** lay eggs nearby, and when they hatch, the larvae crawl toward the aphids and empty them by suction, as do the lacewing larvae. To get an idea of how these battles work, let's look at the case of the **lacewing**. The grower can buy a few boxes that have a hundred eggs each and hang them over the affected plants. They can also be purchased in the form of larvae mixed with rice hulls, and you just have to sprinkle them around.

- **Also to prevent them,** you should avoid excessive fertilizer, sow at the right time, and water when needed, to prevent the plants from oozing, which attracts them.
- **Spray slightly soapy or warm water over the leaves,** with some pressure from a hose to wash them off.
- **Use an infusion based on nettles.**
- **In trees,** it's enough to just hang some sticky tapes to trap them.
- **You must control the ants,** since if there are too many they will protect the aphids that give them honeydew.
- **Concoctions of wormwood,** walnut leaves, tomato sprouts, or garlic are preventative treatments.
- Curiously, **a light sprinkling of very fine dust** will finish them off, since it dehydrates them. And in this vein, some gardeners lay aluminum foil around the plants so that the heat dries them out, although be careful since this can damage the leaves as well.
- **The use of natural insecticides** like rotenone or pyrethrin in late afternoon will help.

The Wooly Aphid
(*Eriosoma lanigerum*)

White in color, it attacks fruit trees and appears in groups on the trunks, branches, and twigs; can be combated with a few dabs of alcohol. It is also effective to mist the trees with nasturtium extract. A sprinkling of lithothamnium will dehydrate the aphids.

- Sodium silicate three times a year will successfully fight off aphids in fruit trees:
  - In winter: a 3 percent solution.
  - Before the buds sprout: 2 percent solution.
  - On the leaves: a 1 percent solution.

Of course, the water that you use in all these preparations, if it is possible, should be rainwater or spring water. This will double the benefits of the preparations.

Types of aphids

The most common are **green aphids**, which on artichokes are *Brachycaudus cardui*; on peas, *Acyrthosiphon pisum*; and on green beans *Cerosipha forbesi*; **gray aphids**, *Brevicoryne brassicae*, on cabbages; **black aphids**, *Aphis fabae,* on fava beans, and many others, such as the black aphid on peaches, *Brachycaudus persicae*.

Flea beetles

Flea beetles are coleopterans between 2 and 3 millimeters in size, that lay eggs on the stems of plants, and whose larvae feed on the roots. They attack potatoes, cabbages, parsnips, beets, and artichokes. They can be fought with soapy water, aromatic plants, tomato plants, and straw laid out in fall to catch them in winter.

Red Spider Mites

These are very small mites of two kinds, *Tetranychus telarius* and *Tetranychus urticae*, which have two spots. They vary in color from red to yellow. They have four legs in the nymph stage, when they attack all kinds of plants: green beans, cucumbers, peas, squash, tomatoes, apples, and strawberries. They plant themselves in the underside of leaves and suck the sap from the plant. They are resistant and easily mutate to adapt to attack.

They can be detected by the blotches that appear on leaves, and you can even see the spider webs around the leaves.

Soapy water, prepared with a little dish detergent, should be used with caution, as it can affect the leaves' stomata.

The easiest way to fight them is by keeping the plants moist, since they love dryness, so with plants that will tolerate it, mist the leaves.

It is important to prevent mites by keeping the soil clean of weeds and making precise rotations. Excess fertilizer will encourage them.

They are repelled by onion skins scattered between the plants, and to mist the leaves you can use infusions of horsetail, nettles, or wormwood, and if they resist, pyrethrin or rotenone.

The natural enemies used to fight red spider mites are three predatory mites, used in greenhouses.

Caterpillars

There are many types of caterpillars that can attack the garden. The cabbage worm (*Pieris brassicae* or rapae) is the biggest threat, although the Beet Armyworm (*Spodoptera exigua*) and others, like the carnation tortrix caterpillar or the geranium butterfly, attack flowers in gardens.

Caterpillars are from the Lepidoptera order; that is, they become butterflies after metamorphosis. Female butterflies lay eggs on the undersides of leaves. The larvae that hatch begin to eat the leaves until, after 15 to 30 days, they descend to the ground, bury themselves, and become pupae. They attack peppers, watermelons, melons, tomatoes, potatoes, cabbages, etc.

The way to combat them is to look for the eggs and squash them with your fingers from April to June. You can also use pyrethrin or rotenone.

Above, the cabbage worm, which produces the moth in the photo above, is easy to identify because they appear in groups when the caterpillars attack the garden.

African Cotton Leafworm

This is a garden pest. They are **caterpillars that gnaw the undersides of leaves**, where the leaf is more tender. They can be eliminated by picking them by hand, or with pyrethrin.

When caterpillars attack

An infestation of caterpillars is one of the worst dangers that a bio gardener can encounter. Their activity is lethal, since an infestation of larvae can decimate a plant in a single night.

Preventative treatments do not always work, so you must pay careful attention, and as soon as you see the first leaf devoured (in some cases, only the veins remain), you must eliminate them.

If the infestation is minor, you can do this manually; if it is massive, you will have to resort to specific products.

On the other hand, not all caterpillars are harmful. Some of them have a very short life cycle and turn into butterflies rapidly, so their impact is minimal and easily controlled.

Whiteflies

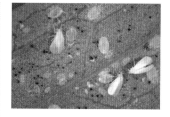

There are various types, although the most common are *Trialeurodes vaporarium*, which occurs in greenhouses and attacks tomatoes, peppers, cucumbers, and green beans. *Aleyrodes proletella*, or the cabbage whitefly, is easy to see because you just have to shake the leaves to observe them all stirred up. They form colonies and are only dangerous when there are a lot of them, since they feed on leaves and their sticky excrement causes fungus such as sooty mold, which is cured with copper.

It seems to be enough to simply maintain a balanced soil in order to prevent them. In any case, the use of soapy water will take care of them. They have three natural enemies: two parasitic wasps and a predatory bedbug. Some plants will repel them, such as Chinese carnations or marigolds. In greenhouses, they hang yellow sticky traps, since the color attracts them; it also works if you place yellow bottles between the plants.

Greenhouses also suffer from attacks from onion flies, cherry flies, and carrot flies, which can be biologically controlled with rotenone.

Mealybugs

Mealybugs are distinguished by their protective shield, a sort of shell that protects them when they stick on a plant. The main problem is not that they suck the sap out, but that they produce a honeydew that causes sooty mold. There are many varieties, of which there are many lice among them. However, it is a pest that affects decorative gardens more than vegetable gardens. The shell makes it resistant to many ecological remedies: spray the plant with warm soapy water and a tablespoon of alcohol per liter of water. After 15 minutes, wash the plant. However, these have so many natural enemies, they are not likely to invade your garden.

Weevils

Like mealybugs, they are not frequent visitors to your garden. Nevertheless, they can attack strawberries, and they will damage rhododendrons, hydrangeas, camellias, fuchsias, begonias, cyclamens, primrose, vineyards, and corn, for example.

The most ecological way to get rid of them is to catch the adults at night with a flashlight as they chow down on leaves. You can also let hens eat the larvae from the soil in winter, or place a net under the tree and shake them out.

These are dark-colored beetles that lay eggs in the spring and summer. In the fall, white larvae hatch that feed on the leaves and stems, like leafminers, and then later move underground and feed on roots.

Turnip beetles

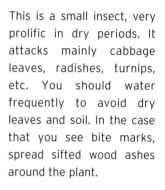

This is a small insect, very prolific in dry periods. It attacks mainly cabbage leaves, radishes, turnips, etc. You should water frequently to avoid dry leaves and soil. In the case that you see bite marks, spread sifted wood ashes around the plant.

Between suckers and chewers

Among the different pests, you must distinguish between **the sucking insects**, such as aphids, mealybugs, spider mites, green flies, and thrips, and **the chewers**, which consist mainly of caterpillars and larvae, snails and slugs, worms, leaf worms, and leafminers.

The fruitfly

This insect (*Ceratitis capitata*) is one of the worst enemies of any gardener who wants to have fruit trees, especially peach trees, although they also attack trees bearing pears, plums, apples, and other fruit trees. The fly lays eggs inside the fruit. **The larvae rot the fruit quickly, causing it to fall to the ground, where they crawl out and go underground, waiting to become a fly that will once again attack the fruit.** This cycle repeats five or six times a year. The only ecological way to fight them is by keeping hens, which eat the larvae, or using pheromones.

Thrips

These are very small insects, between 0.8 and 3 millimeters long, that come in various colors and look like miniature earwigs. There are various types and they are found in flowers. *Kakothrips pisivorous* attacks legumes, *Thrips palmi* attacks cucurbitaceae, *Frankliniella occidentalis* transmits a virus, and there are others that attack ornamental plants, tobacco, olives, citrus fruits, etc. Thrips reproduce by eggs and both larvae and adults feed on sap, leaving characteristic white marks on the leaves. The flowers won't open and the leaves will become deformed and fall off. Their presence can be detected by tapping a flower on your palm and letting them fall into your hand. They like dryness and heat, and can be fought with moisture. Avoid weeds and use blue adhesive traps at the height of the plant. The ecological insecticide recommended against thrips is pyrethrin or pellitory. Biologic warfare in greenhouses is done with predatory mites that are sold in plastic bottles with bran to keep them alive.

Leafminers

Leafminers (*Phyllocnistis citrella*) are lepidopteras, meaning that tiny butterflies lay eggs on the tender leaves and stems. The larvae feed on the leaf tissues, excavating tunnels in the interior. Only the dry cuticle remains, making the leaf wrinkle and curl. Heat stimulates them. Leafminers generally don't affect fruit trees too much; although there are other miners of the genus Liriomyza, that attack lettuce, for example, but generally they are only a danger for decorative gardens. They can be fought with pyrethrin, but since they live inside the leaves it is difficult to reach them. The best method is to pick off the larvae by hand. In biologic warfare, they use three parasitic wasps of the genuses *Dacnusa*, *Opius*, and *Diglyphus*.

Earwigs

Earwigs are beneficial to the garden because they eat aphids, but sometimes they build nests in fruit trees or in corners of dry wood and become a real nightmare. To capture them, use flower pots full of straw turned upside down on sticks, or roll corrugated cardboard around a stick at the same height as the plant.

Leafhoppers

Typhlocyba rosae, also known as leafhoppers, are small insects of about 3 millimeters that live on the undersides of leaves and suck the sap. The leaves will progressively become discolored. They are combated in the same way as aphids.

Control insects with aromatic plants

- **Basil** wards off flies and mosquitoes. It is good to put it next to tomatoes, and inside the house you must keep it in a well ventilated place with plenty of light.

- **Borage** attracts bees.

- **Chives** scare off aphids.

- **Dill and fennel** attract beneficial insects with their strong odor.

- **Lavender** repels ants. Especially when prepared as an infusion.

- **Mint** repels aphids and other insects. Don't hesitate to use it, even in an infusion.

- The variety of mint known as **pennyroyal**, and **rosemary**, are used in wardrobes in the house against fleas and ants.

- **Rue**, when crushed in water with a little **salvia**, is also a strong insect repellent.

- Don't forget **thyme**, which attracts bees and repels aphids and cabbage moths.

Diseases

Squashes, as well as pumpkins, cucumbers, and melons, are attacked by powdery mildew from the Cucurbitaceae, which manifests in the form of powdery white splotches on both sides of the leaves, which end up drying out.

Insects are not the only enemies of the plants. There are other smaller ones that require different attention. Bacteria, fungi, and viruses are waiting for their opportunity to attack your garden. Let's meet them and learn how to defeat them.

Powdery mildew

This is a series of fungi that are very easy to diagnose. It is also called white mildew, or white powdery mildew, because it takes the form of a white or ashy powder that appears on the leaves, stems, and fruits. It makes the leaves and stems yellow. The fungi spores are distributed by wind and when they fall on a stem or leaf, they root themselves. Once they have grown, they stay where they are rooted. This develops during wet springs and dies off with heat

and dryness. It attacks all Cucurbitaceae, and in the flower garden, rose bushes, geraniums, laurel, oaks, begonias, bananas, etc.

Fight back by eliminating weeds from the garden, to prevent trapped moisture. It's best not to wet the plants if the mildew is growing, and as soon as you notice it you must pick off the affected area, or pull the whole plant if necessary. Be careful not to spread the fungus all around when you do so.

Mildew

This is a fungus (*Phytophthora infestans*) that appears with moisture and is detected because it first attacks the edges of leaves with yellow blotches, which then extend to the rest of the leaves. These appear brownish and grey mold appears on the underside of the leaves. It also attacks the stems and fruits, and it's not unusual to find it on potatoes or tomatoes that seem to rot before ripening.

It's also known for attacking grapevines and rose bushes. It only develops when it is hot and the plants are wet for several hours at a time.

It is fought by keeping the crops clean with freely circulating air. Once it appears, you can fumigate with Bordeaux mix (contains copper sulfate) or with horsetail, although the idea would be to do it before the disease appears. When it is hot, you can sprinkle sulfur over the plant.

Bacteria

These are not that common, and tend to affect decorative plants more, but they can also affect green beans, tomatoes, and peas. The symptoms are ulcers that can appear up and down the stem and round stains on the fruits. In tomatoes, black splotches will appear on the leaves, stems, and fruits, although they are very small. The bacteria of mange or scabies will also cause black marks and can even produce large pustules in the fruit. And finally, there are the soft, watery rotten spots on tomatoes that give off a bad odor. In any case, if you start with healthy plants and select the best seeds, you won't have problems with this.

Treatment with copper oxychloride works well.

Virus

Viruses that attack plants are transmitted mainly by aphids, but also by whiteflies, leafhoppers, thrips, or nematodes.

The main characteristic of a virus is its resistance and mutability. There is no way to eliminate them with chemical products and attempting to will cause them to mutate. There can be a million symptoms—dwarfed plants, mosaics, yellowish splotches, or tumors on the leaves. The only way to fight them is by eliminating the sick plants, keeping the garden free of weeds, choosing resistant varieties, or

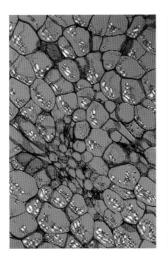

Top: *Phytophthora infestans,* magnified by one hundred. (Photo by Gary Gaugler)
Bottom: A field of potatoes attacked by mildew.

The tomato virus

This Solanaceae is often victim to a number of viruses: for example, **the tomato spotted wilt virus**, which produces dwarfism, discoloration, deformation, and necrosis; **tomato mosaic virus**, which forms a mosaic of green shades on the leaves; **cucumber mosaic virus**, which also attacks Cucurbitaceae, producing light green splotches on the leaves; **yellow leaf curl** virus, which stunts the growth of the plant and produces small fruits; **potato virus**, which also causes green mosaics in the underside of the leaves; and **the tomato bushy stunt virus**, which appears on the stems and extends to the leaves, turning them purple and necrotizing the fruits.

eliminating the carriers, aphids.

You can keep viruses at bay by spraying essences of aromatic plants like lavender, thyme, or rosemary.

Fungi

Fungi attack plants in many different forms: some rot them, others secrete toxins that kill them, and others block light. Ahead, we will take a look at the most common ones.

The mosaics are named for the appearance of the leaves, which take on a colored mosaic of shades of green. Most of the time this is produced by some kind of virus.

White rot

This is produced by the fungus *Sclerotinia sclerotiorum*. It is detected because it forms a white mycelium around the affected parts, which looks like cotton wrapped around the stem of the plant. It is caused by excess moisture and can be controlled by keeping the garden free of weeds and eliminating affected plants.

Botrytis or grey mold

This is caused by the fungus *Botrytis cinerea*. Botrytis starts to produce brownish lesions, then soft rot in the tissues of the plant. It is found in tomatoes when you cut them open and find the grey mycelium of the fungus.

Like the previous one, it is caused by excess moisture and is controlled the same way. It affects plants after they have been damaged by hail or chewed by insects. Therefore, one way to prevent it is to avoid harming the fruits while trimming or harvesting, when you might accidentally scratch the stems. And avoid planting the same species in the same place.

Finally, you can water with nettle broth or wormwood broth.

Sooty mold

This is the fungus that appears on the honeydew that aphids, whiteflies, and wooly aphids excrete. It is named this because it looks like a black powder that weakens the leaves, mainly because it blocks the sun from reaching them. Sooty mold is controlled by eliminating the pests that cause it. Once it appears, mist the plants with soapy water. Some eliminate it from peach trees by planting garlic under the trees.

Alternaria

Alternaria is a fungus from the genus Alternaria, whose presence is announced by spores visible on the affected tissue.

It typically appears on the ground, on dead vegetable material, and in wet spells

Alternaria attacks plants from the soil and spreads on potatoes and tomatoes during wet spells.

can spread rapidly to the plant, which necrotizes and dies in a few days from a toxin excreted by the spores. There are many varieties adapted to different plants or trees that they attack, for example, *Alternaria solani* attacks solanaceae and feeds on the tomato (alternariosis), forming elongated marks and concentric circles on the stems and stalks. It is controlled by keeping the garden clean and preventing excess moisture.

Rust

Rust is a fungus whose symptoms are orangish pustules on the undersides of the leaves and stems. It only appears in cases of extremely moist climates. It is controlled by pulling affected leaves and fumigating with copper, as well as following all the steps already mentioned for preventing moisture, like eliminating weeds and avoiding dense foliage.

Diseases produced by fungi are usually caused by excess moisture, which you can reduce by clearing the mulch and layer of dry plants from the soil.

Anthracnose

It is caused by fungi of the genus *Colletotrichum* and *Glomerella*. The symptoms are well defined brown halos appearing on the leaves, sometimes concentrically like burns. To combat it you must remove the affected leaves and burn them or take them directly to the trash. Otherwise, the spores will return to attack the plant.

Verticillium and *Fusarium*

These "wilting" fungi can be detected when the upper leaves of the plant droop and the lower leaves start to yellow. To avoid infecting nearby crops, remove and burn the diseased plants. Do not add diseased plants to your compost. (Solanaceous plants like tomatoes and potatoes are especially susceptible.)

Blight

What we call blight in potatoes and tomatoes (*Phytophthora infestans*) is also known as potato, eggplant, or tomato smut. That of rose bushes (*Peronospora sparsa*) produces brown spots on the leaves, and corn smut (*Ustilago zeae*) blackens the corn cobs.

Tomato blight is detected, for example, by watery spots on leaves and fruits. It is caused by moisture and can be fought with bicarbonate.

Root rot

There are many fungi that can rot the roots. **Among them are those of the genus *Fusarium*, *Rhizoctonia*, and *Phytophthora*** (image). They are detected because the leaves dry and turn brown. The remedy is in its cause: waterlogged roots by overwatering or in case of rain, poor drainage.

Sunburn

Tomatoes are one of the plants that suffer the most diseases, and also sunburn on the worst summer days, appearing as whitish stains on the skin.

Scarred fruit

These occur when the plant has plenty of water some days and not enough on other days. Cracks appear near the stem.

Rot due to lack of calcium

This occurs at the base of the plant and is not caused by a fungus. It is offset by adding calcium chelates.

Gallery of grievances

After briefly viewing all the enemies of the garden, we classify them with a good science textbook in hand. Let's see the result:

- **Vertebrates**: mammals and birds. Among the former are wild boars, dogs, cats, hedgehogs, rabbits, rats, and mice. Among the latter are all grain-eating birds, although some have a special hatred of corvids, which are not easily fooled by a scarecrow.

- **Arthropods**: insects, arachnids, and crustaceans. Among the former are ants and aphids, among the second group are mites, and among the latter, mealybugs.

- **Mollusks**: snails and slugs.

- **Worms**: white worms, cutworms, and nematodes.

- **Fungi, bacteria, and viruses**: they are numerous, and the smaller they are, the more adapted to the species that they attack.

Keep in mind also that these are not the only enemies we have in the garden, and nature also has something to say, regardless conditions like the following:

- **Lack of light**
- **Sunburn**
- **Excessive heat or cold**
- **Hail**
- **Excess water**
- **Wind**
- **Acidity or alkalinity of the soil**
- **Lack or excess nutrients**

Natural remedies

Running water, especially if it is from a spring, is a good remedy against mites, spider mites, and thrips.

Natural remedies are those that make use of other plants or chemical substances that are accepted by ecological agriculture. We will also comment on more elaborate systems, such as color traps and pheromones.

Mineral oils

To prevent pests in fruit trees, mineral oils are often used in winter and summer. These oils are sold already prepared, they are derived from petroleum, and they are formed from saturated and unsaturated hydrocarbons. They are effective against insect infestations.

Their advantage is that they are cheap, nontoxic to humans, do not create resistance in the insects, and fight all the pests that hide in the trees, preventing them from proliferating. There are winter and summer mineral oils. The winter ones, which will have a milky appearance, are thicker and should be used diluted with water.

They are used when there is a stop in the vegetative cycle, that is, November to December, and you must be careful because they are phytotoxins, which can damage leaves of nearby plants. They fight aphids and spider mites. Paraffin oil should be diluted at a measure of 6 cc (the dose of an espresso is 20 cc) per 10 liters of water, and spray the plants with a sprayer. It should not be used on perennial plants, or at temperatures above 75°F.

Running water

Running water is a good remedy for mites, spider mites, and thrips, which like seasonal heat and dryness. It is enough to just wet the plants, being careful not to do so at the hottest part of the day. Another use for water is pressure washing the plants to get rid of aphids and other insects that are easy to wash off.

Bad company	Remedies
Alternaria	Cleaning soil and affected plants.
Anthracnose	Cleaning out affected plants, weeding, and bicarbonate.
Ants	Traps with sugar or honey in sponges, soapy water, salt on the paths, lemon juice, whitewashing trees, paper funnels, wormwood, pennyroyal, or tansy.
Aphids	Mineral oils, wormwood, garlic, horsetail, potash soap, pyrethrum, tomatoes, nasturtium, ferns, or color traps.
Blight	Sodium bicarbonate.
Botrytis	Potash soap, nettle, and wormwood broth.
Cabbage worms	Cleaning by hand, potash, salt water, pyrethrum, rotenone, neem oil, mint, sage, hyssop, salvia, or potash.
Cats	Fences and water bottles.
Dogs	Train it, establish a place for it to do its business.
Earwigs	Traps.
Fungus in seedbeds	Garlic and cinnamon to keep humidity low.
Mealybugs	Paraffin oil, vegetable oil, wormwood, alcohol, potash soap, and oregano.
Leafminers	By hand, pyrethrin.
Mice	Cats, traps, barriers (yellow melilot and houndstongue).
Mildew	Cleaning, Bordeaux mixture, horsetail, sulfur, or potash soap.
Mole crickets	Traps made from pots or holes with manure, flood tunnels, rotenone, or a blend of coffee, oleander, nicotine, and water.
Mole	Traps, thorn apple, elder, camphor, naphthalene, or ultrasound.
Nematodes	Solarization.
Powdery mildew	Cleaning, drying, sulfur, sodium bicarbonate, potash soap, garlic, or mustard.
Rabbits	Fences (a ring of onion repels them), cats, or traps. Red spider mites and other mites Spray with water, weeding, mineral oils, garlic, wormwood, sulfur, onion skins, soapy water, nettles, pyrethrum, or neem oil.
Snails and slugs	Beer, ashes, orange, or eggshell; avoid lumps.
Sooty mold	Remove pests that cause it, soapy water.
Thrips	Water, paraffin oil, wormwood, color traps, pyrethrum, or neem oil.
Whitefly	Potash, paraffin oil, wormwood, pyrethrum, neem oil, or color traps.
Worms	Solarization.

Although it may seem like a joke, it's not. There are very patient gardeners who entertain themselves by wetting wooly aphids with a Q-tip soaked in olive or sunflower oil.

Alcohol

Another remedy for patient people, to wet aphids with a cotton swab.

Aromatherapy

Natural essences of aromatic plants are useful against aphids, slugs, snails, and mice. Usually these are the same essences used in aromatherapy to cure illnesses in people, since they also reinforce the plants, just like the Bach essences and homeopathy applied to the soil. Of the essences, one teaspoon in a quart of water in the morning is enough.

Artemisia

This plant repels cabbage moths and fruit moths.

Bacillus thuringiensis

This is the only bacterium that is recommended by numerous guides on ecological horticulture. To obtain it, you will have to go to a specialty shop and it is not worthwhile for a small garden.

It has an advantage over the other natural insecticides we've mentioned that it is very specific, and only attacks the species that hosts it. For example, the *kurstaki* variety attacks *processionary* caterpillars, *irraelensis* attacks mosquito larvae, and *tenebrionis* attacks beetle larvae.

It is sold as a powder that contains spores along with the bacteria and the toxin it produces. To use it, follow the manufacturer's instructions.

Basil

Repels all kinds of insects. Some people keep it in the house to get rid of mosquitoes, and some plant it in the garden for aphids.

Top: Basil is a good insect repellant, and in fact, many people keep it in the house for mosquitoes.
Bottom: Garlic, aside from being a good insect repellant, also combats some diseases.

Beeswax

It's not actually the wax that interests us, but a substance that the bees secrete from mixing wax, pollen, and resin from different species, which is called propolis. With this, the bees seal the entrances to the hive and no insect, fungus, or bacteria can enter their domain, since it has insecticidal, fungicidal, and antibiotic properties. Some say it is even antiviral.

It is used in homeopathic doses for humans and the garden, although it is too valuable to waste on the fields.

Bordeaux mix

This is prepared by mixing 3 oz (100 g) of copper sulfate, 5 oz (15 g) of quicklime, and 2.5 gallons (10 liters) of water in a plastic bucket. The preparation requires attention. Wet the quicklime with about a quart of water, wait for it to cool, and dilute with 2 gallons (8 liters) of water. The sulfate is mixed with the remaining quart and finally mixed with the lime when you are ready to use it. Do not save it. It is used for mildew and rot caused by fungi such as botrytis.

Bracken fern

You will have to go looking for it in the forest in wet areas. *Dryopteris filixmas* grows alongside rivers or in the shade of trees. It combats mealybugs, aphids, and slugs, and provides magnesium to compost. It is prepared by steeping two pounds in two and a half gallons of water if the plant is fresh (and three ounces if dry). For aphids, spray on in winter, and for slugs it can be used all year.

Comfrey

Comfrey is excellent to correct potassium deficiency in plants. It is added to compost. Dandelion is similar.

Copper

Copper is used against fungi and other diseases of the leaves (cryptogams). It is generally presented in the form of copper sulfate, and comes in envelopes that you dilute directly in two and a half gallons of water and spray immediately over the plants. These will look "stained" with the typical bluish color of copper, which indicates their health. When the disease is still present and you need more effective remedies, it is used with lime in Bordeaux mix or with sodium carbonate. It can also be found as copper oxyquinoline (for soil deficiencies) or as copper oxychloride.

Dust

Dust from roads is useful for keeping leaves dry and preventing diseases associated with moisture. Too bad there is no dust when the weather is wet. In this case, rock powder or diatomaceous powder is used, but these sophisticated methods risk doing more harm than good by drying the plant out too much or blocking the sunlight.

Eggshells

This is a remedy for snails and slugs, which blocks their path and kills them. Eggshells are a particularly cruel remedy, since the snail cannot get out of them when it finds them on the way to the lettuce. But since the goal is to get rid of them, we can't hide this common method. It is preferable to sprinkle ashes or wood shavings around the plants, to repel them, or the typical dish of beer.

Garlic

The garlic doesn't just repel bad friends, but it also repels mites, aphids, bacteria, and fights certain diseases, as well as eliminating the moisture that causes certain fungi.

Prepare it by mixing 3 to 20 oz of fresh garlic in 2.5 gallons of boiling water for several minutes, depending on how concentrated you want it to be. A mixture of garlic and onion is also effective. In any case, after spraying you better not invite anyone to visit your garden. Raw garlic keeps seeds dry and prevents them from molding, like salt does. Some people use it in seed beds as well, as they do lightly dusted cinnamon powder.

Horsetail

This is a great remedy against aphids and fungi, as it is even taken in infusion form as a diuretic, although there are some toxic species. The easiest way to prepare it is to marinade 3 ounces (100 g) of freshly picked leaves in a quart of water for 24 hours. Then, boil five minutes and allow to cool. Dilute in five quarts of water and apply for three sunny days in a row. It can be prepared quickly, making a decoction in 20 minutes. Mixed with 1 percent sodium silicate in spring, it prevents powdery mildew, regular mildew, and certain viruses. Mixed with nettle purine, it reinforces the plants, and with 0.3 percent potash soap, combats spider mites and aphids more effectively.

Through aromatherapy we will repel aphids, slugs, snails, and mice; even cats are bothered by certain odors. Don't be afraid to experiment.

Egg shell is a questionably humane remedy for slugs, and propolis is too precious a resource to use it in the garden.

Color traps

These consist of **sheets or rolls of plastic in yellow or blue, with an adhesive that catches insects. It attracts the insects** with its color, blue for thrips and yellow for whiteflies and aphids, but if you want to attract other species you can hang a lure with pheromones along with the trap.

Nicotine

Nicotine is a natural insecticide from tobacco that became very popular at the time, because it was very easy to simply prepare three cigarettes in a liter of water and then spray the mixture after letting it marinate a few hours. Works against aphids, but potash is better and doesn't have the toxic effects of nicotine, which the plants absorb.

Neem

This is a tree (*Azadirachta indica*) originating from southeast Asia. A broad-spectrum insecticide can be obtained from the seeds, and is accepted in organic agriculture because it is nontoxic. The seeds are ground and soaked in water for a few hours. Then it is sprayed on the plant and even livestock to free them from parasites.

Onion

This is used mixed with garlic to fight aphids, mites, and bacteria. The skins and leaves can be used in purines to strengthen the plants, and against carrot flies.

Orange rind

This is used to attract snails and slugs. Place them under a tile in the evening and collect your harvest the next morning.

Oregano

This is said to be good against mealybugs. It is a question of trying it out. Make an infusion and wet the plant once it is cool.

Pheromones and traps

● **They are odorous substances that insects release to communicate with the rest of their species**. There are sexual pheromones, tracking ones, alarm ones, etc.

● The ones that you want are the sexual pheromones emitted by females to attract males and to mate, since **these are chemical compounds that can be easily synthesized in the lab.**

● Synthetic pheromones are hung in diffusers throughout the orchards inside traps to trap the insects. **They are totally innocuous to other species and don't create resistance.**

● **They are used for three reasons**: to detect the presence of pests and their growth; to capture insects in large quantities; and to confuse them and prevent mating.

● Traps that use pheromones come in several forms. **The pine processionary trap** consists of an opaque brown plastic bag, with an elongated funnel on the top part and a narrow opening in which the males enter, attracted by the capsule of pheromone inside, and then they can't get out.

● **In fruit trees, they use a bucket with a funnel on top and a lid that contains a pheromone**. It catches all kinds of butterflies, flies, and flying beetles, without harming them.

● Finally, if there are not too many insects, they use triangular traps, that have the shape of a cabin open on the sides. The insects get stuck in the sticky layers on the bottom.

Nettle

It stimulates growth and strengthens the plant's defenses against aphids. Combats mites, chlorosis due to mineral deficiencies, and mildew. Two pounds of fresh plant or three of dried plant in two and a half gallons of water is allowed to ferment for a week. Then dilute twenty times and use it to water the young plants.

If you add horsetail, it is even more effective.

Potash

Potash soap or black soap combat soft-shelled insects such as aphids, mealybugs, and red spider mites, as well as most fungi such as alternaria, botrytis, powdery mildew, or mildew.

Heat 5 quarts of water to 120°F (40°C) and pour into a plastic bucket. Then add two pounds (1 kg) of potassium hydroxide flakes until dissolved, wearing gloves and goggles. Then 5 quarts (5 liters) of used oil is added (kitchen oil is sufficient). Stir for at least one hour and let stand about 15 days.

0.3 ounces (10 g) of this mixture is dissolved in one quart of water to combat whitefly and 0.7 to 1 ounces (20 to 30 grams) in a liter against aphids, mealybugs, and thrips. It can be sprayed on the plant. Potash is effective due to its corrosive power on the chitin of the insects' backs.

It should not be used with hard water, so be careful. It is best to test the mixture before on a few test plants.

Pyrethrum or pyrethrin

Pyrethrum is a natural insecticide extracted from the plant *Chrysanthemum cinerariaefolium*. Dried flowers of the plant are pulverized and mixed with water at a rate of 2 ounces per liter. After 24 hours it can be used. It is toxic to aphids, cabbage flies, whiteflies, mites, fleas, and so on. Be careful, because like rotenone, it is highly toxic to fish.

Rhubarb

Infusions of rhubarb, a common plant in our fields, at 17 ounces (500 grams) per 2.5 gallons (10 liters) of water, will fight black aphids on bean plants.

Horsetail is a potent diuretic in infusion, and also has insecticidal and fungicidal properties against aphids and fungi.

Rotenone

It is an organic insecticide accepted by organic farming. It comes from a plant that grows in the Amazon, the cube or barcasco, grown for this purpose. The indigenous people threw the roots into the river and waited for dead fish to appear, and cooked the roots to extract the poison placed on the tips of their arrows.

Since 1884, the *Lonchocarpus utilitis* and other plant varieties are cultivated to extract the insecticide from the roots. It is effective against whiteflies, aphids, thrips, spider mites, ticks, lice, and fleas, among others, but is also harmful to bees and especially fish, so it should never be dumped in a pond or river.

Seaweed

They bear mentioning, since there is a species called *Lithothamne*, a small calcaric seaweed about an inch long that lives underwater and is not fixed to the ocean floor. In its tiny stem, it crystallizes minerals from the sea water. It is used as a food for humans and a nutritional supplement for the soil, as well as a natural fungicide and insecticide.

We do not recommend the use of a plant that is harvested from the ocean, since its widespread use in agriculture would mean its days are numbered as a species.

Soapy water

This serves to get rid of annoying leaf eaters like aphids, cabbage worms, the ants that accompany aphids, and some fungi, like sooty mold.

It is prepared by diluting 3 to 10 ounces of green soap (like Lagarto) in 2.5 gallons of warm water. Apply it when it is lukewarm, before it gets cold.

Sodium bicarbonate

In addition to helping stomach pain, it is used in the garden to combat anthracnose, blight, mildew, and powdery mildew. It is prepared by mixing a tablespoon with two and a half of vegetable oil, and a half of soap. Apply once a week as long as the infection lasts.

Sugar

This is a good ant trap, since they are irresistibly attracted to honey, condensed milk, or syrup in their path. In reality, it won't get rid of them, but you can entertain yourself by emptying the pots and watching them pour out of the nest.

Sulfur

Sulfur can be used several ways and its effectiveness is directly related to its fineness, purity, and adhesive power. As a preventative measure, it destroys the reproductive structures of fungi, and as a cure, it attacks the mycelium and prevents the growth of the hypha (little roots), which in old fungi interlace so much it prevents the powder from even penetrating them. Wettable sulfur is obtained by mechanical grinding to obtain a very fine powder, with adjuvants added to make it soluble in water.

Tansy

This is another common herb, known as chrysanthemum (*Chrysanthemum vulgare*), whose infusions and decoctions at 10 ounces (300 grams) of fresh grass for two and a half (ten liters) of water will fight all kinds of insects and some worms.

Nettle is hemostatic, astringent, anti-anemic, diuretic, restorative, and is also a good insecticide. We know then that we must not get rid of this plant as enthusiastically as we would other weeds.

Insecticide pellets

It is not a joke. I would not advise anyone to go out and buy a BB gun, but if you happen to have one and **your property has tent caterpillar nests, you can use these pellets invented by the biologist Luis Rejat, pest management technician.** The pellets carry a small dose of insecticide. If only it were ecological!

Tomato

The suckers that you pluck from tomatoes as they grow will serve us not only as fertilizer, but also for making infusions which, after steeping for twelve hours, make a good insecticide against aphids.

White lupin

Lupin beans, salty and sweet, were one of the favorite snacks of moviegoers in other times. They are the seeds of *Lupinus albus*, a plant with blue flowers, and they look like small fava beans. They contain a toxic alkaloid that is eliminated for human consumption when boiled. We want to use raw, chopped beans, though, to extract the oil, and spread on the base of the trees, in order to repel ants.

Wormwood

Take advantage of the leaves and flowers of *Artemisia absinthium*, also known as absinthe, which contain a bitter substance called thujone, which gives absinthe and Pernod their flavor. It can be used by grinding 10 oz of fresh leaves or 1 oz of dry leaves in 1 quart of water for a week. Filter it and spray on every 15 days. This will help control ants, aphids, and caterpillars. As an infusion, it controls mites and slugs, and as a decoction, it fights cabbage worms. To cook, boil 3 oz of dry leaves in a quart of water for 20 minutes, and let sit for a full day. Then dilute it 10 times and sprinkle on plants affected by aphids. Another way to use it is diluting it by 10 and adding classic dish soap. Spray on.

§205.601 Synthetic substances allowed for use in organic crop production.

In accordance with restrictions specified in this section, the following synthetic substances may be used in organic crop production: Provided, that, use of such substances do not contribute to contamination of crops, soil, or water. Substances allowed by this section, except disinfectants and sanitizers in paragraph (a) and those substances in paragraphs (c), (j), (k), and (l) of this section, may only be used when the provisions set forth in §205.206(a) through (d) prove insufficient to prevent or control the target pest.

(a) As algicide, disinfectants, and sanitizer, including irrigation system cleaning systems.
(1) Alcohols.
  (i) Ethanol.
  (ii) Isopropanol.
(2) Chlorine materials—For pre-harvest use, residual chlorine levels in the water in direct crop contact or as water from cleaning irrigation systems applied to soil must not exceed the maximum residual disinfectant limit under the Safe Drinking Water Act, except that chlorine products may be used in edible sprout production according to EPA label directions.
  (i) Calcium hypochlorite.
  (ii) Chlorine dioxide.
  (iii) Sodium hypochlorite.
(3) Copper sulfate—for use as an algicide in aquatic rice systems, is limited to one application per field during any 24-month period. Application rates are limited to those which do not increase baseline soil test values for copper over a timeframe agreed upon by the producer and accredited certifying agent.
(4) Hydrogen peroxide.
(5) Ozone gas—for use as an irrigation system cleaner only.
(6) Peracetic acid—for use in disinfecting equipment, seed, and asexually propagated planting material. Also permitted in hydrogen peroxide formulations as allowed in §205.601(a) at concentration of no more than 6% as indicated on the pesticide product label.
(7) Soap-based algicide/demossers.
(8) Sodium carbonate peroxyhydrate (CAS #-15630-89-4)—Federal law restricts the use of this substance in food crop production to approved food uses identified on the product label.
(b) As herbicides, weed barriers, as applicable.
(1) Herbicides, soap-based—for use in farmstead maintenance (roadways, ditches, right of ways, building perimeters) and ornamental crops.
(2) Mulches.
  (i) Newspaper or other recycled paper, without glossy or colored inks.
  (ii) Plastic mulch and covers (petroleum-based other than polyvinyl chloride (PVC)).
  (iii) Biodegradable biobased mulch film as defined in §205.2. Must be produced without organisms or feedstock derived from excluded methods.
(c) As compost feedstocks—Newspapers or other recycled paper, without glossy or colored inks.

(d) As animal repellents—Soaps, ammonium—for use as a large animal repellant only, no contact with soil or edible portion of crop.
(e) As insecticides (including acaricides or mite control).
(1) Ammonium carbonate—for use as bait in insect traps only, no direct contact with crop or soil.
(2) Aqueous potassium silicate (CAS #-1312-76-1)—the silica, used in the manufacture of potassium silicate, must be sourced from naturally occurring sand.
(3) Boric acid—structural pest control, no direct contact with organic food or crops.
(4) Copper sulfate—for use as tadpole shrimp control in aquatic rice production, is limited to one application per field during any 24-month period. Application rates are limited to levels which do not increase baseline soil test values for copper over a timeframe agreed upon by the producer and accredited certifying agent.
(5) Elemental sulfur.
(6) Lime sulfur—including calcium polysulfide.
(7) Oils, horticultural—narrow range oils as dormant, suffocating, and summer oils.
(8) Soaps, insecticidal.
(9) Sticky traps/barriers.
(10) Sucrose octanoate esters (CAS #s—42922-74-7; 58064-47-4)—in accordance with approved labeling.
(f) As insect management. Pheromones.
(g) As rodenticides. Vitamin D,
(h) As slug or snail bait. Ferric phosphate (CAS # 10045-86-0).
  (i) As plant disease control.
(1) Aqueous potassium silicate (CAS #-1312-76-1)—the silica, used in the manufacture of potassium silicate, must be sourced from naturally occurring sand.
(2) Coppers, fixed—copper hydroxide, copper oxide, copper oxychloride, includes products exempted from EPA tolerance, provided, that, copper-based materials must be used in a manner that minimizes accumulation in the soil and shall not be used as herbicides.
(3) Copper sulfate—Substance must be used in a manner that minimizes accumulation of copper in the soil.
(4) Hydrated lime.
(5) Hydrogen peroxide.
(6) Lime sulfur.
(7) Oils, horticultural, narrow range oils as dormant, suffocating, and summer oils.
(8) Peracetic acid—for use to control fire blight bacteria. Also permitted in hydrogen peroxide formulations as allowed in §205.601(i) at concentration of no more than 6% as indicated on the pesticide product label.
(9) Potassium bicarbonate.
(10) Elemental sulfur.
(11) Streptomycin, for fire blight control in apples and pears only until October 21, 2014.
(12) Tetracycline, for fire blight control in apples and pears only until October 21, 2014.
  (j) As plant or soil amendments.

(1) Aquatic plant extracts (other than hydrolyzed)—Extraction process is limited to the use of potassium hydroxide or sodium hydroxide; solvent amount used is limited to that amount necessary for extraction.

(2) Elemental sulfur.
(3) Humic acids—naturally occurring deposits, water and alkali extracts only.
(4) Lignin sulfonate—chelating agent, dust suppressant.
(5) Magnesium sulfate—allowed with a documented soil deficiency.
(6) Micronutrients—not to be used as a defoliant, herbicide, or desiccant. Those made from nitrates or chlorides are not allowed. Soil deficiency must be documented by testing.
  (i) Soluble boron products.
  (ii) Sulfates, carbonates, oxides, or silicates of zinc, copper, iron, manganese, molybdenum, selenium, and cobalt.
(7) Liquid fish products—can be pH adjusted with sulfuric, citric or phosphoric acid. The amount of acid used shall not exceed the minimum needed to lower the pH to 3.5.
(8) Vitamins, B_1, C, and E.
(9) Sulfurous acid (CAS # 7782-99-2) for on-farm generation of substance utilizing 99% purity elemental sulfur per paragraph (j)(2) of this section.
  (k) As plant growth regulators. Ethylene gas—for regulation of pineapple flowering.
  (l) As floating agents in postharvest handling.
(1) Lignin sulfonate.
(2) Sodium silicate—for tree fruit and fiber processing.
  (m) As synthetic inert ingredients as classified by the Environmental Protection Agency (EPA), for use with nonsynthetic substances or synthetic substances listed in this section and used as an active pesticide ingredient in accordance with any limitations on the use of such substances.
(1) EPA List 4—Inerts of Minimal Concern.
(2) EPA List 3—Inerts of unknown toxicity—for use only in passive pheromone dispensers.
  (n) Seed preparations. Hydrogen chloride (CAS # 7647-01-0)—for delinting cotton seed for planting.
  (o) As production aids. Microcrystalline cheesewax (CAS #'s 64742-42-3, 8009-03-08, and 8002-74-2)-for use in log grown mushroom production. Must be made without either ethylene-propylene co-polymer or synthetic colors.

§205.602 Nonsynthetic substances prohibited for use in organic crop production.

The following nonsynthetic substances may not be used in organic crop production:

(a) Ash from manure burning.
(b) Arsenic.
(c) Calcium chloride, brine process is natural and prohibited for use except as a foliar spray to treat a physiological disorder associated with calcium uptake.
(d) Lead salts.
(e) Potassium chloride—unless derived from a mined source and applied in a manner that minimizes chloride accumulation in the soil.
(f) Sodium fluoaluminate (mined).

(g) Sodium nitrate—unless use is restricted to no more than 20% of the crop's total nitrogen requirement; use in spirulina production is unrestricted until October 21, 2005.

(h) Strychnine.

(i) Tobacco dust (nicotine sulfate).

§205.603 Synthetic substances allowed for use in organic livestock production.

In accordance with restrictions specified in this section the following synthetic substances may be used in organic livestock production:

(a) As disinfectants, sanitizer, and medical treatments as applicable.

(1) Alcohols.
   (i) Ethanol-disinfectant and sanitizer only, prohibited as a feed additive.
   (ii) Isopropanol-disinfectant only.

(2) Aspirin-approved for health care use to reduce inflammation.

(3) Atropine (CAS #-51-55-8)—federal law restricts this drug to use by or on the lawful written or oral order of a licensed veterinarian, in full compliance with the AMDUCA and 21 CFR part 530 of the Food and Drug Administration regulations. Also, for use under 7 CFR part 205, the NOP requires:
   (i) Use by or on the lawful written order of a licensed veterinarian; and
   (ii) A meat withdrawal period of at least 56 days after administering to livestock intended for slaughter; and a milk discard period of at least 12 days after administering to dairy animals.

(4) Biologics—Vaccines.

(5) Butorphanol (CAS #-42408-82-2)—federal law restricts this drug to use by or on the lawful written or oral order of a licensed veterinarian, in full compliance with the AMDUCA and 21 CFR part 530 of the Food and Drug Administration regulations. Also, for use under 7 CFR part 205, the NOP requires:
   (i) Use by or on the lawful written order of a licensed veterinarian; and
   (ii) A meat withdrawal period of at least 42 days after administering to livestock intended for slaughter; and a milk discard period of at least 8 days after administering to dairy animals.

(6) Chlorhexidine—Allowed for surgical procedures conducted by a veterinarian. Allowed for use as a teat dip when alternative germicidal agents and/or physical barriers have lost their effectiveness.

(7) Chlorine materials—disinfecting and sanitizing facilities and equipment. Residual chlorine levels in the water shall not exceed the maximum residual disinfectant limit under the Safe Drinking Water Act.
   (i) Calcium hypochlorite.
   (ii) Chlorine dioxide.
   (iii) Sodium hypochlorite.

(8) Electrolytes—without antibiotics.

(9) Flunixin (CAS #-38677-85-9)—in accordance with approved labeling; except that for use under 7 CFR part 205, the NOP requires a withdrawal period of at least two-times that required by the FDA.

(10) Furosemide (CAS #-54-31-9)—in accordance with approved labeling; except that for use under 7 CFR part 205, the NOP requires a withdrawal period of at least two-times that required that required by the FDA.

(11) Glucose.

(12) Glycerin—Allowed as a livestock teat dip, must be produced through the hydrolysis of fats or oils.

(13) Hydrogen peroxide.

(14) Iodine.

(15) Magnesium hydroxide (CAS #-1309-42-8)—federal law restricts this drug to use by or on the lawful written or oral order of a licensed veterinarian, in full compliance with the AMDUCA and 21 CFR part 530 of the Food and Drug Administration regulations. Also, for use under 7 CFR part 205, the NOP requires use by or on the lawful written order of a licensed veterinarian.

(16) Magnesium sulfate.

(17) Oxytocin—use in postparturition therapeutic applications.

(18) Parasiticides—Prohibited in slaughter stock, allowed in emergency treatment for dairy and breeder stock when organic system plan-approved preventive management does not prevent infestation. Milk or milk products from a treated animal cannot be labeled as provided for in subpart D of this part for 90 days following treatment. In breeder stock, treatment cannot occur during the last third of gestation if the progeny will be sold as organic and must not be used during the lactation period for breeding stock.
   (i) Fenbendazole (CAS #43210-67-9)—only for use by or on the lawful written order of a licensed veterinarian.
   (ii) Ivermectin (CAS #70288-86-7).
   (iii) Moxidectin (CAS #113507-06-5)—for control of internal parasites only.

(19) Peroxyacetic/peracetic acid (CAS #-79-21-0)—for sanitizing facility and processing equipment.

(20) Phosphoric acid—allowed as an equipment cleaner, provided, that, no direct contact with organically managed livestock or land occurs.

(21) Poloxalene (CAS #-9003-11-6)—for use under 7 CFR part 205, the NOP requires that poloxalene only be used for the emergency treatment of bloat.

(22) Tolazoline (CAS #-59-98-3)—federal law restricts this drug to use by or on the lawful written or oral order of a licensed veterinarian, in full compliance with the AMDUCA and 21 CFR part 530 of the Food and Drug Administration regulations. Also, for use under 7 CFR part 205, the NOP requires:
   (i) Use by or on the lawful written order of a licensed veterinarian;
   (ii) Use only to reverse the effects of sedation and analgesia caused by Xylazine; and
   (iii) A meat withdrawal period of at least 8 days after administering to livestock intended for slaughter; and a milk discard period of at least 4 days after administering to dairy animals.

(23) Xylazine (CAS #-7361-61-7)—federal law restricts this drug to use by or on the lawful written or oral order of a licensed veterinarian, in full compliance with the AMDUCA and 21 CFR part 530 of the Food and Drug Administration regulations. Also, for use under 7 CFR part 205, the NOP requires:
   (i) Use by or on the lawful written order of a licensed veterinarian;
   (ii) The existence of an emergency; and
   (iii) A meat withdrawal period of at least 8 days after administering to livestock intended for slaughter; and a milk discard period of at least 4 days after administering to dairy animals.

(b) As topical treatment, external parasiticide or local anesthetic as applicable.

(1) Copper sulfate.

(2) Formic acid (CAS # 64-18-6)—for use as a pesticide solely within honeybee hives.

(3) Iodine.

(4) Lidocaine—as a local anesthetic. Use requires a withdrawal period of 90 days after administering to livestock intended for slaughter and 7 days after administering to dairy animals.

(5) Lime, hydrated—as an external pest control, not permitted to cauterize physical alterations or deodorize animal wastes.

(6) Mineral oil—for topical use and as a lubricant.

(7) Procaine—as a local anesthetic, use requires a withdrawal period of 90 days after administering to livestock intended for slaughter and 7 days after administering to dairy animals.

(8) Sucrose octanoate esters (CAS #s-42922-74-7; 58064-47-4)—in accordance with approved labeling.

(c) As feed supplements—None.

(d) As feed additives.

(1) DL-Methionine, DL-Methionine-hydroxy analog, and DL-Methionine-hydroxy analog calcium (CAS #'s 59-51-8, 583-91-5, 4857-44-7, and 922-50-9)—for use only in organic poultry production at the following maximum levels of synthetic methionine per ton of feed: Laying and broiler chickens—2 pounds; turkeys and all other poultry—3 pounds.

(2) Trace minerals, used for enrichment or fortification when FDA approved.

(3) Vitamins, used for enrichment or fortification when FDA approved.

(e) As synthetic inert ingredients as classified by the Environmental Protection Agency (EPA), for use with nonsynthetic substances or synthetic substances listed in this section and used as an active pesticide ingredient in accordance with any limitations on the use of such substances.

(1) EPA List 4—Inerts of Minimal Concern.

(f) Excipients, only for use in the manufacture of drugs used to treat organic livestock when the excipient is: Identified by the FDA as Generally Recognized As Safe; Approved by the FDA as a food additive; or Included in the FDA review and approval of a New Animal Drug Application or New Drug Application.

§205.604 Nonsynthetic substances prohibited for use in organic livestock production.

The following nonsynthetic substances may not be used in organic livestock production:

(a) Strychnine.

§205.605 Nonagricultural (nonorganic) substances allowed as ingredients in or on processed products labeled as "organic" or "made with organic (specified ingredients or food group(s))."

The following nonagricultural substances may be used as ingredients in or on processed products labeled as "organic" or "made with organic (specified ingredients or food group(s))" only in accordance with any restrictions specified in this section.

(a) Nonsynthetics allowed:

Acids (Alginic; Citric—produced by microbial fermentation of carbohydrate substances; and Lactic).

Agar-agar.

Animal enzymes—(Rennet—animals derived; Catalase—bovine liver; Animal lipase; Pancreatin; Pepsin; and Trypsin).

Attapulgite—as a processing aid in the handling of plant and animal oils.

Bentonite.

Calcium carbonate.

Calcium chloride.
Calcium sulfate—mined.
Carrageenan.
Dairy cultures.
Diatomaceous earth—food filtering aid only.
Egg white lysozyme (CAS # 9001-63-2)
Enzymes—must be derived from edible, nontoxic plants, nonpathogenic fungi, or nonpathogenic bacteria.
Flavors, nonsynthetic sources only and must not be produced using synthetic solvents and carrier systems or any artificial preservative.
Gellan gum (CAS # 71010-52-1)—high-acyl form only.
Glucono delta-lactone—production by the oxidation of D-glucose with bromine water is prohibited.
Kaolin.
L-Malic acid (CAS # 97-67-6).
Magnesium sulfate, nonsynthetic sources only.
Microorganisms—any food grade bacteria, fungi, and other microorganism.
Nitrogen—oil-free grades.
Oxygen—oil-free grades.
Perlite—for use only as a filter aid in food processing.
Potassium chloride.
Potassium iodide.
Sodium bicarbonate.
Sodium carbonate.
Tartaric acid—made from grape wine.
Waxes—nonsynthetic (Carnauba wax; and Wood resin).
Yeast—When used as food or a fermentation agent in products labeled as "organic," yeast must be organic if its end use is for human consumption; nonorganic yeast may be used when organic yeast is not commercially available. Growth on petrochemical substrate and sulfite waste liquor is prohibited. For smoked yeast, nonsynthetic smoke flavoring process must be documented.

(b) *Synthetics allowed:*
Acidified sodium chlorite—Secondary direct antimicrobial food treatment and indirect food contact surface sanitizing. Acidified with citric acid only.
Activated charcoal (CAS #s 7440-44-0; 64365-11-3)—only from vegetative sources; for use only as a filtering aid.
Alginates.
Ammonium bicarbonate—for use only as a leavening agent.
Ammonium carbonate—for use only as a leavening agent.
Ascorbic acid.
Calcium citrate.
Calcium hydroxide.
Calcium phosphates (monobasic, dibasic, and tribasic).
Carbon dioxide.
Cellulose—for use in regenerative casings, as an anti-caking agent (non-chlorine bleached) and filtering aid.
Chlorine materials—disinfecting and sanitizing food contact surfaces, *except*, that, residual chlorine levels in the water shall not exceed the maximum residual disinfectant limit under the Safe Drinking Water Act (Calcium hypochlorite; Chlorine dioxide; and Sodium hypochlorite).
Cyclohexylamine (CAS # 108-91-8)—for use only as a boiler water additive for packaging sterilization.
Diethylaminoethanol (CAS # 100-37-8)—for use only as a boiler water additive for packaging sterilization.
Ethylene—allowed for postharvest ripening of tropical fruit and degreening of citrus.
Ferrous sulfate—for iron enrichment or

fortification of foods when required by regulation or recommended (independent organization).
Glycerides (mono and di)—for use only in drum drying of food.
Glycerin—produced by hydrolysis of fats and oils.
Hydrogen peroxide.
Magnesium carbonate—for use only in agricultural products labeled "made with organic (specified ingredients or food group(s))," prohibited in agricultural products labeled "organic."
Magnesium chloride—derived from sea water.
Magnesium stearate—for use only in agricultural products labeled "made with organic (specified ingredients or food group(s))," prohibited in agricultural products labeled "organic".
Nutrient vitamins and minerals, in accordance with 21 CFR 104.20, Nutritional Quality Guidelines For Foods.
Octadecylamine (CAS # 124-30-1)—for use only as a boiler water additive for packaging sterilization.
Ozone.
Peracetic acid/Peroxyacetic acid (CAS # 79-21-0)—for use in wash and/or rinse water according to FDA limitations. For use as a sanitizer on food contact surfaces.
Phosphoric acid—cleaning of food-contact surfaces and equipment only.
Potassium acid tartrate.
Potassium carbonate.
Potassium citrate.
Potassium hydroxide—prohibited for use in lye peeling of fruits and vegetables except when used for peeling peaches.
Potassium phosphate—for use only in agricultural products labeled "made with organic (specific ingredients or food group(s))," prohibited in agricultural products labeled "organic".
Silicon dioxide—Permitted as a defoamer. Allowed for other uses when organic rice hulls are not commercially available.
Sodium acid pyrophosphate (CAS # 7758-16-9)—for use only as a leavening agent.
Sodium citrate.
Sodium hydroxide—prohibited for use in lye peeling of fruits and vegetables.
Sodium phosphates—for use only in dairy foods.
Sulfur dioxide—for use only in wine labeled "made with organic grapes," Provided, That, total sulfite concentration does not exceed 100 ppm.
Tetrasodium pyrophosphate (CAS # 7722-88-5)—for use only in meat analog products.
Tocopherols—derived from vegetable oil when rosemary extracts are not a suitable alternative.
Xanthan gum.

§205.606 Nonorganically produced agricultural products allowed as ingredients in or on processed products labeled as "organic."

Only the following nonorganically produced agricultural products may be used as ingredients in or on processed products labeled as "organic," only in accordance with any restrictions specified in this section, and only when the product is not commercially available in organic form.
(a) Casings, from processed intestines.
(b) Celery powder.
(c) Chia (*Salvia hispanica L.*).
(d) Colors derived from agricultural products—Must not be produced using synthetic solvents and carrier systems or any artificial preservative.

(1) Beet juice extract color (pigment CAS #7659-95-2).
(2) Beta-carotene extract color—derived from carrots or algae (pigment CAS# 7235-40-7).
(3) Black currant juice color (pigment CAS #'s: 528-58-5, 528-53-0, 643-84-5, 134-01-0, 1429-30-7, and 134-04-3).
(4) Black/Purple carrot juice color (pigment CAS #'s: 528-58-5, 528-53-0, 643-84-5, 134-01-0, 1429-30-7, and 134-04-3).
(5) Blueberry juice color (pigment CAS #'s: 528-58-5, 528-53-0, 643-84-5, 134-01-0, 1429-30-7, and 134-04-3).
(6) Carrot juice color (pigment CAS #1393-63-1).
(7) Cherry juice color (pigment CAS #'s: 528-58-5, 528-53-0, 643-84-5, 134-01-0, 1429-30-7, and 134-04-3).
(8) Chokeberry—Aronia juice color (pigment CAS #'s: 528-58-5, 528-53-0, 643-84-5, 134-01-0, 1429-30-7, and 134-04-3).
(9) Elderberry juice color (pigment CAS #'s: 528-58-5, 528-53-0, 643-84-5, 134-01-0, 1429-30-7, and 134-04-3).
(10) Grape juice color (pigment CAS #'s: 528-58-5, 528-53-0, 643-84-5, 134-01-0, 1429-30-7, and 134-04-3).
(11) Grape skin extract color (pigment CAS #'s: 528-58-5, 528-53-0, 643-84-5, 134-01-0, 1429-30-7, and 134-04-3).
(12) Paprika color (CAS #68917-78-2)—dried, and oil extracted.
(13) Pumpkin juice color (pigment CAS #127-40-2).
(14) Purple potato juice (pigment CAS #'s: 528-58-5, 528-53-0, 643-84-5, 134-01-0, 1429-30-7, and 134-04-3).
(15) Red cabbage extract color (pigment CAS #'s: 528-58-5, 528-53-0, 643-84-5, 134-01-0, 1429-30-7, and 134-04-3).
(16) Red radish extract color (pigment CAS #'s: 528-58-5, 528-53-0, 643-84-5, 134-01-0, 1429-30-7, and 134-04-3).
(17) Saffron extract color (pigment CAS #1393-63-1).
(18) Turmeric extract color (CAS #458-37-7).
(e) Dillweed oil (CAS # 8006-75-5).
(f) Fish oil (Fatty acid CAS #'s: 10417-94-4, and 25167-62-8)—stabilized with organic ingredients or only with ingredients on the National List, §§205.605 and 205.606.
(g) Fortified cooking wines.
(1) Marsala.
(2) Sherry.
(h) Fructooligosaccharides (CAS # 308066-66-2).
(i) Galangal, frozen.
(j) Gelatin (CAS # 9000-70-8).
(k) Gums—water extracted only (Arabic; Guar; Locust bean; and Carob bean).
(l) Inulin-oligofructose enriched (CAS # 9005-80-5).
(m) Kelp—for use only as a thickener and dietary supplement.
(n) Konjac flour (CAS # 37220-17-0).
(o) Lecithin—de-oiled.
(p) Lemongrass—frozen.
(q) Orange pulp, dried.
(r) Orange shellac-unbleached (CAS # 9000-59-3).
(s) Pectin (non-amidated forms only).
(t) Peppers (Chipotle chile).
(u) Seaweed, Pacific kombu.
(v) Starches.
(1) Cornstarch (native).
(2) Sweet potato starch—for bean thread production only.
(w) Tragacanth gum (CAS #-9000-65-1).
(x) Turkish bay leaves.
(y) Wakame seaweed (*Undaria pinnatifida*).
(z) Whey protein concentrate.

Gardening in the home

What we should know about
balcony gardens

Having a terrace is a privilege because it enables us to eat well for several weeks out of the year.

At the moment of truth, you may have no more space than a balcony or terrace for a small home garden. No problem. Look at all the things you can do or fit in a small space:

● A small compost where your organic kitchen waste and scraps from the garden are transformed into compost. The vermi-composters are relatively small, and the worms prevent bad odors.

● A container for growing potatoes. In this case, biodynamic farming recommends stacking several tires, but a can takes up less space and one plant can produce more than twenty potatoes.

● Hang baskets on your balcony to make seedbeds or grow herbs. If you have a terrace you can try to make a grid or wooden lattice to cover the top like a trellis.

● On the lattice that you place on the walls and columns you can grow vines and make vine arbors with any climbing plant, like cucumbers.

● Place the pots in tiers for better use of light and you can have tomatoes, peppers, and eggplants within a short distance of each other.

● Even easier is to buy bags of potting soil and, without tearing them, simply make a hole and sow beans, tomatoes, or peppers.

● Use all containers you have on hand for the garden: an old aquarium, cut drums, and even a bathtub can be useful if you don't want to buy pots.

● Sow germinated seeds in the windowsills.

● Build a corner for aromatic plants.

● Collect rainwater from the roof in a fifty-gallon drum, the kind that are discarded in the chemical industries. You can ask for one; they'll probably give it to you for free.

● Plant species of dwarf fruit trees that produce berries or fruit.

With a few simple drawers, we can build a compost bin on the terrace. Just have a space for new waste and another for the decomposition to occur for several weeks.

The garden on the balcony

Potted plants

The list of plants that can be grown in pots is great. Here's an example: chard, eggplant, zucchini, onions, spinach, beans, lettuce, potatoes, peppers, leeks, cabbage, tomatoes, and carrots. You have to take care of them better than if they were in the ground, getting pots or containers that are 12 to 20 inches deep (the 20 for zucchini and carrots) and watering more often, because if the sun touches them, the pots dry out quickly .

If your balcony is on a low floor and has no more than four hours of sun, you can only grow plants that do not need much light. Forget tomatoes or choose smaller species that are more resistant to lack of light. Sow primarily lettuce and spinach. Parsley also grows well in the shade.

Occasionally, turn the pots, so they do not always grow in the same direction. Try to get seeds of dwarf varieties of tomatoes, cabbage, or lettuce. Do not leave spaces uncultivated, and be always ready with seedlings to transplant a plant when you remove another.

The design of the balcony

Since we will have a very limited space, we have to extract maximum performance: the floor, walls, and ceiling should be utilized fully. Put in shelves, racks, wall planters, and lattices for climbing plants, and also dwarf fruit trees and tiered pots.

Tomatoes planted in pots will soon need a support. Try not to leave more than one or two plants in each of the pots.

The light and the sun

A terrace is not the same as a balcony, nor is living in a wet climate the same as a dry one. In southern Spain, the terraces in summer tend to be uninhabited, but that gives us the possibility to build a lattice with poles that will provide a lovely shade and allow us to have climbing plants, like vining beans, zucchini, or chayote vines.

Soil and water

Having a garden at home involves at least the same obligations as having a plot. The soil must be well fertilized. A mixture of sand or normal soil with 50 percent compost and a layer of gravel at the bottom will work well.

In watering is where you will find more differences, since here the much needed drainage passes through the soil, and more than ever we need to consider drip irrigation. In such a small space it will be easy to set up, and necessary if you plan to go on vacation in the summer. There are other economic tricks, of course. You can purchase water-filled plastic bottles attached to the planters with a narrow tube that makes a siphon, so that they will

Fruit trees in pots

Lemon, orange, pomegranate, persimmon, cherry, pear, apple, quince, plum, currant, and raspberry plants can be grown in pots. **If you want an orange tree in your garden, you can choose between Bunge, Bouquet, and Navelina varieties, but only the latter will offer sweet and edible fruits**. When you choose a fruit for your balcony, pay attention to the species, as most are ornamental and fruits are bitter. Caring for them is very easy. Just get a flower pot and fill it with nutrient-rich soil, like a well-worked garden. In winter to help the fruit stay on the tree, it is best to help the tree with a dose of nutrients including iron, magnesium, zinc, and potassium. **Water it well and wet the leaves in hot weather; prune the shoots in spring to avoid losing the shape and protect it from frost**. The orange tree is best brought indoors if you live in cold areas. Remember that in Seville they are planted in the streets, but in Paris they are stored in warehouses.

Considerations to keep in mind:

- **The orientation** of the balcony.

- **The hours of direct sunlight** available.

- **A terrace is not the same as roofed balcony.**

- **The wind** is an important design factor.

- **Neighbors and regulations** are also important.

- **The** maximum and minimum **temperatures** and humidity.

- **The maximum weight** that the floor can withstand.

Eggplant planted in a pot with a very satisfactory yield. Having plants so close to home allows you to devote more care and attention, and enjoy them more.

Below, pots lined up on a terrace that will allow you to cultivate various vegetables without disturbing the others.

gradually empty; alternatively, you can bore tiny holes into a bottle to make your own irrigation system. It's not like we're in the jungle, and you will have to make a small investment.

The garden

Leaving room for passing, of course, now you have an idea of what your garden on the balcony or terrace will look like with very little space.

You should put sticks in the corners and build an arbor on which to grow a vine with good grapes. If the terrace is large, you can string some wires and have a chayote, a squash, cucumbers, or some climbing beans. Against the wall of the house, build a tiered planter with discarded pallets. A couple of steps should suffice. In the highest and deepest, plant potatoes, for example, and at the bottom, plants that need less soil, like peppers or eggplants. Do not forget the drainage gravel at the bottom of each.

In one corner, you should have a container to collect rainwater, which you will use to fill your watering can or to connect the hose for the drip installation. If the weather is not very dry, a jerrican of just over twenty-five gallons will collect enough water for the entire summer.

In the back, against one of the rails, you can build a table-garden with tables

Mushrooms

The Paris mushroom is so called because, in times of famine, many households grew it in the city, taking advantage of the prevailing moisture. The preparation of the compost is vital for growing them; for example, a hot bed of horse manure and wheat straw works quite well. To enrich this substrate, the producers added urea, chicken manure, and some gypsum. They also add an insecticide and then pasteurize the mixture by injecting hot steam—a method a bit too complicated to do at home, but that properly sanitizes the substrate. The seed is sold on sterile wheat grains whose surface is covered by fungal hyphae. It is mixed with compost and planted in boxes or plastic bags. Humidity must be above 90% and for the first few days it needs a temperature of about 75°F (25°C) for incubation and darkness. Then you need to water daily, spraying water over it; at four weeks you can begin to reap the harvest, which is not more than about 25 kg per hundred of substrate used if the process is followed to perfection or you are very lucky. Pleurotus ostruatus, better known as oyster mushrooms, can also be grown at home by similar methods. Pasteurization can be done by immersion in hot water at 175°F (80°C) for two hours.

and no more than one inch of soil, at a height that does not require you to crouch. Here you have the lettuce, endive, chard, celery, and all those leafy plants that enliven our salads every day; you can also have radishes and carrots. And hanging from the railings are potted herbs.

In the remaining space, you will have one or more homemade pots where there are tomatoes, peppers, and eggplants. And it does not take more than six or ten square meters to have all this.

Containers

The most aesthetic option is clay pots that are heavy and fragile, but very nice and available in every shape and size. Remember that you have to soak them for 24 hours before use to prevent stains with the first watering. The less aesthetic choice is plastic pots, which come in a thousand colors in all shapes and sizes and are stronger, lighter, and can even be hung on the railings of the balcony and expand our useable space with peppers or herbs. Another method is to pick up containers destined for the landfill and put them to better use. Look at the list below:

If you have a simple terrace, do not miss the opportunity to build a small garden, but remember to water it during the holidays.

Useful containers for the balcony

Note that for certain plants, a depth of at least twelve inches (thirty centimeters) is needed. But if you're going to make sprouts or seedlings, just an inch or two is enough.

- **Water jugs,** not made from PVC.
- **Tin cans.**
- **Glass canning jars** of all sizes.
- **Egg cartons.**
- **Cartons** of all sizes.
- **Water bottles** of all sizes, except those made of PVC.
- **Polystyrene trays,** which are used to hold food in stores.
- Wooden or plastic **fruit boxes.**
- **Plastic buckets or basins.**
- **Tires and pallets.**
- **Old drainboards.**
- **Dustbins,** perforated.
- Safe and clean **plastic chemical drums.** (Not recommended.)

Check out any catalog of pots and planters and you will be surprised by the wonders that can be achieved to maximize space.

Sprouts

The germination process transforms the seeds into a prime nutrient that has detoxifying, revitalizing, and regenerative properties. The starch is converted into sugar, proteins become more assimilated, essential amino acids increase, and vitamins and minerals such as iron, selenium, and zinc are at our disposal. And they can grow anywhere, in the simplest way, because you only need a window. To cultivate them, you can buy the trays that are sold for this purpose, and also buy the seeds sold in organic food stores, which should not be chemically treated or irradiated so that they don't germinate. You don't need soil. The list of sprouts is long: alfalfa, watercress, squash, barley, chickpeas, sunflower, peas, lentils, flax, corn, mustard, radish, sesame, and soy are the most common.

Alfalfa is the most popular because it contains chlorophyll. It grows very quickly and will clog germination trays, so it's best to put them in a glass jar with a wide mouth. Put the seeds into the jar and fill with water (spring) halfway. For a couple of days, change the water twice with a sieve, letting the seeds stick to the damp walls. If you do not want to be emptying and filling the jars twice a day, use the plate method: sprinkle a little water so that the seeds get wet without drowning and spread the seeds with a spoon without letting them clump together, as they will sprout all at once. Then put them in the closet and leave them in the dark, replacing the water they absorb. After two or three days the sprouts will be about an inch long. Do not forget about them, because if they get moldy you will have to throw them away.

Handling the sprouts:

- If they get moldy, throw them away.

- Alfalfa leaves hulls, which you should get rid of by rinsing them in a pot of water.

- Soy and lentils don't germinate a hundred percent. When you eat them, you will still notice the raw seed.

- Some sprouts, such as mustard, watercress, and flax, will clog the holes of the germination tray.

- Radish and mustard can be mixed with other sprouts.

- You can make your own container with a bottle, putting holes in the lid and leaving very small holes for the sprouts to emerge.

- You can also use the drip method, so the water spills over and the container never dries.

Chayote

Also known as the **air potato**, it is a squash native to Central America that is very easy to grow and ideal for the balcony or terrace garden. **It has a mild flavor (similar to a pear) and is popular among those who want to lose weight without starving themselves.** It is grown on wires about 15 inches (40 cm) apart and tied to poles, or a pole and the wall, in our case. **If there is space, stagger the height of the wires to let the sun through**, since the idea is that underneath, other plants can be grown, such as spinach and lettuce. **It is sown without burying, placing a whole fruit on the ground**, and every year it sprouts from the rhizome, so all you have to do is reap the rewards, in the best permaculture tradition. They should be picked when they are about the size of a pear, and bear in mind that they can be very heavy for the wires. In an Argentinian magazine, they refer to the stems as asparagus, leaves as spinach, and fruits as cucumbers or potatoes; in other words, they can be eaten boiled or raw.

www.prodiversitas.bioetica.org

Aromatic herbs on the balcony

Aromatic herbs are very easy to grow and anyone can have them on a windowsill or balcony, to season their cooking or put in bags to repel insects. The easiest to grow are basil, chives, tarragon, marjoram, lemon balm, mint, oregano, parsley, rosemary, sage, and thyme. They do not need much care except for generous watering, especially in summer in the morning and afternoon, although many, like thyme and rosemary, are resistant to drought because they come from Mediterranean countries. It is recommended you add fertilizer to the watering can and change the surface soil once a month, and add compost once a year. Remove the weeds, work the surface of the soil often, so that it doesn't form a crust, and watch the ones that propagate through rhizomes, like mint.

If you mulch with bark or gravel, you will prevent weeds, but you also won't be able to dig the surface and will end up mixing it with the substrate. Prune the plant judiciously. After all, you want them to use them, but make sure to leave buds on the stems. A good trim is best after flowering, so they don't get woody. Remove the old flowers and if the plant looks like it may bolt, cut the tips so that it makes lateral branches.

Protect them from spring frosts, strong winds, or lack of light.

The Layout of the Garden

The layout of the garden according to your needs

Each master has his own booklet, according to one proverb. That booklet is experience, so do not hesitate to experiment until you get the best result.

When gardening, it is most common to make straight furrows to facilitate planting and installing stakes in the case of climbing plants. If the ground is slightly sloped, contour lines can be used to keep furrows as horizontal as possible, so that irrigation and rainwater are maximized.

Biodynamic farming suggests that ridges should be oriented north to south along the energy lines, but if the garden is on a hillside you must adapt to the contours. Sometimes there is no choice so an orchard with rows oriented from east to west should work just fine. There will always be plants with more sunlight exposure than others.

Planting in circles

Some experienced gardeners have decided to implement other methods of planting. For example, planting in circles: they begin making a circular ridge, then sowing in the center, and mulching right after. The idea is to compare this type of planting with a linear planting located right next to it and, from this point on, experiment in every possible way. The classic furrows—15 to 20 inches apart, 8" to 12" high, and 15" to 20" wide—can be replaced by circles, spirals, or serpentines, depending on the possibilities of the garden.

When planning the layout of the garden, you must take into account that some plants need more sun than others..

The classical system

In a traditional garden there is a path down the center, which can be paved, and crosses the property, preferably from east to west. Alongside the path, the rectangular beds are in place.

If the weather is dry, furrows and ridges should be of equal width; thus, the gardener creates a jungle in which the plants themselves retain moisture, preventing the sun from reaching the ground. Nevertheless, this has its risks, because if it rains too much, pests and diseases caused by excess moisture could strike. It can also hinder harvest if the beds are too large.

If the weather is wet, furrows are narrow and ridges are wide, thus letting light and air circulate. If the foliage is abundant, it also allows you to walk through the plants. So say the ridge is 3 feet (1 m) wide and the furrow 1.5 feet (50 cm). The plant is rooted half in the wet area and half in the wide ridge's dry zone. With this system, which requires more space, you facilitate harvesting and maintenance work.

Some gardeners prefer very wide furrows and narrow ridges, so irrigation holds more water. This implies that the soil will

If you have trees, make sure that the shadow does not affect the garden, and watch the distance, as some, such as poplar, are harmful to the garden.

Plan carefully the areas you will tread when working in the garden. Sometimes tomato plants are too close together and the precious fruit cannot be reached without damaging plants.

In the image, the three models of furrows that can be used in the home garden. The first two need plenty of space. **Upper left**: circles. **Right**: spiral. They require planning to take advantage of positive associations between plants. **Lower image**: the traditional way.

dry faster and will crack when the sun hits it. Also, you would have to step in the mud to get in between plants.

Tubers, such as the potato, are planted in rows at equal distances; you will not have to get in between, except for removing beetles and weeding. To the contrary, tomatoes and beans involve many trips up and down to clean and harvest. Cabbage, lettuce, onions, and carrots are usually planted close together to maximize the field, because all you need to do between the rows is harvest. They can also be potted without furrows. Garlic, lima beans, peas, string beans, peppers, and eggplant do not offer major trouble to walk through, but it is better if the ridges are not too narrow. Pumpkins, squash, and cucumbers have no problems, because they are always planted apart and can invade their surrounding area for several feet.

The spiral garden

This method has been developed in the field of bio-horticulture. It involves significant initial work but it is reduced in subsequent years.

The cultivation is done on an elevation that has the form of an elongated hill. It is best to mark the spiral on the ground at the beginning. You start to dig a ridge from the outside: 5 ft. (1.5 meters) wide and 20 inches (50 cm) in height. You do this using a big hoe, throwing the soil as loose as possible in the center.

Turn inward progressively to end up in the center of the spiral. As you turn, leave a separation of 32 inches between "ridges" in order to be able to delve into the unique ridge of the garden. Then everything is mulched with straw and only uncovered for planting.

Apparently, this system prevents diseases and maintains good availability of land, spreading positive energy throughout the garden. If you choose this system ensure that the plants do not block the light to each other.

Rotation

It is practiced because of different nutritional needs in the garden. For example, not many plants that need a lot of nutrients are supposed to be planted right after the other; beets will not be planted after cabbages.

Here is a list of plants that need more fertilizer: chard, celery, squash, zucchini, cabbage, spinach, lettuce, corn, cucumbers, leeks, and potatoes. Try not to repeat any of these plants in the same area.

Now look at the plants that are less demanding and can follow the above, provided that the ground is fertilized again: garlic, onions, some lettuce, endive, turnips, beets, and carrots.

And finally, plants that do not only need little fertilizer but also enrich the soil: all legumes, peas, beans, lentils, and chickpeas.

Do not plant vegetables of the same species in the same place two years in a row, like cabbages and cauliflowers. Also do not cultivate plants of the same family like cruciferous vegetables (radishes and turnips), umbelliferae (celery and carrot), or cucurbits (pumpkins and squash). The classic four-year rotation divides the garden into four parts. Look at the box below, which contains two examples. Keep in mind that cabbages can grow after legumes in the same year.

Rotation of crops

● **Tall plants**

First year: beans or peas.
Second year: pumpkins, squash, or cucumbers.
Third year: tomatoes.
Fourth year: corn.

● **Short plants**

First year: cabbage or cauliflower, and radishes.
Second year: carrots, turnips, and celery.
Third year: beets or onions.
Fourth year: peppers, eggplants, and potatoes.

Exceptions to the annual rotation

Tomatoes can be planted several years in the same place, leaving the plants on the ground and burying them to serve as fertilizer. **You may use the same place twice in the same year, for example, to plant lettuce—in spring— and turnips in winter. Follow the criteria of rotation.**
Some plants, like strawberries and turnips, stay several years in the same place. If you have room, reserve some time in the four-year rotation to plant cover crops.

Convenient associations in the garden

Keep in mind when rotating, which plants can be associated with one another and which are incompatible. In the next chapter we will discuss this issue further, but regarding rotation and what plants we can plant together in the square of the garden, here are some convenient associations:

● Garlic, carrot, and onion. Some gardeners also add tomato, because the garlic fights mildew.

● Cabbages, lettuce, cucumbers, beans, leeks, and tomatoes.

● Pumpkins, onions, beans, and peas.

● Pumpkins, spinach, carrots, and onions.

● Eggplants and beans fight potato beetles, onions and leeks repel carrot flies, rosemary and thyme repel cabbage flies, basil repels aphids, and generally aromatic plants are friends with the beneficial insects and enemies of harmful ones. However, you better look at the big chart that we offer on pages 136-137 to study possible associations.

Preparing the layout of the garden

Marianne Hilgers, author of the book *Curso de agricultura ecológica (Organic Farming Course)*, believes that there are four types of associations in the garden:

- **Commensalistic polyculture,** in which one species takes advantage of the other, and the latter does not benefit.
- **Ammensalistic polyculture,** in which one plant is harmed and the other does not feel or suffer, like annuals and perennials interspersed.
- **Monopolistic polyculture,** in which one species benefits and the other is harmed.
- **Inhibitory polyculture,** in which both species are harmed, like when planting sugarcane in a garden interspersed with other plants.

Favorable associations

The main ones are between grasses and legumes, alternating grains, such as barley or rye, with legumes such as alfalfa or clover. This system is used by many farmers that usually plant a legume every two years to recover the lost nitrogen from the soil. However, planting can also be done simultaneously.

The most beneficial association in this sense is the one between corn (a grain) and beans. When the corn reaches a certain height it serves to support beans—planted when they are eight inches (20 cm) tall—and the latter intertwines with the stalk to grow up.

Animals that can help

It is worth remembering that there are many animals that can help us to have an organic garden and to be in communion with nature. So do not be afraid of frogs, as a single one can eat more than ten thousand harmful insects every three months—including crickets, bedbugs, and harmful caterpillars—while at the same

Plan it

- **Divide the work plans for the garden into months and seasons.**
- **Write down the dates for sowing and harvesting vegetables,** using the chart.
- **Divide the space between all species**, taking into account the use you will make of them. **Do not plant too many tomatoes if you do not plan on canning** or giving them away.

There are combinations of favorable and unfavorable plants and every gardener should consider them in order to avoid unexpected problems.

Based on the principle of competition, we combine plants with different root and leaf systems: roots at different depths and leaves that do not compete for light. Also, keep in mind that harvest times are different and that nutritional needs are different. There are associations of plants and insects that need each other. There are also plants with certain fungi that live in the roots and make the nitrogen become assimilable for them, like legumes. Throughout the book and in each plant's description we will mention the rivals and friends, which can be good or bad. For example, chillies planted near tomatoes will give them a particular spicy flavor that some people might like but for most it is not advisable.

Some authors have made their own divisions and classifications. For example, time it respects the earthworms that you lovingly care for. Also, we should respect insectivorous birds, such as swallows, and attract bats, which fly over the orchard fields, getting rid of annoying pests.

Plants that complement each other

- Eggplants and beans fight potato beetles.
- Onions and leeks combat carrot flies. Plant these with tomatoes (onions should be planted first next to the furrow laid down for tomatoes). Also plant them with radishes and strawberries.
- Garlic combats mildew in tomatoes.
- Parsnips and endive get along in alternation.
- Legumes get along with cabbages and carrots in alternate rows, but not with onions and garlic.

Sowing seasons vary depending on climate. Refer to seed packets for specific details.

Six zones for rotation

- In order to maintain soil quality **you should change crops each year.**
- **Divide** the garden into six parts.
- Three of them should be equal for the rotational crops.
- A fourth part will be assigned to perennial crops such as **artichokes, herbs, or small fruits (raspberries, strawberries, or blueberries)**, depending on the climate.
- A fifth part will be meant for crops that occupy a lot of land, such as pumpkins, melons, or cucumbers.
- A sixth one will be to make compost. It may be smaller and it will accumulate organic remains of plants after their growth cycle is finished.
- **Likewise you will need an area to store tools**, hoes, rakes, shovels, watering cans, hoses, and even better if you can cover it so you can prepare the starter pots. Above all, make sure you plan it.

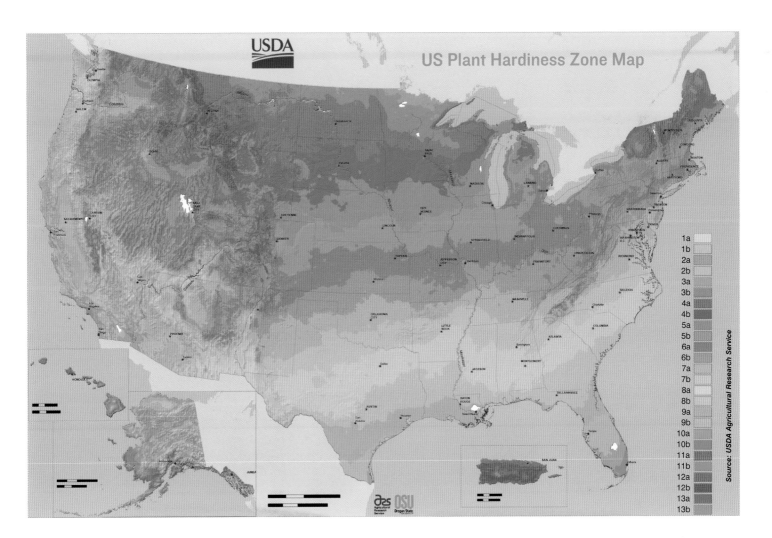

US Plant Hardiness Zone Map

Source: USDA Agricultural Research Service

Association between crops

The data included in this chart is based on experience. Other charts, such as the one from *The Vegetable Gardener's Bible,* suggest different associations—for example, cucumber and tomato are considered friends, whereas potato and tomato adversaries; or cabbage and onions are considered friends while tomatoes and corn enemies—thus contradicting the chart presented below, which indicates that there is no general and absolute law for such relationships.

	Beneficial association	Unfavorable association
chard	celery, lettuce, onions	asparagus, leeks, tomatoes
chicory	lettuce, fennel, tomatoes, onions	cabbage
garlic	strawberries, carrots, turnips, lettuce, peas, beets, potatoes	beans, cabbage, peas
artichoke	lettuce, beans, peas, radish	
celery	lettuce, cabbage, leeks, radish, spinach, tomatoes, cucumbers, beets, beans, chard, peas	corn, parsley, lettuce
eggplants	Beans	potatoes
pumpkin and squash	corn, potatoes, basil, onion, peas, beans	radishes
onions	beets, cucumbers, lettuce, parsley, tomatoes, carrots, strawberries, leeks, spinach, squash, cabbage	cabbage, peas, potatoes, beans
cabbage	beets, beans, lettuce, potatoes, tomatoes, celery, lettuce, peas, cucumbers, leeks	garlic, fennel, chicory, radishes, strawberries, leeks
endive	strawberries, turnip	
asparagus	lettuce, radishes, cucumbers, leeks, tomatoes, parsley, peas	onions, beets
spinach	carrots, onions, turnips, radishes, potatoes, cabbage, beans, strawberries	chard, beets
strawberries	garlic, spinach, lettuce, onions, leek, thyme	cabbage
green peas	asparagus, celery, cabbage, lettuce, turnips, radishes, potatoes, corn, cucumber, carrots	garlic, onions, parsley, leeks
fennel	cabbage, leeks, onions, strawberries, cucumbers, chicory, lettuce, peas	cabbage, tomatoes, beans
beans	eggplant, celery, spinach, lettuce, turnips, radishes, carrots, cabbage, strawberries, corn, potatoes	garlic, fennel, chard, beets, onions
lettuce	beets, chervil, cucumbers, strawberries, onions, peas, carrots, cabbage, lima beans, turnips, leeks, radishes	parsley
corn	cucumbers, peas, beans, tomatoes	beets, potatoes, celery

Indigenous Wisdom

In Central America, subsistence agriculture has always enabled corn, beans, and pumpkins to be planted in the same space. The soil is barely dug on the slopes and the remains of the previous harvest are used as fertilizers. A favorable climate and soil, especially in volcanic areas, allow corn to grow over 13 feet (4 m) and beans thrive between the tall stalks, leaving the ground to the sprawling pumpkins. They are part of a diet that is rich enough to maintain the population.

	Beneficial association	Unfavorable association
turnips	peas, beans, spinach, lettuce tomato, cucumber, cabbage, leek	
potatoes	garlic, cabbage, beans, peas, tomatoes, celery, lima beans, radishes	eggplant, onions, corn cucumber, spinach
cucumbers	asparagus, celery, chives, lettuce, peas, basil, cabbage, beans, corn, fennel	potatoes, tomatoes, radishes beets, parsley, cabbage
leeks	asparagus, spinach, celery, strawberries, onions, carrots, fennel, lettuce, tomatoes	chard, peas cabbage, pumpkins
radishes	carrots, spinach, lettuce, tomatoes, chervil, beans, peas, garlic, cucumber, leek	
beets	celery, lettuce, onions, cabbage	asparagus, beans, leeks, tomatoes, carrots
tomatoes	garlic, basil, celery, onions, leeks, corn, asparagus, carrots, cabbage, parsley, radishes, potatoes	beets, fennel, beans, peas, spinach, cucumber
carrot	onions, lettuce, beans, leeks, radishes, parsley, tomatoes, peas, chervil, garlic	beets, chard

Source: jardínactual.com/html/rinconverde/huerto/compatibilidad.htm (19-XI-2004)

The project of a garden

Shed
Here you can store garden tools, including the sprayer and, if there is enough room, the rototiller which—although it is not recommended because it pollutes the air—can help in large areas and assist people with physical difficulties. Also, you can make starter pots or store the recently purchased ones.

Pond
Here you can have a water source or a pond. It will be dedicated to clean carrots or to make strings of garlic.

Fruit trees and flowers
Here you could plant fruit trees, north of the rest of the garden if possible, to avoid casting shadows on other plants. You could also plant artichokes, beets, asparagus, culinary and aromatic plants, and flowering plants in order to attract insects. Roses are included, though you must be careful because they need sun and are very jealous of their private space. You could add blueberries, strawberries, and currants. If a cherry tree is planted it must be near the fountain or pond for irrigation. The garden will have good shade and splendid flowers in the spring.

Roots
In this area of the three-year rotation you will plant potatoes, carrots, parsnips, turnips, beets, and leeks.

Legumes
Here you can plant legumes for the three-year rotation: beans, peas, lima beans, and any other that makes a proper combination such as onions, garlic, lettuce, spinach, and radishes. On the edges you can plant chard, celery, and leeks. In the middle you can plant basil to ward off insects.

Cabbages
Here you can plant cabbages, cauliflower, broccoli, lettuce, and endive. You can plant tomatoes either here or in the legumes box.

Pumpkins
Here we can leave an area for plants that spread out, such as pumpkins, squash, cucumbers, or watermelons.

The garden, month by month

Below is a basic calendar, which applies to gardens in temperate regions (zones 7 and 8). Remember that growing seasons vary by climate, and you should refer to your seed packets for specifics.

In October

- If we have done well, the garden is still booming.
- You can still harvest beets, squash, cabbage, endive, spinach, lettuce, beets, and carrots.
- The time to let the garden rest is coming, although if the weather is good and the region is warm, we still encourage you to transplant onions, spring cabbage, endive, and strawberries, but it may be better to wait.
- Walnuts, hazelnuts, apples, and chestnuts are harvested.
- We add compost to soils that are becoming bare and begin to clean out the plants for winter.

In November

- Pull up annoying weeds, thoroughly stir the soil, add manure, and level the area you will use for sowing.
- Plant garlic, endives, spinach, lima beans, parsley, and radishes. If it is cold, use quick hoops (plastic tunnels).
- In a dry fall, water plants that are recently planted.
- You can already harvest onions, carrots, chicory, cabbage, and parsley. Regarding fruit crops, you can harvest quinces, pears, apples, oranges, and lemons.
- Apple and pear trees are pruned, fallen foliage is removed, soil is fertilized, and winter mineral oils are used.

In December

- It is probably the only month in which the everlasting chard is scarce, but if you have been prudent you will still have cabbage, endives, spinach, and carrots—not in cold weather though.
- In temperate zones we plant garlic, spinach, peas, and lima beans. We can also plant strawberries.
- Fertilize trees and start pruning.

In January

- Finish spreading the compost or manure and dig the ground deeply. If it is cold you should put mulch around the plants that are still green, like spinach.
- Harvest beets, broccoli, endive, spinach, escarole, cabbages, lettuce, and leeks.
- Sow in hotbeds: tomatoes, eggplant, and squash. If it is hot, plant peppers.
- Sow in single seedling pots: tomatoes, eggplant, endives, leeks, lettuce, celery, and early cabbage.

- Plant—outdoors—garlic, radishes, and carrots if the weather is warm.
- This is the ideal time to prune rose bushes and to plant pitted fruits. If you have vines you can dig them now.

In February

- Continue the work of the previous month if you have not finished all of it yet. The cold continues but in temperate zones you can transplant the seeds planted on hotbeds to starter pots or pots.
- Add green manure to the soil, weather permitting.
- We continue to harvest beets, cabbage, spinach, lettuce, endives, and turnips.
- You can also follow the same planting as in January but this time in a simple seedbed: chard, lettuce, endives, and leeks.
- Plant garlic, red beets, carrots, and radishes.

In March

- This is a month of climatic contrasts, so we have to be careful with the pots because frost could still occur. You must start preparing the soil in order to get going.
- Plant artichokes, cabbages, cauliflower, endives, peas, lima beans, leeks, lettuce, radishes, and carrots.
- Using covered seedbeds, sow eggplants, pumpkins, cucumbers, melons, and peppers.
- Using covered seedbeds, plant garlic, lima beans, spinach, potatoes, radishes, and carrots. If it is hot, also plant green beans.
- We start mulching with grass that has recently been cut.
- Plant mint and parsley. You can also plant rosemary from cuttings.
- You can transplant spring cauliflowers and leeks. Also, if it is hot or in coastal zones, you can plant tomatoes, zucchini, peppers, and eggplant, but use a lot of prudence.

In April

- This month you need to be really careful of late frosts, and the sowings you do will depend on location.
- The green manure will be ready for burial. We can sulfate with horsetail and sulfur to prevent pests.
- Continue the previous month's transplants, still keeping calm, because in inland areas the first days of the month it is still freezing.
- We enrich the compost and adjust the pH of the soil.
- Harvest artichokes, cabbages, spinach, chicory, lima beans, peas, lettuce, leeks, turnips, and carrots.

- Plant indoors: pumpkins, squash, melons, and cucumbers.
- In uncovered seedbeds, plant chard, celery, cabbages, and lettuce.
- Directly sow: squash, spinach, chicory, climbing beans, corn, turnips, potatoes, radishes, beets, and carrots.
- Transplant: onions, cabbages, lettuce, tomatoes (directly and protected), eggplant, squash, and peppers.

In May

- It is the best month. Vegetables and herbs grow joyously, so you will work to keep the garden clean in addition to a lot of harvesting and sowing that must be done.
- Harvest tender garlic, onions, celery, chard, broccoli, lettuce, turnips, leeks, small radishes, and carrots.
- In uncovered seedbeds, sow squash, cabbages, cauliflowers, melons, cucumbers, and leeks.
- Plant directly in the ground squash, pumpkins, onions, cabbages, melons, peppers, leeks, and tomatoes.
- If you have fruit trees, you may pick cherries and loquats.
- Insect prevention begins, such as against the fruit fly. It is time to prepare the traps.

In June

- The hot days start and we must be alert to watering. Tomatoes and squash require water but especially lettuces and endives that could potentially bolt.
- It is also the season of weeds, so you have to weed, especially if it has rained, and mulch generously to prevent them from growing.
- We continue harvesting chard, squash, celery, cauliflower, turnips, carrots, lettuce, and spinach. Add onions, strawberries, peas, tomatoes (in warm weather), potatoes, and beans.
- You can sow in uncovered seedbeds: fall and winter cabbages and cauliflower, endives, and lettuce.
- Plant beans, squash, short-cycle maize, beets, carrots, parsley, and radishes.
- Harvest all kinds of fruits. Plums begin.
- We bravely fight against the aphid.

In July

- It's too hot so you must water with drip irrigation or by furrows, but without wetting the plants. Mulch should cover everything. Select plants that will be used for seeds for the following year.

- Continue harvesting chard, celery, zucchini, cabbage, endives, spinach, lettuce, radishes, and beets. Add watercress, chickpeas, cucumbers, peppers, and eggplant. You can also add beans and tomatoes in cool climates.
- Directly plant beets, endives, spinach, and lettuce.
- Transplant celery, cabbage, and fall cauliflower.

In August

- It is really hot, the garden is at its peak, and it is the worst month to leave for vacation. You have to be there every day, because you have to pick and water daily. You will also need to give away or can the surplus—also a time-consuming task.
- Harvest basically everything except spring products such as artichokes, lima beans, peas, or spinach, although they endure cool climates.
- Directly plant chard, beets, endive, lettuce, and turnips.
- In seedbeds, prepare onions, lettuce, and cabbage.
- Transplant broccoli and fall cabbages.
- Continue to pick fruits: peaches, pears, plums, and the first grapes.

In September

- In some places, harvest will be diminished because sometimes August ends with rains and cool temperatures—though climate change has made some seasons longer.
- We continue harvesting, above all, tomatoes, cucumbers, eggplants, peppers, and beans (some of them already dry). However, spinach, cabbage, lettuce (already scarce when you crave it most), radishes, melons, watermelons, and carrots can also be harvested.
- Plant beets, celery (which is harvested almost all year round like chard), cabbage, spinach, endive, and lettuce.
- Transplant cabbage, onions, cauliflower, lettuce, endive, and leeks.
- It's the season for almonds. Table grapes are replaced with wine grapes. Persimmons ripen.

Harvesting
Vegetables

Vegetables: how to cultivate them, allies, and problems

A good garden requires time to reach its full potential. We will give you some ideas so you can enjoy waiting.

The moment of truth has come. The dream of every gardener is to supply him or herself with the basic, primal products while maintaining a rich and varied diet. You could say that every gardener is a gourmet and also an artist.

The first reason is that he or she must taste his or her own creations and judge for better or for worse—and he/she can always improve them. Do not just accept them as they are—the taste of onions or peppers not only depends on the type of seed and the fact that you fulfill the basic requirements of a good gardener. There are other factors such as type of soil, orientation, the shadow of a wall, an underground river, or even the love given to each plant.

Actually, we wanted to talk about the latter because a good gardener pampers his/her plants, puts all his/her heart into them, and is in some way linked to nature . . . and plants will thank him/her for this.

The good gardener ensures that the garden looks like a piece of art. Proportions are appropriate, the furrows are kept clean of weeds, the water falls and accumulates where it is supposed to do so, there are no harmful insects, the cat does not play in the bushes, and rabbits do not eat the sprouts because the gardener complied with his/her duties in a timely manner. There are no snails or slugs, or aphids, but ladybugs and birds. The soil is loose and its dark color stands out wherever it has not

been covered by dry leaves and herbs to prevent drying or weeds.

Leafy vegetables that we are going to eat—such as chard, spinach, or lettuce—do not have caterpillars. Not a single laboratory-produced chemical has been used.

If there is room, a good gardener has a few fruit trees; to eat an apple or a peach, all he/she needs to do is remove the dust by wiping it on her arm. Above all, a good gardener experiments, and since he/she is not stupid and wants to know what is the best way of doing things, he/she looks for and asks the older gardeners in the area. Yes, those who have spent many years doing the same as taught by their parents who in turn were taught by their grandparents. He/she learns from all of them and seeks ways to reproduce first, and to improve thereafter.

Do not be discouraged; a good garden needs time to reach full potential.

Leafy vegetables

Chard

Chard (*Beta vulgaris*) is a Mediterranean plant first described by Aristotle in the fourth century. It was a staple food for a long time due to its ability to grow anywhere and under all conditions. This is a biennial plant with a long cycle, very much like beets. The edible part is not the root but the leaves, which can reach large sizes.

Cultivation

Chard is a plant of temperate climates that freezes below 23°F (-5°C) and grows well between 43 and 86 °F (6 and 30°C). It does not need much light but does require enough moisture; this is noticeable in dry climates where it grows significantly in rainy seasons. It likes clay soil with a pH between 5.5 and 8. It tolerates salts pretty well, though not acids. It can be grown on ridges, leaving 16 or 20 inches (40 or 50 cm) between each plant. It can also be planted in pots, in an open and clean space. Place two or three seeds in each hole. Maturing period is 50 to 60 days. In warm weather they are planted throughout the year and in cold weather, from October to March; if done in seedbeds they are transplanted when they have 4 or 5 leaves in March-April. If sowing is done in pots, plastic sheeting can be used to cover the soil. Chard does not require an excessive fertilization, although in a manured soil it grows faster. Watering is recommended every 20 days at the most if it does not rain, but more abundant irrigation will also yield larger leaves. It blossoms the second year, and if allowed, its seeds are distributed so it easily grows in other parts of the garden.

Once flowered, you should pull it out and not plant it in the same place for two or three years. In the garden it goes well with low bush beans, carrots, and radishes.

Difficulties

Beware of slugs because chard's large leaves are usually very appealing to them. In this case they appear chewed on.

Aphids, cutworms, beet flies, and flea beetles can also attack. Excessive moisture can rot the leaves and cause other fungal diseases such as mildew, cyclospora, and beet mosaic. Lack of nutrients make the leaves look yellowish. Diseased leaves should be destroyed or burned. Leaves with gray spots should not be transplanted.

Usage

Biennial plant that blossoms every two years. Its leaves can be picked, depending on the weather, from three to six months of age. Chard is emollient, refreshing, digestive, diuretic, and nutritious. It is used against bladder inflammation, constipation, and hemorrhoids. In the kitchen it is used in salads, steamed or in the form of juice for intestinal diseases, and with lemon juice and olive oil to strengthen the stomach and stimulate the brain.

Varieties. Wild chard grows on the edge of fields and road. It is the tastiest, though it needs more cooking time. Moreover, there are many varieties: wide main rib, white or red, thin or narrow, dark or light green, curly or smooth . . .

Chard grows almost wild and reproduces well even in abandoned gardens.

TIP

In the garden, it goes well with celery, lettuce, and onions. Do not plant them with tomatoes.

Lamb's Lettuce

Lamb's lettuce (*Valerianella locusta*) is a highly branched annual herbaceous plant, with fragile stems, and spatulate, ovate, or lanceolate leaves. It has tiny pale lilac flowers in bunches, which are very numerous. It flowers from April to July and reaches 2–17 inches (6–40 cm). It was first cultivated in monasteries of the seventeenth century, hence the name "lamb's lettuce," because it's considered to be able to reduce sexual arousal.

Lamb's lettuce is good in salads with avocado and mushrooms; add lemon juice, garlic, and coarse salt. Enjoy.

Cultivation

It is a winter plant that resists the cold well and that bolts right away when it's hot. It likes firm, bare, clay soils, not dug too deep. Fertilization is low and you just have to water it if the winter is dry. It is planted from July to September in stages from seeds stored for at least two years, as maturity improves their ability to germinate. Plant it in rows spaced about 8 inches (20 cm) apart. Beforehand, you should have those seeds soaked for twenty-four hours, and then, you should cover the soil with straw or some compost to prevent it from getting too dry. Keep this only until they sprout. It is necessary to prevent the plant from being too large when frosts strike. Harvesting begins in October for the ones first planted and lasts all winter.

If it is bitterly cold, cover the plants with straw. You can harvest them until spring. The first heat waves will spoil them, so it is good to plant them in places with some shade by the trees, next to cabbages, lettuce, and chard.

Difficulties

The only difficulty that lamb's lettuce faces is excess moisture, which can cause rotting. To fight this problem you must keep the soil under the plants clean and remove all leaves that show signs of rotting, as they may have powdery mildew and rust fungus. If the rotting spreads, it is advisable to use wettable sulfur.

Usage of lamb's lettuce

As a cleanser, the plant is boiled at 3 ounces (100 grams) per quart (liter) of water for 5 minutes. The dose is 3 to 4 cups daily for ten days. **Helpful in preventing sexual arousal**, the leaves are blanched in boiling water and served with olive oil and vinegar. Eat the salad and drink the scalding water half an hour before bedtime or twice a day.

Cardoon

MAIN RIBS

The edible part of cardoon is the leaves' main rib or midrib.

Difficulties

Cardoon suffers from the same pests artichokes do. When they are young, pesky weeds attack cardoon so you must protect it by mulching, and when mature, due to moisture, it attracts snails and slugs. Voles also find fertile ground among its roots. Make sure you fertilize its soil every harvest.

Cardoon (*Cynara cardunculus*) is a perennial plant that could measure up to 6'6" (2 m) in height. It differs from its relative artichoke (*Cynara scolymus*) because cardoon has longer and fleshier leaves, especially the central ribs, which are the edible part. It is believed that cardoon originated in Egypt or Libya, and was introduced as such in Europe by Greeks and Romans. During the Middle Ages, cardoon varieties began a selection process resulting in the artichoke. Cardoon is low in calories while high in fiber, calcium, and iron. Apparently, it is useful for diabetics because it contains insulin and is free of starch.

Cultivation

Four or five seeds are placed in holes separated by less than three feet (1 meter), along the margins of the garden, in deep and well fertilized soil. Once it has sprouted, leave a couple of plants. The ground should be weeded and mulched. Some people prefer the white main ribs and tie them together, so they do not touch the sun. However, it is unnecessary because once the leaf is boiled the bitterness of its greenish parts is hardly noticeable. As it grows, the gardener picks the outer, more developed leaves; they should still be meaty and tender. Cardoon continues to be productive for three or four years. After that, it is usually pulled out and re-sown in the same area after waiting one year. It becomes evident that cardoon is easy to grow and slightly marginal in the garden. It associates positively with lima beans, which nourish the soil.

Preparing Cardoon

Once harvested and the leaves separated, cardoon's secondary ribs are discarded with a knife, and then the toughest fibers of the main rib are removed from top to bottom. Finally, it is boiled.

Italians and Argentinians of Piedmontese descent cook cardoon with garlic, olive oil, anchovies, and cream, for a typical Bagna Cauda. It is even simpler to grill the leaves—after boiling them—with cheese and tomato.

Cardoon with seitan

A good way to cook cardoon is with seitan or wheat gluten. Put them in water with lemon and cook them in a white broth made with flour, lemon, and oil before adding them to previously roasted seitan.

Endive

Endives with Roquefort cheese

This is the most famous recipe.

- Wash the endives and place them in a dish, adding Roquefort sauce.
- For the sauce, simmer in a pot 3.5 oz (100 g) Roquefort cheese and 7 oz (200 g) of cream, and stir until thickened.
- Spread the sauce over the endives.

True **endive** (*Cichorium endive*) is the edible variety appropriate for the garden and is, in fact, a variety of chicory with a curly endive-like head and its inner leaves whitish.

Endive sold for consumption is grown using a technique called Witloof ("white sheet") so that its leaves do not receive light and acquire that commercial whitish tone you may be familiar with. The method for obtaining these Witloof endives is long and complicated for a family garden, as the ones intended for the store are the offspring of tender leaves that grow in the second year of its life cycle. The wild species has curled leaves and is very bitter to taste, but in the garden we find a substitute cultivating chicory or broadleaf endives. They are similar to lettuce,

Endive is also known as Belgian endive; this is not in vain, since Belgium and Luxembourg offer the greatest harvest around the world.

cold-resistant, and can be whitish if the leaves are tied together or put against each other, thus avoiding sunlight.

Properties

Endive—like chicory—is rich in fiber and regulates intestinal transit, cleaning bothersome substances from the digestive system. It protects the intestinal mucosa, prevents inflammation, fights gases and acidity, and last but not least, it basically has no calories, because

its content is 94 percent water. It is also a diuretic and is used in weight loss recipes. Receiving no light, it lacks vitamin C, but it is antioxidant and anti-carcinogenic; meaning, in other words, it will extend your life.

Difficulties

Endive can be attacked by slugs and cutworms. Its common diseases are sclerotin and lettuce mildew.

TIP

Be careful when you eat endives to not leave them soaking in water because it accentuates the bitterness. Just pass them under cold water and drain before serving with a little oil or Roquefort sauce.

Curly Endive

Endive (*Cichorium endivia L.*) is a variety of endive, which in turn is a variety of chicory. It is believed to be native to India, but was already used in ancient Egypt and around the Mediterranean since time immemorial. Its leaves grow in a cluster without forming a floret. Inner leaves have a lighter color and are more attractive gastronomically because in addition to their curly shape—like the rest of the plant—they are slightly bitter and freshening. Curly endive is cleansing, laxative, refreshing, and contains vitamins A, B, C, and K. It also contains iron, magnesium, cobalt, manganese, and zinc.

Cultivation

Curly endive grows between 43 and 86°F (6 and 30°C) but can resist temperatures down to 21 °F (-6°C). It likes loamy, slightly acidic, rich in potassium, and well-watered soils with low humidity in the air. Heat causes it to bolt. Curly endive can be planted directly in the ground or in a seedbed at any time of the year. After a month it is transplanted to the ground. It is harvested after two or three months. It associates well with lettuce, carrots, beets, and cabbage.

Difficulties

Pests that usually attack curly endive are turnip moth, leafminers, whiteflies, Diptera larvae, caterpillars, aphids, leaf worm, thrips, snails, and slugs.

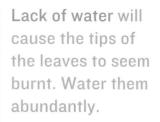

Lack of water will cause the tips of the leaves to seem burnt. Water them abundantly.

Bleaching the endive

Endive's green leaves are more bitter than the white leaves, which should not get any sunlight. In order to achieve this, **it is common to tie them with a rubber band or a cord so the inner leaves remain in the shade one week before harvesting.** It also helps when you grow them tightly close together, or when you cover them with planters fifteen days before picking. Some people do it with a black plastic tarp about ten days before harvest.

Varieties

There are two main types: Curly with very twisted and divided leaves, and escarole, with broad, wavy leaves and not so toothed. The latter are much more resistant to cold. The most popular varieties are: Agora, Brevo, Salonca, and Stratego, perhaps the best among the broad-leaved. Varieties for the curly ones are: Amel, Oxalie, Remix, and Tosca.

Spinach

Spinach is native to Persia, and from there it was brought to Europe in the year 1000, although its industrial production did not begin until the eighteenth century.

This is a plant that sprouts a cluster of edible leaves and later issues a stem in which flowers appear. The main producer is China, with about 8 million tons, followed by Japan and the US, with just over 300,000 tons. Turkey, Belgium, and Korea are next in the list. Spinach has anti-anemic, laxative, and remineralizing virtues.

Cultivation

Spinach is a winter plant that grows from 41°F (5°C), though at least 59°F (15°C) is a condition for an abundant harvest. Permanent cold and heat make it flourish, causing the leaves to become bitter.

Soils should be deep and well fertilized, with the right humidity. However, if you do not wait for too long it is an easy plant to grow. The land should not be fertilized with excessively cold compost. The planting is done in square plots or in buried rows a few inches deep. Sowing is at the end of August, staggered so harvest goes from December to March. Avoid weeds and leave about 4 inches (10 cm) between plants. There are varieties that are planted in spring and harvested in summer.

The largest leaves from around the plant make a suitable harvest. Each plant yields from four to five cuts of leaves. Once pulled out, it has a four- to five-year waiting time. Spinach is friends with legumes, strawberries, celery, lettuce, endive, cabbage, and celery.

Difficulties

Beware of slugs. Aphids—which form colonies behind the leaves—and, more specifically, nematodes and beet leafminers, are likely to attack the spinach. As for diseases, spinach could suffer from spinach mildew and cucumber virus. Spinach is not copper-resistant, so avoid using Bordeaux mixture.

Varieties

They are numerous and are categorized according to season, size, color, thickness, or shape of its leaves. The best known and suitable for fall, winter, and spring are: Polka, Viroflay, winter giant, and Seville for fall, winter, and spring; Valletta, for spring, Viking for summer, etc.

Sweet Fennel

Foeniculum vulgare is native to the Middle East. **Its bulbs, which are the thick segment of the leaves, are the edible part and have a peculiar flavor between anise and celery.** They are good either raw or with Bechamel. Fennel is not cold-resistant and likes well-manured soils. You can sow it in seedbeds from February on or directly in the ground from May on. Harvest it before winter.

Lettuce

Lettuce (*Lactuca sativa*) may come from India, though its true origin is unclear. The only certainty is that wild species are very small compared to the cultivated one. The loose-leaved ones were cultivated by the Greeks and budded ones did not appear in Europe until the sixteenth century.

It is an annual plant, with a root that is not very big, but thick. It has clustered leaves and a cylindrical branched stem that emerges in maturity and spoils the plant.

The main producer is China (with nearly 8 million tons) followed by the United States (more than 4) and Spain (one million tons). Lettuce has few calories and stimulates the intestinal tract, so it is a good slimming food. Moreover, it has vitamins A, B, C, D, and E, as well as calcium, zinc, iron, phosphorus, potassium, and sodium, although all of these minerals come in small quantities.

Cultivation

Lettuce grows anywhere, but it does best in a well-fertilized and well-drained soil, with temperatures between 46 and 64°F (8 and 18°C); it

Varieties

They come in four main types: Romaine, the ones with the central bud or heart, the ones with loosed and scattered leaves, and asparagus lettuce with tasty stems grown in India. The Romaine type is loose-leaved, and its varieties include Romaine and Baby. The hearted ones have a bud of tight leaves. They are blander but easier to conserve and varieties include Iceberg, Batavia, Wonder (with a violet color on top and more heat-tolerant), Trocadero (more cold-tolerant), and the famous Tudela buds. The main varieties for the loose-scatter-leaved type are Lollo Rosa, Red Salad, and Craquerelle. If you want seasonal varieties look for blonde large Romaine, Zaragoza Romaine, Inverna, and Parris Island Romaine for winter. And for summer, there is the Romaine Nogatine, Romaine Pierre Benite, blonde Batavia, Great Lakes, Great Summer, and Kraganer. Tudela buds are a winter variety.

is native to very cool climates. However, it resists temperatures as low as 21°F (6°C) and up to 86°F (30°C), although it does not develop well and gets spoiled.

It likes abundant watering when planting is finished, but if it already has a head, drip irrigation is more suitable. It is sown in winter using seedbeds for later staggered transplanting when it has four to six leaves. It can also be sown directly in the ground, as it is done in the United States with the variety Iceberg, running the risk that birds and insects eat the seed. When transplanting, only the root gets underneath the surface, not the stem. If planted from September to January, harvest takes place in spring; if we do it in spring, harvest is in summer, and if planted after the summer, harvest them in winter.

Romaine lettuces are tied together one week before harvesting, when they are about 5 ½ inches (14 cm) in size, to get a desirable whitish color so they are sweeter. It associates well with almost all plants in the garden. There is no problem in repeated sowing, although it is better not to abuse and follow the quadrennial rotation. When planted on ridges it remains safe from moisture, which spoils the leaves and attracts snails. It is harvested from about two months or sooner when the heads are well compacted after being pressed with hands.

Difficulties

To avoid annoying weeds, you should mulch the

Sow thistle

Sonchus oleraceus is a perennial plant 3 or 4 feet high that can produce flowers (yellow and combined) throughout the year. It is similar to the dandelion. Its most tender leaves are edible in salads or cooked. Those leaves and the root can be the base for diuretic infusions. Latex from its leaves is good for fillings. And since the plant attracts aphids it is planted near cabbage.

ground around lettuces, but that favors the presence of snails and slugs, so you must be aware of them.

It is attacked by thrips, leaf miners, whiteflies, and birds. Regarding diseases, lettuce is prone to anthracnose, botrytis, sclerotin, mildew, and mosaic virus, among others. There is no comparison between organic and industrial crops. In addition, they lose flavor within a few days.

Protection for lettuce

White grub—the cockchafer's larvae—which sometimes destroys lettuce or strawberries, can be neutralized by shaking the adult specimens out of trees and burying the remains of dirty wool.

Against the snails, place wood chips surrounding the lettuce so that they cannot pass.

To obtain seeds, let one of the best-looking lettuce develop a stalk and flower. Then cover the flower stalk with a fine cloth or a plastic bag to protect it from birds. Once the plant gets dry, shake it inside the same cloth and sift.

Leeks

Leek (*Allium porrum*) comes from the Near East and Egypt. Called the "Eastern garlic," it was introduced in Europe during the Middle Ages and is a remarkable food in France. This plant, which can reach 20 inches (50 cm) in height, consists of a bulb and a thick, false stem of 1–2 inches (3–5 cm) thick. The latter is formed by leaves rolled or sheathed into each other. It grows in any climate and all year-round, although its optimum growth temperature is between 55 and 75°F (13 and 24°C).

Cultivation

It likes deep soils rich in organic matter, like onion and garlic; it does not tolerate a pH below 6 and it grows more on stony ground. Planting is done in seedbeds, using 8–10 grams (they are very small seeds) per square meter. When the seedlings are about 8 inches (20 cm) they are transplanted into the garden furrows at a distance of 5 inches (15 cm) apart. It does not tolerate fresh manure, so you should use the previous year's manure and place it deep in the soil, or plant without fertilizer in a place that was well manured the previous year.

In dry weather, it is desirable to water it often. Development takes at least five months. Make a first seedbed (covered) in January, transplant it in March, and begin to pick it in May and throughout the summer. Make another uncovered seedbed in May, which you will transplant in July and harvest all winter.

For it to develop well, you should weed frequently and cover the surrounding soil with straw or organic matter to retain moisture. This plant resists frosts as low as 19°F (-7°C) and some varieties down to -4°F (-20°C).

In France, gardeners often blunt leaves during transplantation and also later on to slow down its growth. To blanch the leaves you can cover them with soil or place a black plastic sheet at the base so that the sun reflects on the leaves.

It should not be planted in the same place for three or four years. It gets along with carrots, celery, strawberries, and tomatoes. It does not get along with beans, cabbages, peas, lettuce, and radishes.

Difficulties

Depending on the latitude, the onion fly larvae, which attacks the green parts of the plant, can be one kind of attacker, as can thrips that attack in dry summers, and nematodes, striking at any time. The leaves can suffer from mildew, rust, blight, and white tip. And once picked, if left for too long, they can be attacked by a bacterium that causes rotting of the soft parts of the plant. If it is humid, they can be attacked by Botrytis and Alternaria.

Usage

Leek is antiseptic, digestive, expectorant, laxative, and tonic. Its nutritional value is small, but it is rich in minerals such as phosphorus, calcium, and potassium. Good for rheumatism and anemia, it is used as a vegetable, or boiled, or in soups such as vichyssoise made with leeks, potatoes, and onions.

Leek varieties, besides wild leek—a variety of strong flavor—are of two types: the first type of leek is short or semi-long, with names like Arcadia and Electra; the second type is the long leek, with names like Alaska or Helvetia.

Virtues

Leeks should be prepared by steaming them or by boiling them in water for soup. Among its virtues we find the laxative, as it cleans everything in its path but without irritating the intestine. It has iron, magnesium, calcium, phosphorus and sulfur, which is good against bronchitis. Also, it has many vitamins and its cooking water is good against pharyngitis. Do not eat it raw because it can be difficult to digest that way.

Watercress

Dandelion

Watercress (*Rorippa nasturtium-aquaticum*) can be found around our region on the banks of all freshwater rivers and streams. However, if you want to grow it in your garden you need to have a flooded ditch, a fountain, or a pond, or other flowing water. Of course not everyone is that lucky, so you should build a tray on the ground, fill it with soil, and flood it during cultivation. Watercress is planted under the course of the water in rows separated by about 6 inches (15 cm) and leaving about 4 (10 cm) between those rows.

Watercress sowing season is during fall and harvest is in spring and summer, when the plant is about 6 inches (15 cm) tall.

After harvest the canal is emptied and fertilized with compost or manure. It is advisable to let some flourish and mature, so the seed expands.

We can also plant it on a nearby stream, and some people have planted it on the saucers used to collect water from the pots, producing an excellent harvest.

Watercress is excellent in salads or simply with garlic and oil, although some people reject it for its spicy and slightly pungent taste. Raw leaves and the tips of the young shoots are good for eating. It is rich in vitamin A, calcium, phosphorus, and iodine and is used against anemia and diabetes.

> TIP
>
> They say that **watercress** protects and helps young orange trees grow. However, keep in mind that they need a lot of water.

The **dandelion** (*Taxacorum officinale*) grows wild and is abundant in good nitrogen wetlands. Its yellow flowers are quite remarkable and its seed pod forms a puffy light ball. Some gardens look like they have a carpet made of this plant. In the shade this plant yields toothed glossy leaves that are very tasty for salads. It is laxative, diuretic, and anti-rheumatic. If root, leaves, and flowers are boiled the mix will produce a liquid that helps with conditions of the liver. It has calcium, phosphorus, iron, potassium, magnesium, and vitamins A, B, and C.

It grows in almost all climates, and even more if the soil is well fertilized and rich in limestone. It can be planted in rows about 8 inches (20 cm) apart, with seedlings about 4 inches (10 cm) apart, between March and June. Or it can also be done on seedbed from January to March, in order to transplant it to the ground when it's not cold, if you are a heavy consumer. Between June and July reproduction is done by dividing the plant root, which is planted again. Dandelion sprouts every spring. Just let the puffy seed balls spread all over the garden.

Although beware, because they do not get along with vegetables and it is better to reserve them a place in the garden or just go out and look for them in the fields. The sunny meadow ones are tastier.

Cabbages

It can be eaten raw, but if you have a sensitive stomach cook it and do not forget to add a little flour to keep it white. Also, in order to avoid the smell spreading all over the house, add a splash of milk.

Varieties

They are numerous and are divided by their cycle:

Extra early
Erfurt (French and very old, with heads weighing about one pound); Succes and Snowball (varieties of the above); Catalina (Spanish variety during October-November); Brestol (Danish origin); Presto (French); Veralto, Primula, and Fortados (Dutch).

Early
Suprimax (Dutch); Idol; Supernova, Zealand, Avans, and Dominant (Danish); Lefert (heat-resistant and very old); Kangaroo (Australian); Rhonia (French); and Florablanca (very large).

Medium
Primus (French), Durato (Dutch), Canberra (Australia), Frankfurter (Germany), Danish Giant and Giant of Naples.

Late
San José (traditional, big, harvested in March, but poor conservation), Late Lent (resistant to cold, from March to April), and Metropol (Italian, large).

Cauliflower

Cauliflower (*Brassica oleracea*) was first cultivated in Italy, before it diversified in the Eastern Mediterranean and spread throughout Europe in the seventeenth century. Cauliflower is supposed to be the cluster containing all those thickened heads of the flowers. Most of those flowers abort and lead to thickened branches that are tight together and tender, creating the heads of cauliflower or pellets. The latter are the remains of the flowers: simple asperities. Cauliflower pel-

lets may be spherical, curved, conical, flat, or hollow.

The world's largest producer is India, with nearly five million tons, followed by China, France, Italy and Spain, with about 300,000 tons. It is rich in potassium and vitamin C, and contains fiber, calcium, phosphorus, iron, magnesium, and zinc. In the Netherlands they recently created a cross between cauliflower and broccoli called Broccoflower.

Cultivation

Cauliflowers like the same temperatures that humans do, between 59 and 77 °F, and like us they are sensitive to low temperatures (below 32 °F) and high ones (over 79 °F). Cauliflowers likes porous, well-fertilized soils with a pH of 6.5 to 7, that is, with not too much limestone. They are planted in greenhouses in winter and early varieties are transplanted in spring to be harvested in late summer. In any case, for transplantation, wait for the fourth or fifth true leaf. Depending on the variety, extra early ones are harvested in September or October, early ones in November, mid-season ones between late December and February, and in March the larger ones. Industrial crops of cauliflower yield between 33,000 and 60,000 per hectare.

Problems

Cauliflower can be stored up to three weeks before eating. Frost damage occurs at 30°F. Pests that affect crops are: cabbage caterpillars (*Pieris Brassicae*, a soft white butterfly with black spots on the wings and *Mamestra brassicae*, a moth); Cabbage moths (*Plutella xylostella* and *Hellula undalis*, gray butterflies whose $2/5$-inch larvae hide in the leaves during the day and at night they eat the inflorescences; pheromones are common to fight them); Cabbage fly (*Chortophila brassicae*, whose larvae attack the tissues on the seedbeds); whitefly (*Aleyrodes brassicae*, which attacks the leaves in cold

Broccoli

weather and leaves honey-dew that attracts fungi); false hernia or cabbage weevil (a black beetle that attacks the seedlings), and the cruciferous waxy aphid (gray-green, attacks the young leaves).

Diseases

Cabbage hernia (*Plasmadiophora brassicae*, a fungus that develops in acidic soils), botrytis, and mildew (that attacks in high humidity), dry rot (*Phoma lingam*, a fungus that attacks the neck of the flower and whose treatment is avoiding fields where the disease has been present), and cauliflower bacteria (bacteria that darkens the top of the flower pellets, and benefits from moisture). To avoid cabbage worm, make a cork collar around cabbage about eight inches (20 cm) in diameter with a hole in the center for the stem.

RECIPE

Cauliflower—the Italian way. Get a medium cauliflower and separate its flowers. Boil them for 5-8 minutes depending on how tender you want them. Separately, combine 3 tablespoons oil, 2 tablespoons balsamic vinegar, ¼ teaspoon of salt, and a chopped garlic. Heat lukewarm. This mix is poured over cauliflower and served.

Broccoli is a plant like cauliflower but more narrow with upright leaves, small flowers, native to the Middle East, and already used by the Romans. Like cabbages, its flower begins to form after a period of time at low temperatures (between 50 and 59 °F). In the terminal bud a pellet is formed surrounded by other smaller ones that grow from leaf branches (at temperatures from 68 to 75 °F). It requires a relatively high humidity (60-70), rather acidic soils, and water low in salt.

It is one of the plants that have more vitamins and minerals by weight, significantly outperforming the cauliflower. It is better when cooked. It has vitamin A, B, C, calcium, phosphorus, and iron. Its name comes from the Latin *brachium* and the Italian *brocco*, meaning "arm" or "branch."

Cultivation

The soil is dug deep and the seed is placed in ridges separated between 2' 7" and 3' 4". It is sown in seedbeds and sprouts within ten days. After 50 days, transplantation is done, when the plant is about 8 inches tall and has 6–8 final leaves. It requires that the soil is rich in potassium and boron and does

Varieties

Like cauliflower, broccoli species are cycle-dependent. Overall, they are harvested much earlier than the former because the main varieties—**Admiral, Coaster, Green duke, and Corvet**—are collected three months after planting. The **Marisa** variety is collected after two months.

not tolerate a lack of magnesium. Broccoli needs enough water until the flower formation begins, after which the soil should not be moist.

Soil should be clean of weeds, and it is suggested to leave enough leaves so the flower is protected as it grows.

Problems

It is attacked by the leafminer, cabbage fly, cabbage worm, false hernia or cabbage weevil, diamondback moth, cabbage flea, and cabbage beetles. Broccoli can be affected by the following diseases: Alternaria, cabbage hernia, cabbage stain, mildew, Rhizoctonia, and rust.

Vulgar cabbage or cabbage sprouts (*Cruciferae Brassica oleracea*) are a variety of cabbage that was already known in Egypt, but would not be grown until the time of the Greeks. Apparently it grows wild in many countries.

This cabbage has a thick taproot, penetrating vertically into the ground. The green and serrated edges of the leaves are rough and curly in the Milanese variety. In the center of the plant a bud or pellet is made up of very tight leaves where the plant stores nutrient reserves for the second year of growth– it is a biennial plant, so it flowers the second year

Cabbages

Cabbage is particularly rich in different vitamins and calcium, though it contains all kinds of minerals as well. It is not demanding and grows in all climates, resisting cold as low as 14 degrees Fahrenheit. It does not mind proximity to the sea or brackish water. It does not need much water either, although lack of water would make the plant smaller. It consumes many nutrients and therefore you should fertilize the soil well.

Cultivation

Cabbages have two planting seasons. The first is autumn-winter, during which sowing is done on seedbeds in late August and transplantation to the fields in late October. Harvest takes place in spring. The sec-

Varieties

They come in many types—some with smoother or rougher leaves—and various sizes, although perhaps the most popular are: Milan cabbage among the curly ones; among the smooth ones we find the early Bacalan of conical head, the Brunswick with a flat and very large head, and the oxheart—also conical. A very early variety is the Market Copenhagen, with a small head, and a variety of winter is the Quintal of Alsace, a large head of a bluish color. The *Asa de Cántaro* variety forms a very attractive white head.

ond is the spring-summer season, in which plants are sown between January and April in protected seedbeds or open until May, and harvested from early summer until December. There is yet another variety that is planted in May-June and harvested during winter.

Transplantation is done one and a half months after planting. Plants should be kept about 1' 7" (50 cm) apart, being careful not to cover the leaves with soil. You have to keep the ground free of grass and earth up the plant as it grows so that it supports its own weight without falling sideways. When grown enough—between 4 and 6 pounds—the plant can be cut at the stem or pulled up as a whole to cut it later.

They get along well with almost everything: legumes, potatoes, onions, cucumbers, and tomatoes—but not with strawberries and beans.

Difficulties

Cabbages have very particular enemies besides the ones that attack the rest of the garden. However, they generally hold up well and give only few problems without too much effort.

The most common one is the cabbage butterfly that lays yellow eggs under the leaves and then larvae eats those leaves, leaving only the veins. The best way to fight them is crushing them with your fingers. As Mariano Bueno was told by his plant biology professor: "The thumb is the organic DDT." Aphids and snails also attack cabbage, but they are not as harmful. Although if you happen to get a list of enemies you may turn pale: cabbage fly, leaf miners, crucifer flea. Cabbage false hernia, cabbage aphid, cabbage bugs, diamondback moth, cabbage looper, cutworms, army worms, and nematodes. There are also some diseases: cabbage hernia, cruciferous mildew, white rust, alternaria, mosaic virus, and so on. But do not get discouraged; cabbages are resilient and you will rarely be out of them.

Lombard cabbages

They are purplish red cabbages, hard and compact, that can be eaten raw. It is a variety of cabbage, among which there is an outstanding one called Black Head, which is well suited to all types of soil and withstands low temperatures very well.

Brussels sprout

In the body and the kitchen, Brussels sprouts are anti-anemic because they contain folate, and have lots of vitamin C, and beta-carotene that stimulates vitamin A so that they also help prevent cancer. You should always consume them cooked, stewed, and by themselves or as a side to meat and vegetable stews or even salads.

Brussels sprout is a variety of wild cabbage characterized for forming—on the stem, at the leaves' branches—small bud-like miniature cabbages, like gems 1–2 inches in diameter. They resemble cabbage heads. They began to cultivate Brussels sprouts more than one hundred years ago near Brussels. It is very popular in Europe, though its digestive properties produce an abundance of intestinal gas. However, it has many properties similar to those of cabbage, and it is interesting, from a culinary perspective, for its mild flavor and texture.

Cultivation

This plant loves temperate climates. It resists temperatures as low as 14 degrees before forming the little heads. It does not tolerate heat and drought. It is sown in seedbeds between April and June, and it likes being transplanted with root balls. It is transplanted in June or July when it is about 4 inches tall, with distances of 1'11"–2'7" between plants. It does not like acidic soils, so they have to be neutralized with lime to pH 7, which is appropriate. You also have to earth up during growth. You should water

frequently, weed, and get rid of yellowing leaves. Picking begins in September, and to accelerate the process, gardeners remove drying leaves when the head is formed. If you plant early and later varieties together, with luck, you'll have sprouts from September to May. It gets along in the same way as the rest of the cabbages, so you have to keep it away from strawberries and lima beans. You should rotate every three or four years. Difficulties are also similar to those of cabbage. One

of the best known is the semi-dwarf varieties of Le Halle, which are not too large and adapted to all kinds of deep soil.

Common Cabbage

Also called forage or common cabbage because it has always been used to feed rabbits and chickens. It grows up to 5 feet, very straight. The leaves open wide apart and defoliate smoothly. **Although its nutrition benefit is high, it is barely used just for human consumption.** In some gardens it is the only plant standing in the middle of winter. Among the most popular varieties there is the Giant horse.

Chinese cabbages

As the name suggests, *Brassica campestris pekinensis* is native to China and has only recently come to Europe. **In outward appearance, it looks like romaine lettuce.** It grows well between 64 and 68 °F—a very small margin. And from planting until harvest there are between two and a half months and three months. The plant is cut at ground level and is served in salads.

Root Vegetables

Garlic

How to store roots in winter

Some people have the habit of building a silo to store carrots, red beets, turnips, parsnips, radishes, or potatoes in winter.

● **To do this**, dig a trench with a slope at the deepest part of the bottom. It should be as deep as necessary depending on the amount of vegetables.

● On the ground, place branches, sand, and straw. Then place the tubers or roots and cover them with some sand, some soil, and a good layer of straw to protect them from the cold. You should try to build—on the ends—an aeration system with the branches. Remove the tops of the carrots and the root tips of the beets.

Garlic (*Allium sativum*) comes from Central and South Asia; Three thousand years ago it was already cultivated in India and Egypt. It is a bulbous root, consisting of 6 to 12 small bulbs, connected by a thin film that gives rise to a clove of garlic. Each clove of garlic has a small white robe or something reddish, membranous, and thin like the one surrounding the whole head. The leaves are pods, like those of an onion, and the stem—whose top takes the shape of a head with flowers and seeds—can reach up to 6' 6" (2 m) in height if allowed to grow.

The main producer is China, with nearly nine million tons; followed by India, with half a million; the United States, with a quarter million; and Egypt, Russia, and Spain, with almost two hundred thousand tons. Garlic is an essential element of Mediterranean cuisine and a major anti-carcinogenic.

Humidity is not suitable for garlic and it does not like over-fertilized or shady gardens.

It contains vitamins A, B, C, and E as well as cobalt, iron, and iodine. It is one of the few that contains selenium. Otherwise it has all the virtues that can be found in the dictionary, from carminative ones to expectorant or worming.

Cultivation

Garlic is a mesetarian crop that grows from 32 to 104 degrees Fahrenheit. It holds up well in the cold when young, and the temperature should be lower than 62 °F at night during summer so it can grow pleasantly. It likes clay or loam soils, rich in potash rather than limestone. The soil must be prepared in advance and must be plowed several months before as well as fertilized, and raked clean.

Planting can be done in beds and ridges. The first is industrial, sown in flat areas and in squares of 6 ½ to 10 feet wide, separating the cloves by a handspan. The second is done on ridges spaced about 1' 7" (20 cm) apart and by placing two garlic facing each other about 8″ apart. In rows around the garden they can be planted about 5 inches (12 cm) apart. The clove is buried about ¾ to 1 ⅕ inches deep (2 to 3 cm).

It can be planted in the Fall, between October and November, or even later, between December and January. In clay and wet soils it can be done between January and March. The tip is left upwards; be sure to choose the days of the waning moon, as in the case of other root crops.

Weeds should often be removed so the soil is clean. In general, it is not necessary to water them except when experiencing extreme dryness during head development period.

Harvest it eight months later if it has been planted in fall and four months if it has been done in spring, that is, between June and August in cold areas. Wait until the leaves are completely dry and the weather is dry to pick up the heads. If rain does not come its way for a while, you should leave those heads three or four days in the open, and then hang them on a string. They can also be harvested tender for tortillas before the bulb fattens. It gets along with strawberries, protecting them from diseases, and also with tomatoes, potatoes, lettuce, and beets. It does not like legumes.

Diseases

Excess moisture or fresh compost can cause fungal diseases. It can be affected by onion maggot, garlic and onion ringworm (*Lita allieta*), which bores the leaves and bulb, garlic weevil (*Brachycerus algirus*), which also pierces the bulb, moths that attack in June, and nematodes. Regarding diseases, it is sensitive to mildew, rust that yellows leaves, white rot, and botrytis.

There is no greater pleasure than putting garlic on a string after harvest.

A good **trick to have the best garlic crop** is to plant it three days after December's or January's full moon.

Putting on a string

To store garlic once dry and clean, tear off the outer leaves and with the inner ones make a braid in a chain and hang them on a dry place. This same technique is also common in the villages for onions and corn when they get dry.

Varieties

There is softneck and hardneck garlic. Hardneck varieties are known because they produce between 4 and 12 cloves, have a stalk with flowers, produce shoots, are difficult to put on a string because of the hardness of the stem, and rot quickly. Softneck or artichoke varieties do not produce shoots, have between 10 and 40 cloves forming layers, are easy to weave, and last for 6 to 8 months without getting spoiled once harvested. There is a variety called elephant (*Allium ampeloprasum*), related to celery, whose head can weigh up to 400 grams.

They take a while to grow, about six months, and are sown from the previous year's garlic cloves.

Celery

The origin of **celery** (*Apium graveolens*) is in the Mediterranean. It is an Umbelliferae that comes in two varieties: common celery (with edible leaves and stalks) and celeriac, or "turnip-rooted celery" (with an edible root). The first variety's leaves have a petiole (the plant part that connects the stem and leaves) of very thick, edible fleshy stalks. Celery requires deep, moist soil, which is neutral and rich in boron. If soil dries the plant becomes tough.

It has antirheumatic, carminative (intestinal gas releases), digestive, and diuretic properties. It is rich in vitamins A, B, and C, and has calcium, iron, magnesium, phosphorus, potassium, and sodium.

Cultivation

Celery's growing cycle is four months. Interestingly, this plant bolts when it's cold, so if the temperature drops in the summer it can be spoiled. It is sown in seedbed between July and August and transplanted between August and October, but can also be planted in a seedbed in November and transplant-ed in January and February. Soil temperature must not fall below 57°F (14°C). Transplantation is done two months later or when they are about 6 inches and have three or four true leaves, separating plants by about 1 foot. You should keep the ground free of weeds when celery is young because it grows very slowly and does not like competitors. You should water in abundance and with good water. It accepts sprinkler irrigation very well. You can earth up to whiten the leaves and they say that it is good to remove the soil around roots. It is harvested when it reaches the right size, in the morning or afternoon, not when it is hot. It is important to avoid the sun after cutting, to keep the leaves crunchy. It gets along with legumes, cabbage, cucumbers, tomatoes, lettuce, and radishes.

Problems

Carrot flies, whose larvae spoil the root. Celery flies, whose larvae attack the leaves. Aphids that bite the leaves. Nematodes that attack the root and prevent the plant from growing, such as cutworms that attack the root collar. Diseases that attack celery are mildew, blight, and septoria leaf blight—fungi that stain leaves.

Celery takes about three months to grow and is planted in the fall and winter because it has good resistance to frost.

Varieties

There are two main varieties, the green one—hardy and easy to grow—and the yellow, more valued, and also considered white, whose varieties include Celebrity, Spartan, Dore Chemin, Golden Boy, and Golden Spartan. In the green variety Isel and Ishtar races standout. The latter is currently consumed mainly for being more resistant.

Celery Root is a variety of celery whose part of interest is the root. It is sown in seedbeds between February and April, passed to root balls when it is about 2 inches (5 cm), and transplanted when it has definitely developed root. It is harvested in the fall. You have to rotate every three or four years. It gets along with legumes, cabbage, cucumbers, tomatoes, and radishes.

A temperature drop or excess moisture or nitrates can hollow out the plant.

Black heart is formed by nutrient deficiency. If the plant lacks boron and magnesium, it will turn brown.

Onions

The **onion** (*Allium cepa*) was first cultivated in Mesopotamia and soon spread throughout the Mediterranean.

It is a plant with a short and flat stalk that has many roots and leaves, whose lower part is the edible bulb. It consists of several thick and fleshy layers that function as reserve when the plant sprouts the second year. The leaves are sheath-shaped and have a pointy end. Its fruit is a capsule of three faces on the end of a stem that extends up to 5 feet tall. This fruit appears when the plant is mature.

More than two million hectares of onions are grown and about 33 million tons are

Onions take three to five months to grow, but can remain in the soil for up to eight months, depending on species.

obtained around the world. The principal producing country is Mexico, with more than one million tons, followed by Korea, Japan, China, and New Zealand. Onion is low in calories but is very rich in minerals, and contains potassium, iron, phosphorus, and magnesium in very usable doses. It also has vitamins A, B, and C.

Furthermore, it protects against infections by stimulating the immune system. For some people, however, it is indigestible

uncooked and, when raw, it produces characteristic bad breath.

Needs

The onion grows in temperate climates, withstands frost when it begins to grow, and needs warm temperatures to develop the bulb. It likes loose soil, as any other tuber does, although if it is sandy it has to be properly fertilized. You should not replant in the same place for three years. It does not like excessive moisture, so you have to water it lightly when the bulb is formed. It does not like excessive acidity either.

Cultivation

Spring-summer varieties are planted from August to September and transplanted from November to January.

Onions are allowed to flower when you want to get the seed for future sowing. The seed should be collected when the plant is completely dry and the flower has fully opened.

Fall-winter varieties are planted from February to March and transplanted from May to June. Depending on the weather, the seeds—which are very small—are sown in seedbeds outdoors, broadcast sown, covering the seed with a layer of mulch of about 1 ½ inches (4 cm) or directly on the ground in rows spaced about 10 inches (25 cm). When they are about 6–8 inches (15 to 20 cm) they are transplanted or, if already in rows, thinned to 4 to 6 inches apart (10 to 15 cm), depending on the species.

Soil should be dug about 11–14 inches (30 to 35 cm) deep to let it be loose and light. For transplantation you will use a transplanter shovel or hoe. They can be planted at ground level or on ridges. Watering is done just after sowing, repeated at 10 days, and then every 15 days, until a month before harvest. In very dry weather it can be watered up until 15 days before. Lack of water makes it more bitter.

Onion gets along with beet, tomato, carrot, cucumber, strawberries, lettuce, and parsley. It does not like legumes.

Difficulties

Onion is quite resistant; however, watch for the onion beetle—which appears in spring and drills the leaves—the onion maggot, whose larvae attack the leaves in the nursery, thrips that bite leaves and make them yellow, nematodes that attack the roots, and the onion moth, which is a ⅗ inch blue-winged butterfly whose caterpillars attack the leaf sheaths from inside.

As for diseases, we have mildew, due to excess moisture, which is noticeable in elongated and violet spots on leaves, treated by weeding thoroughly; rust, which produces more remarkable purplish spots; Powdery Mildew, a silver-gray fungus; Onion smut (*Urocystis cepulae*), a fungus that forms a kind of lead-colored pustules that burst full of black spores; Onion yellow dwarf virus, a virus that yellows the leaves and is transmitted by aphids; White tip disease (*Phytophthora porri*), a white fungus that as its Latin name suggests belongs more to leeks; botrytis because of excess moisture; white rot (Sclerotium cepivorum), fluffy fungus that occurs during sprouting; and Alternaria, white sores that become brown in the leaves.

Harvest

It takes place when the leaves begin to dry. They are pulled by hand in loose soil on dry days and left a couple of days on the ground to dry, turning over at least once. Be careful when storing them as they can be attacked by mold. The black one is treated with low temperatures. The blue one is caused by *Penicillium* and appears at the bruises. To prevent botrytis you must keep them very dry. If they are not picked up once well dried, the bacteria *Erwina carovotora* can also attack them—the plant rots from the neck.

Top: Onions are harvested in spring and are very tasty in salads.
Bottom: Among the dry ones, the Figueras variety is notable because of its durability.

Scallions and chives

Scallions (*Allium fistulosum*) and **chives** (*Allium schoenoprasum*) are wild plants traditionally grown as a condiment. They are very similar and can be substituted for nursery onions, although they are not as tasty. The taste of chives (with violet flowers) and scallions (with green flowers) is slightly different, as is their origin.

Scallions are also known as Japanese chive, since it is native to Japan and is part of the ancient oriental cuisine. Raw scallions are cut above the root and can be eaten raw in salads, considering that is an important source of potassium, it is diuretic, and eliminates worms. Chives are also known as *ciboulette*, come from northern Europe, and serve as a typical condiment for French cuisine.

They belong to the lily family, like garlic, onion, leeks, and scallions. *Ciboulette* leaves are progressively chopped and are used fresh or dried for winter.

Varieties

There are three main types based on size: big, regular, and chives. There are also types based on sowing season, varieties of spring-summer and fall-winter. Spring variety (harvested between April and May), Crystal Wax variety (picked up between May and June), and Liria onion (between June and July, yellow-colored and less spicy) are noteworthy.

Parsnips

Turnips

Mashed parsnips

Nothing easier than this recipe: take four cups of steamed parsnips, ground them in a potato masher, and mix them with 6 oz. cream in a saucepan for about twenty minutes over low heat. Fix with salt and pepper for a Thanksgiving meal.

Parsnips are sometimes called white carrots, although *Pastinaca sativa* is more like a turnip for its color—and it is indeed an intermediate root between the two. It used to grow wild and has progressively been selected in Europe, where it was common before potato, and now has been reduced to making broths.

Parsnip is anti-rheumatic, diuretic, and has calcium, magnesium, potassium, phosphorus, iron, and sodium. It is grown like carrots, to which it similar in all aspects.

It is pulled as needed and lasts a long time buried in the ground. It barely has enemies in either insects or diseases and gets along with radishes, carrots, and onions.

Turnips (*Brassica rapa or Brassica napus*), like parsnips, was a staple food in Europe before the arrival of potatoes, used in grilling, stews, soups, or purees.

Turnips are very interesting for farmers who have animals because, except the small variety for human consumption (it can be eaten raw, grated, or cooked with meat), large varieties are grown generally for feed use, especially for pigs. It is rich in calcium, it is diuretic, and laxative.

For human consumption, the earliest turnip is White turnip, followed by Kohlrabi, which is much larger, Fall turnip (good for meats), Red turnip, and Teltow turnip—a German variety that is eaten roasted.

Seeds are sown directly in the ground from March to June, harvesting in late summer, or July to September for winter picking up, depending on variety and weather. This is done broadcast and on wet ground. The seed is very small and barely buried. Then a clear area is made, separating the seedlings by about 6 inches (15 cm). It is not very demanding, and the only thing that bothers it is the heat.

You will not earth up, but mulch to prevent weeds and conserve moisture. It suffers from the same difficulties as cabbages. It pairs well with legumes, tomatoes, lettuce, and carrots.

The turnip, very popular in Germany, is rich in vitamin C and due to its fiber content it is considered preventive against colon cancer.

Radishes

The origin of **radishes** (*Raphanus sativus*) is not exactly known, but it is believed that the small ones or little **radishes** are native to the Mediterranean area, and the big ones to China. It is a plant with a thick fleshy root, very variable forms, red skin, a short stem, and a bunch of leaves. It likes warm climates but does not like excessive heat and freezes at 29 degrees Fahrenheit. The soil should not be saline and otherwise it grows in any soil. However, if we want large radishes the soil must be loose, similar to the one used for onions.

Cultivation

It grows very quickly. The early varieties are harvested 20 days after planting, which is done by broadcast or in rows, 4 inches (10 cm) apart. After a while thinning is done, so each plant is between ⅘ to 2 ⅓ (2 to 6 cm) inches apart. Harvest usually occurs between 45

Radish gets along with carrots (thinning is not that necessary), spinach, tomatoes, cucumbers, beans, lettuce, peas, and chervil. It does not like cabbage and pumpkins.

Varieties

They come in small and large roots. The former are little **radishes**, round or elongated, with pink or scarlet skin, and white tip. The latter, **radishes** strictly speaking, can be black, pink, or white—in this case Japanese.

and 70 days after planting. You should plant each month starting January, in mild climates, to have radishes all summer. They sprout within 2 or 3 days and because of their speed they need soil permanently moist. If they lack water they will be spicier.

Difficulties

They do not have too many difficulties because of their rapid growth, but they can be attacked by aphids, cabbage looper, armyworm, and mildew. If left too long on the ground they can hollow out or take the form of pitchfork. If water is scarce, they become fibrous. Heat makes them spicy, and if watered too much in maturity they make roots at the sides.

Neeps and kohlrabies

● **Neep** (*Brassica napus var. Napobrassica*) is also known as Swedish turnip and Rutabaga. It is planted in well fertilized soil in late spring or early summer at about 1 in. (3 cm) deep and leaving about 1 foot (30 cm) between seeds. Because seeds are really small (there are a thousand in a sachet) a handful are planted in each hole and thinned. They are harvested after two months. Root and leaves are the edible parts, like if it was a cabbage and a turnip at once. You can also sow it in seedbeds during winter. Moreover, it has the same problems as cabbages.

● The kohlrabi (*Brassica oleracea* var. *Gongylodes*) is very different because what you eat is the thickened stem—from which leaves and roots grow. It is much smaller, has red skin, and is consumed raw or cooked before maturity. In some countries like the United States, it is used for livestock; it is resistant to drought.

Red beet

Red Beet (*Beta vulgaris*)—also known as Table Beet, Garden Beet, and Early Blood Turnip—is very similar to Sugar Beet and Fodder Beet. They are relatives, but the latter are industrial crops. We are rather interested in the variety that is one of the tastiest elements of the garden, though somewhat neglected because of its red color; when cooked it stains the accompanying food. Maybe that is why it is preferable to boil it separately, and then after rinsing it cut it into slices for salad.

Beets are anti-anemic, have vitamins A, B, C, and E, and contain calcium, iron, phosphorus, and magnesium.

Cultivation

It is a crop of Central European type that likes a mild and humid climate and dislikes drought. Like many other root crops, it needs loamy and well fertilized soil where compost is at least two years old.

Beets are usually sold already boiled, keeping their skin, and vacuum packaged. You will soon realize that they have nothing to do with the ones you grow yourself.

They are sown either by broadcast or directly in rows, thinning once they have sprouted. You can even transplant the pulled ones so you avoid wasting them. If you are in a hurry you can sow them in seedbeds from February or March, and if not, sow them on the ground from April. When planted in rows separation should be from 4 to 5 inches (10 to 15 cm) depending on the species, as written in the seeds bag. They are harvested from three months after planting, but you do not need to do it before they ripen. Even in temperate climates some people leave them in the ground for several months and pick them as needed.

It gets along with cabbage, cauliflower, lettuce, tomatoes, onions, and beans.

Since it absorbs many soil nutrients, you should wait several years before re-sowing in the same area.

Difficulties

Beet presents few problems, except those caused by excessive moisture in the garden, including mildew, rot, and aphids—you may pull off the affected leaves.

Varieties

● **Beets can be** oval, round, flattened, or elongated, and of more or less intense color.
The best known in our country are: Flat of Egypt, which has an early cycle and firm and sweet flesh; Cylindra, of mid-late cycle and elongated like a carrots; and Detroit, perhaps the best known, ball-shaped, and very red.
● **There is a pink and white** Italian variety that turns golden color when boiled.

Cooking Beets

They should be boiled before you remove the skin to prevent loss of properties. Then remove it by scraping them. Beet stains are easy to wash, and if you are rushing, use table salt on your hands. **To tell whether they are boiled**, you may pinch them with a fork, and if you grill them instead of boiling they will keep their sugar that is otherwise lost in the water.

Carrots

Carrots (*Daucus carota*) are umbelliferae originating in Mesopotamia, Iran, and the Mediterranean. The ones cultivated in Greece and Rome were purplish, but the Dutch in the eighteenth century selected varieties containing more carotene so carrots turned the pumpkin color they currently have. It is a biennial plant so it blooms during the second year but we are interested only in the first year, when the little leaves and the turnip-shaped elongated roots develop. The world's largest producer is China with almost seven million tons, followed by the United States with two, Russia, Poland, England, Japan, and Italy.

Carrot is rich in vitamin A and contributes to the formation of melanin in the skin, which protects us from the sun and prevents lung cancer.

For its rich content in carotene—a substance that the body converts into vitamin A and that can be noticed from its color—this plant is highly recommended for consumption before summer. Its contribution to melanin will protect us from the sun and anemia. It also has vitamins B, C, D, E, calcium, iron, iodine, magnesium, phosphorus, potassium, etc. In short, it is a nutrient goldmine that can be eaten at any time. "Carrot" in English comes from the Latin *carrota*, derived from a Greek word meaning "to burn."

Method for avoiding carrot thinning

When planting carrots, add a quarter of radish seeds, because their faster growth makes their harvest a way to also thin the carrot.

Cultivation

Carrots like loam, silty clay, or well ventilated soils that are rich in potassium, with a pH between 6 and 7. Above all, fertilizer must not be so fresh because carrots rot easily. It is recommended to sow it where tomatoes, onions, or leeks grew the previous year and wait four to five years to repeat planting because carrots wear out the soil a lot.

Broadcast sowing is used for carrots. It would be nice to mulch about ⅕ inches (5 mm) and thinning is important. When leaves' sizes are about 1 inch (2 to 3 cm), begin thinning, to get plants 1 inch (3 cm) apart, and two or three weeks later thin again to get about 3 inches (8 cm) of separation—although industrial crops are separated about 6 inches (15 cm). Those pulled carrots can be eaten already. They can also be planted in rows, as seen in the Bugs Bunny cartoon series, during which he destroyed the plantations along the ridges. They require a lot of water, being careful with excessive moisture, and knowing that growth of weeds will be encouraged; you have to remove them because carrots do not like competition. They are picked before they grow all the way, between three and seven months after planting—depending on variety. The smaller they are, the more tender they will be.

It is best to plant them in spring, so they sprout in 7 to 10 days. Depending on the variety and planting season harvest is between 3 and 6 months later.

To always have carrots you should plant every month. If you keep them in a cool, dry place, they will last up to six months.

Varieties

They are divided in three: the large kind, especially for industrial use; the fine kind, which are chopped to sell industrially; and the bundle type, sold for direct use in salads. The latter include Nelson and 1901 F. Among industrial varieties we can find Berlina, Bolero, Luxor, Caro, Caro Brite, Caro Pride, Toudo, Tempo, and so on. You should look at the little seeds' bag to figure out what its contents are, whether they are premature, like Tempo or Luxor, whether they resist the cold, such as Bolero or Excellence, whether they grow fast, such as Caro Brite, or whether it is better suited to low sandy soils, like Caro Pride.

Consumption

It can be eaten raw or boiled and some people mash it for children. **It can be eaten at any time**, although people who overeat end up acquiring the color of carrots. Be careful, however, with nitrates, present in large quantities for industrial carrots because of the irrigation water and because the plant accumulates them. When the mash is allowed to stand overnight, these nitrates transform into nitrites, which are carcinogenic, so you should not store it in the fridge.

Difficulties

The carrot does not have too many of them. It is a strong plant but may be attacked by carrot flies in early summer, and by aphids, wireworms, leaf worms, and nematodes that attack after the summer and are treated with coffee grounds in between plants. Diseases that are caused by excessive moisture: mildew, powdery mildew, leaf burns in very hot weather, and Pythium, which forms stains and dark spots in carrots.

RABBIT

Bugs Bunny, the lucky rabbit created by Chuck Jones, prefers carrot fields, which in the US are grown in rows. This rabbit thrives under them and always eats a carrot to mock his opponents.

Vegetables

Difficulties

Eggplants can be attacked by red spider mites (treated by weeding), white spider mites (more typical to peppers), whitefly, aphids, and various caterpillars, including potato beetle (killed with chamomile or by hand), thrips, leaf miners, nematodes, and snails. Diseases can include gray, white, and soft rots, and various viruses (from potato, alfalfa, and tomato), which can be avoided by selecting the strongest plants.

Eggplants

The potato beetle attacks eggplant in the same way it does potatoes, being both of the solanaceae family. Remove them by hand or plant chamomile in between.

Eggplants (*Solanum melongena*) originate in the tropics; from ancient India and China. It was introduced to the pharaohs Egypt and from there—in the Middle Ages—to Europe. It is a herbaceous plant, although its woody stem gives it a bushy appearance. Its flower is small, purplish, and its fruit is an elongated dark berry with small seeds in its fleshy inside. In one gram of seeds there are about 300 units.

The main producer of eggplant is China, with more than fifteen million tons, followed by India, with about seven, and then Turkey, Japan, and Italy.

Cultivation

Eggplant is typical of dry and warm climates (it does not like moisture). It grows between 50 and 104 °F with neutral or alkaline, well fertilized soils.

Since it is sensitive to cold it is sown during January–March in protected seedbeds. When it is a couple of inches tall it is kept in root balls. Once the risk of frost has completely passed, it is transplanted on a crescent moon in May. It must be from 4 ¾ to 6 inches (12 to 15 cm) tall, and each plant must be separated between 1' 4" and 2' 4" (40 and 70 cm), depending on the weather.

Soil should be mulched to keep it free of weeds, and moist. If possible, within two weeks of the transplantation, it may be favorable for the roots to earth up, ensuring that the compost does not touch the stem. One option is pruning, in which two to four stems are kept

and the rest are removed. A four-stem plant can yield from 25 to 30 eggplants. Otherwise, you can thin the leaves and flowers. It is harvested from July, about two months after transplantation, until frosts begin. You should harvest them before they begin to form seeds because then they get bitter. Cut them in the morning with secateurs leaving ⅖ inches (1 cm) of peduncle.

It gets along with low bush beans and potatoes, but prefers to grow alone. Also, you must not grow them on the same soil again for three or four years.

Varieties

Eggplants can be of many types: round, oblong, black lilac, striped, or white, but the two main varieties are the globular and oblong-shaped. Varieties used in America have names like Dark, Epic, Black Magic, and Black Beauty in the round type. Regarding the oblong type there is the Slim Jim or Little Fingers. There's even an ornamental type called Easter Egg, which is beige in color.

Squash

Squash (*Cucurbita pepo*) could have originated in Mexico, although some sources place it in Asia, because it seems Egyptians and Romans had known about it. It is an annual, creeping plant, whose stem grows sinuously across the ground. The stem is cylindrical, hollow, hairy, and rough. Secondary stems tend to grow and should be pruned to leave just the main ones.

Leaves, tendrils, and flowers form in the internodes. Its leaves are webbed and it produces a fleshy fruit (such as cucumber, squash, and melon) that must be harvested in the middle of its growth, before the seeds ripen.

China cultivates more than four million tons, followed closely by India, and then Ukraine, United States, and Egypt.

It is a low-calorie vegetable, but it is cleansing because of its diuretic and laxative properties.

Cultivation

Squash is undemanding in terms of temperature, but prefers to grow in the range of 75 and 85°F (25 and 30°C). It likes slightly acidic soil and a somewhat high relative humidity. Since it contains a lot of water, it also needs a lot of watering.

It is sown in protected seedbeds in late February or in March, and directly on the ground between April and July. The first ones are transplanted when they are of 2 ⅓–2 ¾ inches (6 to

Squash flower

When the yellow flower of the squash is in full bloom and (once the fruit is formed) before the plant spoils, it is a delicious food. **Its fleshy petals can be fried in heavy flour and eggs**, or following the steps of a fashionable Italian recipe. They can also be used to wrap a fish like the now fashionable so-called Saint Peter, grilled.

7 cm), but if you are not going to grow them in a greenhouse, it is best to sow directly on the ground, with 3' 3" feet (1 m) of separation.

You should mulch, earth up the plant two weeks after, and water frequently. Squash gets along with lettuce, cabbage, beans, corn, and pumpkin; it does not like potatoes.

They are harvested between a month and a half or two after flowering, when they are a foot long, and the skin shines like eggplant does.

Difficulties

Squash is targeted by aphids and snails. You can fight aphids with sulfur and snails with glass or plastic jars when they are young. It can also be attacked by spider mites, whiteflies, thrips, and caterpillars. Moreover, it is prone to typical diseases associated with moisture.

Varieties

Squash may be more or less elongated and thick, and has a more or less pale color. However, all varieties are grown equally, so that the choice of one over the other depends on consumers' preferences and on its planting cycles because there are varieties that are planted in April and harvested in June while other greenhouse varieties are planted in winter and harvested in spring—some of them are even planted in August and harvested in October–November.

Planting

To be successful, make a deep hole, put a layer of aged compost, place two or three seeds, cover them with about an inch of soil, and **put a cut plastic bottle over it, upside down**. Once sprouted, leave one single plant per hole.

Winter Squash

overnight. The soil should have a fairly balanced pH of 6.8 to 7, and should be well fertilized, with a lot of compost. Watering must be regular.

Care

If allowed to grow on its own, the plant will lead to chaos in the garden. The best system is the one that looks like a Christmas tree lying on the ground. In other words, the main stem should

fought through crop rotation and keeping the soil with a pH close to 7 and rich in organic matter.

The most common fungus on leaves are powdery mildew and downy mildew. Powdery mildew is more typical of hot places while mildew is of cold places. Both form spots on the leaves, which can be controlled with a sodium hydroxide solution, 1 percent, and summer mineral oil between 1 and 2 percent. Mites and insects depend on the region. The most common are aphids, leafhoppers, caterpillars, spider mites, and yellow mites.

According to the risk of each zone you should design a pest control plan against insects and fungi as a precautionary measure.

Consumption: To eat pumpkin you must air them out several months after harvest, because in this way, pumpkins reduce nitrates and increase sugars and proteins.

Winter squash belongs to a very broad genre: cucurbitaceae, which includes hundreds of species, including the giant pumpkin, spaghetti squash for jams, colored zucchini for decoration, and for consumption, the orange round ones or the elongated pear-shaped ones.

Cultivation

It can be planted in March, but depending on weather it would be better in April or May. They need a little more than a couple of feet on each side to develop, so you need to look for a margin in the garden. They can be sown directly in the ground, and two or three seeds per hole would be enough, except in the case of the giants discussed later. The seeds are soaked in water for a couple of hours and then left on a damp paper

How to tell if they are ripe:

● **The attaching stem of the pumpkin must be dry and brown-colored.**

● **You are not supposed to be able to sink a nail in the pumpkin's skin.**

grow away from its source in a straight line while secondary stems must be perpendicular to the main and shorter as they move away from the plant. You should also practice weeding to keep the ground clean and fluffy. Some people bury the roots that appear under the internodes, from which the emerging ones grow and flower.

Diseases

There are three classes: fungi on the ground, fungi on leaves, and insects on stems. Fungi on the ground are

A giant pumpkin is not ecological

Specimens of pumpkin can weigh more than 440 pounds and records reach 1,100 pounds. It is not grown for food but to brag. However, there are edible pumpkins that can be prepared baked, stewed, pureed, stuffed, as bisque, in flan, in soup, as cream soup, and with potatoes, beans, and rice.

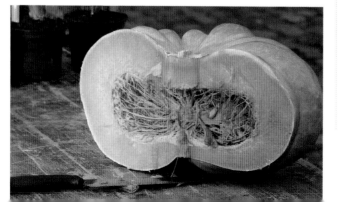

Pollination by hand

● **The Atlantic Giant pumpkin**, developed by Howard Dill in the seventies and eighties, was obtained from various crosses of seeds that have demonstrated ability to produce large fruits.

● **To ensure a certain crossing between two plants pollination by hand is a requirement**—it will allow a maximum output of 500-600 seeds.

● **Each plant produces in each leaf's internode, a flower, which can be male or female**. In the stalk, male ones are more common and in the ends they are balanced. The petiole beneath the corolla is long, thin, and round in the male flowers, and short in the female flowers. Cut early in the morning several newly open male flowers and using the corolla as a brush, rub a newly open female flower inside very gently (it takes three to five male flowers for each female).

Cultivation

Once you get the seed, planting follows a very interesting process. To begin with, in early May in Spain, the seed is disinfected with hydrogen peroxide and let sit overnight on a wet paper. In the morning, it is planted in a pot with peat and kept at about 77 degrees Fahrenheit inside with good light and moisture. It will sprout within a week. Fifteen days later, transplant it to the ground. Reserve room for each plant of 11 x 11 yards and surround it with a weed barrier cloth. Weed throughout June, watch for pests, and water with fertilized water (liquid compost). Flowers come in July, to be protected at night and helped to pollinate. In this phase, fans of pumpkin fertilize with potassium and calcium. Additionally, they select two fruits per plant. In August, you continue to care for the plant, to monitor pests, and those who want a monstrous specimen will have to continue fertilizing.

In September you no longer need to fertilize so much. Watch for aphids, powdery mildew, and cracks that may occur in the plant. So that it does not deteriorate, the plant is washed with disinfectant if it cracks.

It is harvested in October. In order to obtain seeds you have to wait a month.

Some varieties of winter squash acquire really curious shapes.

The pumpkin house

This system was applied in an Argentinean house and it worked perfectly. Thus, it can be done in any country house that has a garden or whose owner wants to take advantage of the roof as the main support for a plant that takes up too much ground space.

Helen Davis put in iron rods on the ground and placed a fence that reached the roof of her house so that the stems of the pumpkin could climb it. She found that, in addition to pumpkins, other climbing vegetables such as squash and cucumbers can be planted. The plants have to be tied to the wire with rope or tape Velcro so that, with a small space next to the wall, we can have a garden on the roof. To complete the tiny garden, which requires a flat and easily accessible roof, we can plant shade species under the arbor: lettuce, endive, beets, carrots, and radishes.

Strawberries

Wild strawberries and strawberries belong to the family Rosaceae, Fragaria variety. It is a herbaceous and perennial plant. The stem is formed by a short axis called a crown, in which leaves are inserted. Strawberries can sprout directly from the crown or from a leaf internode.

Generally, the ones that grow on the edge of the forest are called wild strawberries and the cultivated ones are strawberries, which are much bigger.

Strawberry is depurative, diuretic, laxative, and remineralizing. It has vitamins A, B, C, E, and K, calcium, bromine, iodine, iron, magnesium, potassium, etc. They are also often very digestive.

Cultivation

Strawberries prefer a mild climate. It grows wild in the mountains but crop varieties are more adapted to heat and constant moisture. It does not like drought and direct sunlight causes them to lose too much water so the leaves end up wilting.

If planting from seeds, you have to wait a year to have fruit. Typically planting is done from old bushes and there are two options. In the first one, the plant is pulled and its root divided, selecting the parts with new roots (the old parts are removed) and planted again. In the second option, stolons—those long twigs projecting strawberries and rooted elsewhere—are used. Once the root is grown, it is easy to pull them and take them elsewhere.

Once transplanted you have to water them often. If you live in a climate that frosts, dividing roots or transplanting stolons can be done to indoor pots after summer and transplanted back to the ground from April.

Strawberries like slightly acidic soil, and keeping them free of grass will give you some work. After four or five years you should pull all the strawberries and wait at least five years before planting again. Its root resists down to -4 degrees Fahrenheit but the leaves dry as frost begins. Strawberry gets along with garlic, legumes, spinach, and lettuce. It does not like cabbage.

Difficulties

Industrial crops are usually mulched with a black plastic. In the organic garden, chances are we have to pull weeds by hand. Strawberries form a roof of leaves that remains very damp so all kinds of animals grow under their shade. However, spider mites (which attack when there is drought), thrips, and aphids cause damage to the leaves. Attacks of snails and slugs are even worse, making ripe strawberries full of holes and unpalatable.

Excessive moisture can cause mildew or rot. Leaves turning yellow can also be a symptom of too much lime in the soil, which can be treated with pine humus.

Varieties

There are over a thousand varieties of strawberries.
The most widely grown variety in Spain is the Camarosa, designed at the University of California, which is sold in stores. For our garden, however, we have plenty of options, from creeping to climbing ones, and many different sizes.

Strawberries and snails

Snails are the greatest enemy that strawberry bushes may have. To prevent this, you will need to plant them on a straw or wood chips mulch. Snails will think twice before trying to eat strawberries, because they do not like the roughness and cutting edges of those chips at all. **For protection to be complete, we must ensure that the bushes are as clean as possible** and maintain moisture.

Melon

It is believed that the **melon** (*Cucumis melo*) originated in Africa, although it is likely that its varieties were improved in China and India. Later on, each country might have made their own selections, resulting in an amazing diversity that has been reduced to a few commercial varieties.

It is an annual plant, of the creeping or climbing type, that bears oval leaves with several lobes, toothed borders, and a hairy underside.

The first flowers to appear at the internodes are male and female, and hermaphrodite flowers will bud in the second or third generation of branches. The latter ones will lead to a varying shape and color fruit. Its rind may be smooth or ribbed. The seed appears in a gelatinous placenta located in a hole, in the center of the pulp.

Melon is a refreshing laxative, and diuretic fruit, rich in sugars, with vitamin A, B, C, and calcium, chromium, bromine, iron, phosphorus, as well as other minerals.

Cultivation

Melon is a plant of warm, dry climates typical to the Arab garden, scorched by the sun and properly watered. Hence, it is grown only in hot weather and Europe, except Spain, imports it from tropical countries. However, hybrid varieties grown withstand temperatures as low as 34ºF. It grows in any soil, but better if it is well fertilized with well-rotted humus and after a deep dug soil.

In warm places, it grows all year, but in our latitudes it only does it in summer, so we will sow it directly between April and May and still cover the new seedling to avoid cold temperatures. The soil must be at least 61ºF. Four or five seeds are placed in the hole and, once sprouted, one is allowed to grow.

If you are in a hurry, you can plant them in warm seedbeds in January or February and transplant them in May.

Some people have the habit, as they grow melons, of cutting the tips of the branches so that the nutrients are concentrated in the first fruits, since the last ones are smaller and only absorb energy from the plant. Watering must be abundant during the growth of melon, but you should avoid making the plant wet, and having puddles where the branches are supported. Especially, melons should be protected from contact with the ground with dry

In the kitchen, you can do wonders with melon, from smoothies to melon with ham or with clams, as well as soup, ice cream, and even melon stuffed with chicken.

straw or cardboard. They get along with corn, which in very sunny areas protects them from sunburn and does not reduce their nutrients. Otherwise, it gets along with other garden plants, except for the issue of the space, and it is better not to combine them with cucumbers or squash. Do not plant in the same place for three or four years.

Melons should be harvested at its peak ripeness in a garden, and the way to find out is the same you use when you buy them at the store. You must press the end and ensure that it is slightly soft and sinks a little, while the rest of the melon should be hard. Experience will soon teach you which ones are best.

Difficulties

Excessive moisture can cause mildew, cucurbit powdery mildew, fungi, gummy blight on the stem, and various viruses.

As for pests, although melon usually causes no problems, it has many enemies: spider mites, whiteflies, aphids, caterpillars, thrips, leaf miner, and nematodes. Sulfur should not be abused with melons because they do not like it too much. Other problems include: deformations in the fruit by poor pollination or lack of water; sunburn, which can cause white spots; cracked fruit, caused by lack of or excessive water; and brown spots on yellow melons caused by excessive moisture.

Honey Drew variety is a hybrid with a thick rind and long shelf life.

Plastic accelerator

Industrial crops use the black polyethylene to increase soil temperature and to prevent melons from touching the ground. **In order to accelerate production, little plastic tunnels are placed,** supported on archwires, to increase the temperature. A hive is also placed every half hectare so that bees pollinate the flowers.

Varieties

Melons can be divided by their shape or by their growing cycle; the best known are:

● **Yellow melons**, including the Canary and Golden, that have smooth skin, are more delicate, and have a three-month cycle.

● **The green melons**, involving three classes, the toad-skinned and **Rochet** (which are elongated, about 4 pounds, very sweet, and have a 100-day cycle) and the **Tendral**, which is thicker, with rough skin, low odor, native to Murcia, and with a four-months cycle.

● **The Cantaloupe melons**, that are round, small, yellow, sweet, and have a short three-month cycle.

● **The Galia melons**, which are very similar.

● **The Honey Drew**, which are yellow, with greenish flesh, and very sweet.

● There are shelf-stable varieties that only have an interest to market, designed in order to withstand long journeys.

Watermelon

the technique of squeezing them can be learned from experience. There are other tricks, though. One is that the stain of the area of the shell that has been in contact with the ground has become a creamy yellow color. It should not be white or green. Of course, depending on the species, this may vary. Another trick is to tap with your fingers to listen to it: if it sounds hollow it is ripe. A third trick is to observe that the two leaves on the melons stem are dry. When the stalk itself is dry, it's too late.

Watermelon takes from 90 to 150 days to grow. Those without seeds are obtained from crossing a normal one with another treated with colchicine, and the best known is Alena.

Watermelon (*Citrullus lanatus or vulgaris*) is native to southern and tropical Africa, where it grows freely on the ground. Like other melons, it is a cucurbitaceae, but it is much larger in size, reaching about ten kilos. Its main producers are Turkey, Greece, Italy, Spain, and China.

It is a creeping plant, which emits secondary branches from the fifth or eighth leaf onward, and globose fruit in the internodes.

The seeds may be absent or found in the pulp.

Watermelons are diuretic and cleansing, and have a high water and sugar content. Among the minerals include phosphorus and magnesium, but this is one of the fruits that has the least nutrients.

Cultivation

Watermelon is less demanding than the melon in terms of temperature, and is only damaged by strong contrasts. The soil should be well fertilized. Otherwise, watermelons are grown just as melons, but consume more water. Therefore, drip irrigation is convenient. At the time of harvest, they are nothing like other melons, although

Watermelon is rich in vitamin A and has the same calories as cantaloupe, but much less sodium.

Varieties

The classic is always the diploid or seeded. It is more flavorful and has two categories: the elongated fruit with green rind and lighter bands, among which are the Klondike and Charleston Gray type, and round fruits, with a dark green rind, among which is the small type, the Sugar Baby.

On the other hand, seedless watermelons are being imposed more and more; they are tasteless and are developed in Israel. These are triploid, and the seeds are white and soft enough to eat and go unnoticed. The best known types are Crimson, Queen of Hearts, Jack, etc.

However, local varieties are often tastier than these commercial ones, which accumulate water and have very little taste.

Cucumber

They began to cultivate **cucumbers** in India over three thousand years ago. From there they went to Greece and Rome, and entered France in the ninth century.

It is a creeping and climbing plant. Leaves and tendrils grow out of the knots, and from the internodes grows a flower that will result in a cucumber, which can be rough or smooth depending on the variety.

The main producer is China, with more than 2 million tons, followed by Turkey, with almost 2 million, Iran, the United States, and Japan. Cucumbers have very few calories, and have vitamins A, B, and C and calcium, phosphorus, iron, magnesium, and zinc.

Cultivation

The cucumber grows well between 62 and 86°F. They like a humid climate and well-fertilized soil with low salinity. They can be sown directly in the ground, like zucchini, or in pots or root balls between February and April. Transplant or plant outdoors when the frosts are over in April or May, later than the tomato.

If allowed to grow on the ground, you have to weed thoroughly and if it is very wet, put straw under the cucumbers. It is best to put some reeds or sticks and a system of ropes so that it can climb, until it is going to reach the top; then the broad stems are cut and allowed to grow side branches, which produce flowers.

They are harvested before the seeds ripen. The smaller they are picked, the more tender and sweet. Cut with scissors, a few months after flowering.

They associate well with celery, onions, cabbages, beans, lettuce, and radishes, and do not like tomatoes and potatoes.

Difficulties

The main problem is the red spider mite, which attacks in dry weather. You can fight them by keeping the ground free of weeds on an industrial scale with other predatory insects' larvae. They are also attacked by the white spider mite, whiteflies, aphids, thrips, caterpillars, and worms. In humid environments, they are attacked by powdery mildew, oidiopsis, different forms of rotting, and some viruses.

Lack of light can cause yellowing cucumbers.

The cucumber plant is very grateful, in that if you take good care, it has a very high yield.

Varieties

Most are hybrids and are divided into three types: short or pickle, which does not grow more than 6 inches (15 cm); medium length or French varieties, with thorny or smooth fruit; and large or Dutch cucumbers, over 10 inches (25 cm) long.

Trimming the cucumbers

Trim the side shoots, which should be pinched or pollarded when they have 4 or 5 leaves. From there, other branches will sprout, and in the third generation, trim again with the second or third leaf. Although there are other combinations, and if you have room on the ground in the garden, these operations do not matter.

Peppers

The **pepper** (*Capsicum annum*) is originally from Bolivia and Peru, until the Spanish brought it to Europe in the 16th century. It is an herbaceous plant, whose size ranges from 20 inches (50 cm) to more than six feet (2 m) for hybrid greenhouse varieties. It has deep roots, emits two or three branches from a certain height, and branches out from there. Each knot on the stem grows a flower that gives way to a hollow berry that varies in color.

The main producer is China, with more than 10 million tons, followed by Mexico, Turkey, and Spain, which produce about a million tons, peppers being the main greenhouse crop. It is one of the most versatile foods, to eat fresh, conserved, or as a spice. It is part of gazpacho, escalivada, and pizzas, roasted, stuffed or fried, with very interesting spicy varieties.

It has a high quantity of vitamins A and C, and phosphorous, potassium, iron, magnesium, manganese, copper, and zinc.

Cultivation

The pepper needs well fertilized soil and more heat than tomatoes, so it is best to abstain if you live in a cool climate or settle for small, tough peppers. They grow better in alluvial soils, in the flatlands where the heat combines with the humidity of the nearby river, with loamy soil, well fertilized and drained,

The chili pepper reduces cholesterol, activates circulation, and, taken in small quantities, helps with digestion.

and frequent watering. It can be planted from February in protected seedbeds or a hotbed. When the plant has four leaves, you move it to a seedling pot, and transplant when the temperatures don't go below 50°F (10°C), after the tomatoes. If it is cool, you can cover the plants with a bottle cut in half and inverted, when they are small. The soil should be clear of weeds and mulched. They are harvested according to your taste, either

Peppers grow very well in young, loose soils, near rivers, and added to a good salad while green and meaty they are unforgettable.

Varieties

There are three main types: the sweet ones, the spicy ones (grown in the Americas, longer and thinner), and those used for paprika, one of the sweet varieties.

● Among the sweet greenhouse varieties, the **California** is notable: short and wide, and either yellow or red when ripe.

● The **Lamuyo** type, long and square with thick flesh, and more tolerant of cold.

● **The Italian**, long and narrow, that is used for cooking to accompany meats, for example, and is the most tolerant of cold.

A classification more related to your garden would be the following: the bell pepper, of the Reus variety,

which can weigh up to two pounds, and has thick flesh ideal for salads or grilling; square peppers, which includes the red bell pepper, the piquillo, and the California; the frying peppers, which includes the sweet Italian, the sweet Gerona, the Fushimi, the Shishitoh, Japanese, the Padron, and the Corno di Toro; and finally, the chili peppers, among which the Cayenne and Piri piri are notable.

green or red. The green ones are better for salads, and if you don't let them ripen all the way, the plant will continue producing more. To have big peppers, leave only two or three per plant. Those used for paprika or chili powder are allowed to ripen all the way.

In the greenhouse, peppers are supported with stakes or canes to keep them from breaking, since the stem is very fragile.

They thin out inner branches and take off leaves that are starting to dry. They also remove the fruit grown from the first internode, so that the rest grow bigger.

Peppers get along well with tomatoes and eggplants, and it is worth the trouble to plant basil between the bushes to fight aphids. You must wait three or four years before planting in the same place.

A good string of chili peppers can last a long time in the pantry.

Difficulties

The same as tomatoes and eggplants, although peppers are more sensitive to the climate. Red and white spider mites, aphids, thrips, mole crickets, and nematodes can all attack. And for diseases, oidiopsis, rotting, pepper blight caused by the fungus *Phytophthora capsici*, or the scabies bacteria all present challenges. These require solarization, to eliminate these diseases from the soil.

Corn

Corn is a grateful plant, which requires little care, suffers few diseases, and is compatible with many crops, which grow well at its feet.

The most ancient remains of cultivated **corn** are found in Mexico, and there are still wild species in the mountains, though they are very low production. From there, it spread across America, and then through Europe after the conquest.

Corn (*Zea mays*) is a grass, probably the tallest in the world since, in its ideal habitat, it easily reaches thirteen feet. It has the appearance of a cane, without knots, with long, spear-shaped leaves hugging the stem. It has a masculine florescence called the tassel that appears at the top, marking the end of the plant's growth, and a feminine one, which grows off the stem and forms into the cob or ear, which may contain several thousand grains.

As a food, it is rich in carbohydrates, a diuretic, and a source of energy, but lacking in protein. In part thanks to this, it is easy to digest and is a good, energetic food for athletes to keep up their strength. If it is accompanied by legumes, it is enough for a healthy diet.

Harvest sweet corn and freeze it, to enjoy corn cobs roasted in butter for the rest of the year. The one in this image is at ideal ripeness.

The United States produces 40 percent of the world's corn in the so-called Corn Belt, a region with rich soil that occupies a good portion of the center and east of the country. It produces about 600 million tons, of all different kinds, at such low prices that it is detrimental to the market of poor countries, like Mexico, where the crop is not profitable because of the government subsidies that their neighbor enjoys.

Cultivation

Corn is a tropical plant, which is grown everywhere in Central America, from hot, jungle zones at temperatures from 75 to 95°F, to the mountains, at 2500 meters high, with temperatures from 45 to 70°F. There are so many hybrids developed that current varieties can grow with less water than they did a

few years ago, as little as 3 cm during their growth cycle, although they grow better if they have sufficient water until ripening. The ideal climate is that in the American Corn Belt, with frequent rain, except in fall, when dry, sunny days are perfect for ripening.

It likes deep, well fertilized soil, with a pH between 6 and 7.

Corn can be broadcast sown, or you can put two or three seeds in each hole an inch or two deep, separated by 8 to 10 inches. When they start to grow (within 8 to 10 days), thin to one per hole. In order for them to pollinate, it's best to plant many rows. If you only plant a few, you will have to help with pollination.

Sweet corn can be planted from the end of

Varieties

You must be very careful with the varieties of corn that you use. There are too many and the majority are manipulated hybrids. Don't buy them from a farmer that sells them at a feed mill. Get them from a gardener who has used them for a few years, or buy them in a gardening store. In this case, you will most likely find two kinds: **sweet corn**, to consume before it ripens, either roasted with butter, or raw, and popping corn, whose kernel is round and very hard, and pops when submitted to high heats. Farmers plant two varieties, the one with the longer cycle in spring, and the shorter one in summer, after harvesting grains. Both are harvested in fall.

Corn on the balcony

Planted in a large, elongated pot, **corn will serve as a cane or stake for the high bush beans you will plant underneath**. The root of the corn is small, and it only needs to grow lateral roots to hold itself up. The beans should be planted about two inches from the stem, a few weeks after, so that when they start to grow, they can climb up the stalk. **You must keep in mind that corn can grow up to ten feet high**, but you can cut it when it reaches the desired height. And, in any case, you will have to pollinate it by hand. **When the tassel emerges and begins to release pollen**, collect it in some paper and then, when the feminine flower is ready, dust it on with a paintbrush.

frosts in late April, until July or August, to be able to harvest as soon as it's ready; that is, after two months, when the tassel appears or you can put a fingernail in the yellow kernels. After this, the sugar transforms into starch and it is not as savory.

If you harvest a lot of it, you can freeze it, and simply defrost it when you want to eat it in the winter. Corn used for popcorn, and forage corn, for animals, are harvested when the plant is dry. It is best to wait two or three years before sowing corn in the same plot.

It associates well with legumes and cucurbitaceae—that is, squash and cucumbers—which grow wonderfully together.

Problems

Corn has few problems, but they can begin with birds, since some species love the seeds and tender leaves. Use a scarecrow. In this phase, it may also be attacked by aphids. Once it begins to grow, if you water it sufficiently or it rains, it will not have any problems until it is ripe, when it may suffer sooty mold or corn smut, a fungus that grows on the ear and forms tumors that burst into black powder. The best way to fight it is to pull out the affected plants immediately and burn them.

Tomatoes

Sow tomatoes during the waxing quarter moon, and keep in mind that it gets along well with garlic, onions, carrots, leeks, parsley, and celery, and doesn't like potatoes, cucumbers, or kohlrabi.

In the photo to the right you have one of the numerous varieties of tomatoes, more than fifty, that there are in the world. Look for the one you like the best and plant them. To do so, ask veteran gardeners when their tomatoes are ripe and ask for a healthy one from which to get seeds.

The **tomato** (*Solanum lycopersicum*) is one of the most important crops in the world. It was first grown in the Americas, before the Spanish introduced it to Europe, and from there it spread around the world.

Properties

There are numerous varieties of tomatoes that adapt to the tastes and needs of each consumer or producer. There are large tomatoes to cut up for salads, medium ones for cooking or for making sauce, and small cherry ones to eat whole, which can be grown on a balcony or even on a windowsill.

In any case, the tomato has refreshing properties, it is a diuretic, it is calming and remineralizing, it is a great muscular tonic, and it purifies the liver. Eaten with the skin and the seeds, it is a laxative, and thanks to its lycopene content, it helps with rheumatism, stimulates the heart, and fights cancer. The tomato also has potassium (250 mg per 100 grams of tomato), copper, and vitamin C.

Soil and climate

The tomato grows in any type of soil, but it appreciates a well fertilized one with lots of humus. It tolerates salinity and the only thing that bothers it is puddling.

It is well known that when a wild animal eats a tomato, the seed perfectly withstands the trip through the digestive tract and can sprout from the excrement in any place, as long as it has enough moisture. It likes sun and hot temperatures, but it also grows in cool climates, as long as there is no frost. In very wet, cool climates, you can grow them in a greenhouse. Given that there are many varieties, there is not a single rule, but in general they need sun and heat to ripen. They don't like rainy summers, or excessive heat, above 105°F.

Fertilizer and watering

If you want to get a good crop, you should prepare the soil with a lot of compost or manure (6.5 pounds (3 kg) per square meter). It's best if legumes grew in that spot the year before. You should water abundantly, since the leaves fall off quickly if they lack water. It prefers regular watering, every two to three days, to heavy watering every seven or ten days. Water generously when the flowers appear, and then wait for ten days, earthing up the soil and weeding the rows. When it begins to produce fruit, resume regular watering, especially during harvest, since dry spells will stunt the growth of the fruit.

Sowing

Good gardeners select the best tomatoes each season for the following year. Select the thickest ones from the first crop. Let it ripen well and then open and extract the seeds, and dry them on a paper towel or newspaper.

Sowing can be done in hotbeds from February on, with a cover of glass if possible, which protects them from frost and retains heat from the sun.

On a well conditioned soil with humus, broadcast sow and cover with less than a centimeter of loose dirt. Water and thin when they have the first leaves, then strengthen the remaining plants. Some people sow in seedling trays, and others take advantage of a simple old container. When there is no longer danger of frost, transplant to the ridges, keeping the plants about 20 inches apart.

The hawthorn

The hawthorn is a good indicator that the frosts are over. When it flowers, you can transplant the tomatoes. Don't trust the almond trees, which can flower too soon.

A good stake or support is important when planting tomatoes, and in places where there is a risk of hail, some people cover them with a plastic netting. (See photo on page 187.)

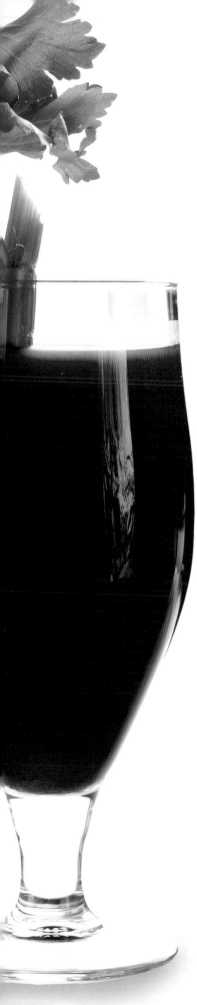

Growth

The tomato is one of the plants in the garden that needs the most care. You cannot leave it for more than a week in summer without suffering the consequences. In the first place, when it reaches a certain height, you will have to put in stakes to support the plant. The most common is to use three or four canes stuck in the dirt around the plant and tied together at the top to form a sort of teepee. Others prefer systems such as hazelnut branches, or even iron stakes, put in vertically with wires connecting the upper portion, like is done with fruit trees. There are also some who cover them with plastic to protect the tomatoes from hail. In order for the yield to be higher, it is good to remove the small secondary stems.

Pruning or Pollarding

During the growth, in the internodes of the stems, small sprouts appear, also called eyes, which should be removed about every ten days to thin the bush. If you don't do this, it will produce a jungle of leaves and smaller tomatoes. Pruning should be done from the top down. Some people only leave the main stem, but others leave various stems to obtain more tomatoes. Given that each master has his own notebook, you will have to trust experience, first that of the gardeners around you, and then your own.

Germination

The seeds of a tomato germinate in about six days, with a temperature of 75 degrees Fahrenheit, when planted in a seedbed with plastic or glass over to protect them.

The prince of tomatoes

In 1998, in the castle of Bourdaisiere, on the shores of the Loire, the **first Tomato Festival** was celebrated, sponsored by Prince **Louis Albert de Broglie**, a passionate gardener and horticulturist. He was also the creator of the brand **Le Prince Jardinier** of gardening tools and a defender of ecological gardening, which seeks to conserve the countless varieties of tomatoes that have been developed throughout European history. In the tasting in the castle, also sponsored by the **Tomato Conservatory**, more than four hundred varieties of tomatoes were displayed, with many recipes to bring out the flavor. Genetically modified, hybrid, or novelty varieties had no place in this festival.

Weeding, mulching, and defoliating

Unless you are making a Fukuoka-style garden, you should lightly dig the ground under the tomatoes to keep the soil loose and eliminate weeds. Mulching should be done when the plant is still small, laying a thin layer of peat or compost around to prevent the soil from drying too much. The tomato is like the palm tree—it wants to have its feet wet and its head dry and warm. In places where the sun is not strong, it is best to take some of the leaves of the plant, to prevent shadows, especially in fall, since the tomato continues producing fruits until the first frost, and from September on it is much harder to ripen.

● **Green tomato**: Contains consistent and fleshy pulp. It should be picked when it is just beginning to turn red, and is ideal for cutting up in salads or eating with oil.

● **Ripe tomato**: Smaller than the previous one, it is ideal for cooking, spreading on toast, or making gazpacho. It is an intense red color and very juicy.

● **Montserrat tomato**: It is aromatic and sweet, of a good size, not very productive but valued for its flavor. It is not very fleshy and has an irregular shape.

● **Vine tomato**: Similar to the ripe tomato, it is a little smaller and very round. You cut the whole little stem and can keep it for a few days.

● **Plum tomato**: It has the shape that its name indicates, is of medium size, and is very meaty. It is harvested when it is very ripe and ideal for canning.

● **Cherry tomato**: It is a very popular variety, genetically modified, of a size comparable to cherries, very aromatic, although sometimes very acidic. It is used in salads,

whole or sliced in half, and to decorate plates. A variety of this is the cherry vine tomato.

● **Raf tomato**: This is a variety of the Montserrat, but with more pulp.

There are more than a hundred varieties of accessible tomatoes; throughout the world there are more than ten thousand varieties, yet you only find two or three in the supermarket. The ones that you are going to plant, you should find them in a nearby place. Most of the time, a gardener friend will have a suitable variety near you. Don't disregard it, and don't hesitate to make your own seedlings.

Harvesting

Depending on the place and the plant, a tomato bush can produce many pounds of tomatoes. They are harvested two months after sowing, and until the cold prevents them from ripening or freezes them, although it depends on the climate and the variety. Some very early types stop producing quickly. The idea is to arrange to have tomatoes for the maximum amount of time by progressively planting from the last frost until May or June, and take care of the plants. Excessive defoliation reduces production.

As far as varieties, hanging tomatoes are good for winter.

Diseases

● **During transplantation**, the plants can be attacked by leaf worms, or cutworms, easy to discover because the plant dies. The best thing is to replace the plant, but first you have to find the worm and get rid of it. Cutworms are eliminated by burying slices of carrot and collecting them the next morning.

● **Powdery mildew** is a fungus that yellows the edges of the leaves, which die in the center. It is combated by clearing out weeds to prevent moisture and is killed with sulfur.

● **Gray rot,** or botrytis, produces lesions on the tomatoes and they end up rotting. It is detected by the white mycelium. It is combated by cleaning the soil and stem, so that it is well ventilated, but it is difficult to get rid of.

- **Excess moisture gives rise to mildew,** a fungus that causes irregular, greasy-looking stains on the leaves, which necrotize little by little. The same thing happens on the stem and the tops of the fruits, with brown spots that end up rotting. You must get rid of the sick parts, not wet the plant, and apply Bordeaux mix when the plant is young, or sulfur. If the weather is wet, it is best to do this before the disease appears.

- **White rot** is a fungus that appears on the stem or leaves, detected by its abundant mycelium. It is fought with cleaning and sulfur, like botrytis.

- **Other fungi that attack the tomato** are Alternaria, *fusarium, verticillium*, and root fungi, which mainly affect the seedlings before transplanting. In all cases, avoid excess moisture and weeds at the base of the plants, since that's where the enemy hides.

- **Bacterial diseases are chancre,** black stain, or scabies, and soft rots; in the first case, the lower leaves wilt, in the following, black spots appear, and in the last one, a watery and bad smelling rot. In all cases, it is combated by using healthy seedlings, not injuring the stem of the adult plant (easy to do when tying or pruning), avoiding excess moisture, eliminating sick plants or fruits, and treating the plants with copper.

• **The viruses** can be of various classes, from the tomato-spotted leaf virus, the mosaic virus, the potato virus, the yellow leaf curl, or the tomato bushy stunt virus. In the first and last cases, the plant does not grow, in the case of the mosaic, potato virus, and bushy stunt, yellow stains appear on the leaves, and in the case of the leaf curl, the leaves are smaller. They are combated by eliminating affected plants, removing weeds, and using resistant varieties, something that you will only discover through experience.

More common problems

• **Rotting at the base of the fruit** is very common, especially from September onward. It can happen due to lack of water, excess of salt, lack of calcium, or unexpectedly cold nights.

• **Splits** are deep cracks that appear on the surface of the tomato from the stem. It is caused by irregular watering, poor fertilization, and sudden cold spells.

• **Sunburn**, can make whitish splotches appear on the fruits and cause them to rot quickly.

• **Lack of nitrogen** produces weak, yellowed leaves.

How to remedy the loss of copper in tomato plants

During the period of growth, tomato plants require supplemental copper. Commercial products can be a great help. However, **you can use a very simple and economical home remedy.**

• **Take a rigid copper wire for electrical conduction**, cut it into 16-inch (40 cm) pieces, and remove the protective plastic coating.

• **Once clean**, stick them in the ground about 8 inches (20 cm) from the tomato plant. Each plant needs four pieces.

• **With the same pieces of copper,** you can also make rings to place around the bush. You must place them on carefully, without damaging the stem, and separated by about 4 inches (10 cm).

Lycopene

The color of the tomatoes indicates that it possesses one of the most interesting pigments that exist in foods, lycopene, the carotenoid that gives them their characteristic red color. **Ten or more weekly servings of foods rich in lycopene**—watermelon, tomato sauce, red grapes, red grapefruit— **contributes to reducing the risk of certain types of cancer, especially prostate, pancreatic, lung, and colon cancer**. It has also been shown to improve the immune system, like the rest of the foods that contain carotenes, such as carrots. Curiously, **blood plasma absorbs lycopene better when it comes from products made at high temperatures** than it does from fresh tomatoes. Tomato sauce is one of the best sources of lycopene, especially when consumed with a little olive oil.

• **Lack of magnesium** causes yellowed leaves with brown spots that you must spray with magnesium sulphate.

• **Lack of phosphorous** makes the flowers dry out.

• **Lack of potassium** makes the leaves curl at the edges, not grow, and yellow.

• **Lack of manganese** makes the leaves whitish along the veins.

• **Lack of copper** can be compensated for by placing pieces of copper near the trunk of the tomato to reinforce its growth.

In all cases, you must fertilize the plant well and water it judiciously, or the harvest will be at risk.

Ripe tomatoes keep better if you keep them upside down, and apart.

Flower crops

Artichokes

The **artichoke** (*Cynara scolymus*) is a perennial plant that can grow up to five feet and sprouts each year after winter. A derivative of cardoon, it originates in North Africa, and the species were selected locally. With cardoon, you harvest the leaves, whose meaty ribs are edible. The artichoke develops a rosette of narrower leaves and the edible part is the flower, covered in membranous, overlapping scales (bracts), meaty at the base, which is what you eat.

The first producer in the world is Italy, followed by Spain. Artichokes possess anti-anemic properties, stimulate hunger, favor the evacuation of bile, are purifying, stimulating, contain vita-mins A, B, an C, and have phos-

phorous, magnesium, and calcium.

Cultivation

The artichoke is a winter crop that grows well between 45 and 85°F (7 and 30°C).

Varieties

The biggest is the Camus of Breton, with a rounded form and about 10 ounces. It is the variety used to prepare canned artichoke hearts, and it is eaten boiled and pickled. Other varieties are the Violet de Provence, the Mosquelina, and the spiny artichoke.

The cold induces flowering, but when the fruit is not formed, frost is not good for it. It likes deep, well fertilized soils, slightly alkaline. It tolerates salinity. It does not like a humid climate, but likes moist soil. Like cardoon, it does very well with drip irrigation. If not, use irrigation by furrows.

It can be planted from seeds, although the wait until harvest will be about eight months to a year, or through shoots or cuttings, which shortens the process to four or five months. The shoots, also called suckers or runners, are picked in February or March; cut leaves and roots and plant them in greenhouses until they take root and then return them to the garden. Cuttings are taken from the mother plant in summer, and planted directly, preferably in a waxing quarter moon. The plants produce artichokes for two years, and after that they are small and not very meaty. It's best to replace half the bushes each year, to have artichokes that are in their first and second years.

The harvest begins in October, and if the weather is good, it can last until May of the following year. The cone of meaty bracts is the flower that is collect-ed before it ripens, keeping in mind that the first few picked will be bigger than the later ones. Lack of water will make them open and dry out too early. They should be cut 3 or 4 inches (8 or 10 cm) below the flower, in a way so that the stem remains a little below the lateral flowers. It associates well with lettuce, cabbage, onions, and legumes, but it prefers to be alone due to its size.

Difficulties

It is less tolerant than cardoon, and if left alone will produce small, hard artichokes. If it is watered too much or has too much nitrate, it is attacked by army worms, which attack the stem, leaf miners, and many types of aphids, some hidden in the folds of the main nerve. It is also victim to snails, artichoke moths, and various beetles. Heat and humidity provoke the attack of mildew and so-called artichoke grease, which causes stains in the bracts.

The main producer of the artichoke in the United States is California, where, since 1949, they celebrate the Artichoke Festival, where Marilyn Monroe was the first Artichoke Queen.

Sunflower

The origin of the **sunflower** (*Helianthus anuus*) is similar to that of corn, but somewhat more North American, since it was grown in New Mexico and Arizona 3,000 years ago. It was introduced in Europe as an ornamental plant and they did not begin to extract the sunflower oil until the 19th century. It is an annual plant with a pivotant root like corn, and not very deep. The stem is consistent and robust, it grows vertically, and can be up to 2 inches (6 cm) thick and up to 6 feet (2 m) tall. At the end is a round head like a plate that contains several thousand tiny yellow flowers, which are dutifully pollinated by bees. The fruit is an achene that ranges from 2 mm to 1 cm. Around the world, more than 16 million hectares of sunflowers are grown. Sunflower seeds are rich in

Sunflowers tend to face south, like all flowers do, in search of maximum sunlight.

Varieties

You can find sunflowers with various branches or just as single stem, which is more convenient for your garden. Choose one that has the biggest flower or head. Industrial crops look for the highest quantity of oleic acid for industrial production. **Buy the ones that produce the best seeds, or, if you want them for decoration,** try a type called **soraya**, which you can plant in a pot in the spring and will flower in summer.

polyunsaturated fats that reduce cholesterol and triglycerides. They are also rich in zinc, iron, potassium, phosphorous, and magnesium, vitamins B and E, and they are antioxidants. If you eat them salted, they have a lot of sodium.

Cultivation

The sowing is very similar to that of corn, but the difference is that these need very little water, since they can get it from very deep in the ground. They are harvested in three months. Cut off the head and let it dry well before separating the seeds.

Before planting in the same place, wait two or three years.

Tubers

more tubers it will form. The plants should be separated by about three feet, since they develop a lot of leaves and are very dense. The harvest comes four months after planting in the soil, and six months after starting the process; when the leaves start to yellow, they are harvested the same way as potatoes.

Difficulties

They don't tend to have problems, however they can be attacked by cutworms, leafworms, and some viruses or fungi.

They require soil rich in potassium and a certain environmental humidity, and they do not get along with any other plants.

Sweet potato flan is made with eggs, milk, sugar, cornstarch, butter, lemon rind, a little rum, and vanilla. Look up a recipe and don't miss out.

Sweet potatoes

The **sweet potato** (*Ipomoea batatas*) is a tropical plant that only grows at temperatures above 70°F (21°C). It is a creeping, herbaceous plant with an edible root, similar to the potato. In some countries, it is essential; for example, in China they grow more than 100 million tons, followed by Uganda and Nigeria, with 3 million. In Spain, they are eaten in the fall, by directly baking the tuber. It is a higher-calorie food than the potato, with as much beta-carotene as carrots, and very easy to digest.

Cultivation

The sweet potato needs heat above all else, so do not plant it until the risk of frost has completely passed. It reproduces through cuttings, and to obtain them, plant the sweet potato tuber in compost and wait for it to sprout. When the stems reach about 8 to 12 inches tall, and have grown

roots, cut a piece of the sweet potato and transplant it into the ground. Some gardeners recommend planting them in pots first to let them finish rooting and grow a little more before transplanting indefinitely. To plant them, dig a deep hole and bury them at the same time you add water to the hole. Make sure that two or three branches of the plant get buried when you plant them, since the more knots there are, the

Varieties

The best varieties for eating are those with red meat. Some notable ones are the Californian, with thick branches, the American Centennial, the Jasper, and the African Eland, although there are varieties native to each country.

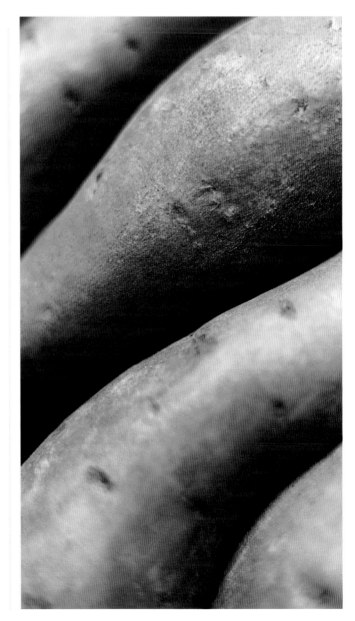

Potatoes

Potatoes originated in the Andes, although they also grow wild in the southern Sierra Madre in Mexico and Guatemala, for example. They were brought to Europe by the Spanish and English, and mass production did not begin until the 18th century.

It is an herbaceous plant (*Solanum tuberosum*) whose importance lies in the tubers that grow on the rhizomes, underground stems. These tubers are large swellings that accumulated starch reserves and function to produce the following year's plants.

In China they produce 65 million tons on more than four million hectares, followed by Russia, with half that, India, and the United States, where the yield per hectare is much higher than in China (400 million as opposed to 150).

The potato is made up of water ($\frac{3}{4}$) and glucides. It is a very complete food, which has sustained entire populations, although it is low in calcium and fiber.

Cultivation

This is a plant of warm or cool climates, which originally grew in the mountains.

However, the plant does not withstand frosts and should be planted when that danger has passed. It grows in any soil, but the more fertilized and looser it is, the more potatoes you will get. Since it's a plant from dry climates, you barely need to water it, and excess moisture favors dis-

How to stop potato beetles

The best way to do so is to **plant chamomile between the potatoes**. The substances that the roots release **repel potato beetles and stop them from laying their eggs under the leaves** of the potato plants.

The growing of potatoes is one of the most rewarding labors of the garden. No matter what, you will have a crop to harvest.

Avoid the use of chemical products when storing potatoes. Some people make a hole in a hillside and cover them with burlap.

eases and rot in the tubers. It does not need much watering, except in case of drought, and the soil should not be flooded. Once the bush is well formed and has flowered, stop watering it.

Planting is done in early spring, in March, although depending on the variety this may be different. The important thing is that, when it sprouts, it does not freeze.

If the climate is mild, you should plant them much sooner, to be able to harvest before the summer heat.

Planting and harvesting

Although you can use seeds and experiment with planting in a covered seedbed to transplant later, the normal method is to get a bag of good potatoes in the vari-

Varieties

They are very numerous and are classified by: color—white or yellow, although the skin can range from white to red; and shape—cylindrical, oval, elongated, flat, irregular, or round.

At the industrial level, they are classified by growing cycle and are divided into:

● Early varieties, of about 90 days (**Royal Kidney and Olinda** among the whites, Palogan and Duchess among the yellows).

● **Semi-early,** between 90 and 120 days (King Edward and Kennebac among the whites, and Belladona and Aura among the yellows).

● **Semi-late,** between 120 and 150 days (**Olalla**, Turia, Majestic, among the whites, and Claudia or Desiree among the yellows).

● **Late,** between 150 and 200 days (**Victor**, among the whites, and Alava or Goya among the yellows).

● Among the potatoes with red skin, the most notable are the **Amorosa, Asterix, Bartina, Cleopatra, Desiree, and Early Rose** varieties.

They say that the red potato is better for frying, due to its consistency, but this depends on the variety.

ety you want, and cut them in chunks, leaving one or two eyes in each chunk, to then plant them in the soil in ridges, separated by about 14 inches. The piece of potato (or whole one if it is very small) is buried about 4 inches deep in a waxing moon.

If it is not cold, the early varieties can be planted in January and wait until they sprout. In inland climates, they are planted in April.

As the plant grows, it is good to earth up, removing the lower leaves as necessary, so that the ground fully covers the new potatoes and they are not touched by the sun, which makes them turn green.

The harvest time depends on the variety: early ones are harvested while the plant is still green, and later ones when it is dried.

Pull them out by hand, pulling the plant first and then dig them out with a hoe or pitchfork, being careful not to cut them, or mechanically if you have a lot and someone will lend you a tractor. If the land is good, you can even pull them out by hand. In dry

Don't forget that there are still ecological varieties among the industrial ones.

weather, leave them out for a few hours in the fresh air, covering the piles with burlap so the sun does not hit them. Then store them in a dry place, in the shade and in an area as cool as possible, as long as it is not less than 40°F.

After planting potatoes in an area, it is best to wait three or four years before repeating. They associate well with cabbages, spinach, and beets, and they don't like tomatoes.

Difficulties

The main problem is the potato beetle, a round yellow or reddish beetle with black stripes, introduced from the United States. It lays orange eggs on the undersides of leaves, and between the larvae and caterpillars, they finish off the aboveground part of the plant. This diminishes production, but not quality.

The most ecological way to fight them is by hand, pulling off the worms and squashing the eggs, even if you have to do it daily.

There is a very effective and simple way to get rid of potato beetles: plant chamomile between the rows. You will see how it scares off worms.

The cut worm attacks from below, making holes in the tubers. There is also the cabbage moth, various aphids, nematodes, fleas and flea beetles, and potato moths, which attack the piles after they are har-

From the roots of the **Jerusalem Artichoke** we obtain a high-quality alcohol.

Jerusalem Artichoke

Helianthus tuberosus, also known as sunroot or earth apple, is a perennial plant, whose underground roots grow tubers that are eaten cooked. They have a flavor similar to artichokes and tend to ferment, producing gas in the intestine (which is why it is sometimes also called the fart potato), but it is considered an aphrodisiac, and a diuretic, and a substitute for potatoes for diabetics. It reproduces from the tubers underground, and can be left year after year and it will grow again in spring. It is undemanding, and grows well with clover. It is also used to fatten livestock, with the stems and leaves making good forage, and fermented alcohol from the stems is very high quality.

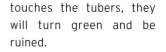

Potatoes grow wild in the high Andean plateaus and are fundamental to the survival of the population in some regions.

vested. In wet seasons, you may also encounter mildew, some viruses, and fungi such as early blight, which is an alternaria. To avoid these kinds of problems, water with a purine of nettles. In industrial farming, they cover the soil with plastic to prevent weeds; you will have to prevent weeds by weeding and using a light mulch of straw or dry grass clippings.

Any of these afflictions is worsened by excessive moisture, but you also have to be careful of the sun, since if it  touches the tubers, they will turn green and be ruined.

The potato on the balcony

You are dealing with a plant that occupies very little space to the sides, but that can grow very deep under the soil, which is what they prefer, and produces an enormous number of potatoes (unlike the sweet potato, which does not produce more than four per plant). It is not unusual for a plant to produce twenty or thirty potatoes. So, if you construct a box about 20 inches high, you can plant as many potatoes as will fit across its width. To get an idea of the size, take a look at the ideal system of permaculture, which consists of stacking two to four tires and filling them with well-fertilized earth. The tires help retain moisture. **In any case, you can obtain quite a few pounds of potatoes with a good tub in the corner of your balcony.**

Legumes

Peas

Originating in the Far East, perhaps Persia or India, and as ancient as lentils—since they were already known in prehistory—peas (*Pisum sativum*) were brought to Europe by the people who lived in the Iranian plateaus. In Rome, they were fed to horses. In the 15th century in Europe, they were eaten dried and cooked with bacon, and they were not eaten green until the 17th century, first in Holland, then France, and then Italy. In central Europe, it's common to eat them when very tender.

The main producer worldwide is India, with

ately, as often is or should be done in industrial agriculture.

They are very rich in sugar and carbohydrates, easier to digest than other legumes, and very nutritious. They are often accompanied by other foods, although they are also very good by themselves.

Harvesting is done when the pod is formed, before it begins to dry. Pull the pods off once they have grown fat, and then open them with a fingernail and extract the peas. Once dry, peas are very good for making compost, and there are even varieties for animal feed. After a couple of

Peas and fava beans are the only legumes that can be eaten raw when picked fresh and tender from the bush.

about four million tons, followed by China, the United States, and France. The pea is a climbing legume, with tendrils to support it up to six feet high. In the crux of the leaves appear one or two flowers, which produce the pods of about 2 to 4 inches (5 to 10 cm), with up to a dozen round seeds. These seeds are very sweet when freshly picked, although in about 20 minutes the sugars transform into starch and it is not as satisfying to eat them raw. You can also freeze them immedi-

Varieties

Peas can be divided according **to shape or color of the seed, the size of the plant, or the use of the product**— this last one is of most interest to us, since there are those for conserving and freezing, for direct consumption, and for consuming the pod before the seeds fully develop.

years, you can plant them in the same spot again. Except for garlic and onions, they get along with all the other plants in the garden.

Cultivation

The pea is a warm-climate crop, which grows between 42 and 95°F, withstands mild frosts, and prefers to be between 60 and 68°F. They like well fertilized clay soil with a pH between 6 and 6.5. Given that it is a spring plant, it probably does not need to be watered.

In mild climates, it can be sown in fall and harvested in early spring, although the most common is to plant them at the end of winter and harvest them in late spring.

They are planted directly in the ground, about 2-2.5 inches (4 to 5 cm) deep, or on top of the soil and covered with wood chips to protect them from frost and keep them moist, in rows about 12 to 20 inches (30 to 50 cm) apart, depending on the variety. When they sprout and are about 4 inches (10 cm) tall, weed thoroughly if you have not mulched. Since it is a very tender plant and

Lentils

The lentil (*Lens esculenta*) originated in Southeast Asia or Mesopotamia, and from there spread through Europe. It is mentioned in the Iliad, and seems to have saved Europe from famines during the Middle Ages. **Today, its main producers are Turkey and India.**

It is a free-standing plant, with a maximum height of about 20 inches (50 cm). The leaves are made up of 15 leaflets around a rachis. **The small flowers are found in a floral peduncle, which produces a diamond-shaped fruit with two lentils inside.**

Among the varieties, notable ones are the Armuña, pardina, verdina, and the biggest, the Laird lentil.

They are rich in protein and iron, and in mild climates they are grown in winter, since they are a cool-weather plant, but they do not like extreme cold or heat. **The lentil is generally an industrial crop, which is not worth the effort in a garden, but you can still do it: plant in October in rows about 12 inches (30 cm) apart, leaving an inch or two (3 to 5 cm) between the seeds.** It is a dry crop, so you don't need to water it. It should be harvested in June or July. In the fields, they used to do this with a scythe when the plant was yellow, and then they threshed them and cleaned them. You can do it by hand, but in a small garden, you will hardly get a plateful. They can be attacked by aphids and weevils, and if it is wet, also by some fungi.

very attractive to birds, until they are about 8 inches (20 cm) tall you should protect them with a netting or some other system designed to keep hungry critters away. Otherwise, you will have to get up very early to chase them away. In climbing varieties, you should put in stakes or supports so that the tendrils grab on, whether they are canes, sticks, or iron.

Difficulties

In addition to birds, snails and slugs like the tender leaves of the sprouts. Once they have grown, they can be attacked by aphids, beetles, thrips, and pea moths or their larvae (*Laspeyresia nigricana*), a moth that lays eggs on the leaves and whose caterpillars go into the pods, then the peas, and eat them from the inside.

Fava beans

to fertilize with manure. The roots of the fava bean have a symbiotic bacteria, *Rhizobium leguminosarum*, which fixes nitrogen in the soil and benefits other crops.

Difficulties

It is often attacked by a parasitic plant called bean broomrape (*Orobanche crenata*), which is combated by crop rotation, eliminating affected plants, or pulling them out by hand.

The most common pest is the black bean aphid, which causes the leaves

Varieties

● **Aquadulce or Sevillana**, an early variety with large pods that take 6 to 7 months to ripen, although you can pick them earlier to eat.

● **Granadina**, is the most tolerant of cold.

● **Mahon blanca or morada** is sensitive to cold, but resistant to drought; it produces narrow pods.

● **Muchamiel** is called the "forty-something", since it can be eaten forty days after sowing.

Fava beans can be picked while tender, before the seed has fully developed, if you want to eat the shells, or when the bean is still green in the pod.

The **fava bean** (*Vicia Faba L.*) is a plant that originated in the Near East, but spread rapidly through the Mediterranean region. The Romans selected the species of large, flattened beans that are recognized today.

This is a leguminous plant whose fruit is a legume (in the form of a pod) that can be up to 14 inches (35 cm) long. You can eat the pod and the bean together, when the legume is tender, or just the bean, when it is ripe.

The fava bean is rich in phosphorous.

The main producer of fava beans is Algeria (125,000 tons), followed by China, Cyprus, Morocco, and Spain.

Cultivation

The fava bean is not very demanding, although it prefers mild, coastal climates. It does not sprout above 68°F and does not ripen at more than 86°F. It likes clay or siliceous soils, and if they are limestone, it must be rich in humus and well drained. Its ideal pH is between 7.3 and 8.2.

For planting, the soil should be deeply dug. The seeds are buried every 10 to 12 inches (25 to 30 cm) in ridges or rows about 20 to 24 inches (50 to 60 cm) apart. They sprout after 8–12 days and are harvested in three months. They can be planted from September to November for early varieties, and in spring in cold climates. It is good

Chromotropic trap

This is a yellow **sheet that you hang from a nearby tree or pole, which is impregnated with a pheromone substance** and an adhesive substance. You can also try fly traps made from a plastic bottle cut in half, with the top part inserted into the bottom part. By planting nasturtium, you will keep out ants, which carry aphids.

to curl and produces a honeydew that favors the presence of fungi. It is fought by keeping the soil clear of weeds, with yellow chromatic traps, or by taking them out by hand.

The sitona (*Sitona lineatus*) is a beetle that chews on the leaves in its adult stage, and attacks the nodules of Rhizobium as larvae. The pea thrip (*Kakptrips robustus*) gives the leaves a silvery appearance.

The diseases of the fava bean are mildew, rust, and botrytis (reddish brown tips or spots), always in the case of excessive moisture.

Beans

The bean is one of the plants that has the most names.

Although beans were already grown in Europe before the discovery of the Americas, there were few known species. Neither the Egyptians, Hebrews, nor Romans ate them, even though the name comes from the Arabic *al'lubiyas*. In America, they discovered better species, the popular green bean or string bean, and the dry beans, such as black beans and pinto beans. Napoleon was a bean enthusiast.

It is an easy plant to grow, but at the same time, there are so many varieties that it's best to get to know them and select one that is best suited for your environment.

These are herbaceous plants, which can be climbing (six to ten feet), in which the stems wrap around anything they can find, or low bushes (up to 16 inches). From the internodes of the leaves grow little clusters of

4 to 8 flowers, which form pods that contain 4 to 6 seeds. Beans can be grown for the seed, or tender, in which case you eat the pods before the seed develops.

Green beans are much more digestible than dried beans, but you have to freeze them for them to last. Dry beans can be stored in a sack, and they can last up to a year with no more help than being kept in the shade and free of mice.

They are diuretic and very digestive, and contain vitamins A, B, C, and E, and calcium, copper, iron, sodium, nickel, silicon, and zinc.

Cultivation

The bean lives at temperatures between 35 and 95°F, and sprouts at 50°F, but it is really happy between 68 and 86°F. The humidity should be relatively high (no more than 70 percent), and the soil should be clay, with a pH between 6 and 8. In limestone soils, the beans will be harder and more fibrous. The ground does not need to be that fertilized, but rather the opposite, as beans are great producers of nitrates. It also does not want too much water—it mainly needs water before flowering, and always in the morning or evening. Yet of course, it is a plant from cool, wet climates, so if you are in a dry, hot climate, you will have to water it every day, watching out for excess moisture, since it protects the soil from the sun. Beans are planted in groups of four or five in holes about 12 inches (30 to 40 cm) apart, in rows about 20 inches (50 cm) apart, and an inch (2.3 cm) deep. Plant them from March to June, for the climbing varieties, and until July for bush varieties, which grow faster.

It is essential to provide support for the climbing varieties.

Cooking beans

If they are green, you just have to boil them a few minutes, and **if they are dry, you must soak them for 12 hours before.** Once they swell up, rinse and drain them, put them in fresh cold water, and boil. **A trick to make them more tender is to add cold water just as they start to boil, to "scare" them.** Another way is to eat beans, before they dry, harvested in September.

Varieties

As we already said, **there are bush beans and climbing beans**. This is the first division. Another division is created by the shape of the pod, and finally, by the use. For example, beans eaten fresh can be perona (with a wide, flat, long pod), **pinto** (with purple stripes), **white butter beans, yellow, or cylindrical beans**, known as Bobby beans.

Among the dry varieties, some highlights are: **white kidney beans**, large in size and often grown in northern Spain; white butter beans, for conserving; **Judion de la Granja**, which are very large; **Caparron**, which are reddish in color and from Rioja; **Palmena jaspeada,** wine-colored, elongated, and large; **the pinto bean,** like the previous one but round; **Tolosana**, dark red, for stews, and the **Asturian fava bean**, with large, elongated grains.

Beans on the balcony and *Ipomea violacea*

These are perfect, since **a simple string is enough for them to climb, and with just a few plants you will have beans for two months, harvesting every week your ration of beans to cook.** If you use an elongated planter (it does not to be very deep), you can have half a dozen plants and leave some to dry to make your own conserve. *Ipomea violacea* is a great healer and is planted between bean plants to protect them from aphids and fungal diseases.

it can be done in many ways, although the classic way is by sticking a cane in each bush, at least six feet high, and connecting them with string at the top. In industrial farming, they use cords tied to a grate up high, for the beans to climb along.

Harvesting is done by hand and begins at two months for tender beans, and at four months for dry ones. You can harvest beans from the same plant for two or three months. When you have picked enough, it's best to thin the plants, taking off leaves so they continue producing. You must do rotations of two years. Beans get along well with all plants, especially corn, and only dislike garlic, leeks, onions, and fennel.

Difficulties

Beans don't have many problems if the weather cooperates, but they can suffer attacks from aphids, red spider mites (which attack in dry spells), white mites, whiteflies, thrips, leafminers, caterpillars, and nematodes, and if there is too much moisture, they endure rotting, sooty mold, rust, and various viruses.

You will most likely have the most problems at the beginning, since worms and caterpillars love young, tender beans, and you will likely have to replace a few.

White beans, the largest, are used in all kinds of stews; black beans go well with rice and are more common in Central America.

Beans grow well in wet climates, since they do not need that much sun to ripen, but they still deserve a well-watered Mediterranean garden.

Chickpeas

The **chickpea** (*Cicer arietinum*) is originally from the southeast of Turkey. **Today, India grows more than half of the 10 million tons harvested each year around the world.** This is a bean with a round stem, no more than 20 inches (50 cm) high, with toothed leaves, from the internodes of which emerge the flowers, producing one fruit with one or two chickpeas. It is a plant of dry climates that does not need watering, although it appreciates it when the seed is developing. It grows well between 77 and 95°F (25 and 35°C), although it will grow from 40°F (10°C) on up.

It likes clay soils, with a pH between 6 and 9, and low salinity, and it should not be repeated for 4 or 5 years.

It can be planted in fall, although it's more common to plant in spring.

Bury two or three chickpeas in a hole, keeping the plants about 20 inches (50 cm) apart, and wait. They even grow well among lots of weeds, although that makes them difficult to harvest.

Harvest when the plants are dried, pulling them out like lentils, and then separating the pods and choosing the best chickpeas by hand.

● There are three main types: the **kabuli**, which are medium to large in size; the **desi**, which are smaller, and grown in India; and the **gulabi,** which are medium-sized.

● **Garbanzo flour is rich in protein and carbohydrates, and contains calcium, sodium, and iron.** Its enemies are garbanzo flies, weevils, various moths, and some fungi.

Hummus

Even if it is just to make this dish, it is worth it to use a field that is too far away to tend to daily for growing chickpeas. **Hummus is a dish from the countries of the Near East and is made from cooked chickpeas (9oz/ 250g), garlic (1 clove), lemon juice, and tahini (two tablespoons of sesame paste).**

Mix the tahini with the lemon juice and a little water. Add the clove of garlic, like when you make mayonnaise, and the chickpea puree, and it's ready. For variations, you can also add cooked potatoes, cumin, salt, pepper, and olive oil.

fruit

trees

A brief introduction
to fruit trees

At a country house, any corner is good for a fruit tree: at the edges of the garden, along paths, in little-used corners, along an irrigation channel, by a pond . . .

The cherry tree by the acequia

Fruit trees are an accessory to the garden that you will really appreciate at harvest time. I will never forget the first garden I knew in my childhood. A huge cherry tree shaded the reservoir that the gardener used to irrigate. With great skill, he watered beans, tomatoes, peppers, and eggplants by conducting the water through furrows, in those summers that expired on the 15th of September, when climatic changes brought on the long autumn and made spring a treacherous friend.

A shadow in the garden

Most gardeners don't like the shade of the trees, or their roots. There are trees that are not permitted near a garden: poplars and shaking poplars have very shallow and extensive root systems that impede the growth of plants; pines acidify the soil around them and their shade is perennial. There are trees that get along well with uncultivated corners: the cherry, a walnut beside the fountain, a fig tree against the wall, a pear tree over the garden bench, with the bundle of canes you will use for the beans and tomatoes leaning against it.

To reinforce the immune system of fruit trees, you can add minerals to the base of the trunk.

In small gardens, it's not unusual to see delicate peach trees and wizened olives accompanying the work of the gardener, as well as vines, among which you can plant melons or squash. Beans grow well at the feet of olive trees, and even gain protection from intense frosts. Under peach trees, you can plant early lettuce or peas, and even garlic and strawberries grow well under the trees, but the rest of the crops prefer to be far away, in a corner where their sunlight is uninterrupted.

The climate

In countries like El Salvador or Guatemala, which are in the tropics and have mountains that produce every climate, the list of fruit trees grows considerably. For example, at sea level, you can plant avocados, custard apples, myrtle, coconut, guava, plums, lemons, cashews, mangoes, macadamias, papayas, pineapples, tamarinds, and sapotas, all trees that are impossible to grow in a temperate-Mediterranean climate, for example. Even oranges need to be grown higher than 300 meters, and as you go up you will find loquats, mandarins, mameys, plums, cherries, figs, blackberries, and peaches. In any case, the climate is a determining factor for fruit trees. The Chinese that introduced the lychee to the Mexican state of Sinaloa knew this well, since this state has a climate similar to the southeast of China, from where the plant originates.

Keep in mind that there are species that need the winter cold to bear fruit, that is, a certain number of hours at below 45°F (7°C) for the tree to grow fruit, depending not just on the species but the variety. In general terms, almonds, hazelnuts, peaches, quince, Japanese plums, figs, and grapes need less than 100 hours; apples and pears need more than 200, although they do best with more than 600 hours; a minimum of 300 for the apricot tree; 400 for the walnut; 500 for the cherry; and 800 for the European plum. Except for the almond, the apricot, the quince, and the fig, most trees do better with at least 1,000 hours of winter cold below 45°F (7°C) during the three winter months. Therefore, this kind of tree is found inland, with oranges and lemons on the coast, as they don't need any cold (although they tolerate near-freezing temperatures and grow well in tropical regions).

Conditions for growing

Fruit trees are permanent plants, although some last more than others, from the ten years of a peach tree to the hundred years of a walnut. You have to keep this in mind when choosing the placement. Also keep in mind that the soil must be deep, with more than a meter of soil before reaching the bedrock. The fig tree likes to be beside walls or fences, which retain moisture longer. The majority of species need good drainage. In sandy soils you will have to water much more frequently than in clay soils with a lot of organic material. To make sure the yield is sufficient, the trees need enough water. You also have to keep in mind the risk of diseases. There are species that are more sensitive than others, like peaches, which get sick easily and require more care.

Fruit trees don't like too much air, and so they grow best when protected by a wall or in an inner patio, or behind the house, sheltered from wind. Some people plant big trees to protect them, although the most common in this area is not barriers of fir trees but rather cypresses; you can plant many flowers at the base of them.

Pruning fruit trees

• **Fructification pruning** is part of the previous category, since it is done to get rid of weak branches and let the young branches bear more fruit.

• **Rejuvenation pruning** is done in old trees to get rid of sick branches, leaving only the young sprouts. Some trees with a short life, like the peach tree, do not allow it. In pear and apple trees, it is normal to get rid of very long branches that do not produce fruit anymore, or graft young branches from other trees. In olives, it is even possible to cut the tree off at the ground and re-grow from suckers. It is a common operation in places where every ten years, severe frosts cause lots of branches to die.

Calcifugous trees

Test the pH of the soil through the methods suggested in the chapter on soils, with pH paper, phenolphthalein, or hydrochloric acid. If it is acidic or alkaline, you have the option to neutralize it. If you are not strong enough to dig five feet (1.5 meters) down as is necessary, here is a list of **trees that don't tolerate alkaline soils with too much limestone: avocado, persimmon, chestnut, pomegranate, lemon, mandarin, peach, orange, and papaya**. Among those that are not fruit trees you have **a silver fir, ash, spruce, magnolia**, and **oak**.

Pruning fruit trees is different than pruning shade trees, which live longer and are meant for the long-term.

Pruning is necessary for any tree to give it shape. It was practiced in the Middle Ages to get firewood with the maximum yield, and it has always been done with fruit trees, to get rid of dead branches, increase the yield, and make it easier to pick the fruit. There are three or four types of pruning:

• **Shape pruning** is practiced on young plants to give them a proper shape, as you will see in the following section that describes the varieties.

• **Sanitary, maintenance, or cleaning pruning** is done so that the tree has enough light and air, and also to eliminate the dry or dead branches in the winter.

Shape pruning

This begins as soon as you buy the tree, at one or two years old, and continues for the next three or four years. The goal is to encourage the top to grow to the most convenient height, and make a solid tree, which can bear the weight of the fruit. The majority of fruit trees also need the sun to reach all the fruit; therefore, we prune inner branches, and choose a shape that suits the species, since it is not the same to grow a cherry tree for cherries as an ornamental tree with lots of shade and little fruit.

Of the many shapes you can give a fruit tree, the most common are: **vase, pyramidal, central leader, cordon, and palmette** Let's look at each one by one.

Vase pruning

This consists of getting three main branches, at a height of 20 to 40 inches (50-100 cm) from the ground, with each branch leading to two- or four-tiered secondary branches, each 24 to 40 (60-100 cm) inches to each side. It is a very geometric shape, which takes up a lot of space, but it gives the tree a certain

Pruning is an art that requires learning a technique and quite a bit of practice to know what works for each species.

bearing and is convenient for harvesting the fruit. To do this, follow these steps: when you plant the young tree in the winter, cut the trunk at a height of 32 inches (80 cm) and prune the lateral branches, leaving two shoots on each one from the trunk. In June, choose which three branches you are going to keep, at least 4 to 8 inches (10 to 20 cm) apart vertically, not all coming from the same point, and which form a circle or vase. Cut off all the little shoots that have sprouted and leave 4 or 5 buds and wait for winter. In this season, begin to give shape to the tree, making sure that all the empty spaces are filled, but also that no branch is over another one, so that they all get light. Leave all the branches that grow upward from the trunk at a 45 degree angle from the vertical, and cut the tips. The third year, continue the same process but pick off all the fruits, since you will harvest the fourth year, when the quality is better.

This is appropriate for apricot, almond, hazelnut, persimmon, cherry, plum, citrus, pomegranate, fig, apple, peach, quince, olive, and pear trees.

Pyramidal shape

This is used almost exclusively for pear trees, although it is also the shape of the fir and is the most ornamental shape. Unlike the vase shape, what you want is a straight trunk with various levels, about 30 inches (80 cm) apart, each with 3 to 5 open, almost horizontal branches. The trick is to leave only the shoots that are convenient, and leave empty spaces every 16 to 20 inches (40 to 50 cm). The central trunk is cut off at the top, since if it is too strong it will take strength away from the lower branches. Each year, lop it off slightly higher, so that the branches closest to the top start to go vertical; this way the trunk has a tiered shaped. If you want the pyramid to be irregular, leave the branches at different distances.

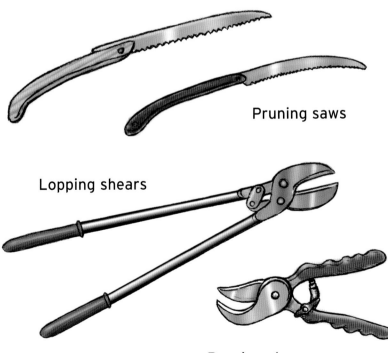

Pruning saws

Lopping shears

Pruning shears

Central leader pruning system

This is the simplest and most natural for the tree, since it allows the central trunk to grow as it pleases, and then starting 16 to 20 inches (40–50 cm) from the ground, leave 4 or 5 secondary branches, about 8 inches (20 cm) apart in height. One meter up, do the same. The branches are selected the same way as in the vase shape, making sure that the light always gets through the tree. This is good for peaches and pear trees.

Cordon pruning

This is useful because the tree takes up very little space and can be placed almost anywhere. The result is a smaller tree without thick branches, and very narrow, as if it was only two-dimensional. It can be horizontal, with two branches growing out to the sides about 12 to 16 inches (30 or 40 cm) from the soil, and from there, other vertical ones supported by wires lattice-

Water sprouts and suckers

Careful with the names of the trees. We tend to generalize too easily, although it usually does not matter, since we understand each other, but it's good to know that water sprouts come out of the branches, grow vigorously, and bear no fruit, while suckers sprout from the soil, from the base of the tree or the root, and are very common in olives and hazelnuts. Both should be removed, although olive suckers are good when a tree has dried up in a cold year.

The buds emerge in the first year, the shoots in the second, and by the third year they are called branches, but of course only specialists make that distinction.

work against a wall. It may also be vertical, if it has a main branch going upward, with smaller branches sprouting off the side, but on only one plane (the best shape is to put it in front of a door or arch). The oblique cordon has branches that lean to the same side, from which horizontal secondary branches emerge, and in the shape of a U, two main branches that open up and grow upward from very low on the main trunk.

All of these shapes require a support to which you will tie the branches, and frequent pruning to direct it. Above all, you have to slow down the growth of the branches by lopping them off (cutting off the ends) or buying dwarf species, since they exist for this purpose, of apple, pear, peach, and cherry trees. The most common application of this system is for grapevines.

This style, and the following, are also known as trellis pruning, since they need the support to grow.

Palmette pruning

This is the most commonly seen style in orchards of pitted fruits, pears, and apples. It consists of leaving the central trunk 6 to 12 feet (2 to 4 meters) in height, with two symmetrical branches to each side, at a 45 degree angle, every 20 inches (50 cm), approximately. The tree typically has four levels, and the first one starts about 28 inches (70 cm) from the ground. These trees are planted in rows between two posts about ten feet (3 m) high, with wires every 20 inches (50 cm), from the first 28 inches (70 cm) off the ground. The first year, lop off the tree to a height of about 32 inches (80 cm). The following year, begin to select the three strongest branches, directing them with stakes, so that each year you get another layer, until you have a flat tree with four or five layers, and as wide as you want. This pruning style is good for walls with lattices, upon which you can have beautiful trees in the shape that you wish.

This works for apricot, persimmon, plum, apple, quince, peach, nectarine, and pear trees.

Grafts

This is another way to propagate plants. In grafts, part of one plant is combined with another, with the goal of improving it, as is often done with vines. In many fruit trees, they combine the root of a species adapted to the soil and resistant to the pests of a certain place, with the trunk of a species that produces the best fruit. This operation is done by grafting a bud onto the stem. The easiest example to understand is that of rose bushes, in which it is common to graft a domesticated species onto the much hardier roots of a wild species.

The grafts that you can do will be in the branches, to add better species or to graft them with other species, for example, a plum branch onto a pear or apple tree. Additionally, in a single tree you can do various grafts, for example, several types of apples on an apple tree. Some trees are best reproduced through grafting, like pear trees.

Grafting is done when you have a tree that produces spectacular fruit; then you select a branch and graft it onto a tree of the same species or family, to get more fruit of the same quality.

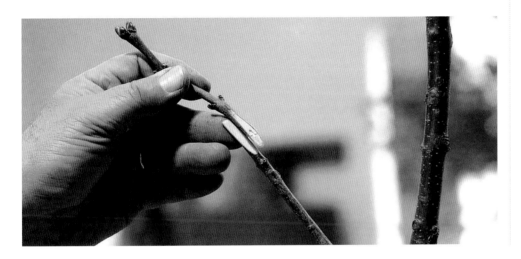

Air layering

We are going to make a branch develop roots without separating it from the mother plant.

● **Select a good branch, make two circular cuts** more than 12 inches (30 cm) from the end so that you can take out a ring of bark. Then take transparent plastic (so you can see inside it) and tie one end around the base of the ring, like a cone. Fill the cone with peat and tie the end of the plastic above the ring, holding the peat tight against the peeled branch. Then inject water with a syringe to wet the peat.

● **Repeat this operation every 15 days.** Finally, wrap the whole thing in aluminum foil or newspaper so the sun does not touch it. After about two months, you can take off the opaque layer to observe the growth of the roots. When they go around the whole plastic, it is time to cut the branch below and transplant it into a pot or in the soil.

● **There are some methods that professionals use to make this process easier**; for example, vitamin B1 injections combined with the water, the use of rooting hormones sprinkled on the ring before covering it, etiolation, which consists of covering the area where you are going to make the cut a few months before with a thick packing tape, or the use of special plastic pots that can be opened on the side and are sold especially for layering.

● **Layering can be done in fall or spring**. The time depends on the species. Cherries form roots in three months, and can already be transplanted. Azaleas, on the other hand, need more than a year. The list of species that permits layering is very long. Among those of interest for our gardens, are cherries, plums, apples, figs, laurels, strawberry trees, quince, olives, pears, and sycamores.

Types of Grafts

The two main types are stem grafts and bud grafts.

Stem grafts

This consists of inserting a piece of stem with various buds onto a host. **There are various methods.**

The whip graft

This consists of joining two thin branches cut diagonally with a sort of tongue in each that fits together when they are connected. Tie securely with a string or adhesive tape and wait until the buds are more than 2 inches (5 cm).

The cleft graft

Going under the bark is perhaps the best known and simplest method: make a cut in the shape of a T in the host, and lift the bark, under which you insert a scion that you have cut diagonally, with the cut edge in contact with the sap of the tree. Then tie and wait for it to sprout; when it does, cut the host branch so that the sap goes to the new branch, and later untie it so you do not strangle it.

The bark graft

This is the same as the previous one, but the process is longer, since it is used to join different varieties. In winter, cut the scions destined for grafting, about 4 inches (10 cm) or two or three buds, and put them in the refrigerator, wrapped in newspaper, unless it is an evergreen like pine, which you must graft directly so it doesn't dry out.

In spring, cut the branch or host stock that you want to graft onto with a saw, and  with a knife, make a vertical cut in the bark, separating it from the trunk. In the branches, make a beveled cut and stick at least two scions between the bark and the trunk. Then, bind the whole thing and wait until the buds sprout.

Above, whip graft, the easiest to do and rather secure. Practice with rose bushes.

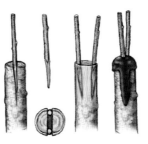

Cleft grafting

This is also very popular, since it consists of making a horizontal cut in the branch of the host stock. Then make a cut in the center about 2 to 2 ½ inches (5 to 7 cm) deep, and introduce the new branches, cut at an angle on both sides, as if sharpening a pencil. Seal the union with grafting paste, and that's that. The same graft can be done double, putting two branches, one on each side of the cut. Always use a putty to cover the wounds and don't untie them until the scions have sprouted and grown more than 2 inches (5 cm).

Approximation grafting

This is done with small plants, joining two branches from which the bark has been removed in shapes that fit together perfectly. It is done with different types of pines. Each branch has its own roots, which it can maintain.

Oblique graft

This is also very easy to do. It is as simple as cutting the stem and scion diagonally and joining them; they should always be the same size.

Bud grafts

This consists of putting the bud of a tree you want to graft onto the stock tree. Cut a piece of bark around the bud and lift it up, separating it from the mother tree. The next step is to make a cut on the stock tree, which can be one of three shapes:

T-shaped

In this one, the bark will have the shape of a pointed shield at the base, and insert the bud between the bark of the host and the trunk.

Square or rectangular

The bark to be added will have the same shape and will simply be placed over the cut.

Square with a cut at the base

This is done with the bud being grafted is found on a small branch, and so that the weight does not pull it out the base is inserted into the tree. In any case, the graft is bound with adhesive tape or string. Then cut the branch above the graft so that the tree puts its efforts into the new branch. A characteristic of bud grafts is that they should be untied after 15 days to avoid strangling the tree. In both types of grafts, you should get rid of the buds that are below the graft, always with the goal of putting more strength into the graft. It is very important to make contact between the cambium layers.

The cambium

This is a layer of very small cells in the plant that is found between the bark and the vascular tissues that carry water and nutrients through the tree. For a graft to work, the cambium of the tree must be put in contact with that of the scion or grafted branch. Therefore, it is best if the bark of each touches on the sides.

Grafting tools

Stem grafts can be done between January and March, and bud grafts in the spring or fall. The majority of grafts are done with plants of the same species, although there are exceptions, such as pear being grafted onto quince.

You need very few tools:

● **A very sharp knife** to make the cuts.

● **Tape to bind the grafts.** There are many brands, among them grafting bands of various widths and lengths, with types for trees, roses, and vines, with their corresponding rubber bands. The tape does not need to be adhesive.

● **Wax** to cover the wounds on the tree and seal the grafts.

● For grafts on small branches or shoots, they sell clips to keep them straight, **and other special systems.**

Planting fruit trees

This is another delicate subject, since the first thing you have to figure out is if the condition of the soil and climate will suit the tree you want to plant. The best way to be sure is to buy it from a local nursery that has the same climatic conditions. And don't forget to talk to an expert there and be sure of what you're getting. I have had many surprises due to incompetent vendors, who can sell you one species for another when they don't have leaves. If you want a fruit tree, don't end up with an ornamental one, and vice versa.

The most common practice is to buy the trees in pots or with root balls, sometimes inside a bag. If it does not have too many roots curled up in the pot, it can be planted at any time of year. The tree will notice the difference when it starts to grow in the spring and finds the new soil around it.

If you buy one with naked roots, it has to be fall or winter, and you must plant it right away, but it's best to make a big hole with anticipation, with good compost in the bottom. Also mix compost into the soil you use to fill the hole. Don't force the roots to fit in the hole; there should be plenty of room. It is good to cut the dry roots and bury at the same depth as it was originally. It is also suggested that you dip the roots in a mixture of soil and liquid compost. Then rest it in the bottom of the hole and cover it with earth, forming a mound around the trunk. Surround it with a circular furrow for watering.

Trees and the climate

The mango is a type of fruit that is reproduced through grafting, since planting the fruit does not produce enough quality.

In cold northern countries, they can only enjoy a few species of trees that produce nuts: walnuts, chestnuts, hazelnuts, and beechnuts. In the Mediterranean and other subtropical regions, there are countless species and varieties you can grow.

Fruits of very temperate climates

These trees are not very tolerant of frost and especially not in the spring, once they have flowered. The temperature should not go below 28°F (-3°C). When they are grown inland, you will need to protect them from late cold snaps, using smoke to produce artificial fog:

Lemon, mandarin, orange, grapefruit, prickly pear, palm, and banana trees.

Fruits of somewhat temperate climates

These species tolerate frost well, not so much in late spring, but they need a lot of sun and not a lot of fog. The temperature can go below 23°F (-5°C) on occasion, but persistent or colder spells will freeze the trees:

Apricot, mesquite, almond, persimmon, pomegranate, fig, jujube, kiwi, loquat, olive, and stone pine trees.

Fruits of cold climates

Fruit trees specific to climates with freezes in winter, spring, and fall, which need cold and tolerate late frosts to a certain point. It is not unusual for the temperatures to go below 15°F (-10°C):

Blueberry, hazelnut, chestnut, cherry, raspberry, gooseberry, plum, apple, quince, peach, nectarine, walnut, pear, and grape vines.

Fruits from hot climates

List of the most common species that grow in the tropics. They do not tolerate frost at all.

● **Jackfruit**	*Artocarpus integriflora*
● **Avocado**	*Persea americana*
● **Cacao**	*Theobroma cacao*
● **Coffee**	*Coffea arabica*
● **Coconut**	*Cocoa nucifera*
● **Cherimoya**	*Annona cherimolia*
● **Guava**	*Psidium guajaba*
● **Lychee**	*Litchi chinensis*
● **Mango**	*Mangifera indica*
● **Papaya**	*Carica papaya*
● **Pineapple**	*Ananas cosmosus*
● **Rose apple**	*Eugenia jambos*
● **Tamarind**	*Tamarindus indica*

Citruses   Orange

Oranges, mandarins, lemons, and grapefruits originated in Asia. With the conquest of Alexander the Great, the first specimens of lemon trees came to Europe (*citrus* comes from the Latin for lemon), and with time, oranges appear with all their variations, until the 19th century, when the delicious mandarins arrived.

Citruses originated in the subtropical and tropical regions of Asia, from which they have spread all over the world. Of all the varieties, the orange is the most common, and of all the types, the Valencia orange is the most sold, followed by the Navel. The orange tree is a perennial tree with simple, coriaceous leaves, and white, aromatic flowers, called azahar, which give off an unmistakable aroma in the spring. It is so fragrant that it is worth including one in your garden just for that reason, as long as you live in an area that does not get too many frosts, and that does not go below 25°F (-3°C) after January, when they flower.

Others

● **Mandarins, grapefruit, and lemons** follow the same guidelines, although lemons tolerate more heat and mandarins tolerate more cold.

● **The mandarin** has been generally displaced by the clementine, which is easier to grow commercially.

● **The lemon** is reproduced through grafting onto the trunks of bitter oranges, and like orange trees, you can always graft new varieties when they are adults.

Cultivation

The orange tree likes deep, clay soils that are well-drained, without too much calcium or sodium, and it needs abundant watering to be sweet. Normally, you buy a young plant and plant it in the garden. After that, you can graft to improve it. If you want to grow one from a seed, the process is complicated. Plant the seed in a seedling pot, and when it is about 8 inches (20 cm) tall, move it to a protected covering on the ground, keeping the plants a meter apart, where they will remain for at least a year. After that, transplant them to the garden, and it will take 6 to 8 years for them to produce fruit.

They require quite a bit of fertilizer and it is best to use drip irrigation to save water, although many gardeners use flood irrigation every ten to fifteen days.

Pests include ants, aphids, and mealybugs, and

diseases include nematodes, gummy blight, and tristeza virus.

Only about 4 percent of the flowers bear fruit, and harvest should be done a year after flowering. Although if your main goal is to have a pretty tree to decorate the garden, you may want a more rapid-growing variety.

Types of oranges

To avoid the lengthy ripening process, from 12 to 13 months for the sweet Valencia orange, and to get fruit more than just once a year for a short period of time, they use all sorts of systems that we do not recommend, like storing them in warehouses or harvesting them well before they are ripe, then accelerating the ripening with chemical products that reduce the flavor.

If you want to enjoy fresh oranges for several months, you should plant different species. The Navel orange matures fastest, around November, and does not have seeds. It is light in color.

Then come the blood oranges, red in color, which ripen in January; the imperials, and late Navels, from February to April; and finally, the Bernas and Valencia, which can be picked until June.

Pitted fruits

These grow in temperate climates, with long periods of cold. They tolerate temperatures as low as 15°F (-10°C) and even need cold in order to bear fruit.

Apricot tree

This is a fairly short (6 meters) rosaceae, originally from China, with a brownish-violet, craggy trunk; scarce, reddish branches; and leaves that curl when young and are dark green with lighter undersides. It tolerates cold well, although it flowers early and you must be careful with late frosts. It tolerates dry weather well, and does not like saturated soils; it needs well-drained soil. Depending on the soil, it can be commonly grafted on to roots of plum trees, or almond roots in very dry land. It should be pruned in a vase shape and keep in mind that branches that are two or three years old flower well, so leave them be. The most common varieties are: Harcot, which has large, sweet fruit, is very hardy, and is harvested in June; Royal Rosa, which has large, yellow fruit and is very vigorous; Blenheim, which has very large fruits that fall easily, is slightly tart, and is harvested in July; King, with large orange fruit and white flesh; and Goldcot, which has white flesh and is very juicy and fragrant, harvested in June or July.

Cherries

This is a rosaceae whose cultivated varieties can grow up to 80 feet (75 meters) high and make splendid shade trees. There is a European variety that grows wild in the mountains, not very large, at an altitude of around 1500 meters, producing small, tart fruits.

The bark is smooth, with a ringed appearance and a reddish color.

It has few branches and the leaves are slightly toothed. The white flowers appear at the same time or before the leaves. The fruit is a red or black drupe. Fields of cherries are magnificent in the summer.

The cherry blossoms have turned some places into tourist attractions, such as the valley of Jerte, in Cáceres, Spain, where their spectacular flowers cover the mountainsides.

It is the national tree of Japan, for its beauty, and anyone who has a cherry tree in their garden will feel inspired when it flowers, and when harvesting, since there is nothing sweeter than a ripe, fresh-picked cherry.

The main producers are Russia, the United States, Germany, Italy,

Plum

France, and Spain. It is a species that needs many hours of cold (at least 900 hours) in order to bear fruit. It tolerates temperatures below zero in winter, and the flower tolerates freezing temperatures. It flowers late, in April, and between the flower and the fruit, there is about 100 days. The cherries do not ripen if picked while green. It needs a lot of water to grow well, more than 260 gallons a year, and if it does not get enough, you will have to water it.

It grows when grafted onto stock of sour cherry and other cherries, and can be transplanted in a year.

It does not like to be pruned, although you can do a vase or pyramidal pruning if you don't cut the thick branches. If you prune it, do so just after the leaves fall, so it has time to scar, and when it is small, it's good to lop off the top so that it spreads from the beginning.

In the world today, they use few varieties of cherries for rootstock, basically *Prunus avium*, or sweet cherry, *Prunus cerasus*, or sour cherry, and various hybrids of the two.

On these rootstocks, you can graft **Ambrunes**, **Napoleon**, **Burlat**, **Stella**, **Sunburts**, etc. Look for the variety best adapted to your area in a local nursery.

Birds

Blackbirds, starlings, and magpies, among equally gluttonous birds, are the nightmare of cherry tree owners. To fight them off, we suggest hanging black string from the tree, since the birds don't see it and get scared when they trip over it.

More comfortable is hanging something shiny that moves in the wind, like aluminum foil or cans. **To stave off mice, which are also common visitors when there are cherries**, put out traps or let your cat get a little hungry.

Solitary plum trees, near running water or embankments, **produce excellent fruit.** Enjoy.

Another medium-sized rosaceae, like the apricot tree, these do not grow more than 20 feet. They have a smooth trunk, bluish dun in color, and the branches are small. The root is long but shallow, so it does not get along with nearby crops. The flowers appear on branches that are a year or older. The fruit is a yellow, red, or violet drupe with two seeds that can sprout within a month of ripening.

The plum tree tolerates frosts well, and even the flowers are hardy, but it does not like dry weather.

If you have limestone soil that is not very deep, this is your tree. I have seen them grow admirably in slopes near streams: they are well drained, and they have water within reach. They are reproduced by grafting onto rootstock depending on the type of soil: among others, there is the **Franco**, for all kinds of soils; **San Julian**, for calcareous soils; **Damas Blue**, for rich, deep soils; or **Marianna**, for Japanese varieties and siliceous soils. As for trees, there are the **Santa Rosa**, with large, red fruits; **Queen Claudia**, green in color; and the **Golden Japan**.

The tree is pruned in a vase shape or palmette, leaving the branches of more than a year and getting rid of those that sprout from the trunk. To know if the plums are ripe, shake the tree. If some fall, then they are perfect.

Peach tree

It is reproduced by T-shaped bud grafting, and it is important to choose the variety best suited to your area.

The most popular variety are those with white flesh, which can be American or European; the ones with yellow flesh, with hairy skin and a pit that separates easily; and the nectarine, with firmer flesh. Grafts can be done on rootstock of wild varieties, of plums, or hybrids of peach and almond. Peach trees are pruned in vase or palmette, and you must thin the fruit, leaving a peach every 6 to 8 inches (15 to 20 cm).

The peach originated in China, then passed to Persia, through Greece, and to Europe. The tree is no more than 20 feet (6 meters) high, with a very powerful root that does not like competition in the soil. Its flowers range from pink to intense red and the peaches appear on branches sprouted the year before. The fruit is a large drupe with a hard endocarp inside and an edible mesocarp. The main producer is China, and that is still just a fifth of the apples, followed by Italy, United States, Spain, Greece, and France.

The peach tree is very tolerant of cold, below zero Fahrenheit, and needs at least 400 hours of temperatures below 40 degrees Fahrenheit (7°C) to bear fruit, depending on the variety. Therefore, in tropical climates, they are grown at high altitudes. It is a delicate tree that wants cold and light but suffers from sunstroke and tends to get sick easily.

The peach is a delicate tree, so you will have to find the ideal variety for your area.

Some producers, as done with the peaches of Calanda, Spain, put each fruit in an individual paper bag to prevent pests and reduce treatments.

Loquat

The loquat originates in Southeast Asia and entered Europe as an ornamental tree. Tall, it can reach up to 35 feet (10 m) in the best of cases. It is distinguished by its large, perennial leaves—coriaceous, spear-shaped, and hairy. The flowers are white and fragrant, and flower from the previous year's branches. They flower at the end of fall or winter, and the fruit ripens in April to June. The fruit is small, about 2 inches (5 cm) in diameter, and has various large seeds that are very flavorful.

It is a tree of temperate climates, that does not need cold—the frost harms the fruit. The main producer is Japan, followed by Brazil, **Algeria**, and India.

It is reproduced by grafts on hybrids and quince trees.

Pruning is best done in a pyramid shape, and you should thin the fruit when they are a little bigger than a hazelnut.

Underground pruning

If the fruit trees grow and produce too much wood—that is, grow too many branches—you can **cut one or two thick roots near the trunk.** This way, the tree will be weakened and can be controlled, and floral **buds will sprout from the wood buds.**

Flowering branches

In maintenance pruning with stone fruit trees, certain terms come up a lot: for example, flowering branches are those on which the flowers appear. **They are new branches, between 6 and 12 inches (15 and 30 cm), which have the flower buds. They are so delicate, that in peach, nectarine, and some apricot and plum trees, if you let it, the weight of the fruit will break them, and so it's best to prune them.** Chifonas are even smaller branches, long and weak, which must be pruned from the base, but in cherries and almonds, leave the strongest ones and cut the rest off, because the fruit does not weigh as much.

Mixed branches are about 12 inches to 36 inches (30 cm to 1 m), and have flower and wood buds (from which new leaves will sprout). **These are pruned two different ways: French style,** leaving some mixed branches and cutting others off at the second bud—the next year eliminate the mixed branches and leave the ones that were pruned; and **American style,** leaving very long branches so that they bow with the weight of the fruit and produce new branches near the base, which will be the ones you leave for the following year.

Wood branches and water shoots, which don't produce flowers, should be eliminated, unless you need to fortify the tree by lopping off the woody branches.

Seeded fruits

Apple, quince, and pears have an endocarp that contains the seed in the middle. These trees can live more than fifty years.

Apple trees

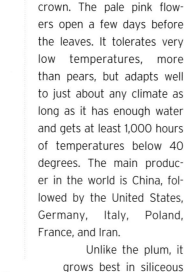

The apple tree originated in Asia, where the first varieties came from and were crossed with European species. It was introduced to Spain from North Africa. It is a tree that grows up to 35 feet (10 m) high, with a straight trunk and round crown. The pale pink flowers open a few days before the leaves. It tolerates very low temperatures, more than pears, but adapts well to just about any climate as long as it has enough water and gets at least 1,000 hours of temperatures below 40 degrees. The main producer in the world is China, followed by the United States, Germany, Italy, Poland, France, and Iran.

Unlike the plum, it grows best in siliceous soil. It is reproduced from seeds or from bud grafts. There are over a thousand varieties of apple, and the most well known are:

Apple or Pear Worms

Cydia pomonella is a moth about an inch in length, which lives from May to September and lays **eggs on the fruits at the end of the summer. The larvae hatch a week later and dig into the fruit in search of the seeds.** When it has grown, it hides under the bark or underground and waits to become a moth the following spring. **To combat them, you have to burn the wormy fruits or put traps out in August,** like corrugated cardboard under tiles.

Golden Delicious, whose fruit is large and golden yellow, and harvested in early fall; **Red Delicious**, whose fruit is large and red and is more difficult to grow because it is more sensitive to diseases; **Starking**, which is a mutation of the previous variety; **Reineta**, of Canada, is a strong tree that produces oblong, greenish fruits; **Verde doncella**, which gives a fruit that is wider than it is tall; **Gala**, originating in New Zealand, and well adapted to irrigated land, with abundant yellow fruit; and an Australian variety, the **Granny Smith**, bright green with a large tree that is easy to grow.

Pests

The main pest of apple trees is the apple blossom weevil, which, as the name indicates, harms the flowers of the tree.

Pear tree

Quince tree

Nectarine

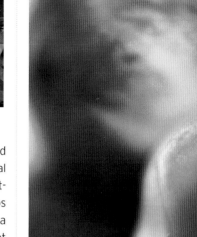

The pear originated in Eastern Europe and Asia. It is a medium-sized tree, which can grow up to 70 feet (20 m) and live more than fifty years. Not that long ago, I cut one down in my garden that had been there more than half a century, and it continued to support the bundles of canes for the beans up to the last moment. It was still producing fruit at that point.

It is a tree that naturally forms a pyramidal shape once fully grown. The fruits have smooth, green skin, and get narrower at the top, taking on the characteristic shape.

The main producer is China, followed by Italy, the US, and Spain. They like temperate climates and prefer cold to heat. They need about 1,000 hours below 40 degrees Fahrenheit (7 degrees Celsius) and a deep, clay soil with sufficient moisture.

They reproduce through seeds and grafts onto hybrids or quince. The most well known varieties are the **Conference,** the **Blanquilla,** and the **Dr. Jules Guyot** A variety that is resistant to calcareous soil is the **Bartlett.** Depending on the variety, they are picked from August to September. The pear tree can be pruned in a pyramid, cordon, or palmette shape, and once formed you must eliminate the branches that don't produce fruit.

Pear trees are grown on rootstock of quince, since this makes the trees smaller and more accessible.

The quince tree is found in its natural state in central Asia. It was already cultivated in Babylon, and the Arabs used it as a laxative. It is a small tree of 15 to 20 feet (5 to 6 meters), similar to the apple, with single white or pink flowers that grow in the internodes of the leaves. The fruit is a bulb of coarse, yellow flesh, full of seeds.

The main producer is Turkey, with 100,000 tons, followed by China, Morocco, and Argentina.

You can find quince trees in almost all country homes, since they need very little care. They tolerate cold, although they do not need it that much—100 hours is enough—and they tolerate intense heat of summer without too much water, unlike apples. They reproduce by cuttings of the same year, which you can pull off when the leaves fall, stick in the ground, and transplant in February or March. If you grow from seeds, you will have to graft.

Of the different varieties, the most acceptable is the common one, which, like the others, produces fruit in October. Pruning should be limited to thinning the branches, since it is a slow-growing plant that does not have

any problems in a vase or palmette form.

This is a mutation of peach trees, mainly differentiated by the fruit, whose skin is smooth, with a different flavor and a free stone. Other differences are that the nectarine does not need as much cold, and tolerates it less, and tends to be planted near the coast. The known varieties mainly come from the United States. It is reproduced through seeds, then grafted onto a peach tree, peach-nectarine hybrid, almond tree, plum, or apricot tree, depending on the climate and soil.

Otherwise, it should be cared for like a peach tree.

Other trees

Here we will brief-ly review some of the varieties not included in the previous three categories, but that are common in gardens.

Plastering the trees

Often trees have wounds to the trunk that can get infected or attract para-sites. **To prevent any cuts or scratches from harm-ing the tree, you can pre-pare a putty of polymer clay, manure, and fine sand, mixed in equal parts, with which you will cover the trunk, branches, and sprouts**. In the case that you have many trees, you can use 80 percent clay and 20 percent manure. It is best to apply this mixture in fall, after all the leaves have fallen, or at the end of winter or early spring.

Almond tree

It is originally from Central Asia, from which it reached Persia and Mesopotamia and Spain two thousand years ago. It has a smooth trunk that grows rough over the years, with greenish bark when young that turns brown to gray as it ages. The flowers are formed on flowering branches most-ly and appear when the cold sets in. The fruit is a long-lasting drupe, and is one of the most valued nuts. It requires cross-pollina-tion to bear fruit, done by bees, like in cherries. A sin-gle tree will not bear fruit. It does not like late frosts, and blooms too early, so that sometimes the crop is lost. They reproduce by grafting on host stock of almond, peach, or plum (the latter in wet climates). Among the many varieties, some notable ones are: the Marcona, with a rounded shell, Desmayo Largueta, with elongated fruit, the Desmayo Rojo, with thick fruit, Guara, Cristo Morto, Garrigues, Moncayo, etcet-era. Almond trees are grown in dry areas, so you don't need to water, but if done, it increases produc-tion. Pruning is done in the vase shape, but can also be done on a trellis against a wall.

Hazelnut

Originally from Asia Minor, it was introduced to Europe by the Greeks. It is believed that the name comes from the city of Avella, Italy. It is a tree of no more than 15 feet high, quite irregular in shape, with many branch-es coming from the trunk. When young, the branch-es are quite straight, as anyone familiar with the practice of detecting water with a hazel wand knows well, and when they are old they become twisted. The leaves are large and round and the result is a cup-shaped achene.

It grows in temperate climates. It needs at least 700 hours below 45 degrees Fahrenheit (7 degrees Celsius), but can be found anywhere from near the coast to 1,500 meters above sea level in the Pyrenees mountains, where it bears excellent fruit. It likes moisture and rich, deep soils, and if it lacks water, it will drop the fruit. The main producer is Turkey, followed by Italy, the US, Spain, Azerbaijan, China, and Iran. It breeds in many ways: by seed, cutting, layering, stake, and graft (bud or approximation). The varieties are numerous, and it is best to find one adapt-ed to the place where you want to plant. Pruning is done to favor new growth, in which the fruit appears in the following year.

Chestnut

Like the walnut tree, you can cultivate this tree for shade or fruit. Its ori-gin is in Eastern Europe. It is a large tree, with spear-shaped leaves, an upright trunk, and a leafy canopy, which blooms from May to June. It is happiest in the mountains, between 500 and 1,200 meters of altitude, especially in wet places sheltered from exces-sive sun. If you want to have it as a fruit tree, you must pollard it to about 6 feet tall when the trunk is about 3 in (7 cm) in diameter, so it will grow side branches.

Walnut

Originally from Persia, it is even bigger than the chestnut tree and is sensitive to late frosts, which can easily kill the new buds and leave the tree in a very sorry state. It is propagated by grafting, and grows well along rivers, where it has plenty of water, since like the chestnut, it needs more than 260 gallons (1,000 liters) of rain per year.

Olive

It is believed that the olive comes from the eastern coast of the Mediterranean and that the Phoenicians were those charged with taking it to Greece and Italy, where it spread across the world, introduced by the Spanish to Peru, Mexico, and California. Many gardeners have received land that was an olive grove before and still have been able to plant garlic, beans, peppers, and tomatoes at the base of the trees, since the old olive tree is deeply rooted and earth can be worked and composted around the tree, pruning well to not block the sun. The oil is the juice from the fruit, but to be profitable, you must have an olive grove. However, with one or two trees, you can have olives for quite some time. If left to grow freely, *Olea europaea* can reach a significant size, as occurs in gardens where the gardener waters a lot but is not skilled. The tree has a smooth and crooked trunk, and over the years acquires fantastic shapes that make it very attractive. It is also attractive because of its small, pointed leaves, gray-green in color and very dense. The fruit is a dark drupe when ripe and green when unripe. It does well in limestone soils, and likes the light. It does not need watering and tolerates cold as low as 15 degrees Fahrenheit (-10 degrees Celsius). If it freezes, suckers sprout, and when it needs water, it may lose fruit and leaves, but is very difficult to kill. Reproduction is performed by stakes 20 to 40 inches (50 cm to 1 m) in length obtained from old and vigorous branches, stuck directly into the ground, although in smaller industrial crops advantageously treated cuttings are used. Then they are improved by grafts. The best known table varieties are manzanilla and gordal, and for oil production, Picual, Arbequina, hojiblanca, picudo, and cornicabra.

Grapevine

The grape vine is one of the oldest plants used by humans. This is a bush that has a root, a stalk, and what we call vine shoots, which grow vigorously every spring and where the grape bunches form that so often decorate trellises and shade gardeners as they sit and watch their plants grow.

Vines grow on lattices and cover the tops of pergolas and trellises.

Choose a variety that can climb if you want to have grapes in autumn.

Herbs and Spices

A corner dedicated to
herbs and spices

Aromatic and culinary herbs are not demanding; you can even have them on a windowsill, and they are a joy for the senses.

The majority of spices, aromatic plants, and medicinal plants can be grown in very little space, even on a little balcony, which is ideal for our garden.

Light

These types of plants generally need a lot of light, so they should be in places where there are no trees in the garden, or if it is a balcony, as close to the railing as possible, or even hung over it in pots. They also like walls that face the sun, like rose bushes do, and you can even have them on a sunny windowsill.

Water

Although they are very hardy plants and many can survive with rainwater alone—like thyme, rosemary, lavender, oregano, fennel—if they are planted in pots they will need abundant watering because the sun dries the soil very quickly. Some, like rosemary and thyme, can tolerate a week of strong sun, while others, like sage and mint, need daily watering at sunrise and sunset.

Fertilizer and mulch

Herbs and spices should not be fertilized too much because our main goal is to keep their aroma and flavor.

It is best to keep the ground free of weeds, and for this, the best option is mulch, which for herbs could be gravel or pine bark.

Pruning

Once they have flowered, remove the dry flowers and trim the plant all over so that it grows new sprouts. If you let the plant grow too much, it will look like it's bolted and will be less pretty and weaker. Another thing is to take the points off the central branches so that they grow to the side and develop a round shape.

A small space

Select your favorite plants. The most common are rosemary, which grows very well with **lavender; thyme**, which is drier and does not need much water; **oregano, sage**, and **marjoram**, which can all share a pot. In another pot you can put **mint** or **spearmint**, **basil**, and **parsley**, which need more water. In any case, after a year you will have to trim the plants well.

Many herbs grow wild in the mountains. Thyme, for example, grows in dry terrain in mild climates, but you will also find rosemary, lavender, oregano . . .

Herbs and spices, one by one

The difference between an herb and a spice is just like the difference between a plant you use for poultices and teas, and those that you add to dishes to flavor them: many have both uses.

Basil

Basil (*Ocinum basilicum*) is an annual, herbaceous plant, with small white flowers and aromatic leaves—the new ones are more fragrant and should be used when the plant is about a foot high. It grows well in dry, sunny climates.

There are about forty types of basil, some purely decorative, like the Red Rubin with red, toothed leaves, and the Large Leaf, and the Sweet Thai with small leaves, although for culinary uses the Genovese and Napolitano varieties predominate. The former is more fragrant and the latter smells a bit like mint.

Uses

The leaves are used either fresh or dry. If they are fresh, they are finely chopped and good with scrambled eggs

or omelets, fish, and veggie dishes.

If they are dried, they can be used in soups and stews. In Egypt, they used it in mummification, and in Rome it was the herb of lovers. It is also used to repel mosquitoes and aphids when planted in the garden between peppers or eggplants.

Cultivation

It is planted in pots, near the window, or in the ground, in areas with good sun, although if it is in direct sun you must be sure to water it frequently, and not too much at once.

Plant in a seed bed with soil rich in humus between February and April, and once the cold has passed, transplant outside, leaving one or two hand widths between plants. If you keep it inside and it never gets sun, it will dry out soon. To conserve basil, we recommend freezing it in ice cube trays, or once dried, in glass jars.

Savory

Savory (*Satureja hortensis*), also known as royal thyme or olive herb, since it is added to give them flavor, is an herbaceous plant that is planted in seedbeds in February and transplanted in May, although it is best to separate a few branches that have roots. It prefers very basic limestone soils, with good sun exposure, and hot, dry climates. There are two types of savory—summer or winter. The former is a plant that is grown in pots or in gardens, delicate with a gentle aroma. The latter (*Satureja montana*) is a perennial herb, with a stronger scent and flavor.

The flavor is similar to that of mint and thyme, and it is used in cooking for sauces and for flavoring vinegar. It is mainly used as a marinade for olives, but also goes well with trout and cheeses. The essential oil has antibacterial properties.

As an infusion, it is an aphrodisiac, digestive, tonic, stimulant, and antioxidant. The decoction is used in poultices to cure cuts.

Wormwood

Anise

Celery

Wormwood (*Artemisia absinthium*) is a lively plant with a pale appearance, with divided leaves and yellow flowers on white heads.

It is one of the bitterest plants that exists to cure intestinal problems. The Latin name *absinthium* gives us a hint about its use, to make absinthe, and also as a component of vermouth.

Due to its unpleasant odor, it is useful in the garden to ward off insects, especially aphids. The infusion of wormwood is a tonic and digestive.

It can be reproduced through its tiny seeds, by cuttings, or by dividing the plant at the root. It likes cool, dry, mountain climates best.

Green anise (*Pimpinella anisum*) is an annual plant from the umbelliferae family, of a certain bearing, with flowers in clusters and seeds in the form of small, oval, fragrant grains.

It does not like wet, clay soils, and is susceptible to aphids. In September, when the flowers dry, cut the plant and store it in a well ventilated place, until it is totally dry, then remove the seeds.

The seeds are useful for their essence, anethol, which loses its medicinal properties and is toxic when isolated, but in the seed and combined with the other components, it has tonifying and digestive properties, cleans the intestines, is good for asthma, helps people quit smoking, cleans the lungs, and freshens breath. It also increases milk production in lactating mothers.

The infusion is made with a teaspoon of seeds per cup of water.

Aromatic herbs

These are a selection of plants used in cooking to add flavor to the dishes. **The main ones are the bunch herbs (parsley, thyme, and bay), the fine herbs (parsley, chervil, chives, and tarragon), basil, mint, angelica, pimpernel, sage, and others, depending on the taste of the individual.**

To use them, you should **pick them fresh**, a little before they flower, and if they are not hard plants like thyme or rosemary, you should chop them very finely and add them at the end of cooking, to keep them from losing their flavor.

Celery (*Apium graveolens*) is an herb as well as a vegetable, and can be used raw in salads or juices, and boiled in soups or with vegetables for its richness in vitamins and its many digestive, diuretic, and remineralizing qualities. It has a strong flavor that not everyone likes. It grows up to 16 to 24 inches (40-60 cm) and you use the stems with the greenest leaves.

Cultivation

Celery is planted from March to June in open air or covered seedbeds, as long as the temperature does not go below 57°F (14°C). It is transplanted two months later, after the waxing moon, with the plants about two feet apart. If the climate is very dry, it requires frequent watering.

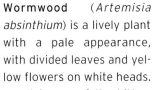

Starflower

Marigold

Watercress

Watercress (*Nastrutium officinalis*) is a plant that grows naturally on the banks of rivers and even in the water. It is a perennial plant from the cruciferae family. It grows up to two hands and each leave has five to seven leaflets, and small white flowers. The leaves are of more interest, since they have a strong flavor and are used in salads, with garlic and salad dressing to taste. They became popular in France in the 17th century.

Watercress has a slightly spicy and penetrating aroma, reflected in the Latin name *Nasturtium*, which means "makes the nose twist" and *officinalis*, due to its use in pharmacies. It is also used in sauces and with fish, and even in soups. The Romans used it to prevent hair loss.

Its cultivation is not necessary, but if you choose to, starter pots are convenient. It grows along freshwater sources and can be harvested there.

Starflower, or borage (*Borago officinalis*) is a great pollinator. It is an annual plant of certain size that has two varieties—a wild one with blue flowers, and a domestic one with white flowers, very appealing as a green, although the hairs that cover the leaves and give it a certain look mean that its use is limited to the north of Spain, where it is very popular.

Use

This is a plant with very low caloric content, but a high content of water, good for weight loss regimes, since it is rich in fiber and slightly laxative. It is also diuretic due to its potassium content. "Borage water" is the name of a soup made from the leaves in times of famine, since it grows in the mountains. The flowers can be used in an infusion to fight colds. In the kitchen, you only use the leaves and the tenderest stems, finely chopped for preparing a salad, although it is more common to drink it boiled (not too long) as a vegetable.

Cultivation

It is planted from March to June in loose soil rich in humus, although it can be started in seedbeds and transplanted after two months. It is harvested before flowering; you should leave a few plants be, because they only reproduce once a year.

The bunch of herbs

This consists **of a few stalks of parsley, a little thyme, and a bay leaf tied with a string, which can be added to soups or stews,** so it can be removed from the pot before serving. Some people add some fennel or a few celery leaves, but be careful not to go overboard and cancel out the flavors.

Marigold (*Calendula officinalis*) is a medium-sized plant, imported from Egypt in the time of the Crusades. It is a strong plant that requires little care, with large orange flowers with numerous petals, similar to daisies.

The word "calendula" comes from calends, which in the Roman calendar was the first day of every month, since the plant flowers all year if it does not freeze.

Harvest fresh flowers and store in tightly sealed glass jars. As an infusion, it is used to prevent digestive upset, but its most important function is for its virtues for the skin. Marigold oil is made by marinating a handful of flowers in a quart of olive oil for forty days, and is used to treat sunburn. The tincture is obtained by marinating 3.5 oz (100 g) of flowers in 2 cups of alcohol, and then applying with a cotton ball.

It can also be applied in compresses, or by using the petals directly on the wound.

Scallions and chives

Scallions (*Allium fistulosum*) and chives (*Allium schoenoprasum*) are very similar. Scallions grow wild in many places and can easily be found by its scent and appearance, but it is also easy to grow, much like chives.

Cultivation

They are planted in seedbeds in March or April and transplanted a month and a half later, being careful not to put them near legumes. They do not produce a bulb, but rather many stems that you can cut periodically. If they grow in the wild, they will re-sprout after winter, but if you grow them it is best to re-seed every spring.

Use

Only the leaves are used, fresh cut, as a seasoning or as an ingredient in fine herbs for omelets or sauces. They contain many minerals, like calcium, iron, and phosphorous, and vitamins A, B, and C, but consuming just a small quantity is not relevant in this sense.

Garden Herb Mixture

This is a **mixture of parsley, chervil, chives, and tarragon, very finely chopped.** It is used in cooking to **season fish,** like flatfish, for **poached eggs,** and for **omelets.** These herbs can be added to roasted chicken, mixed with melted butter and a bit of lemon juice, and can also be added to **mashed potatoes or vegetable purees** right before they reach a boil in the cooking process.

In some countries, the scallion is known as the Japanese onion, since it has been a feature of the Japanese garden for two thousand years. From the stems, two to six per plant, you remove the green leaf that covers them and a false white stem appears, similar to a leek. This is the part you eat. The Japanese earth them up so that they remain more white and tender. In many stores, they sell recently planted onions as if they were chives, but they are really young onions.

Lavender

Lavender (*Lavanda angustifolia, officinale*), or *spica* are varieties of a single plant that is industrially grown for its aromatic properties. The leaves and flowers are used to make perfumes, colognes, and soaps, but they also serve as a flavoring in the kitchen. Lavender grows well in dry land, especially calcareous soils, and tolerates cold well. The stems of the plant, straight and square, form bunches of bluish flowers. The greenish-blue color of the plant is very characteristic. It is reproduced by seeds, but it is a very slow system, so it's better to pull out a few cuttings with roots from a fully grown plant, or buy a small one, since they are easy to find.

Grown along the edge of a path, in the garden, or under the pines, they make a very pretty border with their fluffy appearance. You harvest the tips of the stems with flowers and let them dry, hanging upside down.

Once dry, you can use them as an air freshener, in small cloth bags or bags of herbs, or you can put them in perfume boxes or with other herbs in aromatic pillows. The dry flowers are used as a sleep aid under the pillow. The infusion or tinctures are good for insomnia, fever, rheumatism, intestinal spasms, kidneys, and as a tonic.

Lavender essential oil is an important anti-rheumatic and is a disinfectant for wounds and scars. It is said to scare off mosquitoes if you add a few leaves in distilled water and alcohol, it makes a good insect repellent.

Cress

Fennel

Plantain

Cress (*Lepidium sativum*) is also known as garden cress. It is easy to confuse it with watercress (*Nasturtium officinale*), by its appearance and the name that it is marketed with, both used in salads with garlic and lemon. These garden cress are rich in minerals and salts, fiber, and minerals C and A.

If you want to grow in the garden, you have to be near a spring, as it will need about four inches of soaked soil, rich in humus, to sprout. Propagation is by cuttings, which are stuck in the mud, or with seeds in a pot, kept wet until the seedling is about 4 inches (10 cm) and transplanted.

Once transplanted, it is covered with water, leaving the upper leaves projecting out. To harvest, cut off the top 3 inches (7 or 8 cm). In winter you have to submerge them completely in the water with some stones on the stems.

Fennel (*Foeniculum vulgare*) is a perennial plant with bright stems and very divided leaves. Its small, yellow flowers, arranged in large umbels, are very characteristic. It adapts to any soil, but if it is well fertilized and watered, it can reach up to 60 in (150 cm) tall. In temperate climates, it flowers twice a year, in summer and in winter, but in cold climates it only blooms in summer. It is very aromatic. It is sown in February and March in a warm bed and passed to seedling pots when you have a pair of leaves. It is transplanted from May onward. You can sow outdoors from March to June, with a waning moon.

The flowers contain essential oil and the root contains coumarins. The bulb is harvested and used in salads while fresh. The flower umbels are used in infusions to reduce flatulence, and with milk and honey for a cough. Buds and leaf buds are used as a stimulant, cooked and eaten. Seeds and dried flowers boiled in water makes compresses used for inflammation of the eyes. Do not plant near tomatoes, and sparingly around beans. Essential oils should not be drunk and is contraindicated in case of pregnancy, gastritis, ulcers, liver disease, or neurological problems.

The greater **plantain** (*Plantago major*) and the English plantain (*Plantago lanceolata*) is a wild herbaceous plant that blooms between spring and summer, when the leaves are picked. Mix four tablespoons of juice from the leaves with 3.5 oz (100 grams) of butter and 0.3 oz (10 grams) of dried powdered leaves for an ointment against hemorrhoids, fistulas, eczema, and varicose veins. The leaf tea with honey is restorative and cleansing. Water obtained from macerating the leaves is also useful against conjunctivitis, insect bites, sore throat, and mouth sores.

Preserving herbs

As it is not possible get them fresh all year round, and if you do not want to buy dry ones, **the best ways to keep them as fresh as possible are: freezing,** once chopped and clean, for example, in ice cube trays or with blotter paper; **in oil or vinegar;** and **in salt,** alternating layers of salt and herbs. In all these cases, the herbs will preserve in some way their original appearance. But **you can also dry them in the sun** or near a heat source, tied into small bunches and hung upside down. Then grind them with a kitchen roller, and store in jars.

Bay

Hollyhock

Chamomile

The **sweetbay** (*Laurus nobilis*) is an evergreen tree or shrub, with leathery, alternate, long, spear-shaped leaves, very aromatic when broken. The plant can reach ten to thirty-five feet (3 to 10 m) high. It tolerates the cold but dies if the temperature goes below 15°F (-10°C). It is reproduced either through cuttings, seeds, or layering. Cuttings can be planted in July or August, but it will suffice to transplant one of the suckers you find growing wild in your garden, and you will have an evergreen tree whose leaves are used to season stews. Dried leaves retain the aroma well. They contain essential oil, resin, tannin, mucilage, and a bitter taste. Crush fresh leaves to make a paste and apply directly to the wasp stings, and as a poultice for rheumatism or shock. The juice extracted from crushed fruits is snorted to decongest the head and infusions of leaves with honey help against the flu.

Hollyhock (*Althaea rosea*) is a biennial herbaceous plant with a long stem, which reaches up to six feet (two meters) high, along which alternate branches open with large single flowers. Flowers appear in summer the second year after planting; the first year they only grow leaves. The infusion of dried flowers and leaves is taken with honey to fight colds. The crushed root with fresh leaves is applied to gumboils. Water and boiled leaves are used against redness and sunburn, and the water from leaves boiled for two minutes can be gargled to soothe throat inflammations. However, the most important element of the plant is the mucilage, which makes the infusion slightly viscous and helps to strengthen the mucus that lines the walls of the stomach. Hollyhock is a good indicator of the balance of the soil in your garden.

There are several annual herbaceous plants of the family Asteraceae, although we will use *Matricaria recutita*, or German **chamomile**. This is an annual plant, erect, with rigid branches, whose very showy and fragrant yellow flowers have yellow-green buds and white petals. It blooms from May to September. Chamomile grows wild, but just pick the seeds and scatter them, as it is not picky about soil or temperature, although it grows best in fertile ground. It is sown from February onward.

The infusion of flowers is used against stomach discomfort, indigestion, gas, or gastritis. The name Matricaria comes from its use against menstrual pains. The infusion, once lukewarm, is very good for washing sore eyes and lightening blond hair. If you add honey, you can drink it throughout the day as an invigorating tea. With white willow leaves, lemon rind, and honey, it is useful for fighting insomnia before bedtime.

The four seeds of spagyric medicine

Alchemy divides the seeds of the garden into four classes:

● **The freshest seeds,** which are melon, watermelon, pumpkin, and cucumber.

● **The least fresh seeds,** which are lettuce, curly endive, chicory, and purslane.

● **The warmest seeds,** which are fennel, anise, cumin, and caraway, from which you prepare a delicious tea.

● **The least warm seeds,** which include celery, parsley, and carrot.

Lemon balm

Oregano

Parsley

Lemon balm (*Melissa officinalis*) is an herbaceous plant, with bunched stems and small white flowers that appear from June to September. It reaches a height of about 32 inches (80 cm) and smells like lemon. Its main use is to attract bees.

It is a rustic, non-demanding plant that forms large bushes if fertilized. It is planted with young branches and roots of a grown plant. You just need to water it in dry regions and it needs a good pruning every year to re-grow strongly.

It contains essences, alcohols, and essential oils. The juice of the leaves is useful against bites and stings, the infusion helps nervous states, and it is antispasmodic, sedative, soothing, and refreshing. It also acts against vertigo and headaches. It is part of water of Carmen. Lemon balm is also a great pollinator.

Oregano (*Origanum vulgare*) is a wild, herbaceous plant with straight, branched stems and red or white flowers in corymbs. It blooms from June to October, reaches 24 inches (60 cm) in height, and gives off a strong aromatic odor. It is also very melliferous and attracts beneficial insects like bees. It is sown from March to April in the nursery and transplanted in autumn or spring. It likes calcareous soils and tolerates drought and cold, so it is popular in the mountains. It is good to neutralize the excess heat in the neighboring plant.

A handful of leaves and flowers cooked for 8 minutes produces water that helps fight against colds. Cooked in wine for about three minutes, it produces a liqueur for mouth rinses and a plaster for abscesses in the mouth. The infusion fights breathing and digestive problems, and is used as a tonic.

Parsley (*Petroselinum sativum*) is an herbaceous plant native to the island of Sardinia. It was first used on the graves of the deceased until the Middle Ages, when it was introduced into the kitchen. It is an essential herb in the kitchen, which is now very easy to get in stores, but it is far more exciting if you can get in your own garden. It can also be grown in a pot. It flowers the second year after planting, which is done in a waning moon in early August to have leaves in winter, and in February to have leaves in summer. It likes rich and well-watered soils, but grows freely along walls and terraces, along with tomatoes, roses, onions, and asparagus, but does not like lettuce.

In addition to enriching any dish with its flavor, ground fresh leaves are used as a poultice for ulcers or sores. You can prepare a juice with some leaves and water in a mortar, and mixed with hot milk it is good for

asthma and coughs. Crushed and applied with a thin gauze to the chest, it helps reduce breast milk in lactating women. In addition, parsley is a diuretic, stomachic, vasodilator, stimulant, and tonic. It can be stored frozen in ice cube trays, or wrapped in a cloth or newspaper. It should not be taken by people with heart or renal failure.

How to protect mint from the cold

To protect mint leaves from the cold, **sprinkle wood ash over the whole plant until it is well covered.** Thus, frost will not affect it too much. In the case of strong winds blowing off all the ash, you will have to repeat the operation.

Pennyroyal

Rosemary

Sage

Pennyroyal (*Mentha pulegium*) is a perennial herbaceous plant that repels fleas if rubbed on the skin. It tolerates the loss of moisture from the leaves very well. It has quadrangular stems, small white to purple flowers in verticils, and does not reach more than two feet tall. It is very aromatic and similar to mint. It can be grown in any soil, but it prefers those that are well maintained and fertilized.

Plant the seeds in seedbeds and transplant when the risk of frost has passed. You have to water frequently.

Infusions, which are often paired with mint, are used against stomach aches. If you live in a place with fleas, you can put a bunch on the bed and carry a few leaves with flowers in your pockets, because the scent drives them off. It is also good against migraines and nerves.

Rosemary (*Rosmarinus officinalis*) is a perennial, shrubby plant with small, purplish or bluish white flowers that blooms almost all year, but prefers the spring and fall. Scrappy plants are found in the most unusual places, such as dry loam, but in the shade of pine trees and with good soil it can reach a meter and a half tall in a Mediterranean climate (although it grows worldwide). To dry the branches, it is better to cut them in the summer, after flowering. It reproduces by seeds, which are planted in spring and transplanted when they are 2 inches (5 cm), or through some twigs or root cuttings, which is the best method in our case. You can also find pots with small plants that will latch on even in the worst spots in the garden (where Hartmann lines intersect and do not allow us to have tomatoes). Cuttings take two months to root.

Leaves of rosemary have essential oils and camphor; the flowers and stem have starch, oils, tannins, fat, sugar, and albumin. An infusion of fresh leaves is used in compresses for circulation problems and it is even good to wet the whole body with infusion. Water used to cook flowers for two minutes is good to wash wounds and make compresses for abscesses. Boiled, the leaves are used in a poultice against torticollis. The infusions are digestive, are favorable to circulation, and calm nerves. The oil is antiseptic, anti-inflammatory, anti-rheumatic, anti-parasitic, and is good against hair loss.

Sage (*Salvia officinalis*) is an almost shrubby plant, which forms large bushy plants and flowers from April to June. The flowers grow in spikes and are small and purple. Its various species grow anywhere except in waterlogged clay soil. It reproduces by seeds—seedlings are planted in February or March and transplanted in May—or by cuttings. It is also layers like strawberries.

The branches and leaves are cut just before they flower. You can store them dried and in the shade for its antiseptic and astringent properties, estrogens, tonic, or as a food seasoning. Use fresh on bites and stings, rubbing directly on the wound. Cooked with white wine for a few minutes, it can be used to clean wounds and make compresses. This mixture can also be used as a tonic. It has even been recommended to smoke a cigarette of dry sage leaves for asthma.

It is not recommended during pregnancy and breastfeeding, or if you have epilepsy or kidney failure.

Elderberry

Elderberry (*Sambucus nigra*) is a branchy bush, which can grow into a tree in good conditions. It has spear-shaped leaves and is easily distinguished by its black fruits, which grow in bunches and are edible when cooked.

It grows at certain elevations, from 500 to about 1500 meters in the mountains, and is very tolerant of cold. It tolerates acidic or basic soils, and likes water. It propagates well through cuttings at any time of year, and in spring with shoots, which take root easily when watered frequently. If you have one in the garden, you will have to thin the branches, since it tends to sprout from the bottom. The fruits produce a purple juice that is used to dye wool, so be careful with cement paths under the tree, since they will be stained by the abundant fruits in the fall.

It flowers from May to August, and with the water from boiled flowers you can obtain a remedy for respiratory afflictions.

The juice of the leaves mixed with lard is used against gout. The flowers ground in vinegar for 15 minutes and applied with a cloth to the forehead will help with a migraine. The leaves, when boiled, serve as a poultice for hemorrhoids.

Finally, an infusion of the leaves has antitussive, anti-inflammatory, and antipyretic properties, and when cold it works well as an eyewash. The leaves are purgative and boiled fruit can be eaten, but be careful because it has a toxic compound. Sticking the leaves in mole hills fights off moles.

Thyme

Thyme (*Thymus vulgaris*) is a lively plant that does not grow more than 20 inches (50 cm), but has the appearance of a tiny bush because of its woody stems and diminutive leaves. It flowers every year in spring and fall. It grows in the poorest soil and is adapted to droughts, although in rainy years it flowers even more splendidly. You should not water it in the garden. To reproduce it, you can use seeds in spring, divide the plant with some pieces of root, use layering in spring or fall, or use cuttings in early summer.

Cultivated plants lose a lot of their aroma after four or five years, and must be replaced. They tend to grow in the sunniest part of the garden. Its intense aroma is found in the leaves and flowers.

The twigs are collected when they are flowering, and can be used fresh or dry to season foods or make a delicious soup. An infusion with lemon and honey is anti-catarrhal and digestive. Cooked, in poultices, it alleviates neuralgia. It is used fresh in stews, soups, marinades, sauces, etc.

Thyme has disinfectant properties and can be taken when you have an upset stomach.

Valerian

Verbena

Purslane

Blackberry

Valerian (*Valeriana officinalis*) is an herbaceous plant that grows wild in all kinds of climates, although it prefers the middle mountain. It grows best in fertilized soil but is more aromatic in dry soil. If you use seeds to plant it, they must be sown immediately because they cannot be saved. It's better to use parts of the plant pulled off with a bit of root, like with thyme.

Since you will use the root, it is best to cut off the flowers to stimulate its growth, and harvest after two years in the fall. Then you should not plant in the same spot for many years.

Valerian is known as a relaxer for its hypnotic properties. Once dried, the root is ground to a powder and used as a decoction to promote sleep, as a sedative for the nervous system, and against insomnia, migraines, and rheumatic pains.

Verbena (*Verbena officinalis*) is an herbaceous plant that grows up to 20 inches (50 cm) and was considered magical in ancient times by the druids of Wales. The leaves are coarse and very divided. The flowers grow in spikes and are pink or lilac.

It is a wild plant that grows well in the fields and is easily grown from seeds. The infusion can be used for digestive problems, but with caution, as it can be emetic. The tender leaves, ground and steeped in vinegar for an hour, is used as a poultice on ulcers, and hot for osteoarthritis. The water used to cook leaves, roots, and flowers is also good for ulcers and wounds to heal them. The infusion of flowers and leaves is also a purifier; for example, 0.3 oz (10 g) of leaves in a half liter of water, boiled for 10 minutes, and let rest for 20 minutes.

Common purslane (*Portulaca olearacea*) is considered a weed by many gardeners, since as soon as good weather arrives in the spring, it invades the fields with its small, fleshy leaves and creeping stems. When cut, it forms a dry cover over the ground that impedes the growth of grasses. It is an annual plant that does not grow more than 12 inches (30 cm), and in ancient times it was eaten as a vegetable. It is perfectly edible when boiled, and the Sativa variety is even edible when raw. In fact, you can make a good salad of tender leaves mixed with watercress.

It has purifying and anti-diarrheal properties due to the mucilage of the plant, which is obtained by crushing the leaves. Take three spoonfuls a day. The infusion, when taken while fasting, is a diuretic that stimulates the kidneys and eliminates body fat. The juice of the plant, when used as a poultice, soothes eye irritations.

The **blackberry** (*Rubus fructicisus*) deserves a place here because the fruits have tonic and energetic virtues. This is a robust bush, with thick spines, which in proper conditions can grow up to 12 feet high and form enormous, leafy thickets. In some cases, it becomes a pest, since wherever there are roots underground, it will sprout again.

The young sprouts of the plant can be chewed to help with weak, bleeding gums. The ripe fruit or drupes are eaten for energy. An infusion of the leaves is recommended for diarrhea. And with the fruit you can also make excellent jam.

Edible
flowers

Some useful facts about
edible flowers

Sometimes we are not aware that although gardens, meadows, and forests can be a source of food, you should get to know them well before consuming anything from them.

Flowering plants—commonly called flowers—are not only an aesthetic element of the first order, which also provide a wonderful fragrance to our garden, but also attract beneficial insects, and, last but not least, give us their flowers as food.

The consumption of flowers is an established custom in the East. In the West, where it is starting to develop, nurseries can already be found in countries such as Spain, France, or Brazil.

Beware that not all flowers can be eaten and many are toxic, so be attentive and well informed. The information on the following pages serve as recommendations, but please consult an expert if you're unsure as to which parts or species of flowers can be consumed.

With flowers (and we do not mean cauliflowers) we only eat the petals. Some violets are eaten whole; however, remove the pistil from most of them, as well as the little white fraction at the base of the petals, which is bitter. They can be eaten raw, in salads, but also in the form of soup or batter, such as squash flowers. Of course, if you are eating the flowers, you should not use any chemicals to kill insects. You must treat them with natural products recommended in this book. Also, weeds must be removed by hand.

Artichoke is an edible flower, but setting it aside as one of our favorites of the garden, the most accessible one is the squash flower.

Squash flowers can be prepared in many ways. Among the most delicious recipes you can find the ones stuffed with monkfish and prawns, or with meat and vegetables, or with fried cheese, accompanied by noodles and shrimp or a rich salad.

A non-exhaustive list of edible flowers:

Borage (*Borago officinalis*)
Flower, preferably blue—but also pink or white—is eaten raw in salads or in ice cubes for cocktails.

Gourds and Squash
Their flowers, bright yellow in color and very large and fleshy, are eaten cooked in stews or soups, but mostly fried with egg and flour batter.

Common daisy (*Bellis perennis*)
It flowers all year round and is eaten raw in salads.

Field marigold (*Calendula arvensis*)
It flowers in winter and spring for very long periods. It is used as a healing ointment. From its orange flowers, sometimes used as a colorant in place of saffron in rice and soups, petals are separated (the center is **not** edible) and added to salads or desserts and even yogurt.

Carnations and pinks
It belongs to the family *Dianthus*; their bright petals are used in salads and creams.

Chrysanthemums (*Chrys. x mori-follium*) Belonging to the *Dendranthema* family, it blooms in autumn and the petals are eaten raw in salads and with oranges, but beware against abusing them, because they can be dangerous.

Aztec marigold or Tagetes (*Tagetes erecta*)

Bloom in summer, in full sun; remove the white parts and eat the colored part, especially for rice. In the garden it is a healing plant and neutralizes nematodes.

Hemerocallis or daylily

From the asphodel family, are common in Asia, are grown in full sun and flower throughout the warm season; the flowers are consumed whole, in stews or soups, and roots (raw) and young sprouts (cooked).

Spring or cowslip (*Primula spp.*)

In northern Spain it is yellow if it grows wild, but is also dark blue, purple, or light blue. As the name suggests, it blooms in spring, although it is perennial, and consumed in salads.

Pansy (*Viola vittrockiana*)

It is used in salads and desserts and has diuretic properties.

Chamomile (*Matricaria recutita*)

Or feverfew. It is grown for its flowers when dried to make teas, for its calming and digestive properties, and essential oils for their aroma. Its petals, whose collection requires a great deal of patience, can be eaten in salads.

Rose (*Rosa spp.*)

Its petals are used in baking, for syrups, jams, and marmalades, and rose water is very good for the skin.

Tulip (*Tulipa spp.*)

Petals, of any color, are eaten in salads to which you can add tuna or boiled potatoes

Top: Stuffed endive leaves with marigold petals.
Bottom: Not a bad idea to combine rose petals and pansies.

to give more substance.

Garden nasturtium (*Tropaeolum majus*)

Its orange petals, somewhat spicy, are eaten in salads or cheese.

Violet (*Viola arvensis*)

Blooming in spring, violet or white and everything in between them, their petals are eaten raw and are used to make liquor.

If you dare, try orchid flowers, bougainvillea, chives, nasturtium, sunflowers, geraniums, daisies, yucca flower (big and white), amaranth, lemon, papaya, and orange. But keep away from lilies (of which *only* the bulb is eaten) especially tiger lilies (*Lilium lancifolium*); violas (eat leaves and buttons); Christ thorn; and the poinsettia.

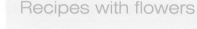

Recipes with flowers

- **Chrysanthemums or gladioli salads.**
- **Pansy jello.**
- **Thyme flower ice cream with candied violets.**
- **Jasmine, hollyhock, chamomile, or lavender ice cream.**
- **Rose petal jam.**
- **Zucchini flowers with mozzarella and anchovies.**
- **Flower butter.**
- **Hollyhock soup.**
- **Marigold or rose petal omelets.** To make the last one, the petals are crushed and mixed with cheeses in portions; add well beaten eggs with salt and place directly in the pan with a little oil.

Never eat flowers bought from a florist

They contain all sorts of chemicals and preservatives added to the water for maintenance. **Ideally, consume your own, but if you want to buy them you must do so in a greenhouse or in a place where they are sold** in pots for planting in the garden itself.

Poisonous Plants

The rediscovery of the benefits of medicinal plants in herbal medicine has led to some abuses. Therefore, in some countries, there is legislation to regulate their consumption. The prohibition of a number of plants and their preparations on the basis of their toxicity and their possible poisonous or narcotic action seems logical: its use for the development and commercialization of pharmaceutical specialties, master formulas, officinal preparations, homeopathic stocks, and research is restricted. The following is a list of some of these toxic plants, organized by toxic syndrome, as per the United States Department of Agriculture.

Abortifacient and Reproductive Toxins
Ponderosa Pine Needles (*Pinus ponderosa*)
Broom Snakeweed (*Gutierrezia sarothrae, microcephala*)

Cardiac Glycoside-Containing Plants
Hemp Dogbane (*Apocynum cannabinum*)

Cyanide or Prussic Acid-Containing Plants
Arrowgrass (*Triglochin spp.*)
Chokecherry (*Prunus spp.*)

Gastrointestinal Irritants and Toxins
Bitterweed (*Hymenoxys odorata*)
Colorado Rubberweed or Pingue (*Hymenoxys richardsoni*)
Sneezeweed (*Helenium hoopesii*)
Copperweed (*Oxytenia acerosa*)

Hepatotoxic and Pyrrolizidine Alkaloid-Containing Plants
Groundsel (*Senecio riddellii, S. longilobus*)
Tansy Ragwort (*Senecio jacobaea*)
Horsebrush (*Tetradymia glabrata, T. canescens*)

Neurotoxic and Myotoxic Plants
Deathcamas (*Zigadenus spp.*)
Larkspur (*Delphinium spp.*)
Locoweed (*Astragalus, Oxytropis spp.*)
Selenium Accumulators (*Astragalus spp.*)
Milkvetch (*Astragalus spp.*)
Rayless Goldenrod (*Haplopappus heterophyllus*)
Lupine (*Lupinus spp.*)

Poison-hemlock (*Conium maculatum*)
Water Hemlock (*Cicuta douglasii*)
Western False Hellebore (*Veratrum californicum*)

Nitrate-Accumulating Plants
Crops such as oat hay, sorghum, corn, sudangrass, Johnsongrass, beets, and weeds such as carelessweed, kochia, pigweed, Russian thistle, and nightshade, are examples of plants that accumulate nitrate. There are many more.

Oxalate-Containing Plants
Greasewood (*Sarcobatus vermiculatus*)
Halogeton (*Halogeton glomeratus*)

Photosensitizing Plants
St. Johnswort (*Hypericum perforatum*)
Spring Parsley (*Cymopterus watsonii*)

Miscellaneous Poisonous Plants
Bracken Fern (*Pteridium aquilinum*)
Oak (Quercus spp.)
Other Toxic Plants: Cocklebur (*Xanthium strumarium*), Desert baileya (*Baileya multiradiata*), Drymary or inkweed (*Drymaria pachyphylla*, Horsetail (*Equisetum spp.*), Jimsonweed or thornapple (*Datura spp.*), Tansy mustard (*Descurainia pinnata*), Yellow star thistle (*Centaurea solstitialis*)
Yew (*Taxus spp.*)

Above: The whole plant *Nierembergia veitchii* is very toxic.
Right, top: *Papaver somniferum* or opium poppy.
Right, below: In the *Magnolia officinalis*, the whole plant is also very toxic.

Above: Hellebore or Christmas rose is a violent purgative and toxic to the heart.
On these lines: Ipomoea violacea L. or black Bodo, whose seeds were used by the Nahuatl of Latin America as hallucinogens.

Above: Lily of the valley causes a disease of the same name that begins to manifest with blurred vision.
Below: The laburnum is a dangerously toxic medicinal plant.

The making and uses of compost

State of organic material	Fresh organic material	Unfermented compost Organic material. Beginning of decomposition
Approximate weight	22 lbs (10 kg) (initial weight)	18 lbs (8kg)
Proportion of water	70-85%	40-50%
C/N (carbon/nitrogen) ratio	C/N 20-80/1 (very variable)	C/N 20-80/1 (very variable)
State, form, or presentation	Plants from the garden ashes dry leaves kitchen scraps branches grass clippings hair scissors cardboard and paper seaweed manure straw	Compost bins mulch compost pile
Recommended uses	As padding A Do not bury	On the ground (protected) B Do not bury
Use in horizontal composting	Mulch for trees, hedges, and crops Does not yet nourish the crops	Surface composting Does not yet nourish the crops
Convenience in terms of soil type	Rocky or sandy soil	Calcareous soils, hot and well aerated.
How to improve the structure of the soil	Add bentonite and clay to the compost	

Fresh compost (2-3 months) O. M. semi decomposed	Ripe compost (6-9 months) O. M. decomposed	Old compost or humus (more than a year) O.M in mineralization phase
13 lbs (6kg)	9 lbs (4kg)	4.5 lbs (2kg)
30-40 %	20-30%	10-20%
Compost sieve	C/N 15-20/1	C/N (variable)

Compost sieve

Very fine, can be bagged and stored

Ideal for pots and see-dbeds.

On the ground (protected)

C

On the ground

D

Or slightly mixed

E

Mix with the soil or bury beneath

Compost on the surface

Does not yet nourish the crops

Un-mulched crops

Directly nourishes the plants.

| Loamy soils | Clay soils | Heavy soils |

Add dolomite, perlite, vermiculite, coconut fiber . . . to the compost or directly to the ground.

Index

Bibliography

Ecological and biodynamic agriculture, permaculture, agroecology

● ALTIERI, M. A. (1984). *Agroecología*. Cetal. Valparaiso. (*Agroecology*)

● ARAÚJO, J. (1990). *Cultivar la Tierra*. Manual de técnicas ecoló-gicas en agricultura. Ediciones Penthalon. Madrid (*Manual of Ecological Techniques in Agriculture*)

● AUBERT, C. (1979). El huerto biológico. Integral. Barcelona. (The Biologic Garden)

● BUENO, Mariano (2002). El huerto familiar ecológico. Integral RBA, Barcelona. (The Ecologic Family Garden)

● BUENO, Mariano (2003). Agenda del huerto y el jardín ecoló-gi-cos. Integral RBA, Barcelona. (Agenda of the Ecologic Home Garden)

● BOCHER, L. *De la homeopatía a la agricultura biodinámica*. Asociación Biodinámica de España. (*From Homeopathy to Biodynamic Agriculture*)

● CÁNOVAS, A.; Hilgers, M; Jimenez, R; Mendizabal, M; Sanchez, F. (1993).Tratado de Agricultura Ecológica. Instituto de Estudios Almerienses. Departamento de Ecología y Medio Ambiente. Almería. (Treaty on Ecologic Agriculture)

● FUKUOKA, M. (1995). *La senda del cultivo natural*. Terapión. Valencia. (*The Path to Natural Cultivation*)

● GUIBERTEAU Cabanillas, A. (1993). *Guía de productos utilizables en Agricultura Ecológica*. Junta de Extremadura. (*Guide to Usable Products in Ecologic Agriculture*)

● LEGASA LABURU, A. M. (1993). *Agroecología y sistemas agrarios*. Monográficos Bio-Lur. Asociación Bio-Lur Navarra. Tafalla. (*Agroecology and Agrarian Systems*)

● MOLLISON, B.; Slay, R. M. *Introducción a la permacultura*. Permacultura Montsant. Cornudella. (*Introduction to Permaculture*)

● PFEIFFER, E. Introducción al método biodinámico. Asociación de Agricultura Biodinámica de España. Madrid. (Introduction to the Biodynamic Method)

● SEIFERT, A. (1988). *Agricultura sin venenos*. Integral. Barcelona. (*Agriculture Without Poisons*)

● STEINER, R. Curso de agricultura biológico-dinámica. Editorial Rudolf Steiner. Madrid. (Course on Biologic-Dynamic Agriculture)

● VV. AA. (1989). *Lecciones de agricultura biológica*. Mundi-Prensa Libros, S.A. Madrid (*Lessons in Biologic Agriculture*)

● *Denominación de calidad Demeter: normas generales de producción agraria para su certificación* (vigentes desde 1990). Asociac. Agricultura Biodinámica de España. Tordera (Barcelona) (*Demeter Quality Approval: General Rules of Agrarian Production for Certification* [*current since 1990*])

Ecologic livestock

● FÖLSCH, D. W.; Pfirter, H. P.; Zülig, M. *Guía para una avicultura ecológica*. Publicaciones de Can Ricastell. (*Guide to Ecologic Aviculture*)

Biodiversity, Associations and rotation, cover crops, hedges

● ARBUNIÉS, J; GARDE, M; HERRANZ, E. (1995). *Los setos en el medio rural. Manual para su conservación y adaptación*. Monográficos Bio-Lur. Asociación Bio-Lur Navarra. Tafalla.

(*Hedgerows in Rural Areas: Manual for Conservation and Adaptation*)

Fertilizing, use of the soil, compost

● BOURGUIGNON. (1989). *El suelo, la tierra y los campos*. Vida Sana. Barcelona. (*The Soil, the Land, and the Fields*)

● LABRADOR, Moreno, J. (1996). *La materia orgánica en los agrosistemas*. Mundi Prensa—MAPA. Madrid. (*Organic Material in Agrosystems*)

● URANGA Balanzategi, J. (1995). El compostaje. Monográficos Bio-Lur. Asociación Bio-Lur Navarra. Tafalla. (Composting)

Plant health

● LEGASA LABURU, A. M. (1993). *La protección vegetal en Agricultura Ecológica. I parte: limitación de plagas y enfermedades en la naturaleza*. Monográficos Bio-Lur. Asociación Bio-Lur Navarra. Tafalla. (*Plant Protection in Ecologic Agriculture Part I: Limiting pests and diseases in nature*)

● LEGASA LABURU, A. M. (1993). *La protección vegetal en Agricultura Ecológica. II parte: resistencia de la planta y efectos de los pesticidas en su metabolismo*. Monográficos Bio-Lur. Asociación Bio-Lur Navarra. Tafalla. (*Plant Protection in Ecologic Agriculture Part II: Plant resistance and the effects of pesticides on their metabolism*)

● SAMWAYS, M. J. (1990). *Control biológico de plagas y malas hierbas*. Oikos-Tau. (*Biologic Pest and Weed Control*)

● VILLARÍAS Moradillo, J. L. *Atlas de malas hierbas*. Mundi-Prensa Libros, S.A. Madrid. (*Weed Atlas*)

Crops

● DEMETER. *El arroz*. Cuadernos Demeter. Tordera. (Barcelona) (*Rice*)

● DEMETER. *La cebada*. Cuadernos Demeter. Tordera. (Barcelona) (*Barley*)

● DEMETER. *El mijo*. Cuadernos Demeter. Tordera. (Barcelona) (*Millet*)

● DEMETER. *El trigo*. Cuadernos Demeter. Tordera. (Barcelona) (*Wheat*)

● *Los cereales: apuntes para una alimentación consciente*. La Cebada . Asociación de Agricultura Biodinámica de España. Federación Demeter.Tordera (Barcelona) (*Grains: Notes for Conscientious Eating*)

● LEGASA LABURU, A. M. (1993). *Cultivo ecológico del olivo*. Monográficos Bio-Lur. Asociación Bio-Lur Navarra. Tafalla. (*Ecological Olive Cultivation*)

● LEGASA LABURU, A. M. (1993). *Cultivo ecológico de la vid*. Monográficos Bio-Lur. Asociación Bio-Lur Navarra. Tafalla. (*Ecological Grapevine Cultivation*)

● LEGASA LABURU, A. M. (1993). *Cultivo ecológico del espárrago blanco*. Monográficos Bio-Lur. Asociación Bio-Lur Navarra. Tafalla. (*Ecological Cultivation of White Asparagus*)

● *Organización de las Naciones Unidas para la Agricultura y la Alimentación. Agroecología, cultivo y usos del nopal*. Mundi-Prensa Libros, S.A. Madrid. (*Organization of the United Nations for Agriculture and Nutrition. Agroecology, growing, and uses of prickly pear*)

Energy and agriculture

● DOMINGO, J. *Aplicaciones de energías renovables.* Permacultura Montsant. Cornudella. (*Applications of Renewable Energy*)

Commercialization, consumption, quality

● GLÖCKLER, M.; Bockemühl, J.; Tesson, M.F. (1993). *La calidad de los alimentos.* Cuadernos Demeter. Tordera. (*Quality of Foods*)

● LEGASA LABURU, A.M. (1993). *Certificación y comercialización de productos de agricultura ecológica.* Monográficos Bio-Lur. Asociación Bio-Lur Navarra. Tafalla. (*Certification and Commercialization of Ecological Agricultural Products*)

Other subjects

● AKIZU, X.; GARDOKI, M. *Viaje por nueve granjas ecológicas junto al lago Constanza.* Asociación de Agricultura Biodinámica de España. Madrid. (*A Journey Through Nine Ecological Farms Near Lake Constanza*)

● LIEVEGOED, B. C. J. *Las acciones de los planetas y los procesos vitales en el ser humano y en la tierra.* Asociación Biodinámica de España. Madrid. (*The Actions of the Planets on Vital Processes in Human Beings and the Earth*)

● MOLLISON, B. *El agua en permacultura.* Permacultura Montsant. Cornudella. (*Water in Permaculture*)

● VISIONS, D. *Temas claves sobre sostenibilidad.* Permacultura Montsant. Cornudella. (*Key Themes in Sustainability*)

● WISTINGHAUSEN, C.; Scheibe, W. (1996). *Indicaciones para la elaboración de los preparados biodinámicos.* Ed. Rudolf Steiner. Madrid. (*Guide to the Making of Biodynamic Preparations*)

● Ministerio de Medio Ambiente. *Desarrollo de un sistema de identificación/clasificación de peligrosos para el medio ambiente terrestre. Posición y aportaciones españolas en la Unión Europea.* Mundi-Prensa Libros, S.A. Madrid. (*Development of a System of Identification and Classification of Dangers for the Environment. Spanish Position and Contributions to the European Union.*)

Publications

● *Ecoagricultura* Editor: Coordinadora de Agricultura Ecológica (CAE). Address: Apdo. Correos nº 2580. E-08080 Barcelona. Language: Catalán. (*Ecoagriculture*)

● *Ecology and Farming. The International IFOAM Magazine* Editor: IFOAM. Address: Ökozentrum Imsbach. D-66636 Thorley-Theley, Alemania. Language: English www.ecoweb.dk/ifoam/pub/index.aspl

● *Les quatre saisons du jardinage* Editor: Asociación Terre Vivante. Address: Domaine de Raud. F-38710 Mens, Francia. Language: French

● *Permaculture International Journal* Editor: Permaculture International Lt Language: English. www.nor.com.au/environment/perma/data/pij.aspl

● *Permaculture Magazine* Address: Hyden House Limited. Little Hyden Lane. Clanfield. Hampshire. PO8 0RU. England. Language: English. www.gaia.org/permaculture/cover.aspl

● *Savia. Revista de Agricultura Ecológica* Editor: Federación de Agricultura Ecológica FANEGA. Address: Apdo. correos nº 10. E-31300 Tafalla. Tel y fax 948 75 54 04. Language: Spanish. (*Sage. Magazine of Ecological Agriculture*)

Articles, papers, etc.

● *Documentación Primeras Jornadas de Agricultura Ecológica.* (1993). ADAE - SPUPV (*Documentation of the First Seasons of Ecological Agriculture*)

● Prácticas ecológicas para una agricultura de calidad. Actas del I Congreso de la S.E.A.E. (1994). SEAE. Toledo. (Ecological Practices for Quality Agriculture: Acts of the First SEAE Congress)

● Ponencias de los cursos de la Escola Agrària de Manresa. (www.visca.com/esagrari/ponenc-c.aspl Email: esagrari@minorisca.es (Course Presentations from the Agrarian School of Manresa)

Connections with other libraries

● Biblioteca de Eco-agro. (Eco-agro Library) www.arrakis.es/~ecoagro/bibliografia.asp

● Permanent Publications Earth Repair Catalogue. www.permaculture.co.uk/menu.asp

● Publicacións do IFOAM. (Publications of the IFOAM) www.ecoweb.dk/ifoam/pub/index.aspl

● Publicacións do Departamento de Agricultura Ecológica da Universidade de Kassel (En Alemán) www.fserv.wiz.unikassel.de/foel/Publicat.aspl (Publications of the Department of Ecological Agriculture of the University of Kassel (In German))

Publishing houses and distributors

● Asociación Vida Sana. Àngel Guimerà, 1, 1º 2ª - 08172 Sant Cugat (Barcelona). Tel. 93 580 08 18. www.vidasana.org

● Can Ricastell (Demeter en España; Asociac. Biodinámica de España). Can Ricastell. 08399 Tordera (Barcelona). Tel: 93 765 03 80. Fax: 93 764 17 84.

● Junta de Extremadura, Address General de Investigación, Producción y Capacitación Agraria. C/ San Vicente, 3 (Apdo. Correos nº 217). 06071 Badajoz.

● Permacultura Montsant C/ Nou, 6. 43360 Cornudella (Tarragona).

● Savia. Apdo. Correos 10. 31300 Tafalla. Tel. y fax 948 75 54 04. Pódese a Savia tanto a revista do mesmo nome coma os monográficos de Bio-Lur Navarra.

● Terapión. C/ Médico Esteve, 2. 46007 Valencia. Tel.: (96) 380 67 67. Fax: (96) 380 86 95.

● Mundi-Prensa Libros. Castelló 37 - 28001 Madrid Tf: 914363700 E-mail: librería@mundiprensa.es Consell de Cent, 391 - 08009 Barcelona Tf: 934883492. E-mail: barcelona@mundiprensa.es www.mundiprensa.com